Ewa Dąbrowska and Dagmar Divjak (Eds.)
Cognitive Linguistics – A Survey of Linguistic Subfields

This volume is part of a three-volume set on Cognitive Linguistics

1 **Cognitive Linguistics** – Foundations of Language
   Ewa Dąbrowska and Dagmar Divjak (Eds.)

2 **Cognitive Linguistics** – A Survey of Linguistic Subfields
   Ewa Dąbrowska and Dagmar Divjak (Eds.)

3 **Cognitive Linguistics** – Key Topics
   Ewa Dąbrowska and Dagmar Divjak (Eds.)

Cognitive Linguistics
A Survey of Linguistic Subfields

Edited by
Ewa Dąbrowska and Dagmar Divjak

ISBN 978-3-11-062298-0
e-ISBN (PDF) 978-3-11-062645-2
e-ISBN (EPUB) 978-3-11-062315-4

Library of Congress Control Number: 2018968017

Bibliographic information published by the Deutsche Nationalbibliothek
The Deutsche Nationalbibliothek lists this publication in the Deutsche Nationalbibliografie; detailed bibliographic data are available in the Internet at http://dnb.dnb.de.

© 2019 Walter de Gruyter GmbH, Berlin/Boston
Cover image: borchee/iStock/Getty Images Plus
Typsetting: Meta Systems Publishing & Printservices GmbH, Wustermark
Printing and Binding: CPI books GmbH, Leck

www.degruyter.com

Cognitive Linguistics
A Survey of Linguistic Subfields

Edited by
Ewa Dąbrowska and Dagmar Divjak

DE GRUYTER
MOUTON

Contents

Geoffrey S. Nathan
Chapter 1: Phonology —— 1

Dirk Geeraerts
Chapter 2: Lexical semantics —— 25

Holger Diessel
Chapter 3: Usage-based construction grammar —— 50

Christopher Hart
Chapter 4: Discourse —— 81

Martin Hilpert
Chapter 5: Historical linguistics —— 108

Dirk Geeraerts and Gitte Kristiansen
Chapter 6: Variationist linguistics —— 133

Danielle Matthews and Grzegorz Krajewski
Chapter 7: First language acquisition —— 159

Nick C. Ellis and Stefanie Wulff
Chapter 8: Second language acquisition —— 182

Peter Stockwell
Chapter 9: Poetics —— 208

Index —— 231

Geoffrey S. Nathan
Chapter 1: Phonology

1 Introduction

Phonology is a branch of Cognitive Linguistics which has developed more slowly than fields such as lexical semantics or morphology (Lakoff 1987; Brugman 1981; Lindner 1981; Langacker 1990; Rubba 1993). In the history of the journal *Cognitive Linguistics*, only eleven articles on the topic have been published, an average of fewer than one per year. This author made some preliminary suggestions in an early article (Nathan 1986), and has since expanded these explorations in various directions (Nathan 2007, 2008; Donegan and Nathan 2014). A number of others have also written Cognitive Linguistics-based works on phonology including Nesset (2008), Bybee (1999, 2001), and Pierrehumbert (2002), as well as the articles in Mompeán-González (2006).

The question of how speech sounds are stored, perceived and produced, which is the essence of phonology, is an old one. The earliest theorizing in what we would now call synchronic phonology can be traced back to the late nineteenth century, where two different strands emerged. One, originating with the work of Baudouin de Courtenay (1972), and to some extent Sapir ([1933] 1972), exemplifies the active processing, psychologically oriented view still current in Natural Phonology and in one version of Cognitive Phonology, while another, founded by Saussure ([1916] 1974) emphasizes the structuralist, oppositional/contrastive view of how speech sounds are stored, with little or no interest in how sounds are actually produced. Generative Phonology, classically defined in Chomsky and Halle (1968) constituted somewhat of a compromise between the contrast-only storage model introduced by Saussure and the active production model championed by Baudouin, and, to some extent, Sapir. In recent years generative phonology has mostly been succeeded by a computationally-based model, Optimality Theory (OT), that is somewhat neutral on the actual psychological mechanisms of production and perception and storage. OT, however, takes other aspects of how phonology works very seriously (particularly the tension between "naturalness" and minimization of divergence be-

---

Note: This paper has benefited from comments by Patricia Donegan, José Mompeán-González and three anonymous reviewers.

Geoffrey S. Nathan, Detroit, USA

tween underlying form and surface form – "faithfulness") (Prince and Smolensky 2004; Kager 1999; McCarthy 2008).

This chapter will examine the active theoretical issues that arise in trying to understand how phonology would work within a cognitive linguistics worldview. We will discuss the question of the nature of the entities stored (the "underlying form" or "phoneme" question), the nature of the production and perception mechanism (how psychologically real are "rules"?) and the extent to which physiology and perceptual mechanisms constrain or influence the answers to the preceding questions (the "naturalism" question).

I will focus my discussion primarily on the question of why there might be a field of "phonology". That is, why there might be general principles governing how the phonologies of individual languages are constrained, rather than being simply a massive list of individual variants of lexical items. The task, from a Cognitive Grammar (CG) point of view, is to find governing principles that are not attributable to an innate language organ, since CG has no analog to the generative notion of Universal Grammar to fall back on. Hence, every explanatory principle must be based on pre-existing cognitive principles. I will argue that such principles as categorization, embodied perception and motoric organization account for all that is "universal" in (phonological) grammar. I should briefly mention that I will not be discussing questions of "phonetics", which some earlier scholars did not distinguish from "phonology". I will assume that phonetics deals with "raw materials" (anatomy, physiology, acoustics, perceptual psychology) and can be a source of explanation for phonological facts, but is not itself part of "the structure of English (or any other language)". I consider it the same as the contrast between materials science and architecture – the former constrains the latter, but is not identical to it.

2 Invariance, segmentation and storage of units: The fundamental issues

2.1 The problem of invariance and variation

It has been known since the beginning of linguistics that the same *word* is pronounced differently every time it is uttered. To take a concrete example, the English word *banana* might be pronounced [bə.ˈnæ.nə] or it can be pronounced [ˈbnæ.nə], and there are a number of intermediate possibilities as well. And, of course, it can be pronounced by men, women, boys, girls, speakers from Detroit – [ˈbnẽə̃nə̃]) or RP – [bə̃ˈnɑnə], and each one is different. Yet, to all intents and purposes, these variations are not even perceived by naive native speakers. Yes, anyone can recognize that Suzy or Daddy or Pierre said *banana*, but a child acquiring the language never thinks that the words refer to different objects, and it would be beyond imagination to try to spell each version differently – nobody (other than trained phoneticians) could perceive enough of a difference to know which spelling to use when.

It has also been known since very early in linguistics that the same *sound* is not the same either, but instead varies according to strict rules or principles based on such parameters as the nature of the preceding or following sound, or the prosodic status of the sound in question. The variation that has come to be known as "allophony" is classically illustrated by cases such as the American English phoneme /t/, which can be pronounced as a voiceless aspirated alveolar stop in *tall*, an unaspirated equivalent in *stall*, a voiced alveolar tap in *flatter*, a voiceless glottal stop in *flatten* and nothing at all in an allegro pronunciation of *Saturday*. Not only do native speakers not normally perceive this variation, it takes many months of phonetic training to get them to be able to transcribe it reliably. Similar facts pertain to Parisian French /e/, whose allophones [e] in open syllables and [ɛ] in closed syllables are completely opaque to most younger speakers (as noted by their inability to differentiate which way to spell the sound, among the traditional spellings for [e], namely <é> or <et> versus the traditional spellings for [ɛ]: <ais, ait, aient> etc.). To take one further example, Mandarin allophones [h] (as in *hao* 'good') and [x] (as in *heng* 'very') are indistinguishable to even moderately phonetically aware native speakers. The fact that speakers of a language are unable to hear the difference between sounds that are not only phonetically distinguishable, but are contrastive in other languages I consider to be significant evidence that phonemic perception is real.

2.2 The nature of units and storage

The vast majority of phonologists (of any stripe) accept that human beings segment the speech stream into roughly phoneme-sized segments. A few British phonologists in the nineteen-forties and fifties suggested that there might be some "segments" that were longer than a single phoneme (so that contrastive features such as nasalization might span a longer stretch of speech), but even contemporary autosegmental-based phonological models assume that the initial ("underlying", phonemic) string consists of segment-sized units (X-nodes or root-nodes), even if subsequent processing operates on larger stretches.[1] The

---

[1] Goldsmith discusses this issue in his seminal work (Goldsmith 1990), and even in his dissertation (Goldsmith 1976).

fact that the vast majority of even minimally phonetically oriented writing systems are segment-based,[2] with a minority being syllable-based with segmental additions (Japanese Hiragana, Cuneiform Hittite) suggests that segment-sized entities are readily accessible to speakers of most languages.[3]

Some researchers over the years have suggested that the notion of speech as consisting of phoneme-sized units is an illusion brought on by the high level of literacy in (at least) the western world (see, e.g., Port 2010) and suggests that the existence of segments is not justified by the physically continuous nature of the speech signal, the absence of invariant cues for phonemes, and the fact that certain kinds of speech error do not seem to occur. Some of these issues will be dealt with below. Note however that storage of units larger than the segment does not preclude the notion that those units are *made up of smaller units*. The existence of puns, spoonerisms and taboo avoidance behaviors in some cultures suggest strongly that speakers have access to identities at the segmental level, and, as Stampe (1979) noted, this identity is not at the level of fine phonetic detail but rather at a more abstract, schematic level that is equivalent to the phoneme of the "psychological realist" school of phonology that includes Baudouin, Sapir and others. Just to take a simple case, *Batman* is an illustration of assonance, despite the fact that the two vowels are enormously different – one is short and oral, the other long and nasalized, yet this difference is a revelation to students in an introductory phonetics course.

The history of phonology has ranged widely over the possible answers to this question. Baudouin held that phonemes are mentally-stored sound images, but his colleague Saussure argued that they are systems of oppositions. European Structuralists such as Trubetzkoy ([1939] 1969) argued that phonemes were *defined* solely by their system of oppositions, so that if some sound was lacking in an opposition in some context, it wasn't even a real phoneme, but an *archiphoneme*. So, for example, English [ŋ] in *thank* was different from the [ŋ] in *thing* because there was an opposition *thing:thin* but none in *thank:*thamk*. So *think* would have been represented phonemically as /θɪNk/ but *thing* would be "spelled" /θɪŋ/.

---

[2] Roman and Cyrillic-based writing systems, for example, and also Devanagari-based and most Semitic alphabets represent objects that are at least roughly segment-sized, although some Devanagari-derived alphabets are CV-based, but with diacritics to mark the non-default vowels, and additional segments to mark onset clusters (the coda symbols are diacritically-marked CV symbols).

[3] Note also that no orthography writes anything corresponding to what would be 'long segments' (in the Firthian sense). Even languages that mark tones orthographically mark them on individual segments or syllables.

Most American Structuralists were wary of archiphonemes. Hockett (1942: 10) for example, says they "confuse the facts without adding anything", but within various streams of Generative Phonology underspecified segments have become quite popular (there are various flavors of "underspecification theory" that go beyond the scope of the current chapter).

Natural Phonology has always agreed with Baudouin that phonemes are mental images of concrete sounds held in long-term storage, and thus are completely specified (i.e., all features are "filled in"). To the extent that cognitive linguists working within the usage-based model have considered the issue they have allowed for "schematic" sound storage, but with little exploration of how that concept would play out in a model of speech production or perception.

The question of whether phonological processes are psychologically real has been debated since at least the nineteen fifties (see, e.g, Hockett 1954; Baudouin de Courtenay 1972). Baudouin argued that physiophonetic "divergences" were calculated in the course of speaking, and Sapir ([1933] 1972), in his discussion of native speaker phonemic perception implied the same. Later Structuralists were either agnostic on the subject, or, in the case of Bloomfield's Behaviorist discussion (Bloomfield 1933) argued that the relationship among allophones was one of operant conditioning (as we would now say), thereby implying again that such "categorization" occurred in real time.

Generative phonologists have varied in their view of whether this kind of processing is or ought to be part of a model of linguistic performance (a competence model, of course, is agnostic on the subject). Because of an inherent bias against derivations (the essence of generative grammar) CG has assumed that there is no online "transformation" of linguistic structures. Langacker (1987) explicitly makes this claim, and virtually all subsequent work has continued to accept it.

The amount of detail stored for each phoneme (assuming sounds are stored as units) varies as well. Sounds are affected by their prosodic position, as well as proximity to neighboring sounds. If stress is predictable, are vowels stored as long if the language marks stress with length? If vowels are nasalized before nasal consonants, is that feature stored for each vowel in the lexicon that is so located?

In versions of Generative Phonology following closely on the classic Chomsky and Halle (1968) all morphophonemically related allomorphs were represented with a single form, so that *collide* and *collision* would be represented in the lexicon with a single underlying form, roughly /kolīd/. The alternations in the second syllable would be derived through the operation of several "rules" – Vowel Shift and/or Trisyllabic Laxing, which accounts for the two different vowels, and palatalization, which accounts for the /d ~ ʒ/ alternation. At the opposite extreme, many usage-based theorists have argued that each distinct pronunciation, whether "rule-governed" or governed by sociolinguistic or style-based factors, or perhaps even indexing individual speakers, is stored separately (Bybee 2010; Pierrehumbert 2002)

Again, this is a matter of the nature of phonological representations. Prague School linguists and generative phonologists argued that storage is not in actual sounds, but rather in lists of features. The set of features has, of course, varied over the seventy or so years since the concept was introduced, but this view continues to be popular among non-cognitive phonologists. Bybee argued that features are not relevant to phonological behavior (Bybee 2001; 2010). Natural phonologists have argued that features are not elements of storage but rather dimensions of categorization that govern the operation of processes (Donegan and Stampe 1979, 2009). For natural phonologists, as for usage-based theorists, representation is of real sounds (again, with the caveat that there is some question about the nature of sound schemas).

Finally, there is the question of what kind of mental unit a phoneme is. Structuralists generally did not deal with this question, with the exception of those experimenting with a behaviorist model, such as Bloomfield (1933: 33–41), for whom phonemes were behavioral units united by learned associations. Generative phonologists do not normally ask this question, because for most generative linguists linguistic units are sui generis, and thus not comparable to other units of cognition. This author proposed that phonemes were radial prototype categories (Nathan 1986), and the notion that phonemes are some kind of category has been considered fundamental for all cognitive linguists since then, although the issue of whether they are radial prototype categories or exemplar-based categories has remained contentious.

On a higher level of abstraction is the question of the nature of phoneme inventories. It has been known since at least Trubetzkoy ([1939] 1969) that there is much less variation among the phoneme inventories of the languages of the world than would be expected if they were randomly distributed. Greenberg (1966) was the first to investigate this statistically, and it has become a staple of phonological theorizing since then (a good source for relatively recent research is Ladefoged and Maddieson 1996). To illustrate with a few randomly-chosen examples: there are no phoneme inventories that consist solely of fricatives, nor any that have only low vowels. Although the overwhelmingly uniform nature of phonological inventories cannot be merely coincidence, there is disagreement among cognitively-oriented linguists on the reasons for the uniformity, with some, like the present author, arguing for physiological/perceptual pressures, while others, notably Blevins (2004) and Bybee (2001: 204) have argued that the influence of embodied processes is indirect, operating through sound change rather than synchronically. In addition, we should at least mention the fact that some have recently claimed that there are indeed no universals in phonology. The controversial paper by Evans and Levinson (2009: 431) argues that not even the existence of sounds is universal, since there are signed languages. This forces virtually all "universals" to contain "if-then" clauses. We would have to say "if languages have sounds, they have consonants and vowels", and similar contingent laws would have to obtain in the finer details of stop or vowel inventories.

Finally, phonology has long concerned itself with how (or whether) segments are grouped into larger units, particularly syllables, feet, prosodic phrases and so forth. The evidence for syllables is quite strong (although there have been serious questions raised about how universal they are [Hyman 2011]), and some evidence (albeit somewhat theory-dependent) for feet (McCarthy 1982) and perhaps phonological or intonational phrases. Finally, there is the somewhat contentious issue of whether there exist overall phonological typologies – traditionally syllable-timed, stress-timed and mora-timed. Although some phoneticians have, on the basis of measurements (or actually, the inability to find appropriate measurements [Dauer 1983, 1987]) questioned the essential typology, other researchers have found confirmation of at least some kind of division, using it to explain perception not only of speech but of music (Patel 2008).

3 The invariance problem

Much of the history of phonology consists of accounting for the fact that phonetic entities (however defined) that seem the same to native speakers (even linguistically-trained ones) are actually physically quite different. This first became evident with the nineteenth century development of phonetics, but after the invention of the sound spectrograph it became inescapable. As vowels succumbed to precise measurement it became obvious that no occurrence of any vowel was ever exactly the same. For consonants this is less strikingly obvious, but true nevertheless, as voice onset time, frication duration and similar parameters susceptible to precise measurement will demonstrate. The additional, linguistically significant detail is that much variation appears to be rule-governed. American English voiceless stops are aspirated at the beginning of words, except if preceded by /s/. Sanskrit and Thai stops are all voiceless unaspirated word-finally, even though there are minimal quadruples (triples for Thai) in word-onset position.

The consensus among most practicing phonologists in the first decade of the twenty-first century is that regular variation within phonemes is accounted for by some set of regularity principles. The more orthodox of the generative phonologists derive allophones from underlying phonemes through the operation of phonological rules, while Optimality Theory enthusiasts (McCarthy 2004; Kager 1999) prefer a set of ranked "markedness constraints" that permit deformation of target forms. Recent phonology texts (e.g, Hayes 2009; Gussenhoven and Jacobs 2005; Odden 2005) tend to present both models, the former in the earlier chapters and the latter in the later ones.

The present author has argued, near the beginning of the development of CG, and in subsequent publications over the years (Nathan 1986, 2007, 2008; Donegan and Nathan 2014), that the systematic variants of target sounds represented members of a radial prototype category, with the "underlying form" itself being the prototype sound. Non-prototypical instantiations of the phoneme are generated online via "image schema transformations" (Nathan 1996), a cognitive operation explored first in semantic lexical representations by Lakoff (1987).

There is, however, another set of variants that raise far more complex questions, both of storage and of what and how much is computed online vs. what remains in long-term memory. The same word can be pronounced in many different ways, depending on social and individual speech-act factors. Casual speech variants, as well as socially-indexed variants (such as the Northern Cities Vowel Shift in the US, as well as variable consonant cluster simplification in African American Vernacular English) raise additional questions. This will be discussed below.

4 The allophone question

As was discussed above, the existence of large numbers of variants of "single sounds" is a crucial fact in our understanding phonemes, and the fact that this variation goes unremarked by native speakers is an important aspect of this variation. For example, in many dialects of American English there are (at least) two distinct lateral sonorants, a clear [l] and a dark [ɫ] in *leaf* and *feel*[4] respectively. While children acquiring English often have difficulty producing these sounds (frequently replacing the former with [j] and the latter with [w], or even both with [w]) there are no reported cases of children having difficulty *spelling* the two with the same letter. And, for those who have taught phonetics to native speakers of American English, it is clear that the difference between these two

---

4 Note also that there are actually more variants. /l/'s are voiceless after aspirated stops and voiceless fricatives (*please, floor* etc.). Again, this variation is largely unheard.

sounds is *very* hard for their students to hear. In fact, it has been my experience that students never end up being able to hear the difference, and just memorize the rules for when to use which example (and when the language, due to morphological differences, contrasts the two, as in *really* [ɹɹəɫi][5] vs. *freely* [frili], the difference is perceived as a vowel difference or as a morphological boundary).

Similarly, the four English words *bang* [bæ̃ɪŋ], *bad* [bæːd], *Hal* [hæ̞əɫ] and *bat* [bæt] have four distinct vowels, each of which would be phonemically distinct in some other language, yet, again, children do not balk at spelling them with the same letter, and phonetics students have difficulty hearing the differences.[6] All of this leads to the inescapable conclusion that in some sense native speakers of a language do not "hear" allophonic differences, categorizing all instances of allophonically-related sounds as the same.

Stampe (1979) presented a number of pieces of evidence that phonemes are the units that are cognitively most active, including the well-documented fact that spoonerisms and other speech errors appear to move phonemes, with allophones being expressed according to their new environments. Thus, a speaker I recently heard referred to *thynsesis* [θɪnsəsɪs] rather than *synthesis* [sɪn̪θəsɪs] with a dental /n/. The assimilation of the /n/ to the /θ/ clearly "followed" the transposition of segments, a point that has been repeatedly documented since Fromkin (1973). Similarly, rhyme, even in folk poetry, is at the phonemic rather than allophonic level. For example, at a recent musical I attended, one of the singers "rhymed" *pretend*, pronounced as [priˈtɛnd], with *friend*, pronounced as [frɛntʰ]. This was possible because American English allophonically devoices final voiced consonants, but I am sure nobody in the audience, nor the singer himself was aware that these words did not have the same final codas, because, despite the physical realization, the codas are phonemically identical (/ɛnd/). Physically distinct sounds are perceived as identical, because rhyme is about phonemic rather than phonetic perception.

So, we have to do here with *categorization*, with speakers physically distinct objects into a single category. This forces us to consider the nature of human categorization behavior.

The structural phoneme was a traditional Aristotelian category, in which all members shared common characteristics, traditionally called *features*. This

---

[5] The phonetic transcriptions in this paper vary in degree of detail, depending on the particular point being made. For example, since it is not crucial to this point, the American English [ɹ] is represented in most examples as 'r'.

[6] In fact, the mind boggles at attempting to teach second grade students to attend to these differences simply to learn how to spell. It is notable that no contemporary (and virtually no historical) orthographies mark allophones. Sanskrit Devanagari may be virtually unique in this respect.

Aristotelian definition of phonemes led to problems first debated within the structuralist community and then during the phonological part of the "Linguistic Wars" in the late nineteen sixties and early seventies. There are several problems with an insistence on distinctive features and what came to be called "phonemic overlapping".

Classic cases in this debate included (for American English) the fact that both /t/ and /d/ seemed to have a common allophone [ɾ] (*betting:bedding*), and that sometimes there seemed to be predictable phonemes. The latter was particularly interesting. In American English vowels are longer before syllable final voiced stops than before voiceless ones (so Midwest *cot:cod* are [kʰɑt kʰɑːd], for example). But, on the other hand, there seem, at the same time, to be contrasts, such as *bomb:balm*. This led Bloch ([1941] 1966) to argue that the different vowels in *cot* and *cod* are distinct phonemes. "The words in the last pair, instead of exhibiting shorter and longer allophones of the same phoneme, have totally different phonemes" (Joos 1966: 96). While this permits the theory to maintain the Aristotelian character of the phoneme, it is challenged by the phonemic perception facts alluded to above.

Two distinct developments in categorization theory offered a way out. First, the development of fuzzy logic, which permitted objects to be members of some category to a measurable degree, allowed there to be overlap between categories. Secondly, the advent of the work of Rosch (1975, 1978 et seq.) permits us to understand how phonemic overlapping might be accommodated within a theory of phonemes as categories. Nathan (1986) proposed that phonemes were radial prototype categories, following the detailed notions developed in Lakoff (1987). There is a single, central sound which speakers perceive to be "the sound", and which in traditional phonological theory was identified as the principal allophone, or "underlying form". Each non-principal allophone constitutes a modification of the primary sound via the Lakoffian notion of *image schema transformation*. Each modification is phonetically-motivated (albeit sanctioned by the particular language and dialect), but a modification is subject to additional modification (as is found in all radial categories) such that long chains of extension in two distinct directions lead to sounds that share no common characteristics.

Just to take a hackneyed example, the American English phoneme /t/ can be instantiated by a glottal stop (as in *button*) and by a voiced alveolar tap (as in *butter*). These sounds share no distinctive features at all (other than being consonants). Furthermore, one of the allophones is identical to the allophone of a distinct phoneme – that in *rudder*. But, of course, this is not a theoretical problem in a non-Aristotelian category. What unites the members of the /t/ category is not that they have *features* in common, but that they are all traceable back to a common sound, via distinct routes. Just as the fact that a *cup* can be both a hole in the ground (the 18th hole) and a sports championship (the World Cup) is not a problem, because each can be traced back, via the undoing of mental transformations that are well understood (image schema rotations, metaphors, metonymies). This view explains accounts for the traditional phoneme as well as the anomalies that "killed" it, such as phonemic overlap and the lack of common "distinctive features". Allophones do not need to share common features, nor do they need to have an overarching "schema", as long as each one can be felt as an appropriate instantiation of the target, or of an instantiation of a substitute for the target. The fact that a chain of substitutes might run into a neighboring phoneme was further explored by Mompeán-González (2004) within this framework.

5 Alternative views of categorization

As mentioned above, there is a competing theory of how humans form categories, namely *exemplar theory*, extensively outlined (along with prototype theory) in Murphy (2002: 73–114) as well as Ramscar and Port (volume 1) and Baayen and Ramscar (volume 1). Within phonology, Pierrehumbert proposes that people have detailed long-term memories of particular percepts and these are the "exemplars" of the theory. Exemplars are categorized using a label set, and each label is associated with a large set of remembered percepts. The label can be thought of as equivalent to a phoneme (Pierrehumbert 2002: 113).

Exemplar theory has become very popular in recent work in Cognitive Grammar, because it is inherently frequency-based, and seemingly requires no pre-existing linguistic apparatus, and hence no notion of innate linguistic categories, or of innate linguistic processing.

An additional facet of exemplar theory is that every percept is stored, in great phonetic detail. This has certain consequences that represent either an advantage or a disadvantage, depending on one's theoretical proclivities. What is stored is an image of each instance of an utterance, which would include both high-level information (what word was said) as well as low-level information such as the identity of the speaker, the rate of speaking, dialect and register information, and so on. The image, cited above, of instances continually superimposed on a perceptual map can be thought of as analogous to making a rubbing over a number of similar coins (or medieval etchings). Each additional coin adds detail, and some of the detail, that which is common to all the coins, will become progressively clearer, even as the differences will disappear into a blur. A particularly striking example of this notion is provided by the photographer

Corinne Vionnet (Vionnet nd.), who collected hundreds of photographs of famous landmarks, both sent in by volunteers and collected from the web, then electronically superimposed them on top of each other. The results are somewhat blurry but clearly recognizable images of, for example, the Eiffel Tower and Tiananmen Square in Beijing.[7]

Another, related proposal for how sounds are stored is discussed in various works by Langacker (most extensively in Langacker 2007: 443–447). Langacker argues that allophones are nodes in a complex network of sounds, and that the contextually least restricted variant is the prototype. Langacker suggests that "higher-level nodes represent further abstractions capturing whatever is common to different sets of allophones" (Langacker 2007: 445). Features are "abstracted segments that are specific in regard to just a single property", while other higher-level schemas represent "syllables, words, prosodic patterns, and intonation contours". Further, "The phonotactic patterns of a language are thus embodied in schemas for phonologically complex clusters. As part of a dynamic processing system, such units function as templates (routinized packets of processing activity) with varying degrees of accessibility for the categorization of new expressions" (Langacker 2007: 445-6).

A similar argument (with considerably more detail) can be found in Kristiansen (2007). Kristiansen argues that a more generalized network model of speech sounds, rather than a specifically radial prototype structure can appropriately account for the fact that speakers of one dialect can, after relatively short exposure, understand speakers of different dialects, in which the allophones may not map in the same way.

For example, in some vernacular British dialects, glottal stops are exponents not only of /t/ but of all voiceless stops. Similarly, the same sound [ɑ] could represent, to a speaker of a Southern American dialect the vowel /ai/ as in *buy*, while to a speaker of the dialect of Boston or Maine it might represent /ɑr/ as in *bar*. What is crucial, for Kristiansen, is that speakers of both dialects may well be aware of what the other's dialect sounds like, and may have associated sociolinguistic and cultural reactions. Thus she argues that there is no reason to privilege a single dialect's array of variant forms with a single central prototype form, but rather have a loose network of related forms, over which a schematic generalization extracts some commonality.

---

[7] I am grateful to Diane Larsen-Freeman for directing my attention to Vionnet's work, and pointing out the relevance to usage-based models.

6 The role of frequency in phonology

In Bybee's seminal works (Bybee 2001, 2010) she has argued that frequency of occurrence of forms has a powerful explanatory role in the acquisition, production and perception of phonology. In her view words are the fundamental unit of storage (Bybee 2001: 30), but schemas capture commonalities among words such as similar segments (allophones), and structural units such as syllables. One goal of her work is to argue against the structuralist/generative view of the phoneme as an abstract contrastive unit (her arguments are not quite as effective against the concrete, pronounceable storage unit proposed by non-structuralist phonologists such as Baudouin, Stampe and myself). She presents evidence of phonological variation that appears related to frequency of specific words. This includes distributionally predictable features that are lexically contrastive.

In a widely cited work, Hooper [Bybee] (1978) examined "schwa-deletion" in English. As is exemplified by words such as *every, memory,* and *mammary,* word-internal schwas are optionally deleted (actually schwa-deletion is much more widespread than these cases, but deletions such as in the *banana* example discussed in section 1.1 and cases like *police* are not relevant to the current discussion). In the examples she discusses she reports that "high frequency words undergo the deletion to a greater extent than do low-frequency words" (Bybee 2001: 41). She notes that some words such as *every* are almost never pronounced with schwa, some variably with and without, such as *memory,* and some always have schwas, such as *mammary.* Since a structuralist analysis can be made that syllabic [ɚ] and non-syllabic [r] are allophones of a single phoneme, this would be an instance of allophony on a purely statistical basis. She notes that the non-syllabic version occurs post- and pre-consonantally (*trap, tarp*), while the syllabic version occurs elsewhere (*bird*). This, however, is not true, because the non-syllabic version also occurs intervocalically, in *arrange* and *berry*. In addition it is not a traditional view of allophones that the choice of allophones determines the syllable structure of a word – rather it is for most phonologists the reverse.

An alternative view would be that syllabic [ɚ] in *bird* is bi-phonemically /ər/, while its nonsyllabic equivalent [r] is a single phoneme /r/ which can occur intervocalically as in /bɛri/ or in codas as in /tɑrp/. Schwa-deletion, an optional process, is, like many other stylistic processes, sensitive to frequency. Put another way, speakers are aware of how common or rare are the words they are saying, and are more likely to choose a more "relaxed" (lenited) pronunciation when the word is more likely to be recognizable, while a rarer word is more likely to be pronounced closer to its underlying, prototypical pronunciation.

Gahl (2008), in a corpus-based study, presented evidence that speakers store fine phonetic detail, such as the small differences associated with differences in frequency of occurrence of words that might otherwise be identical, such as homonyms. Gahl found that the more frequent of pairs of English homonyms (such as *thyme* vs. *time*) are significantly shorter than the less frequent of the pair. This suggests that allophonic length might be determined by frequency in addition to the more usual conditions, such as word position, neighboring sounds and so on. On the other hand, the lower-frequency words were on average 7% longer than their higher frequency counterparts (396 vs. 368 ms.) (Gahl 2008: 481). A roughly 7% difference is enormously different from what is traditionally considered allophonic (say the English vowel length difference in *cot* vs. *cod*, which is roughly 100%) and much smaller than the differences that mark phonemic differences in various languages. A difference that small is within the normal range of error for the length of aspirated stops, for example. It would be interesting to see whether native speakers could identify the more frequent vs less frequent member of a homophone pair given these differences, out of context.

On the other hand, Cutler and her associates (Cutler et al. 2010; McQueen et al. 2010) found what might be considered exactly the opposite conclusion – namely that short-term adjustments hearers make to small acoustic differences in phonemes among individual speakers immediately generalize to words that the hearers had not previously been exposed to. Cutler and her colleagues showed that speakers adjust their phonemic representations of all the words containing a particular phoneme if they are exposed to subtly adjusted renditions of that phoneme (analogous to hearing someone with a different accent or a speech defect). The adjustment (in this case of an ambiguous /f/ – /s/ stimulus) affected all words presented to the subjects, not only the ones that served as the initial "training" stimuli, arguing that perceptual adjustments apply "online" as the embodied perception discussed above suggests.

Notably, it is also clear that children must abstract and separate personally-identifiable information (such as gender or dialect) from lexical information, because no investigator has ever reported a child who has decided that *dog* spoken with a fundamental frequency of 200 Hz refers to a different object than the same word spoken by someone else with an F_0 of 100 Hz. There is evidence that children attend to and acquire different *languages* as spoken by different caretakers, but each individual *lexical* learning task does not appear to be linked in any way to gender, size or regional or social accent.

The other area where frequency is closely correlated with phonological variation involves processes that are sociolinguistically marked, such as the famous New York City /oh/-raising in words like *fourth*. For extensive discussion of this point, see Labov (2010: 282–286) who shows that there is a distinction between phonetically-conditioned variation, which is not socially sensitive, and socially-sensitive variation, which is not phonetically-conditioned. It may well be that this kind of variation is subject to a different kind of processing than the allophonic alternations we have been discussing above.

7 The nature of perception

One issue on which very little has been written is what it means, exactly, to perceive a speech sound. Following the fundamental tenets of CG, we are required to look outside linguistics proper to understand how human beings perceive and store speech, since we would expect that such perception and storage would not be modular, but rather work in the same fashion as perception and storage of other aspects of external reality. What makes speech perception "special", however, is that we are storing aspects of external reality that happen to correspond (for the most part) to aspects of "internal reality", because when we hear speech, we are hearing performances of objects that we ourselves also produce. To the extent that we are hearing speech of a language we speak, this kind of perception would be different from, say, the sound of an airplane, or the sight of an oak tree. And, in fact, to some extent we even treat the sound of an airplane as speech, because we can imitate the sound, and in so doing, we use our vocal tracts to do so.

Perception and production of external sounds produced by other animals, in fact, can even be conventionalized within our language, and, just as there are similarities within the phonologies of different languages, there are similarities in the imitation of animal sounds across related, and even unrelated languages.[8] Recent research shows that speakers are quite capable of exploiting the whole range of human vocal tract affordances in imitating the sound of percussive musical instruments. Proctor et al. (2013) show that artists can produce sounds from various places in the IPA chart that their native language does not possess while imitating snare drums and cymbals, for example.

One of the major tasks for a theory of perception of speech sounds is to deal with the connections that exist between the articulatory and auditory channels that are involved. Articulation is physiological (although, of course, we perceive

---

8 Comparison of words for 'bow-wow' across languages has been done both seriously and in various websites around the world, but goes beyond the scope of this paper. For an interesting take on how we perceive bird sounds, see Donegan and Stampe (1977).

our own productions). Conversely, perception of others' speech is, of course, primarily aural. Many have tried to develop theories of perception that bridge this gap. My own view has been strongly influenced by the work of the psychologist Gibson and his school (see Gibson 1982, 1986). More recent work within the Gibsonian framework is Spivey (2007). One of the mysteries surrounding how children acquire language (and how adults understand those around them, including those who speak different dialects or have non-native accents, or speech impediments, or even food in their mouths), is how they are able to recognize the words that they hear.

It is clear from the beginning of child language acquisition that children are engaged in considerable "pre-processing" of the sounds they hear and store. The speech of a prototypical father has a fundamental frequency in the realm of 120 Hz, while prototypical mother's speech has F_0's in the 210 Hz realm. (Grabe nd.) Children below the age of five are physically incapable of producing pitches in these ranges (their frequency ranges from 250–400 Hz), yet they have no trouble perceiving (and presumably acquiring) intonation contours, and, for tone languages, the tones of the language.

Even more puzzling, however, is children's ability to hear vowels and consonants. The raw waveforms that they hear have formants at very different values from those they can produce given the size of their vocal tracts. This makes any model based on reproduction of stored instances much more difficult to implement. For example, a study of contemporary American English vowels noted that average F1 and F2 values for /i/, /u/ and /ɑ/ were as follows:

Tab. 1.1: (from Hillenbrand et al. 1995: 3103).

Vowel	i		a		u	
	F1	F2	F1	F2	F1	F2
Men	342	2322	768	1333	469	1122
Women	437	2761	936	1551	519	1105
Children	452	3081	1002	1688	568	1490

In absolute terms, children's vowels are acoustically nowhere near the adult's, yet to adult ears (and presumably to the child), the vowel systems are not different at all.

Furthermore, information about point and manner of articulation is found in the transitions at the ends of formants, as well as some inherent pitches (for fricatives, for example). Although children may very well store this as a set of absolute values, they could not produce it themselves – their vocal tracts are incapable of it. Instead they must perform a complex transformation so that their vocal tracts can produce (what we call) the same vowels, stops and other consonants. This is also true, of course, for adults speaking with other adults, and, of course with children as well. If we assume a motor theory (see A. Liberman and Mattingly 1985 for the classic statement of this theory), or alternatively, an embodied theory of perception, this is no puzzle at all. Virtually speaking, perception of vowel values is perception of "what I would have to do to make that sound" – that is, perception of the interlocutor's intentions. It is likely that the human perceptual system is in fact designed to translate the sensory data of other's actions directly into percepts of our own actions. The fact that this complex transformation is accomplished automatically (and not limited to hearing, or to human beings[9]) suggests that perception of language is far more complex than an averaging of the storage of many individual instances, and that image schema transformations are part and parcel of our perceptual apparatus.

8 Higher levels of structure

Generally very little has been written on prosody within the CG framework. Although it might be tempting to argue that stress, for example, is simply part of the phonetic detail that is stored with each lexical item, there is strong evidence that overall sentence rhythm is part of the overall production computation system, primarily because it interacts with other aspects of human rhythmic behavior. In fact, I would argue, following (Donegan and Stampe 1983, 2009), that linguistic accent/stress simply is human rhythmic behavior to which strings of segments are mapped, much as hand-clapping and foot-tapping is mapped to internally generated or externally perceived rhythms.

Consider, for example the fact that speakers are able to map words to music without any training in either music or prosody. Children in English-speaking North America sing a playground song designed to embarrass two of their number by suggesting a romantic relationship between them. The first two lines are

(1) X and Y, sitting in a tree
     K-I-S-S-I-N-G

---

[9] Gibson notes that spiders flinch if they see a pattern projected on a wall that suddenly expands – they perceive (as do humans in the same conditions) that something is rushing towards them. But spiders have eight eyes, and those eyes don't focus the way ours do.

where X and Y are first names. What is of interest is how Y is sung. M. Liberman (1979) provided an elegant analysis of the process of setting words to tunes (he used the taunting melody usually quoted as *Nyah nya nya NYAH NYA*, but the principle is the same).

Y is sung on two notes (descending third). If the name is monosyllabic the name is broken into two syllables with an inserted glottal stop:

(2) Jo-ohn [ˈdʒɔ ʔɔn]
              | |
              H L

If the name is bisyllabic and has initial stress, the high tone (and accented syllable) falls on the first syllable and the low tone on the second syllable. However, if the name is iambic the first syllable is shortened and receives a slightly lower pitch and a "grace note", while the second syllable is broken in the same way as the previous example:

(3) E-lai-aine [i ˈle ʔeɪn]
              | | |
              M H L

As names get longer a similar principle is followed. The primary stressed syllable aligns with the high note, preceding syllables are reduced (even if secondarily stressed) and following syllables are mapped onto the low note:

(4) Alexan-dra [æ lɪg ˈzæn drə]
              \ / | |
              M   H L

The ability to do this (that is, to synchronize two aspects of temporally extended behavior, such as bodily movement and patterns of beats, or segmental and suprasegmental strings) is not a linguistic ability but simply an instance of entrainment (see London 2012: 32 and Repp 2005: 978 for extensive discussion). But it is possible to take this identity further and argue that stress systems in language are simply instantiations of this ability as well. Work by Goswami (2012: 58) argues that attention to syllable structure and attention to rhythmic beat in music are the same cognitive task. In addition, she notes that appropriately shaped onsets of rhythmic beats facilitate the ability to entrain (that is, to get the listener in sync with the music being heard). This fact underlies the claim made in Nathan (2008: 36) that the universal preference for CV syllables is driven by the perceptual preference for clearly demarcated beats with an audible onset. In addition, Goswami (2012: 60) has found evidence for a correlation between dyslexia and difficulty in perceiving speech prosody and syllable stress.

A brief comment here about the acquisition of constituents such as syllables. Although usage-based theorists have suggested that speakers extract information about the constituency and "relatedness" of pieces of (say) a syllable from statistically-based generalizations over multiple instances, this view of syllables as beats suggests that the acquisition of onset plus coda is more like the acquisition of how to hammer a nail. Hammering a nail requires a backstroke, the strike, and some kind of control over the rebound of the hammer, perhaps blending with the next hammer blow. While it is possible that the unit "hitting a nail with a hammer" is extracted from the statistical coincidence of backstroke–stroke–rebound in that order over numerous instances (both of the hammerer and others around the learner) it is more likely that hammering has an inherently "natural" structure based not on UG but on how hammers are best manipulated as users have learned through doing hammering. Exactly the same argumentation could be made for the near preference of CV structures over CVC, VC and more extreme cases.

Linguists have long puzzled over the nature of stress or accent. It is often easy to hear, but very difficult to measure in any simple way. The current consensus is that stress is a combination of length, amplitude and rapid pitch change (Ladefoged 2005; Rogers 2001; see also Lerdahl and Jackendoff 1983). However, as Stampe (p.c.) has pointed out, accent in the musical sense can easily be sensed in harpsichord music, which uses neither length nor amplitude (harpsichord strings are plucked by a mechanical device that does not respond to how hard the key is pressed, nor does the musician control how long the note lasts, unlike a piano). The only control a player has is the micro-timing of the pluck, but attention to that timing only makes sense against some internal representation of regular beats against which deviations could be perceived.

Given this, we can explore what is known about cognition of rhythm. London (2012) argues that there are universal parameters for the kinds of rhythms that human beings can perceive and entrain. It is notable that those rhythms align quite closely with normal speech delivery rates (London 2012: 27–30), and also with the natural periodicity for human jaw movement and perhaps also foot stomping and finger tapping.[10]

---

[10] Finger tapping proceeds at a faster pace than either head bobbing or foot stomping, and seems to correspond more to syllables, while the latter corresponds more to accentual feet. That is, finger rhythms correspond to subdivisions of larger limb movements. I am grateful to

9 Conclusions

The status of phonology in CG is far from settled. One can identify at least three distinct strands – a usage-based, frequency-oriented view relying on exemplar theory, a related view in which the extraction of schemas from a network of instances permits the generation of higher-level abstract elements such as features, syllables and similar traditional linguistic units, and an active construction/realist view in which phonology is the immediate construction of physical action as a task to be accomplished, and the sympathetic reception of the results of others' similar constructions within the parameters set by each speaker's system. This appears to be a difference in vision about the fundamental nature of linguistic behavior that is represented in the tenor of the field in general. Work in lexical semantics and construction theory tends to emphasize the creative role of speakers in extending meanings and valence possibilities through well-known pathways such as metaphorical and metonymic extension, while work in grammaticalization theory and historical change has tended to focus more on the gradual change of units based on frequency. In addition, usage-based models tend to focus much more strongly on purely linguistic data (distributional factors, for example) while work in metaphor and metonymy looks at extralinguistic factors virtually by definition. My view has been that linguistic representations are embodied (i.e., that phonological storage is of images of sequences of vocal tract states) and that phonological processing is conventionalized adaptation of those states to each other. From this point of view, incidentally, phonological change is a change in which conventionalized adaptations have become more acceptable to the speech community, perhaps leading to a recoding of the target states over time (see Donegan and Nathan 2014 for details). Additionally, from this point of view, all phonological processing is conventionalization of independently-motivated facts about vocal tracts, auditory processing, categorization, rhythmic behavior, interpersonal activity (such as speaker/hearer estimation of recoverability of information during conversation, which determines degree of phonetic reduction) and so forth. By taking non-modularity of language seriously I believe we can get much closer to a truly explanatory view of the nature of phonology.

David Stampe for discussion of this isomorphism, but see also Tovey (1957: 175–176) and London (2012) for further discussion.

10 References

Baayen, Harald and Michael Ramscar. Abstraction, storage and naive discriminative learning. Volume 1. Boston: De Gruyter Mouton.
Baudouin de Courtenay, Jan (1972): An attempt at a theory of phonetic Alternations. In: E. Stankiewicz (ed. and trans.), *A Baudouin de Courtenay Anthology: The Beginnings of Structural Linguistics*, 144–213. Bloomington/London: Indiana University Press.
Blevins, Juliette (2004): *Evolutionary Phonology: The Emergence of Sound Patterns*. Cambridge and New York: Cambridge University Press.
Bloch, Bernard ([1941] 1966): Phonemic overlapping. In: M. Joos (ed.), *Readings in Linguistics* I, 93–96. Chicago: University of Chicago Press.
Bloomfield, Leonard (1933): *Language*. New York: Holt.
Brugman Claudia (1981): *Story of Over*. Bloomington: Indiana Linguistics Club.
Bybee, Joan L. (1999): Usage-based phonology. In: M. Darnell, E. A. Moravcsik, F. Newmeyer, M. Noonan and K. Wheatley (eds.), *Functionalism and Formalism in Linguistics*, Volume II: *Case Studies*, 211–242. Amsterdam: Benjamins.
Bybee, Joan L. (2001): *Phonology and Language Use*. Cambridge/New York: Cambridge University Press.
Bybee, Joan L. (2010): *Language, Usage, and Cognition*. Cambridge/New York: Cambridge University Press.
Chomsky, Noam and Morris Halle (1968): *The Sound Pattern of English*. New York: Harper and Row.
Cutler, Anne, Frank Eisner, James M. McQueen, and Dennis Norris (2010): How abstract phonemic categories are necessary for coping with speaker-related variation. In: C. Fougeron, B. Kühnert, M. D'Imperio and N. Vallée (eds.), *Laboratory Phonology* 10, 91–111. Berlin: De Gruyter Mouton.
Dauer, R. M. (1983): Stress-timing and syllable-timing reanalyzed. *Journal of Phonetics* 11: 51–62.
Dauer, R. M. (1987): Phonetic and phonological components of language rhythm. *Proceedings of the 11th International Congress of Phonetic Sciences* 5: 447–450.
Donegan, Patricia J. and Geoffrey S. Nathan (2014): Natural phonology and sound change. In: J. Salmons and P. Honeybone (eds.), *The Oxford Handbook of Historical Phonology*. Oxford: Oxford University Press.
Donegan, Patricia J. and David Stampe (1977): Old Sam Peabody Peabody Peabody: Verbal imitations of bird song. LSA Summer Meeting. Honolulu.
Donegan, Patricia J. and David Stampe (1979): The study of natural phonology. In: D. Dinnsen (ed.), *Current Approaches to Phonological Theory*. Bloomington: Indiana University Press.
Donegan, Patricia J. and David Stampe (1983): Rhythm and the holistic organization of language structure. In: J. F. Richardson, M. Marks, and A. Chukerman (eds.), *Papers from the Parasession on the Interplay of Phonology, Morphology, and Syntax*, 337–353. Chicago: Chicago Linguistic Society.
Donegan, Patricia J. and David Stampe (2009): Hypotheses of natural phonology. *Poznań Studies in Contemporary Linguistics* 45(1): 1–31.
Evans, Nicholas and Stephen Levinson (2009): The myth of language universals: Language diversity and its importance for cognitive science. *Behavioral and Brain Sciences* 32(5): 429–492.

Fromkin, Victoria (1973): Introduction. In: V. Fromkin (ed.), *Speech Errors as Linguistic Evidence*. The Hague: Mouton.

Gahl, Susanne (2008): Time and thyme are not homophones: The effect of lemma frequency on word durations in spontaneous speech. *Language* 84(3): 474–496.

Gibson, James J. (1982): *Reasons for Realism: Selected Essays of James J. Gibson*. Hillsdale: Lawrence Erlbaum.

Gibson, James J. (1986): *The Ecological Approach to Visual Perception*. Hillsdale: Lawrence Erlbaum.

Goldsmith, John (1976): *Autosegmental Phonology*. Bloomington: Indiana University Linguistics Club.

Goldsmith, John (1990): *Autosegmental and Metrical Phonology*. Oxford: Blackwell.

Goswami, Usha (2012): Entraining the brain: Applications to language research and links to musical entrainment. *Empirical Musicology Review* 7(1/2): 57–63.

Grabe, Esther and John Coleman (n. d.): *Leaflet*. http://www.phon.ox.ac.uk/files/apps/IViE/leaflet.pdf.

Greenberg, Joseph H. (1966): *Language Universals: With Special Reference to Feature Hierarchies*. The Hague: Mouton.

Gussenhoven, Carlos and Haike Jacobs (2005): *Understanding Phonology*, Understanding Language Series. London: Hodder Arnold.

Hayes, Bruce (2009): *Introductory Phonology*. Malden/Oxford: Wiley-Blackwell.

Hillenbrand, James, Laura Getty, Michael J. Clark, and Kimberlee Wheeler (1995): Acoustic characteristics of American English vowels. *Journal of the Acoustical Society of America* 97(5): 3099–3111.

Hockett, Charles F. (1942): A system of descriptive phonology. *Language* 18(1): 3–21.

Hockett, Charles F. (1954): Two models of grammatical description. *Word* 10: 210–234.

Hooper [Bybee], Joan (1978): Constraints on schwa-deletion in American English. In: J. Fisiak (ed.), *Recent Developments in Historical Phonology*, 183–207. Amsterdam: North Holland.

Hyman, Larry M. (2011): Does Gokana really have no syllables? Or: What's so great about being universal? *Phonology* 28(1): 55–85.

Kager, René (1999): *Optimality Theory*. Cambridge/New York: Cambridge University Press.

Kristiansen, Gitte (2007): Towards a usage-based cognitive phonology. *International Journal of English Studies* 6(2): 107–140.

Labov, William (2010): *Principles of Linguistic Change: Cognitive and Cultural Factors*. Oxford: Wiley-Blackwell.

Ladefoged, Peter (2005): *Vowels and Consonants*. Malden/Oxford: Blackwell.

Ladefoged, Peter and Ian Maddieson (1996): *The Sounds of the World's Languages*. Oxford/Cambridge: Blackwell.

Lakoff, George (1987): *Women, Fire and Dangerous Things – What Categories Reveal About the Mind*. Chicago: University of Chicago Press.

Langacker, Ronald W. (1987): *Foundations of Cognitive Grammar*. Stanford: Stanford University Press.

Langacker, Ronald W. (1990): *Concept, Image and Symbol*. Berlin: Mouton/de Gruyter.

Langacker, Ronald W. (2007): Cognitive grammar. In: D. Geeraerts and H. Cuyckens (eds.), *The Oxford Handbook of Cognitive Linguistics*, 421–462. New York: Oxford University Press.

Lerdahl, Fred and Ray S. Jackendoff (1983): *A Generative Theory of Tonal Music*. Cambridge: MIT Press.

Liberman, A. and Ignatius Mattingly (1985): The motor theory of speech perception revisited. *Cognition* 21: 1–36.

Liberman, Mark (1979): *The Intonational System of English*. New York: Garland.

Lindner, Susan Jean (1981): A lexico-semantic analysis of English verb particle constructions with *out* and *up*. Ph.D. Dissertation. University of California, San Diego.

London, Justin (2012): *Hearing in Time: Psychological Aspects of Musical Meter*. New York: Oxford University Press.

McCarthy, John J. (1982): Prosodic structure and expletive infixation. *Language* 58(3): 574–590.

McCarthy, John J. (2004): *Optimality Theory in Phonology: A Reader*. Malden: Blackwell.

McCarthy, John J. (2008): *Doing Optimality Theory: Applying Theory to Data*. Malden/Oxford: Blackwell.

McQueen, James M., Anne Cutler, and Dennis Norris (2010): Phonological abstraction in the mental lexicon. *Cognitive Science* 30(6): 1113–1126.

Mompeán-González, José A. (2004): Category overlap and neutralization: The importance of speakers' classifications in phonology. *Cognitive Linguistics* 15(4): 429–469.

Mompeán-González, José A. (ed.) (2006): Cognitive phonology issue. *International Journal of English Studies* 6(2).

Murphy, Gregory L. (2002): *The Big Book of Concepts*. Cambridge: MIT Press.

Nathan, Geoffrey S. (1986): Phonemes as mental categories. *Proceedings of the 12th Annual Meeting of the Berkeley Linguistics Society* 12, 212–224. Berkeley: Berkeley Linguistic Society.

Nathan, Geoffrey S. (1996): Towards a cognitive phonology. In: B. Hurch and R. Rhodes (eds.), *Natural Phonology: The State of the Art*, 107–120, Berlin: Mouton de Gruyter.

Nathan, Geoffrey S. (2007): Phonology. In: D. Geeraerts and H. Cuyckens (eds.), *The Oxford Handbook of Cognitive Linguistics*, 611–631. Oxford: Oxford University Press.

Nathan, Geoffrey S. (2008): *Phonology: A Cognitive Grammar Introduction*. Amsterdam/Philadelphia: Benjamins.

Nesset, Tore (2008): *Abstract Phonology in a Concrete Model: Cognitive Linguistics and the Morphology-Phonology Interface*. Berlin/New York: Mouton de Gruyter.

Odden, David (2005): *Introducing Phonology*. Cambridge/New York: Cambridge University Press.

Patel, Aniruddh D. (2008): *Music, Language, and the Brain*. New York: Oxford University Press.

Pierrehumbert, Janet (2002): Word-specific phonetics. In: C. Gussenhoven and N. Warner (eds.), *Laboratory Phonology* 7, 101–139. Berlin/New York: Mouton de Gruyter.

Port, Robert F. (2010): Language as a social institution: Why phonemes and words do not live in the brain. *Ecological Psychology* 22: 304–326.

Prince, Alan and Paul Smolensky (2004): *Constraint Interaction in Generative Grammar*. London: Blackwell.

Proctor, Michael, Erik Bresch, Dani Byrd, Krishna Nayak, and Shrikanth Narayanan (2013): Paralinguistic mechanisms of production in human 'beatboxing': A real-time Magnetic Resonance Imaging study. *Journal of the Acoustical Society of America* 133(2): 1043–1054.

Ramscar, Michael (volume 1): Categorization. Berlin/Boston: De Gruyter Mouton.

Repp, Bruno (2005): Sensorimotor synchronization: A review of the tapping literature. *Psychonomic Bulletin and Review* 12(6): 969–992.

Rogers, Henry (2001): *The Sounds of Language: An Introduction to Phonetics*. Harlow: Pearson.
Rosch, Eleanor (1975): Cognitive representations of semantic categories. *Journal of Experimental Psychology: General* 104: 192–233.
Rosch, Eleanor (1978): Principles of categorization. In: E. Rosch and B. B. Lloyd (eds.), *Cognition and Categorization*, 27–48. Hillsdale: Lawrence Erlbaum.
Rubba, Jo (1993): Discontinuous morphology in modern Aramaic. Ph.D. dissertation. University of California San Diego.
Sapir, Edward ([1933] 1972): La réalité pschologique des phonemes [The psychological reality of phonemes]. In: V. Becker Makkai (ed.), *Phonological Theory: Evolution and Current Practice*. New York: Holt Rinehart and Winston.
Saussure, Ferdinand de ([1916] 1974): *Course de Linguistique Générale*. Edition critique préparée par Tullio de Mauro. Paris: Payot.
Spivey, Michael (2007): *The Continuity of Mind*. Oxford/New York: Oxford University Press.
Stampe, David (1979): *A Dissertation on Natural Phonology*. New York: Garland.
Tovey, Donald Francis (1957): *The Forms of Music: Musical Articles from the Encyclopedia Britannica*. Oxford: Oxford University Press.
Trubetzkoy, N. S. ([1939] 1969): *Gründzüge der Phonologie* [Principles of Phonology]. Translated by A. M. Baltaxe. Los Angeles: University of California Press.
Vionnet, Corinne (n. d.): corinnevionnet.com (retrieved 21 May 2014).

Dirk Geeraerts
Chapter 2: Lexical semantics

To the extent that linguistic categorization is a focal area for Cognitive Linguistics, lexical semantics provides a crucial source of inspiration for the cognitive approach: to a considerable degree (see Taylor, Volume 3), the research strategy of Cognitive Linguistics is characterized by an extrapolation to other areas of linguistics of theoretical insights and descriptive models initially developed in the study of word meaning. The present chapter provides a brief survey of the main lines of lexical semantic research in Cognitive Linguistics, organized in two groups: contributions to semasiology (the study of the internal semantic structure of words), and contributions to onomasiology (the study of the semantic structure of the vocabulary and the relations between words). The concluding section considers current methodological developments. For more details for the position of Cognitive Linguistics in the history of lexical semantics at large, see Geeraerts (2010), specifically chapter 5.

1 Contributions to semasiology

Cognitive Linguistics advances semasiology primarily by the development of a prototype-theoretical model of lexical-semantic structure. We will first introduce the prototype as such, and then discuss a related (but foundational) topic, viz. the mutual demarcation of meaning and vagueness, and the indeterminacy of polysemy. An overview of the development of prototype theory within Cognitive Linguistics may be found in Mangasser-Wahl (2000). Foundational monographs like Lakoff (1987) and Langacker (1987), and successful textbooks like Taylor (1989, third edition 2003b) and Aitchison (1987, third edition 2003) contributed considerably to the expansion of prototype-based descriptions. Testifying to the early adoption of prototype-based models in Cognitive Linguistics are collective volumes like Craig (1986), Rudzka-Ostyn (1988), Tsohatzidis (1989), and monographs like Kempton (1981), Geeraerts (1985), Sweetser (1990), Schmid (1993). Since then, a prototype-based form of semantic description has become a standard ingredient of a Cognitive Linguistic view of categorization.

Dirk Geeraerts, Leuven, Belgium

https://doi.org/10.1515/9783110626452-002

1.1 Semantic salience: prototype effects and radial sets

Prototype models in linguistics were inspired by the psychological work of Eleanor Rosch. We will first present the original experimental results of Rosch and her colleagues, and then consider the general model of prototypicality effects that was developed in linguistic lexical semantics on the basis of the results obtained by Rosch. Characteristically, this model is applied on two different levels: within individual senses (in a monosemic context), and among different senses (in a polysemic context).

1.1.1 Prototypicality in a monosemic context

Rosch's results initially relate to perceptual categories, building on Berlin and Kay's anthropological study of colour terms (1969). Studying primary colour terms in a wide variety of languages, Berlin and Kay concluded that all languages select their primary colour terms from a set of eleven: black, white, red, yellow, green, blue, brown, purple, pink, orange and grey. There is a hierarchy among these terms, with five levels, in the sense that in a language with two colour terms, these terms will be *black* and *white*. A language with three terms invariably has *red* as the additional one. The fourth, fifth, and sixth term are chosen from among the colours on the third level (yellow, green, blue), and so on. Rosch inferred from these results that particular areas of the colour spectrum are more salient than others, and conjectured that these focal colours would be more easily encoded linguistically and more easily remembered than less salient colours. Both predictions were supported experimentally, and an extrapolation to other semantic domains turned out to be possible (see Rosch 1977: 15–18). Rosch concluded that the tendency to define categories in a rigid way clashes with the actual psychological situation. Perceptually based categories do not have sharply delimited borderlines, but instead of clear demarcations one finds marginal areas between categories that are only unambiguously defined in their focal points. Rosch developed this observation into a more general prototypical view of natural language categories, specifically, categories naming natural objects. The range of application of such categories is concentrated round focal points represented by prototypical members of the category. The attributes of these focal members are the structurally most salient properties of the concept in question, and conversely, a particular member of the category occupies a focal position because it exhibits the most salient features. This view of category structure is summarized in the statement that "much work in philosophy, psychology, linguistics, and anthropology assumes that categories are logical bounded entities, membership in which is defined by an item's possession of a simple set of criterial features, in which all instances possessing the criterial attributes have a full and equal degree of membership. In contrast, it has recently been argued ... that some natural categories are analog and must be represented logically in a manner which reflects their analog structure" (Rosch and Mervis 1975: 573–574).

Rosch's prototype results were introduced in linguistics in the early 1980s. In the course of the linguistic elaboration of the model, it became clear that prototypicality is itself, in the words of Posner (1986), a prototypical concept: the concept refers to various categorization phenomena that need not co-occur. The following four features in particular are important. First, prototypical categories exhibit degrees of typicality; not every member is equally representative for a category. Second, prototypical categories exhibit a family resemblance structure, or more generally, their semantic structure takes the form of a radial set of clustered and overlapping readings. Third, prototypical categories are blurred at the edges. Fourth, prototypical categories cannot be defined by means of a single set of criterial (necessary and sufficient) attributes.

These four features are systematically related along two dimensions. The first and the third characteristic take into account the referential, extensional structure of a category. In particular, they have a look at the members of a category; they observe that not all members of a category are equal in representativeness for that category, and that the referential boundaries of a category are not always determinate. These two aspects (non-equality and non-discreteness) recur on the intensional level, where the definitional rather than the referential structure of a category is envisaged: non-discreteness shows up in the fact that there is no single definition in terms of necessary and sufficient attributes for a prototypical concept, and the clustering of meanings that is typical of family resemblances and radial sets implies that not every reading is structurally equally important. The concept of prototypicality, in short, is itself a prototypically clustered one in which the concepts of non-discreteness and non-equality (either on the intensional or on the extensional level) play a major distinctive role. Non-discreteness involves the existence of demarcation problems and the flexible applicability of categories. Non-equality involves the fact that categories have internal structure: not all members or readings that fall within the boundaries of the category need have equal status, but some may be more central than others. Figure 2.1 schematically represents these relationships.

Going through Figure 2.1 in counter-clockwise fashion to illustrate the characteristics, we may have a look at the category *fruit*, which is also among the categories originally studied by Rosch. Her experimental results exemplify (a): for American subjects, oranges and apples and bananas are the most typical

	extensional characterization (on the level of exemplars)	intensional characterization (on the level of definition)
non-equality (salience effects, core/periphery)	a) differences of typicality and membership salience	b) clustering into family resemblances
non-discreteness (demarcation problems, flexibility)	c) fuzziness at the edges, membership uncertainty	d) absence of necessary- and-sufficient definitions

Fig. 2.1: Prototype effects and their relations.

fruits, while watermelons and pomegranates receive lower typicality ratings. But is a coconut a fruit? We are not concerned here with the technical, biological reading of *fruit*, but with folk models of fruit as a certain category of edible things. Technically, any seed-containing part of a plant is the fruit of that plant; as such, nuts in general are fruit. In ordinary language, however, nuts and fruit are basically distinct categories: nuts are small, dry and hard, while fruits are typically somewhat bigger, soft, sweet, and juicy; also, the situations in which nuts and fruits are eaten are typically different. But coconuts are neither a typical nut nor a typical fruit, and so language users may hesitate how exactly to categorize coconuts – an indeterminacy about membership that establishes (c).

Intensionally, membership indeterminacy reflects on the definability of a category. If people hesitate about membership, evaluating the adequacy of a proposed definition may be difficult: should the definition cover coconuts or not? But even if we ignore the boundary problems and concentrate on bona fide cases of fruit, (d) emerges. A definition in a classical sense, in fact, would be one in which we can list a number of features that are shared by all fruits and that together distinguish fruits from other categories. The obvious candidates, however, do not apply to all fruit (not all fruits are sweet, they do not all grow on plants with a wooden structure, they are not all used for dessert ...), and the ones that do are not collectively sufficient to distinguish fruit from nuts and vegetables. Assuming then that we cannot define the uncontroversial core members of *fruit* in a classical, necessary-and-sufficient fashion, we can appreciate the importance of (b). If *fruit* receives a classical definition in terms of necessary and sufficient attributes, all the definitional attributes have the same range of application (viz. the entire category). However, if such a classical definition cannot be given, the attributes that enter into the semantic description of *fruit* demarcate various subsets from within the entire range of application of *fruit*. The

	edible seed-bearing part	of wood-plant	juicy	sweet	used as dessert
apple	+	+	+	+	+
strawberry	+	–	+	+	+
banana	+	+	–	+	+
lemon	+	+	+	–	–

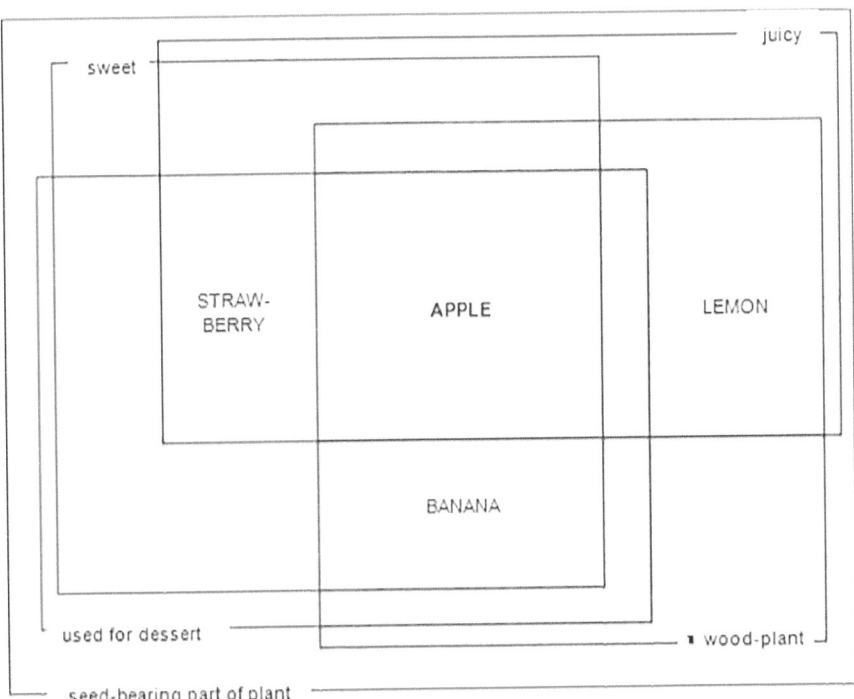

Fig. 2.2: The prototype structure of *fruit*.

overall description of *fruit* then takes the form of a cluster of partially overlapping sets. Characteristics (d) and (b) are illustrated in Figure 2.2.

In the *fruit* example, all the relevant features of prototypicality are present, but as suggested before, that need not be the case for all categories. Armstrong et al. (1983), for instance, showed experimentally that even a mathematical concept like *odd number* exhibits representativity effects. This might seem remarkable, since *odd number* is a classical concept in all other respects: it receives a clear definition, does not take the form of a family resemblance or a radial set, does not have blurred edges. However, degrees of representativity among odd numbers are not surprising if the experiential nature of concepts is taken into account. For instance, because the even or uneven character of a large number can be determined easily by looking at the final digit, it is no wonder that uneven numbers below 10 carry more psychological weight: they are procedurally of primary importance. 'Odd number', then, is a peripheral case of prototypicality: it has one out of four features, whereas 'fruit' has all four.

1.1.2 Prototypicality in a polysemic context

The importance of family resemblance structures may be illustrated in yet another way, by looking at clusters of different senses rather than the structure of a single meaning. So far, we have been concerned only with the most common, everyday meaning of *fruit* (roughly, 'soft and sweet edible part of a tree or a bush'). There are other meanings to *fruit*, however. In its technical sense ('the seed-bearing part of a plant or tree'), the word also refers to things that lie outside the range of the basic reading, such as acorns and pea pods. In an expression like *the fruits of nature* the meaning is even more general, as the word refers to everything that grows and that can be eaten by people, including for instance grains and vegetables. Further, there is a range of figurative readings, including the abstract sense 'the result or outcome of an action' (*the fruits of his labour, his work bore fruit*), or the archaic reading 'offspring, progeny' (as in the biblical expressions *the fruit of the womb, the fruit of his loins*). Moreover, the 'result or outcome' sense often appears in a specialized form, as 'gain or profit'. These meanings do not exist in isolation, but they are related in various ways to the central sense and to each other. The technical reading ('seed-containing part') and the sense illustrated by *the fruits of nature* are both related to the central meaning by a process of generalisation. The technical reading generalizes over the biological function of the things covered by the central meaning, whereas the meaning 'everything that grows and that can be eaten by people' focuses on the function of those things for humans. The figurative uses in turn are linked to the others by metaphor. The overall picture, in short, is similar to that found within the single sense 'soft and sweet edible part of a tree or a bush': we find a cluster of mutually interrelated readings, concentrating round a core reading (the basic sense as analysed in the previous paragraph). Family resemblance effects, then, do not only apply *within* a single sense of a word like *fruit*, but also characterize the relationship *among* the various senses of a word.

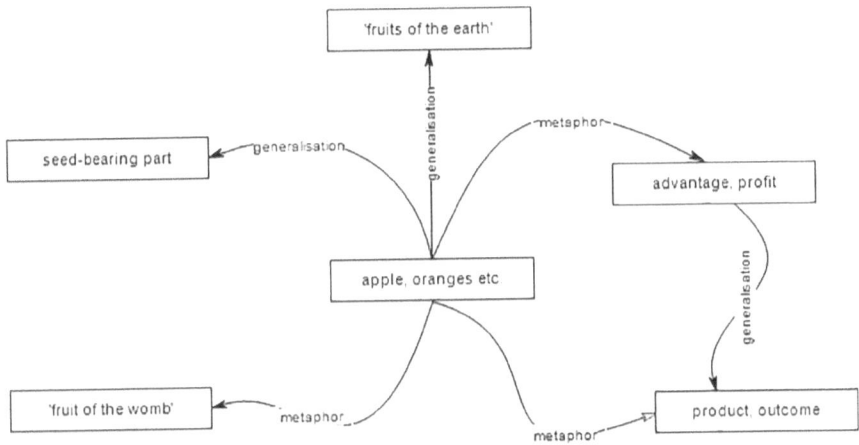

Fig. 2.3: The radial set structure of *fruit*.

A popular representational format for such prototype-based polysemous structure is the radial network model, first introduced by Brugman (1988, originally 1981) in her analysis of the English preposition *over*, and popularized through Lakoff's influential *Women, Fire, and Dangerous Things* (1987). In a radial network, senses are related to the prototype and to each other by means of individual links, possibly labelled with the appropriate semantic relation, as in Figure 2.3. Labelling of this type brings metonymy and metaphor into the picture: whereas all the examples of prototype-based category structure that we captured in Figure 2.2 involved relations of literal similarity, metaphor and metonymy need to be included in the description of polysemy.

But radial network representations as illustrated in Figure 2.3 have the disadvantage of representing the meanings as relatively isolated entities. The radial network representation suggests that the dynamism of a polysemous category primarily takes the form of individual extensions from one sense to another. This may hide from our view that the dimensions that shape the polysemous cluster may connect different senses at the same time. For a discussion and comparison of the various representational models of prototype effects, like radial sets in comparison to family resemblance models, see Lewandowska-Tomaszczyk (2007). More generally, the preposition *over*, with which Brugman introduced the radial network model, remained a rallying-point for discussions of semasiological structure in cognitive semantics, from Vandeloise (1990), over Cuyckens (1991), Geeraerts (1992), Dewell (1994), and Tyler and Evans (2003) to Deane (2005) – the list is not complete.

1.2 Flexibility and change: polysemy and contextual dynamics

Apart from representational questions, the transition from prototypicality within one meaning to salience effects among meanings raises a theoretical issue: is it acceptable to situate prototypicality both among senses and within senses (see Kleiber 1990)? Are the phenomena studied at the level of different senses really so theoretically similar to the phenomena studied at the level of a single sense, that they can be lumped together? One answer to this question could be purely practical. Even if it is not legitimate, in a theoretical sense, to equate the within-sense and the among-sense levels, the prototype-based phenomena that we discover on the level of polysemous clusters are worthy of description, and if a prototype model helps to describe them, so much the better. But a more principled answer is necessary too. It touches upon the possibility of systematically distinguishing between the within-sense and the among-sense levels: how stable is the distinction between the semantic level (that of senses) and the referential level (that of category members)? In other words, how stable is the distinction between polysemy and vagueness? This distinction involves the question whether a particular semantic specification is part of the stable semantic structure of the item, or is the result of a transient contextual specification. For instance, *neighbour* is not polysemous between the readings 'male dweller next door' and 'female dweller next door', in the sense that the utterance *my neighbour is a civil servant* will not be recognized as requiring disambiguation in the way that *this is rubbish* ('material waste' or 'worthless arguments and ideas'?) does. The semantic information associated with the item *neighbour* in the lexicon does not contain a specification regarding sex; *neighbour* is vague as to the dimension of sex.

Research in cognitive semantics suggests that the borderline between polysemy and vagueness (i.e. between variation at the levels of senses and variation at the level of membership within one sense) is not stable – and this, in turn, justifies the application of a prototype model to both levels. The synchronic instability of the borderline between the level of senses and the level of referents is discussed, among others, in Taylor (1992), Geeraerts (1993), Tuggy (1993). The common strategy of these articles is to show that different polysemy criteria (i.e. criteria that may be invoked to establish that a particular interpretation of a lexical item constitutes a separate sense rather than just being a case of vagueness or generality) may be mutually contradictory, or may each yield different results in different contexts.

To illustrate, let us consider one of various polysemy criteria that are discussed in the literature. So-called linguistic tests involve acceptability judgements about sentences that contain two related occurrences of the item under consideration (one of which may be implicit); if the grammatical relationship between both occurrences requires their semantic identity, the resulting sentence may be an indication for the polysemy of the item. For instance, the identity test described by Zwicky and Sadock (1975) involves 'identity-of-sense anaphora'. Thus, *at midnight the ship passed the port, and so did the bartender* is awkward if the two lexical meanings of *port* are at stake; disregarding puns, it can only mean that the ship and the bartender alike passed the harbour, or conversely that both moved a particular kind of wine from one place to another. A 'crossed' reading in which the first occurrence refers to the harbour, and the second to wine, is normally excluded. By contrast, the fact that the notions 'vintage sweet wine from Portugal' and 'blended sweet wine from Portugal' can be crossed in *Vintage Noval is a port, and so is blended Sandeman* indicates that *port* is vague rather than polysemous with regard to the distinction between blended and vintage wines. Similar arguments might involve coordination rather than anaphora. The case against a strict distinction between vagueness and polysemy then takes the form of showing that the test does not just rely on the words in question, but also on the specific context in which they are evaluated. For instance, Norrick (1981: 115) contrasted the odd sentence *Judy's dissertation is thought provoking and yellowed with age* with the perfectly natural construction *Judy's dissertation is still thought provoking though yellowed with age*. If the coordination generally requires that *dissertation* be used in the same sense with regard to both elements of the coordinated predicate, the sentences show that the distinction between the dissertation as a material product and its contents may or may not play a role: whether we need to postulate two senses or just one would seem to differ from one context to the other.

It now appears that the contextual flexibility of meaning, which is a natural component of a cognitive semantic conception of lexical semantics, may take radical forms: it does not just involve a context-driven choice between existing meanings, or the on-the-spot creation of new ones, but it blurs and dynamizes the very distinction between polysemy and vagueness. In the context of cognitive semantics, next to the papers already mentioned, discussions of the theoretical issues concerning prototypicality and polysemy include Wierzbicka (1985), Sweetser (1986, 1987), Geeraerts (1994), Cruse (1995), Schmid (2000), Janssen (2003), Taylor (2003a, 2006), Zlatev (2003), Allwood (2003), Riemer (2005), Evans (2006, 2009). These authors do not all take a radically maximalist approach, though: some pursue a more parsimonious position. The focus on the flexibility of language use has also sparked an interest in diachronic semantics. The prototype structure of semantic change in its various aspects is acknowledged and illustrated in one form or another in many studies, among them Dirven (1985), Dekeyser (1990), Casad (1992), Goossens (1992), Nerlich and Clarke (1992), Geeraerts (1997), Soares da Silva (1999, 2003), De Mulder and Vanderheyden (2001), Tissari (2003), Molina (2005). For a broader view of diachronic semantics in a cognitive context, see the collective volumes edited by Winters et al. Allan (2010) and Allan and Robinson (2011), and compare Hilpert (this volume).

2 Contributions to onomasiology

The contribution of Cognitive Linguistics to onomasiology is situated on two levels. On the first level, Cognitive Linguistics draws the attention to specific forms of onomasiological structure in the lexicon. On the second level, it introduces and develops the notion of salience in onomasiological research.

2.1 Structures in the lexicon: conceptual metaphor, conceptual metonymy, and frames

Structures in the lexicon above the level of the individual word are a traditional topic in lexicological research: structuralist theories (which dominated lexical semantics from roughly 1930 to 1970) focused on lexical fields or lexical relations like synonymy and antonymy, which link separate lexical items on the basis of their meaning. In the context of Cognitive Linguistics, the attention for supralexical structures in the lexicon focuses on three different types of structure: conceptual metaphor, conceptual metonymy, and frames. This does not imply, to be sure, that lexical relations are totally neglected, but they occupy a less central role than in structuralist approaches to the lexicon. Cognitive perspectives on lexical relations are explored in Cruse (1994) and Croft and Cruse (2004). More recently, the study of lexical relations is witnessing a renewal through the introduction of the experimental and corpus-based methods that will be discussed in section 3 below: see for instance Paradis, Willners and Jones (2009) for experimental approaches to antonymy, and Glynn (2010), Arppe (2008), Divjak (2010) for corpus-based approaches to synonymy.)

2.1.1 Conceptual metaphor

Metaphor constitutes a major area of investigation for Cognitive Semantics. The major impetus here came from Lakoff and Johnson's *Metaphors We Live By*

(1980), a book that worked like an eye-opener for a new generation of linguists. In the linguistic climate of the 1970s, dominated by the formal framework of generative grammar, semantics seemed a peripheral issue, but *Metaphors We Live By*, more perhaps than the other foundational publications in Cognitive Semantics, was instrumental in putting semantics back on the research agenda. Conceptual Metaphor Theory, as introduced by Lakoff, includes two basic ideas: first, the view that metaphor is a cognitive phenomenon, rather than a purely lexical one; second, the view that metaphor should be analysed as a mapping between two domains. From an onomasiological point of view, the first feature is particularly important, because it now defines metaphor not primarily as a semasiological link between the sense of a single lexical item, but as a mechanism that pervades the lexicon (and, more broadly, non-linguistic systems of cognition and signification – but that lies beyond the scope of this chapter). In fact, metaphor seems to come in patterns that transcend the individual lexical item. A typical example is the following.

LOVE IS A JOURNEY
Look how *far* we've come. We are at a *crossroads*. We'll just have to go our separate *ways*. We cannot *turn back* now. We are *stuck*. This relationship is a *dead-end street*. I don't think this relationship is *going anywhere*. It's been a long, *bumpy road*. We have gotten *off the track*.

Groups of expressions such as these, tied together by a specific conceptual metaphor, constitute so to speak a metaphorical lexical field, an onomasiological structure of a type not envisaged by structuralist theorizing about onomasiological structures.

Metaphor studies within Cognitive Linguistics have developed explosively, specifically also if we take into account productive theoretical offshoots like the Conceptual Integration Theory developed by Fauconnier and Turner (2002; and see Turner, Volume 1). An indispensable handbook for metaphor research is Gibbs (2008), while Steen (2007) and Kövecses (2002) are excellent starting-points for getting acquainted with the literature. Edited volumes of specific interest include Paprotté and Dirven (1985), Ortony (1979, 1993), Gibbs and Steen (1999), Barcelona (2000), Dirven and Pörings (2002), Coulson and Lewandowska-Tomaszczyk (2005), Baicchi et al. (2005). Popular areas of application for metaphor theory (the domain is huge) include the study of emotion concepts (Kövecses 2000), literary and stylistic studies (Turner 1987; Lakoff and Turner 1989; Turner 1996), religious discourse (Feyaerts 2003), and cultural models (Kövecses 2005). For a more extensive treatment of relevant issues in metaphor studies, see Gibbs (Volume 1).

2.1.2 Conceptual metonymy

The emergence of Conceptual Metaphor Theory also led to a revival of the interest in metonymy. In Lakoff and Johnson (1980) already, metonymy figured next to metaphor as one of the conceptual mechanisms behind the semantic structure of language. That clearly should not come as a surprise: an approach that is interested in the semantic mechanisms behind language use and linguistic structures is likely to rediscover the traditional mechanisms of semantic extension. Lakoff and Johnson (1980: 38–39) list a number of metonymic patterns (like PART FOR WHOLE, LOCATION FOR LOCATED, or PRODUCER FOR PRODUCT) that might have been taken straightforwardly from a traditional pre-structuralist treatise on semantic change of the type that was dominant in lexical semantics before 1930. As in the case of conceptual metaphors, all expressions illustrating a particular metonymical pattern can be thought of as an onomasiological group.

Lakoff and Johnson emphasize that such metonymic patterns are conceptual and not purely linguistic, in much the same way that metaphorical concepts are. In the first place, metonymical concepts allow us to think of one thing in terms of its relation to something else. In that sense, we can distinguish a source and target in the description of metonymy just like we can for metaphors. In the second place, metonymies are systematic in the sense that they form patterns that apply to more than just an individual lexical item. In the third place, metonymic concepts structure not just the language, but also the language users' thoughts, attitudes and actions. From the late 1990s on (somewhat later than the rise in popularity of metaphor studies), the renewed interest in metonymy led to an upsurge of publications. Important collective volumes include Panther and Radden (1999), Barcelona (2000), Dirven and Pörings (2002), Panther and Thornburg (2003), and Benczes et al. (2011). On the classification of metonymical patterns, see Peirsman and Geeraerts (2006).

Like conceptual metaphor studies, the interest in metonymy branches off in various directions. Without trying to be exhaustive (for more details on the scope of metonymy research in the framework of Cognitive Linguistics, see Barcelona, Volume 1), the following topics may be mentioned. First, a fair amount of attention is devoted to the mutual demarcation of metaphor and metonymy. Against the tradition in lexical semantics of defining the difference between both mechanisms in terms of similarity-based versus contiguity-based changes, a number of alternatives have been debated in Cognitive Linguistics: among other contributions, see Croft (1993), Peirsman and Geeraerts (2006), and Ruiz de Mendoza Ibáñez (2000). Second, Feyaerts (2000) and Panther (2005) explore the existence of metonymical hierarchies, in which more schematic and more specific metonymical patterns co-exist. Third, Paradis (2004) argues for a distinction between 'facets' and metonymy, building on Cruse (1995). Fourth, the function of metonymy in texts has not yet been studied as extensively as that of metaphors (for the latter, see Semino 2008), but see for instance Nunberg (1978) for pragmatic constraints on referential metonymy, Panther and Thornburg (1998, 2003) and Ruiz de Mendoza Ibáñez and Peña Cervel (2005) for the role of metonymy in inferences and speech acts, and Barcelona (2005) for an analysis of the functions of metonymies in discourse.

2.1.3 Frame semantics

The third type of onomasiological grouping that Cognitive Linguistics focuses on is the concept of frame as introduced by Charles Fillmore (Fillmore 1977, 1985; Fillmore and Atkins 1992, 1994, 2000). In contrast with metaphor and metonymy – traditional concepts that were part of linguistics long before the advent of Cognitive Linguistics – frame theory is an entirely original contribution to the field. Frame theory is specifically interested in the way in which language may be used to perspectivize an underlying conceptualization of the world: it's not just that we see the world in terms of conceptual models, but those models may be verbalized in different ways. Each different way of bringing a conceptual model to expression so to speak adds another layer of meaning: the models themselves are meaningful ways of thinking about the world, but the way we express the models while talking, adds perspective. This overall starting-point of Fillmorean frame theory leads to a description on two levels. On the one hand, a description of the referential situation or event consists of an identification of the relevant elements and entities and the conceptual role they play in the situation or event. On the other hand, the more purely linguistic part of the analysis indicates how certain expressions and grammatical patterns highlight aspects of that situation or event.

To illustrate, we may have a look at the standard example of frame theory, the COMMERCIAL TRANSACTION frame. The commercial transaction frame involves words like *buy* and *sell*. The commercial transaction frame can be characterised informally by a scenario in which one person gets control or possession of something from a second person, as a result of a mutual agreement through which the first person gives the second person a sum of money. Background knowledge involved in this scenario includes an understanding of ownership relations, a money economy, and commercial contracts. The categories that are needed for describing the lexical meanings of the verbs linked to the commercial transaction scene include Buyer, Seller, Goods and Money as basic categories. Verbs like *buy* and *sell* then each encode a certain perspective on the commercial transaction scene by highlighting specific elements of the scene. In the case of *buy*, for instance, the buyer appears as the subject of the sentence and the goods as the direct object; the seller and the money appear in prepositional phrases: *Paloma bought a book from Teresa for €30*. In the case of *sell* on the other hand, it is the seller that appears as a subject: *Teresa sold a book to Paloma for €30*.

In its further development, frame semantics was enriched, first, by the systematic use of corpus materials as the main source of empirical evidence for the frame-theoretical analyses, and second, the development of an electronic dictionary with frame-theoretical descriptions. These two developments go together in the Berkeley FrameNet project (Johnson et al. 2002; Ruppenhofer et al. 2006). The position of Fillmore's frame theory in comparison with structuralist field approaches is discussed in Post (1988) and Nerlich and Clarke (2000); more broadly, a comparison between different approaches to lexical structure (semantic fields, frames, prototypes, and lexical relations) is pursued in Lehrer and Kittay (1992), Lutzeier (1992). Examples of descriptive work in the frame approach include Dirven et al. (1982), Lawler (1989), Rojo and Valenzuela (1998), Martin (2001). The impact of the frame approach on applied lexicography may be measured in Atkins et al. (2003). Frame theory, incidentally, is not the only aspect of lexical semantics to have had an impact on lexicography: for the impact of prototype models on lexicography, see Geeraerts (1990, 2007) and Hanks (1994).

2.2 Onomasiological salience: basic levels, entrenchment, and sociolexicology

Possibly the major innovation of the prototype model of categorization is to give salience a place in the description of semasiological structure: next to the qualitative relations among the elements in a semasiological structure (like metaphor and metonymy), a quantifiable centre-periphery relationship is introduced as part of the architecture. But could the concept of salience not also be applied to the onomasiological domain?

The initial step in the introduction of onomasiological salience is the *basic level hypothesis*. The hypothesis is based on the ethno-linguistic observation that folk classifications of biological domains usually conform to a general organizational principle, in the sense that they consist of five or six taxonomical levels (Berlin et al. 1974; Berlin 1976, 1978). Figure 2.4 illustrates the idea with two sets of examples. The highest rank in the taxonomy is that of the 'unique

	ethnobiological examples		clothing terms
kingdom	animal	plant	garment
life form	tree	fish	outer garment
intermediate	evergreen	freshwater fish	...
generic	pine	bass	trousers
specific	whitepine	black bass	ski pants
varietal	western whitepine	large-mouthed bass	stretch ski pants

Fig. 2.4: Taxonomical levels.

beginner', which names a major domain like *plant* and *animal*. The domain of the unique beginner is subdivided by just a few general 'life forms', which are in turn specified by 'folk genera' like *pine, oak, beech, ash, elm, chestnut*. (The 'intermediate' level is an optional one.) A folk genus may be further specified by 'folk specifics' and 'varietal taxa'. To the extent that the generic level is the core of any folk biological taxonomy, it is the basic level: it is the most commonly used, everyday set of categories of folk biological knowledge. The generic level, in other words, is onomasiologically salient: given a particular referent, the most likely name for that referent from among the alternatives provided by the taxonomy will be the name situated at the basic level.

As the basic level model was developed for the description of the folk classification of natural kinds; it is an open question to what extent it may be generalized to all kinds of taxonomies, like the taxonomical classification of artefacts. If we apply the basic level model to the lexical field of clothing terminology, items like *trousers, skirt, sweater, dress* are to be considered basic level categories: their overall frequency in actual language use is high, they are learned early in acquisition, and they typically have the mono-morphemic form of basic level categories. A further extrapolation yields the right-hand side of Figure 2.4, in which *garment* is considered a unique beginner in contrast with, say, *utensil* or *toy*.

Crucially, the basic level model contains a hypothesis about alternative categorizations of referents, i.e. it is a hypothesis about onomasiological salience: if a particular referent (a particular piece of clothing) can be alternatively categorized as a garment, a skirt, or a wrap-around skirt, the choice will be preferentially made for the basic level category 'skirt'. But differences of onomasiological preference also occur *among* categories on the same level in a taxonomical hierarchy. If a particular referent can be alternatively categorized as a wrap-around skirt or a miniskirt, there could just as well be a preferential choice: when you encounter something that is both a wrap-around skirt and a miniskirt, the most natural way of naming that referent in a neutral context would probably be 'miniskirt'. If, then, we have to reckon with intra-level differences of salience next to inter-level differences, the concept of onomasiological salience has to be generalized in such a way that it relates to individual categories at any level of the hierarchy (or what is left of it when all forms of hierarchical fuzziness are taken into account). Terminologically, this concept of *generalized onomasiological salience* can be seen as a specification of the notion of *entrenchment*, introduced by Langacker (1987: 59–60) in connection with the process of unit formation: a particular linguistic construct (such as a new compound, or the use of a word in a new reading) may gradually transcend its initial incidental status by being used more often, until it is so firmly entrenched in the grammar or the lexicon that it has become a regular well-established unit of the linguistic system. (Basic levels, entrenchment and salience in linguistics are discussed in Geeraerts (2000) and Schmid (2007); see also Divjak and Caldwell-Harris, Volume 1)

The concept of generalized onomasiological entrenchment was studied and further developed in Geeraerts et al. (1994). Using corpus materials, this study established that the choice for one lexical item rather than the other as the name for a given referent is determined by the semasiological salience of the referent (i.e. the degree of prototypicality of the referent with regard to the semasiological structure of the category), by the onomasiological entrenchment of the category represented by the expression, and by contextual features of a classical sociolinguistic and geographical nature, involving the competition between different language varieties. By zooming in on the latter type of factor, a further refinement of the notion of onomasiological salience is introduced, in the form of the distinction between *conceptual* and *formal* onomasiological variation. Whereas conceptual onomasiological variation involves the choice of different conceptual categories for a referent (like the examples presented so far), formal onomasiological variation merely involves the use of different names for the same conceptual category. The names *jeans* and *trousers* for denim leisure wear trousers constitute an instance of conceptual variation, for they represent categories at different taxonomical levels. *Jeans* and *denims*, however, represent no more than different (but synonymous) names for the same denotational category. The addition of 'denotational' is not without importance here, because the assumption is not that the words are equivalent in *all* respects. They may have different stylistic values (which will show up in their distribution over different types of text), or they may belong to different lects (dialects, regiolects, sociolects, national varieties – whatever variety of a sociolinguistic nature that might be relevant).

The latter observation may be generalized: all forms of lexical variation considered so far may be subject to contextual, 'lectal' variation. Different dialects may use words in different meanings (semasiological variation). Experts are more likely to use specific, technical terms than laymen (conceptual onomasiological variation). And denotationally synonymous expressions may have different sociolinguistic distributions (formal onomasiological variation). This recognition then leads to an upsurge of socio-lexicological studies, as a practical consequence of the idea that all aspects of lexical variation (the semasiological, the conceptual onomasiological, and the formal onomasiological) are sensitive to lectal variation, and therefore require to be studied from a sociolinguistic point of view. Sample studies include Robinson (2010) for semasiological variation, Szelid and Geeraerts (2008) for conceptual onomasiological variation, and for formal onomasiological variation, the socio-lectometrical studies in which the distribution of denotational synonyms over language varieties is used as a measure of the distance between language varieties: see Speelman et al. (2003), Soares da Silva (2005), Zenner et al. (2012). More generally, the development of sociolexicological studies in Cognitive Linguistics is an element of a broader tendency towards variationist studies, often referred to as Cognitive Sociolinguistics: see Geeraerts and Kristiansen (this volume).

3 Current developments

The foregoing pages have highlighted the theoretical and descriptive contributions of Cognitive Linguistics to lexical semantics, either as a revival of traditional topics (the renewed interest in metaphor and metonymy as cognitive mechanisms), or as foundational innovations (the incorporation of salience effects in semasiological and onomasiological structure, and the recognition of the contextual instability of the distinction between polysemy and vagueness). Continuing these theoretical and descriptive lines of research, current developments in Cognitive Linguistic lexical semantics seem to be primarily of a methodological nature. Two trends may be mentioned.

First, a number of researchers enrich and support their linguistic analyses with data derived from psycho-experimental and neurobiological studies. This trend is perhaps most outspoken in metaphor studies, where a belief in the embodiment of metaphorical thinking leads to an active interest in psychological and neurophysiological evidence; see Gibbs (Volume 1) and Bergen (Volume 1). In the context of the developments sketched in the previous pages, this turn towards psycho-experimental and neurobiological data diminishes the gap between the psychological and the linguistic study of meaning and the lexicon. In fact, in spite of the psycholinguistic origins of linguistic prototype studies in the work of Rosch (see above), linguistics and psychology went remarkably separate ways in their development of that common starting-point. In contrast with the linguistic studies mentioned above, psychologically oriented prototype-based studies do not as a rule go beyond prototype effects in monosemic concepts, and at the same, they focus more than the linguistic studies on the formal modelling of the effects (see Murphy 2002 for an overview of the psychological developments, and compare Geeraerts 2010: 240–249 for a more extended discussion of the relationship between psychological and linguistic approaches in lexical semantics). A methodological rapprochement of the kind mentioned here will help to narrow the divide.

Second, we witness an increased emphasis on quantitative corpus analysis, specifically in the form of so-called distributional approaches that model meaning on the basis of the corpus contexts that a given word or expression occurs in: see Gries (Volume 3), and compare Geeraerts (2010: 165–178, 263–266) for a positioning of this trend in the history of lexical semantics. Such a corpus-based approach is attractive for any theoretical framework in lexical semantics, for the basic reason that it provides an unparalleled empirical basis for lexical research. The wealth of data contained in the corpora – regardless from what perspective they are analysed – will simply benefit any research endeavour in lexical semantics, Cognitive Linguistics no less so than other approaches. But more specifically and more importantly, there is a certain theoretical affinity between Cognitive Linguistics and the distributional analysis of corpus data, an affinity that rests on at least the following two features. First, both approaches are explicitly usage-based ones. In fact, it is difficult to see how Cognitive Linguistics can live up to its self-declared nature as a usage-based model if it does not start from actual usage data and a methodology that is suited to deal with such data. And second, the quantitative elaboration of a distributional corpus analysis provides a formal perspective on semantic data that is specifically congenial to Cognitive Linguistics. Quite a number of the phenomena that Cognitive Linguistics is interested in – fuzzy boundaries, graded category membership, differences of structural weight, onomasiological salience – are characteristics that are not optimally described by the discrete, all-or-none categories of classical linguistic formalization, but that require a quantitative perspective.

Both methodological developments mentioned here are emerging trends: in neither case have they reached a stable state – but that merely means that they testify to the continued dynamism of lexical semantics in the framework of Cognitive Linguistics.

4 References

Aitchison, Jean (1987): *Words in the Mind. An Introduction to the Mental Lexicon.* Oxford: Blackwell.
Aitchison, Jean (2003): *Words in the Mind. An Introduction to the Mental Lexicon.* 3rd edition. Oxford: Blackwell.
Allan, Kathryn and Justyna A. Robinson (eds.) (2011): *Current Methods in Historical Semantics.* Berlin/New York: Mouton de Gruyter.
Allwood, Jens (2003): Meaning potentials and context: Some consequences for the analysis of variation in meaning. In: H. Cuyckens, R. Dirven and J. Taylor (eds.), *Cognitive Linguistic Approaches to Lexical Semantics*, 29–66. Berlin: Mouton de Gruyter.
Armstrong, Sharon L., Lila R. Gleitman, and Henry Gleitman (1983): What some concepts might not be. *Cognition* 13: 263–308.
Arppe, Antti (2008): *Univariate, Bivariate, and Multivariate Methods in Corpus-Based Lexicography. A study of synonymy.* PhD dissertation, University of Helsinki.
Atkins, B. T. Sue, Michael Rundell and Hiroaki Sato (2003): The contribution of FrameNet to practical lexicography. *International Journal of Lexicography* 16: 333–357.
Baicchi, Annalisa, Cristiano Broccias, and Andrea Sansò (eds.) (2005): *Modelling Thought and Constructing Meaning. Cognitive Models in Interactions.* Milan: FrancoAngeli.
Barcelona, Antonio (ed.) (2000): *Metaphor and Metonymy at the Crossroads: A Cognitive Perspective.* Berlin: Mouton de Gruyter.
Barcelona, Antonio (2005): The multilevel operation of metonymy in grammar and discourse, with particular attention to metonymic chains. In: F. Ruiz de Mendoza Ibañez and S. Peña Cervel (eds.), *Cognitive Linguistics: Internal Dynamics and Interdisciplinary Interaction*, 313–352. Berlin: Mouton de Gruyter.
Barcelona, Antonio (Volume 1): Metonymy. Berlin/Boston: De Gruyter Mouton.
Benczes, Réka, Antonio Barcelona, and Francisco Ruiz de Mendoza Ibáñez (eds.) (2011): *Defining Metonymy in Cognitive Linguistics: Towards a Consensus View.* Amsterdam: John Benjamins Publishing Company.
Bergen, Benjamin K. (Volume 1): Embodiment.
Berlin, Brent (1976): The concept of rank in ethnobiological classification: Some evidence from Aguaruna folk botany. *American Ethnologist* 3: 381–400.
Berlin, Brent (1978): Ethnobiological classification. In: E. Rosch and B. B. Lloyd (eds.), *Cognition and Categorization*, 9–26. Hillsdale: Lawrence Erlbaum Associates.
Berlin, Brent, Dennis E. Breedlove, and Peter H. Raven (1974): *Principles of Tzeltal Plant Classification: An Introduction to the Botanical Ethnography of a Mayan-speaking People of Highland Chiapas.* New York: Academic Press.
Berlin, Brent and Paul Kay (1969): *Basic Color Terms: Their Universality and Evolution.* Berkeley: University of California Press.
Brugman, Claudia (1988): *The Story of 'Over': Polysemy, Semantics and the Structure of the Lexicon.* New York: Garland.
Casad, Eugene H. (1992): Cognition, history and Cora 'yee'. *Cognitive Linguistics* 3: 151–186.
Coulson, Seana and Barbara Lewandowska-Tomaszczyk (eds.) (2005): *The Literal and Nonliteral in Language and Thought.* Frankfurt: Peter Lang.
Craig, Colette (ed.) (1986): *Noun Classes and Categorization.* Amsterdam: John Benjamins Publishing Company.
Croft, William (1993): The role of domains in the interpretation of metaphors and metonymies. *Cognitive Linguistics* 4: 335–370.

Croft, William and D. Alan Cruse (2004): *Cognitive Linguistics*. Cambridge: Cambridge University Press.

Cruse, D. Alan (1994): Prototype theory and lexical relations. *Rivista di Linguistica* 6: 167–188.

Cruse, D. Alan (1995): Between polysemy and monosemy. In: H. Kardela and G. Persson (eds.), *New Trends in Semantics and Lexicography*, 25–34. Umeå: Swedish Science Press.

Cruse, D. Alan (1995): Polysemy and related phenomena from a cognitive linguistic viewpoint. In: P. Saint-Dizier and E. Viegas (eds.), *Computational Lexical Semantics*, 33–49. Cambridge: Cambridge University Press.

Cuyckens, Hubert (1991): *The Semantics of Spatial Prepositions in Dutch: A Cognitive Linguistics Exercise*. Ph.D. dissertation, University of Antwerp.

De Mulder, Walter and Anne Vanderheyden (2001): L'histoire de centre et la sémantique prototypique. *Langue Française* 130: 108–125.

Deane, Paul D. (2005): Multiple spatial representation: On the semantic unity of 'over'. In: B. Hampe (ed.), *From Perception to Meaning: Image Schemas in Cognitive Linguistics*, 235–282. Berlin: Mouton de Gruyter.

Dekeyser, Xavier (1990): The prepositions 'with', 'mid' and 'again(st)' in Old and Middle English: A case study of historical lexical semantics. *Belgian Journal of Linguistics* 5: 35–48.

Dewell, Robert B. (1994): 'Over' again: On the role of image-schemas in semantic analysis. *Cognitive Linguistics* 5: 351–380.

Dirven, René (1985): Metaphor as a basic means for extending the lexicon. In: W. Paprotté and R. Dirven (eds.), *The Ubiquity of Metaphor. Metaphor in Language and Thought*, 85–120. Amsterdam: John Benjamins.

Dirven, René, Louis Goossens, Yvan Putseys, and Emma Vorlat (1982): *The Scene of Linguistic Action and Its Perspectivization by 'Speak', 'Talk', 'Say' and 'Tell'*. Amsterdam: John Benjamins.

Dirven, René and Ralf Pörings (eds.) (2002): *Metaphor and Metonymy in Comparison and Contrast*. Berlin: Mouton de Gruyter.

Divjak, Dagmar (2010): *Structuring the Lexicon: A Clustered Model for Near-Synonymy*. Berlin: Mouton de Gruyter.

Divjak, Dagmar and Catherine Caldwell-Harris (Volume 1): Frequency and entrenchment.

Evans, Vyvyan (2006): Lexical concepts, cognitive models and meaning-construction. *Cognitive Linguistics* 17: 491–534.

Evans, Vyvyan (2009): *How Words Mean: Lexical Concepts, Cognitive Models, and Meaning Construction*. Oxford: Oxford University Press.

Fauconnier, Gilles and Mark Turner (2002): *The Way We Think: Conceptual Blending and the Mind's Hidden Complexities*. New York: Basic Books.

Feyaerts, Kurt (2000): Refining the Inheritance Hypothesis: Interaction between metaphorical and metonymic hierarchies. In: A. Barcelona (ed.), *Metaphor and Metonymy at the Crossroads: A Cognitive Perspective*, 59–78. Berlin: Mouton de Gruyter.

Feyaerts, Kurt (ed.) (2003): *The Bible through Metaphor and Translation: A Cognitive Semantic Perspective*. Bern: Peter Lang.

Fillmore, Charles J. (1977): Scenes-and-frames semantics. In: A. Zampolli (ed.), *Linguistic Structures Processing*, 55–81. Amsterdam: North-Holland Publishing Company.

Fillmore, Charles J. (1985): Frames and the semantics of understanding. *Quaderni di Semantica* 6: 222–254.

Fillmore, Charles J. and B. T. Sue Atkins (1992): Toward a frame-based lexicon: The semantics of 'risk' and its neighbors. In: A. Lehrer and E. Feder Kittay (eds.), *Frames, Fields and Contrasts. New Essays in Semantic and Lexical Organization*, 75–102. Hillsdale: Lawrence Erlbaum Associates.
Fillmore, Charles J. and B. T. Sue Atkins (1994): Starting where dictionaries stop: The challenge of corpus lexicography. In: B.T. S. Atkins and A. Zampolli (eds.), *Computational Approaches to the Lexicon*, 349–393. Oxford: Oxford University Press.
Fillmore, Charles J. and B. T. Sue Atkins (2000): Describing polysemy: The case of 'crawl'. In: Y. Ravin and C. Leacock (eds.), *Polysemy: Theoretical and Computational Approaches*, 91–110. Oxford: Oxford University Press.
Geeraerts, Dirk (1985): *Paradigm and Paradox: Explorations into a Paradigmatic Theory of Meaning and its Epistemological Background*. Leuven: Leuven University Press.
Geeraerts, Dirk (1990): The lexicographical treatment of prototypical polysemy. In: S. L. Tsohatzidis (ed.), *Meanings and Prototypes: Studies in Linguistic Categorization*, 195–210. London: Routledge. (Also in Geeraerts 2006, Words and Other Wonders 327–344.)
Geeraerts, Dirk (1992): The semantic structure of Dutch 'over'. *Leuvense Bijdragen: Leuven Contributions in Linguistics and Philology* 81: 205–230. (Also in Geeraerts 2006, Words and Other Wonders 48–73.)
Geeraerts, Dirk (1993): Vagueness's puzzles, polysemy's vagaries. *Cognitive Linguistics* 4: 223–272. (Also in Geeraerts 2006, Words and Other Wonders 99–148.)
Geeraerts, Dirk (1994): Classical definability and the monosemic bias. *Rivista di Linguistica* 6: 189–207. (Also in Geeraerts 2006, Words and Other Wonders 149–172.)
Geeraerts, Dirk (1997): *Diachronic Prototype Semantics: A Contribution to Historical Lexicology*. Oxford: Clarendon Press.
Geeraerts, Dirk (2000): Salience phenomena in the lexicon: A typology. In: L. Albertazzi (ed.), *Meaning and Cognition*, 79–101. Amsterdam: John Benjamins. (Also in Geeraerts 2006, Words and Other Wonders 74–96.)
Geeraerts, Dirk (2007): Lexicography. In: D. Geeraerts and H. Cuyckens (eds.), *The Oxford Handbook of Cognitive Linguistics*, 1160–1175. New York: Oxford University Press.
Geeraerts, Dirk (2010): *Theories of Lexical Semantics*. Oxford: Oxford University Press.
Geeraerts, Dirk and Gitte Kristiansen (this volume): Variationist linguistics.
Geeraerts, Dirk, Stefan Grondelaers, and Peter Bakema (1994): *The Structure of Lexical Variation: Meaning, Naming, and Context*. Berlin: Mouton de Gruyter.
Gibbs, Raymond W. (ed.) (2008): *The Cambridge Handbook of Metaphor and Thought*. Cambridge: Cambridge University Press.
Gibbs, Raymond W. Jr. and Gerard J. Steen (eds.) (1999): *Metaphor in Cognitive Linguistics*. Amsterdam: John Benjamins.
Gibbs, Raymond W. Jr. (Volume 1): Metaphor.
Glynn, Dylan (2010): Testing the hypothesis. Objectivity and verification in usage-based Cognitive Semantics. In: D. Glynn and K. Fischer (eds.), *Quantitative Methods in Cognitive Semantics: Corpus-Driven Approaches*, 239–269. Berlin: Mouton de Gruyter.
Gries, Stefan Th. (Volume 3): Polysemy. Berlin/Boston: De Gruyter Mouton.
Hanks, Patrick W. (1994): Linguistic norms and pragmatic exploitations, or why lexicographers need prototype theory and vice versa. In: F. Kiefer, G. Kiss and J. Pajzs (eds.), *Papers in Computational Lexicography*, 89–113. Budapest: Hungarian Academy of Sciences.
Hilpert, Martin (this volume): Historical linguistics.

Janssen, Theo (2003): Monosemy versus polysemy. In: H. Cuyckens, R. Dirven and J. Taylor (eds.), *Cognitive Approaches to Lexical Semantics*, 93–122. Berlin/New York: Mouton de Gruyter.

Johnson, Christopher R., Charles J. Fillmore, Esther J. Wood, Josef Ruppenhofer, Margaret Urban, Miriam R. L. Petruck, and Collin F. Baker (2002): *FrameNet: Theory and Practice*. Berkeley: International Computer Science Institute.

Kempton, Willett (1981): *The Folk Classification of Ceramics: A Study in Cognitive Prototypes*. New York: Academic Press.

Kleiber, Georges (1990): *La sémantique du prototype. Catégories et sens lexical*. Paris: Presses Universitaires de France.

Kövecses, Zoltán (2000): *Metaphor and Emotion: Language, Culture and Body in Human Feeling*. Cambridge: Cambridge University Press.

Kövecses, Zoltán (2002): *Metaphor: A Practical Introduction*. Oxford: Oxford University Press.

Kövecses, Zoltán (2005): *Metaphor in Culture: Universality and Variation*. Oxford: Oxford Uiversity Press.

Lakoff, George (1987): *Women, Fire and Dangerous Things: What Categories Reveal about the Mind*. Chicago: University of Chicago Press.

Lakoff, George and Mark Johnson (1980): *Metaphors We Live by*. Chicago: University of Chicago Press.

Langacker, Ronald W. (1987): *Foundations of Cognitive Grammar*, Volume 1: *Theoretical Prerequisites*. Stanford: Stanford University Press.

Lawler, John M. (1989): Lexical semantics in the commercial transaction frame: Value, worth, cost and price. *Studies in Language* 13: 381–404.

Lehrer, Adrienne and Eva Feder Kittay (eds.) (1992): *Frames, Fields, and Contrasts: New Essays in Semantic and Lexical Organization*. Hillsdale: Lawrence Erlbaum Associates.

Lewandowka-Tomaszczyk, Barbara (2007): Polysemy, prototyes, and radial categories. In: D. Geeraerts and H. Cuyckens (eds.), *The Oxford Handbook of Cognitive Linguistics*, 139–169. New York: Oxford University Press.

Lutzeier, Peter Rolf (1992): Wortfeldtheorie und kognitive Linguistik. *Deutsche Sprache* 20: 62–81.

Mangasser-Wahl, Martina (2000): *Von der Prototypentheorie zur empirischen Semantik*. Frankfurt: Peter Lang.

Martin, Willy (2001): A frame-based approach to polysemy. In: H. Cuyckens and B. Zawada (eds.), *Polysemy in Cognitive Linguistics*, 57–81. Amsterdam: John Benjamins.

Molina, Clara (2005): On the role of onomasiological profiles in merger discontinuations. In: N. Delbecque, J. Van der Auwera and D. Geeraerts (eds.), *Perspectives on Variation: Sociolinguistic, Historical, Comparative*, 177–194. Berlin: Mouton de Gruyter.

Murphy, Gregory L. (2002): *The Big Book of Concepts*. Cambridge: MIT Press.

Nerlich, Brigitte and David D. Clarke (1992): Outline of a model for semantic change. In: G. Kellermann and M. D. Morrissey (eds.), *Diachrony within Synchrony: Language History and Cognition*, 125–141. Frankfurt: Peter Lang.

Nerlich, Brigitte and David D. Clarke (2000): Semantic fields and frames: Historical explorations of the interface between language, action and cognition. *Journal of Pragmatics* 32: 125–150.

Norrick, Neal R. (1981): *Semiotic Principles in Semantic Theory*. Amsterdam: John Benjamins.

Nunberg, Geoffrey (1978): *The Pragmatics of Reference*. Bloomington: Indiana University Linguistics Club.

Ortony, Andrew (ed.) (1979): *Metaphor and Thought*. Cambridge: Cambridge University Press.

Ortony, Andrew (ed.) (1993): *Metaphor and Thought*. 2nd edition. Cambridge: Cambridge University Press.

Panther, Klaus-Uwe (2005): The role of conceptual metonymy in meaning construction. In: F. Ruiz de Mendoza Ibañez and S. Peña Cervel (eds.), *Cognitive Linguistics: Internal Dynamics and Interdisciplinary Interaction*, 353–386. Berlin: Mouton de Gruyter.

Panther, Klaus-Uwe and Günter Radden (eds.) (1999): *Metonymy in Language and Thought*. Amsterdam: John Benjamins Publishing Company.

Panther, Klaus-Uwe and Linda Thornburg (1998): A cognitive approach to inferencing in conversation. *Journal of Pragmatics* 30: 755–769.

Panther, Klaus-Uwe and Linda Thornburg (eds.) (2003): *Metonymy and Pragmatic Inferencing*. Amsterdam: John Benjamins.

Paprotté, Wolf and René Dirven (eds.) (1985): *The Ubiquity of Metaphor: Metaphor in Language and Thought*. Amsterdam: John Benjamins.

Paradis, Carita (2004): Where does metonymy stop? Senses, facets, and active zones. *Metaphor and Symbol* 19: 245–264.

Paradis, Carita, Caroline Willners, and Steven Jones (2009): Good and bad opposites: Using textual and experimental techniques to measure antonym canonicity. *The Mental Lexicon* 4: 380–429.

Peirsman, Yves and Dirk Geeraerts (2006): Metonymy as a prototypical category. *Cognitive Linguistics* 17: 269–316.

Posner, Michael (1986): Empirical studies of prototypes. In: C. Craig (ed.), *Noun Classes and Categorization*, 53–61. Amsterdam: John Benjamins.

Post, Michael (1988): Scenes-and-frames semantics as a neo-lexical field theory. In: W. Hüllen and R. Schulze (eds.), *Understanding the Lexicon. Meaning, Sense and World Knowledge in Lexical Semantics*, 36–47. Tübingen: Max Niemeyer Verlag.

Riemer, Nick (2005): *The Semantics of Polysemy. Reading Meaning in English and Warlpiri*. Berlin: Mouton de Gruyter.

Robinson, Justyna A. (2010): Awesome insights into semantic variation. In: D. Geeraerts, G. Kristiansen and Y. Peirsman (eds.), *Advances in Cognitive Sociolinguistics*, 85–110. Berlin/New York: Mouton de Gruyter.

Rojo, Ana and Javier Valenzuela (1998): Frame semantics and lexical translation. *Babel* 44: 128–138.

Rosch, Eleanor (1977): Human categorization. In: N. Warren (ed.), *Studies in Cross-cultural Psychology*, 1–49. New York: Academic Press.

Rosch, Eleanor and Carolyn B. Mervis (1975): Family resemblances: Studies in the internal structure of categories. *Cognitive Psychology* 7: 573–605.

Rudzka-Ostyn, Brygida (ed.) (1988): *Topics in Cognitive Linguistics*. Amsterdam: John Benjamins.

Ruiz de Mendoza Ibáñez, Francisco (2000): The role of mappings and domains in understanding metonymy. In: A. Barcelona (ed.), *Metaphor and Metonymy at the Crossroads. A Cognitive Perspective*, 109–132. Berlin: Mouton de Gruyter.

Ruiz de Mendoza Ibáñez, Francisco and Sandra Peña Cervel (2005): Conceptual interaction, cognitive operations and projection spaces. In: F. Ruiz de Mendoza Ibañez and S. Peña Cervel (eds.), *Cognitive Linguistics: Internal Dynamics and Interdisciplinary Interaction*, 249–279. Berlin: Mouton de Gruyter.

Ruppenhofer, Josef, Michael Ellsworth, Miriam R. L. Petruck, Christopher R. Johnson, and Jan Scheffczyk (2006): *FrameNet II: Extended Theory and Practice*. Berkeley: FrameNet.

Schmid, Hans-Jörg (1993): *Cottage und Co., idea, start vs. begin. Die Kategorisierung als Grundprinzip einer differenzierten Bedeutungsbeschreibung.* Tübingen: Max Niemeyer Verlag.

Schmid, Hans-Jörg (2000): *English Abstract Nouns as Conceptual Shells: From Corpus to Cognition.* Berlin: Mouton de Gruyter.

Schmid, Hans-Jörg (2007): Entrenchment, salience, and basic levels. In: D. Geeraerts and H. Cuyckens (eds.), *The Oxford Handbook of Cognitive Linguistics*, 117–138. New York: Oxford University Press.

Semino, Elena (2008): *Metaphor in Discourse.* Cambridge: Cambridge University Press.

Soares da Silva, Augusto (1999): *A Semântica de 'deixar'. Uma Contribuição para a Abordagem Cognitiva em Semântica Lexical.* Lisboa: Fundação Calouste Gulbenkian.

Soares da Silva, Augusto (2003): Image schemas and category coherence: The case of the Portuguese verb 'deixar'. In: H. Cuyckens, R. Dirven and J. Taylor (eds.), *Cognitive Approaches to Lexical Semantics*, 281–322. Berlin: Mouton de Gruyter.

Soares da Silva, Augusto (2005): Para o estudo das relações lexicais entre o Português Europeu e o Português do Brasil: Elementos de sociolexicologia cognitiva e quantitativa do Português. In: I. Duarte and I. Leiria (eds.), *Actas do XX Encontro Nacional da Associação Portuguesa de Linguística*, 211–226. Lisboa: Associação Portuguesa de Linguística.

Speelman, Dirk, Stefan Grondelaers, and Dirk Geeraerts (2003): Profile-based linguistic uniformity as a generic method for comparing language varieties. *Computers and the Humanities* 37: 317–337.

Steen, Gerard J. (2007): *Finding Metaphor in Grammar and Usage: A Methodological Analysis of Theory and Research.* Amsterdam: John Benjamins Publishing Company.

Sweetser, Eve E. (1986): Polysemy vs. abstraction: Mutually exclusive or complementary? In V. Nikiforidou, M. Van Clay, M. Niepokuj and D. Feder (eds.), *Proceedings of the Twelfth Annual Meeting of the Berkeley Linguistics Society*, 528–538. Berkeley: Berkeley Linguistics Society.

Sweetser, Eve E. (1987): The definition of 'lie': An examination of the folk models underlying a semantic prototype. In: D. Holland and N. Quinn (eds.), *Cultural Models in Language and Thought*, 43–66. Cambridge: Cambridge University Press.

Sweetser, Eve E. (1990): *From Etymology to Pragmatics: Metaphorical and Cultural Aspects of Semantic Structure.* Cambridge: Cambridge University Press.

Szelid, Veronika and Dirk Geeraerts (2008): Usage-based dialectology: Emotion concepts in the Southern Csango dialect. *Annual Review of Cognitive Linguistics* 6: 23–49.

Taylor, John R. (1989): *Linguistic Categorization: Prototypes in Linguistic Theory.* Oxford: Clarendon Press.

Taylor, John R. (1992): How many meanings does a word have? *Stellenbosch Papers in Linguistics* 25: 133–168.

Taylor, John R. (2003a): Cognitive models of polysemy. In: B. Nerlich, Z. Todd, V. Herman and D. D. Clarke (eds.), *Polysemy: Flexible Patterns of Meaning in Mind and Language*, 31–47. Berlin: Mouton de Gruyter.

Taylor, John R. (2003b): *Linguistic Categorization.* 3rd edition. Oxford: Oxford University Press.

Taylor, John R. (2006): Polysemy and the lexicon. In: G. Kristiansen, M. Achard, R. Dirven and F. Ruiz de Mendoza Ibañez (eds.), *Cognitive Linguistics: Current Applications and Future Perspectives*, 51–80. Berlin: Mouton de Gruyter.

Tissari, Heli (2003): *LOVEscapes. Changes in Prototypical Senses and Cognitive Metaphors since 1500*. Helsinki: Société Néophilologique de Helsinki.
Tsohatzidis, Savas L. (ed.) (1989): *Meanings and Prototypes*: *Studies in Linguistic Categorization*. London: Routledge.
Tuggy, David (1993): Ambiguity, polysemy, and vagueness. *Cognitive Linguistics* 4: 273–290.
Turner, Mark (1987): *Death is the Mother of Beauty: Mind, Metaphor, Criticism*. Chicago: University of Chicago Press.
Turner, Mark (1996): *The Literary Mind*: *The Origins of Thought and Language*. New York: Oxford University Press.
Turner, Mark (volume 1): Blending in language and communication.
Tyler, Andrea and Vyvyan Evans (2003): *The Semantics of English Prepositions*: *Spatial Scenes, Embodied Meaning and Cognition*. Cambridge: Cambridge University Press.
Vandeloise, Claude (1990): Representation, prototypes, and centrality. In: S. L. Tsohatzidis (ed.), *Meanings and Prototypes*: *Studies in Linguistic Categorization*, 403–437. London: Routledge.
Wierzbicka, Anna (1985): *Lexicography and Conceptual Analysis*. Ann Arbor: Karoma.
Winters, Margaret E., Heli Tissari, and Kathryn Allan (eds.) (2010): *Historical Cognitive Linguistics*. Berlin/New York: Mouton de Gruyter.
Zenner, Eline, Dirk Speelman, and Dirk Geeraerts (2012): Cognitive Sociolinguistics meets loanword research: Measuring variation in the success of anglicisms in Dutch. *Cognitive Linguistics* 23: 749–792.
Zlatev, Jordan (2003): Polysemy or generality? Mu. In: H. Cuyckens, R. Dirven and J. Taylor (eds.), *Cognitive Approaches to Lexical Semantics*, 447–494. Berlin: Mouton de Gruyter.
Zwicky, Arnold and Jerry Sadock (1975): Ambiguity tests and how to fail them. In: J. Kimball (ed.), *Syntax and Semantics*, Volume: 4, 1–36. New York: Academic Press.

Holger Diessel
Chapter 3: Usage-based construction grammar

1 Introduction

The general goal of research on grammar in cognitive linguistics is to develop a framework for the analysis of linguistic structure that is grounded in general cognitive processes, i.e., processes that are not only involved in language, but also in other cognitive phenomena such as vision, attention, and abstract thought. The cognitive approach to the study of grammar contrasts sharply with the generative theory of grammar in which the core of the language users' grammatical knowledge (i.e., competence) is assigned to a particular faculty of the mind including innate categories and constraints that are exclusively needed for language (Pinker and Jackendoff 2005). In the cognitive approach there is no particular language faculty and grammatical knowledge is derived from linguistic experience. On this view, grammar is an "emergent phenomenon" (Hopper 1987) shaped by general psychological mechanisms such as categorization, analogy, and entrenchment (see volume 1; see also Diessel 2011a for a review).

Early research in cognitive linguistics emphasized the importance of non-linguistic (spatial) concepts for the analysis of grammatical categories. Word classes, for instance, were described by means of conceptual primitives such as "boundedness" (e.g., count nouns and telic verbs are "bounded" vs. mass nouns and activity verbs are "unbounded"), and complex sentences were analyzed in terms of the figure-ground segregation, which gestalt psychologists proposed for the analysis of visual perception (Langacker 1982; Talmy 1978, 1988). In this early research, linguistic structure is immediately based on conceptual structure; but soon it became clear that an important aspect is missing in this approach, namely usage and development.

There is good evidence that linguistic structure and conceptual structure are related; but the relationship between them is indirect – it is mediated by language development, which in turn is driven by language use. This view of grammar underlies the "usage-based approach" – a term that Langacker (1988) proposed to emphasize the importance of usage and development for the analysis of linguistic structure. The general idea of this approach may be summarized as follows (cf. Hopper 1987; Langacker 2008; Bybee 2010):

> Grammar is a dynamic system of emergent categories and flexible constraints that are always changing under the influence of domain-general cognitive processes involved in language use.

The usage-based approach challenges central assumptions of linguistic analysis that have influenced grammatical research throughout the 20th century:
- It challenges the rigid division between the language system and language use, or competence (i.e., langue) and performance (i.e., parole).
- It abandons the structuralist dictum that the study of (synchronic) linguistic states must be separated from the study of (diachronic) language change.
- And it rejects the common assumption that syntactic analysis presupposes a set of primitive categories such as subject and noun phrase, which in other grammatical theories are often used as a "toolkit" for linguistic analysis (Jackendoff 2002: 75).

If we think of grammar as a dynamic system of emergent structures and flexible constraints, we cannot posit the existence of particular syntactic categories prior to grammatical analysis. On the contrary, what we need to explain is how linguistic structures evolve and change, both in history and acquisition. This explains why cognitive grammarians have turned to the study of language acquisition (e.g., Goldberg 2006) and why cognitive research on grammar has formed such a close liaison with research on grammaticalization (e.g., Bybee 2010; Hilpert 2013; Traugott and Trousdale 2013; see also Diessel 2007, 2011b, 2012 for some discussion of the parallels between L1 acquisition and language change). In the structuralist paradigm, grammatical theory seeks to provide formal representations of linguistic structure; but in the usage-based approach, grammatical research is primarily concerned with the dynamics of the grammatical system. This does not mean, however, that grammar is completely unconstrained in this approach. Like any other grammatical theory, the usage-based model rests on particular assumptions about the nature of grammatical elements and the overall organization of the grammatical system. As I see it, there are two general principles that underlie or constrain the analysis of linguistic structure in this approach:
- First, linguistic structure can be analyzed in terms of complex signs, i.e., constructions, combining a specific structural pattern with a particular function or meaning.
- Second, all linguistic signs (i.e., lexical signs and grammatical signs) are connected with each other by various types of links so that grammar (or language in general) can be seen as a dynamic network of interconnected signs.

The first principle has been discussed extensively. There is a large body of research on the symbolic nature of grammar and the importance of constructions in the usage-based approach (see Croft 2007 and Fried 2010 for two recent reviews of this research); but the second principle has not yet been sufficiently described and will be in the focus of this chapter. Section 2 provides a short discussion of the notion of construction and the nature of linguistic signs; and the rest of the chapter is concerned with the general architecture of grammar in the usage-based approach.

2 Signs, constructions, and lexemes

2.1 Some basic definitions

The ability to use signs or symbols is a fundamental capacity of the human mind providing a prerequisite for disembodied cognition and language (cf. Deacon 1997; Tomasello 1999). The classic example of a linguistic sign is the word (or lexeme). According to Saussure ([1916] 1994: 67), a word is a "two-sided psychological entity" that combines a particular form, i.e., the "signifier" (or "significant"), with a particular meaning, i.e., the "signified" (or 'signifié'). The English word *head*, for instance, consists of a specific sound pattern (i.e., [hɛd]) that is associated with a particular concept (or more specifically, with a network of related concepts, e.g., head as a body part, head of department, head of table; see Gries Volume 3).

Traditionally, the notion of sign is reserved for lexical expressions; but in cognitive linguistics it has been extended to grammatical entities, notably to constructions. A construction is as a grammatical unit in which a particular structural pattern is associated with a specific function or meaning. Construction grammar has played an important role in the development of the usage-based approach. In fact, in the literature construction grammar is often described as an integral part of the usage-based approach to the study of grammar

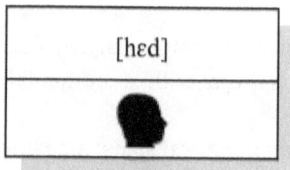

Fig. 3.1: Linguistic sign.

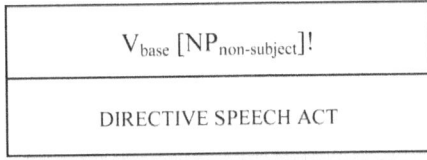

Fig. 3.2: The imperative construction.

(cf. Bybee 2010; Goldberg 2006; Hilpert 2014; Langacker 2008; Tomasello 2003; see also Diessel 2004: chapter 2); but the notion of construction grammar refers to a whole family of theories which are not all usage-based (see Hoffmann and Trousdale 2013 for a recent survey of different construction-based theories). Indeed, one of the earliest and most influential construction-based theories, i.e., the sign-based theory of construction grammar developed by Fillmore and Kay (1999), adopts the generative division between competence and performance and disregards usage and development (see also Michaelis 2013; Sag 2012). Other varieties of construction grammar, such as Cognitive Grammar (Langacker 2008) and Radical Construction Grammar (Croft 2001), take a dynamic perspective and have made important contributions to the usage-based approach (see also Bybee 2010; Goldberg 2006; Tomasello 2003; Steels 2011).

Constructions vary across a continuum of schematicity or abstractness. The term applies to both grammatical units that are associated with particular lexemes, e.g., idioms such as *kick the bucket* and prefabricated expressions such as *I don't know*, and grammatical units that are defined over abstract categories, or "slots", which can be filled by certain types of expressions. Consider, for instance, an imperative sentence such as *Open the door*, which is based on a "constructional schema" (Langacker 2008: 167) combing a particular syntactic configuration of linguistic elements with a particular function or meaning. In English, an imperative sentence includes an uninflected verb form at the beginning of the sentence, it usually lacks an overt subject, may include a postverbal element, e.g., a noun phrase or prepositional phrase, and functions as directive speech act. Imperative sentences can be analyzed as grammatical signs, i.e., constructions, that speakers use to express a particular illocutionary force (cf. Figure 3.2).

Like lexemes, constructions can be polysemous, i.e., they can have multiple functions or meanings. The imperative construction, for instance, can express a command, a request, an instruction, a warning, a permission, or good wishes (cf. 1–6) (cf. Stefanowitsch 2003; see also Searle 1979 for a general discussion of this point).

(1) Open the door!   Command

(2) Please pass me the salt.   Request

(3) Melt the butter in the saucepan.   Instruction

(4) Uh yeah go on there.   Permission

(5) Just be careful!   Warning

(6) Have a great birthday!   Good wishes

The notion of construction has a long history in linguistics. Traditionally, the term applies to particular clause types and phrases, e.g., imperative sentences, relative clauses, complex NPs including genitive attributes. However, in construction grammar the term has been extended to all grammatical patterns including highly productive clause types (e.g., transitive clauses) and phrases (e.g., ordinary PPs) (see below).

Note that in some of the usage-based literature, the notion of construction is not only used for grammatical patterns but also for lexical expressions (cf. Goldberg 1995; Croft and Cruse 2004: chapter 9). Both constructions and lexemes are signs, i.e., conventionalized form-function pairings; however, given that the parallels between lexemes and constructions are already captured by the notion of sign, there is no need to extend the notion of construction to lexical expressions. I will therefore restrict the notion of construction to grammatical units consisting of at least two elements (e.g., two lexemes or two categories) and will use the notion of sign as a cover term for both lexemes (i.e., lexical signs) and constructions (i.e., grammatical signs).[1]

2.2 Some general aspects of constructions

While construction grammarians have emphasized the importance of constructions for syntactic analysis, generative linguists have questioned the usefulness of this term. In fact, in Minimalism, i.e., the most recent versions of generative grammar, the notion of construction has been abandoned in favour of a fully compositional approach in which all syntactic structures are derived from atomic primitives and combinatorial rules (cf. Chomsky 1995: 4). Cognitive linguists

---

[1] Morphologically complex words consisting of multiple morphemes (e.g., *armchair*, *untrue*) can be seen as particular types of constructions, i.e., as "morphological constructions" (cf. Langacker 1987: 83–85).

NP *be* V-*ed* [*by* NP]
X IS AFFECTED [BY Y]

Fig. 3.3: The passive construction.

do not deny the compositionality of linguistic structure. In fact, if we restrict the notion of construction to grammatical patterns, i.e., if we exclude single lexemes from the notion of construction (see above), constructions are generally divisible into particular components that contribute to their meanings. However, compositionality is a matter of degree, and constructions are also associated with holistic properties, i.e., properties that are linked to the entire grammatical pattern rather than to particular components.

The best evidence for this comes perhaps from structures such as imperative sentences, which have always been analyzed as constructions. In traditional grammar (and early versions of generative grammar) these structures were described by means of construction-particular rules (or "transformations" in the "aspect model" of generative grammar; cf. Chomsky 1965), i.e., rules that are exclusively needed to derive a particular morphosyntactic pattern from atomic primitives. However, in Minimalism all construction-particular rules are eliminated and replaced by general syntactic operations such as "Move alpha" (Chomsky 1995). In contrast to Minimalism, usage-based construction grammar is a surface-oriented theory in which construction-particular properties are seen as an important aspect of grammar that cannot be explained by general rules (i.e., rules that are independent of particular constructions).

Take, for instance, a passive sentence such as *The door was opened by Peter*, which involves a particular configuration of grammatical elements: a clause-initial NP encoding the subject, a particular verb form consisting of the past participle of a transitive verb and the auxiliary *be*, and optionally a *by*-phrase denoting a semantic argument, i.e., the agent of the activity expressed by the verb. While passive sentences share important properties with other clause types (e.g., word order, subject-verb agreement), this configuration of syntactic elements is unique and associated with a particular meaning or function (i.e., a particular perspective on a causative event and a particular information structure, cf. Langacker 1991: 200–207). One way of analyzing this mixture of general and idiosyncratic properties is to assume that passive sentences are licensed by a constructional schema (cf. Figure 3.3).

The holistic properties of the passive are reminiscent of idiosyncratic properties of idiomatic expressions. In the generative approach, idioms are analyzed as irregular expressions that are stored together with words in the mental lexicon. But in the cognitive approach, idioms are analyzed in the same way as non-idiomatic grammatical expressions, i.e., constructions. On this view, there is no principled difference between a passive sentence such as *The door was opened by Peter* and an idiom such as *Where are you headed?* Like the passive, this idiom shares certain properties with other grammatical entities: It has the same word order as ordinary content questions and the auxiliary is inflected as in any other sentence type; but the meaning of the verb is of course idiosyncratic and cannot be derived by means of general (semantic) rules.

Idioms have played an important role in the development of construction grammar (cf. Fillmore et al. 1988; Nunberg et al. 1994). There is a wide range of idiomatic expressions that overlap to different degrees with regular grammatical patterns. Semantically, most idioms are unpredictable (e.g., *kick the bucket*); but some idiomatic expressions are semantically transparent in that their meaning can be derived by means of pragmatic principles (e.g., *answer the door*) (cf. Nunberg et al. 1994). Similarly, while some idiomatic expressions are syntactically irregular (e.g., *all of a sudden*), most idioms share some of their morphosyntactic properties with non-idiomatic grammatical expressions (e.g., *Curiosity killed the cat* has the same structure as an ordinary transitive clause) (cf. Fillmore et al. 1988). What is more, some idioms include "slots" like regular grammatical expressions. The comparative correlative construction (e.g., *The bigger, the better*), for instance, can be seen as a schematic idiom consisting of a lexically-specific frame, two comparative adjectives, and two slots that may or may not be filled by regular expressions (i.e., *The ADJ_{er} ___ the ADJ_{er} ___*).

Taken together, this research suggests that idiomaticity constitutes a continuum ranging from structures that are completely idiosyncratic and lexically particular to structures that share most of their semantic and syntactic properties with other grammatical patterns. On this view, there is no rigid division between idioms such as the comparative correlative construction, particular clause types such as the passive, and fully productive grammatical patterns such as basic declarative sentences. In fact, there is evidence that even the most productive and most variable clause types, e.g., the transitive SVO, have holistic properties, i.e., properties that are associated with the entire structural pattern.

2.3 The English transitive construction

In English, a (prototypical) transitive sentence consists of a clause-initial NP encoding the subject, a transitive verb denoting a causative event, and a post-

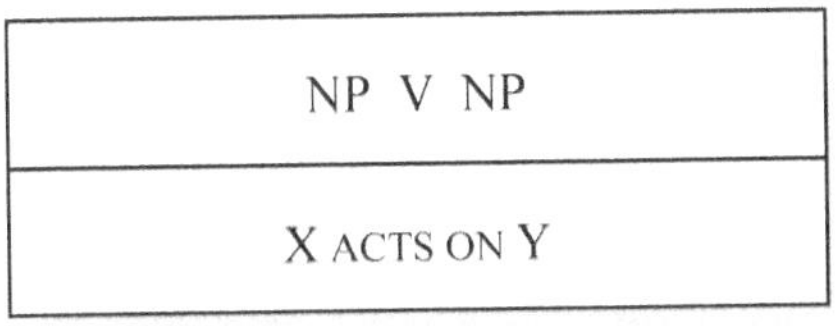

NP V NP
X ACTS ON Y

Fig. 3.4: The transitive construction.

verbal NP encoding the object (e.g., *Peter closed the door*). In the syntactic literature, transitive sentences are commonly analyzed as fully compositional expressions formed from primitive categories by means of general rules; but research in psycholinguistics suggests that speakers of English conceive of the NP-V-NP sequence (or SVO) as a holistic entity that is associated with a particular scene involving an actor (or experiencer) and undergoer (or theme).

In a seminal study on sentence processing and language acquisition, Thomas Bever (1970) showed that English-speaking children often misinterpret passive sentences as active transitive clauses if the active interpretation is compatible with the meaning of the words in a (given) passive construction. For instance, a passive sentence such as *The girl was kissed by the boy* may be interpreted as an active sentence, meaning 'The girl kissed the boy', despite the fact that the structure occurs with passive morphology. There is evidence from psycholinguistic research that in English word order provides a stronger cue for grammatical relations than morphology so that English-speaking children often ignore the morphological marking of passive sentences and interpret them as active transitive clauses (cf. Slobin and Bever 1982). Since this type of mistake also occurs with several other clause types involving the order NP-V-NP (e.g., cleft sentences, reduced relative clauses), Bever suggested that children interpret these sentences based on a grammatical "template", which he called the "canonical sentence schema" of English. Subsequent research revealed that the same type of mistake occurs in comprehension experiments with adult speakers when they are put under time pressure while processing passive sentences or reduced relative clauses (cf. Ferreira 2003; see also Townsend and Bever 2001). Bever interpreted the canonical sentence schema as a "pseudosyntactic" device that children (and adults) use in lieu of true syntactic rules, as described in generative grammar; but from the perspective of construction grammar, the canonical sentence schema is a construction combining a particular structural pattern, i.e., NP-V-NP, with a particular meaning (cf. Figure 3.4).

2.4 The network architecture of language

In accordance with this view, cognitive research on grammar analyzes all clausal and phrasal patterns as constructions; i.e., as complex linguistic signs combining a particular structural pattern with a particular function or meaning. If grammar consists of grammatical signs, i.e., constructions, there is no principled difference between grammar and lexicon as in other theoretical approaches. This view of grammar has far-reaching implications for grammatical analysis. If linguistic structure consists of signs it is a plausible hypothesis that grammar is organized in the same way as the mental lexicon, which is commonly characterized as a network of related signs or symbols (cf. Figure 3.5).

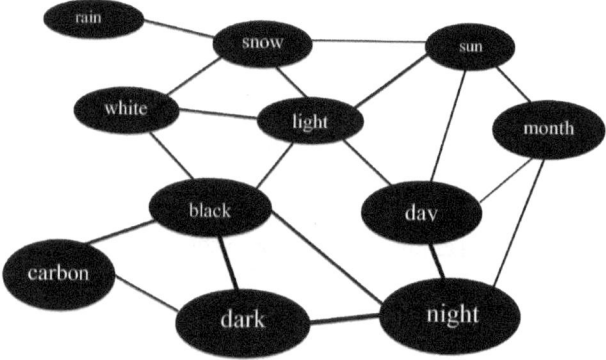

Fig. 3.5: Lexical network.

In accordance with this view, cognitive linguists think of grammar as a network of interconnected signs, or a "structured inventory" of "symbolic units" (Langacker 1987: 57), that are related to each other by various types of links reflecting overlapping aspects of their structure, function, and meaning (cf. Goldberg 1995; Croft 2001; Bybee 2010; see also Diessel 1997). In generative linguistics, grammar and lexicon are two strictly distinguished components (or "modules"); but usage-based construction grammar has abandoned the division between lexicon and grammar in favour of a network model in which all linguistic elements are potentially connected with each other.

Network models have a long tradition in cognitive science. There are many different types of network models – some theoretical, some computational – that vary with regard to a wide range of parameters (see Elman 1995 for an overview); but what all network models have in common is that they are designed to "process" data and to "learn" from experience through data processing. Network models are thus usage-based models by definition.

In the remainder of this chapter, I will consider four different types of links between linguistic elements that are important to understand the network architecture of grammar in the usage-based approach, namely the links between ...
– constructions at different levels of abstractness [taxonomic links]
– constructions at the same level of abstractness [horizontal links]
– constructions and syntactic categories [syntactic links]
– constructions and lexical expressions [lexical links]

3 Constructions at different levels of abstractness [taxonomic links]

The first type of link concerns the hierarchical organization of grammar. As argued in section 2, constructions are schematic representations of linguistic structure that are instantiated in concrete utterances, sometimes referred to as "constructs" (cf. Fried 2010). The relationship between constructs and constructions is based on a process of schematization, which can be seen as a type of implicit learning (see Matthews and Krajewski this volume and Baayen and Ramscar volume 1) (cf. Figure 3.6).

Constructions emerge as generalizations over strings of concrete lexical expressions with similar forms and meanings. While this may happen at any time, most constructions are learned during childhood. The study of first language acquisition plays thus an important role in the usage-based analysis of linguistic structure (see Diessel 2013 for a recent review of usage-based research on the acquisition of constructions).

There is abundant evidence from psycholinguistic research that children are very good in detecting distributional regularities in strings of lexical expres-

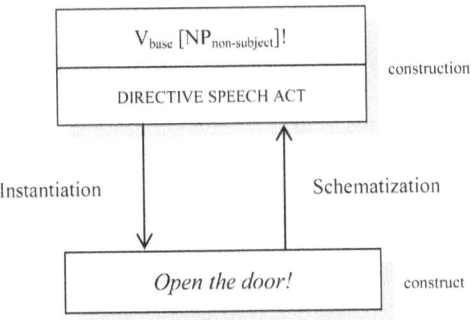

Fig. 3.6: Constructions and constructs.

Tab. 3.1: Sample sentences of an artificial grammar, adopted from Gómez and Gerken (1999: 114).

Condition 1	Condition 2
VOT PEL JIC	PEL TAM RUD RUD
PEL TAM PEL JIC	VOT JIC RUD TAM JIC
PEL TAM JIC RUD TAM RUD	VOT JIC RUD TAM RUD
REL TAM JIC RUD TAM JIC	VOT PEL JIC RUD TAM
VOT PEL PEL JIC RUD TAM	PEL TAM PEL PEL PEL JIC

sions. For instance, in a series of studies Gómez and Gerken (1999) exposed 12-month-old infants to strings of monosyllabic nonce words (e.g., vot, pel, jic) that appeared in different structural patterns, or constructions, defined by linear order and the number of words they include. Each word the children learned occurred in one or more constructions in particular structural positions (e.g., after the first word, at the end of the construction). After training, i.e., after the infants had been exposed to the constructions for a few minutes, they were tested under two conditions (cf. Table 3.1).

In condition 1, they listened to the same constructions as the ones they had heard during training, but with different words; that is, each word the children had learned during training was replaced by a novel nonce word with the same distributional properties. And in condition 2, the infants were exposed to others constructions (i.e., constructions involving other word orders and including different numbers of words), but with the same novel nonce words as in condition 1. Using the head-turn preference procedure, Gómez and Gerken found that the infants recognized the constructions to which they were exposed during training although they had not heard any of the words of the test sentences before, suggesting that children as young as one year of age are able to abstract beyond specific words and to acquire abstract syntactic categories or schemas (see also Marcus et al. 1999).

However, a number of studies have argued that children are conservative learners who tend to restrict syntactic generalizations to particular lexical expressions that are commonly used in a constructional schema (cf. Gerken 2006). This is consistent with the hypothesis that children's early constructions in speech production are organized around particular words (cf. Lieven et al. 1997; Tomasello 1992, 2000, 2003). In a classic study, Martin Braine (1976) suggested that children's early multi-word utterances are "pivot schemas" that are composed of specific "pivot words", i.e., relational terms, and "open slots" that can be filled by various expressions as long as these expressions are semantically compatible with the pivot word (cf. Table 3.2).

Tab. 3.2: Pivot constructions (Braine 1976).

Pivot word	More __	All __	No __
Examples	More car	All broke	No bed
	More cereal	All clean	No down
	More cookie	All done	No fix
	More fish	All dressed	No home
	More juice	All dry	No mama
	More toast	All shut	No pee

Building on this research, Tomasello (1992) characterized children's early pivot schemas as "verb-island constructions" because most of them are based on pivot verbs; but there are also pivot schemas that revolve around other types of words (cf. Lieven et al. 1997; Dąbrowska 2004). Children's early questions, for instance, are usually organized around particular question words.

Like verb-argument constructions, questions originate from fixed expressions (e.g., *What-s-this?*) and formulaic frames (e.g., *Where-s __?*). As children grow older, their questions become increasingly more complex and variable. Consider, for instance, the sentences in (7) to (15), which illustrate the development of a particular type of question in the speech of a two-year-old child named Naomi (cf. Dąbrowska 2000).

(7) What doing? (many times) 1;11.11

(8) What's Mommy doing? (many times) 1;11.21

(9) What's donkey doing? (4 times) 2;0.18

(10) What's Nomi doing? (2 times) 2;0.18

(11) What's toy doing? 2;0.18

(12) What's Mommy holding? 2;0.26

(13) What's Georgie saying? 2;1.19

(14) What is the boy making? 2;11.17

(15) What is Andy doing? 2;11.18

As can be seen, the development originates from a pattern consisting of the question word *what* and the verb *doing*, which Naomi used many times before *what* appeared in any other context. Later, the child inserted the noun *Mommy* into this pattern; but it was only after the second birthday that she began to

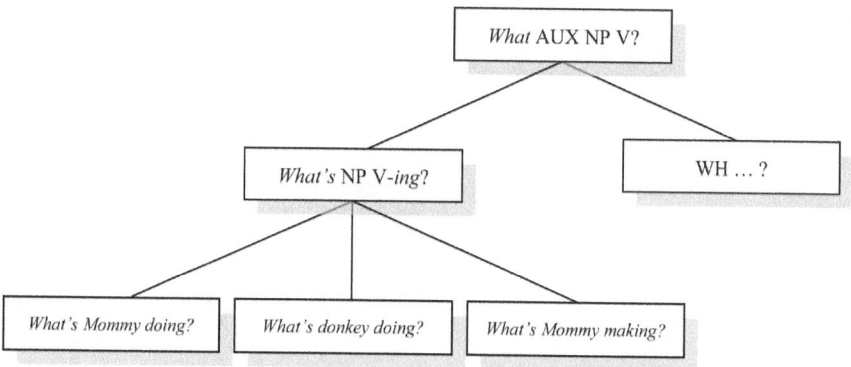

Fig. 3.7: Emerging taxonomy of WH-constructions in child speech.

produce questions with different types of nouns and a bit later also with different types of verbs. At the end of the analyzed period, Naomi recognized that the question word *what* and the auxiliary *is* are separate words and abandoned the contracted form *what's*, which only recurred after a few months. Note that the overall structure of the question did not change throughout the entire period. In all of these examples the question word functions as patient (or object) of the activity expressed by the verb providing a lexical frame for the utterance (see also Dąbrowska and Lieven 2005).

Such lexically particular constructions are characteristic of early child language (cf. Braine 1976; Lieven et al. 1997; Tomasello 1992, 2000, 2003); they provide a link between children's early holophrases and schematic representations of grammatical structure. The development involves a piecemeal, bottom-up process whereby children acquire increasingly more abstract syntactic patterns.

The emergence of grammatical schemas enriches the child's grammatical knowledge, but does not necessarily efface the memory of lower-level constructions and frequent strings of lexical expressions. In the generative approach, syntactic representations are maximally abstract and economical; but in the usage-based approach, linguistic information is often stored redundantly at different levels of abstractness (cf. Langacker 2000). What children eventually learn is a hierarchy of grammatical patterns reaching from prefabricated strings of lexical expressions to highly abstract constructional schemas. Figure 3.7 shows a simplified fragment of the taxonomy of WH-questions that one might extract from the analysis of Naomi's questions.

4. Constructions at the same level of abstractness [horizontal links]

The second type of link concerns the relationships between constructions at the same level of abstractness. These horizontal links are similar to the associative links between lexical expressions in the mental lexicon. There is abundant evidence from psycholinguistic research on speech errors and lexical priming that lexemes are related to each other by various types of links that influence language comprehension and production (cf. Harley 2001). For instance, research on lexical priming has demonstrated that words are more easily accessible if they follow a prime, i.e., a word that shares some of its semantic and/or phonetic features with the target item (McNamara 2005).

Priming effects have also been observed in research on grammatical constructions (see Tooley and Traxler 2010 for a recent review). The classic example of constructional priming in speech production involves passive sentences. As first noted by Weiner and Labov (1983), one factor favoring the use of a passive sentence in language production is the presence of another passive sentence in the preceding discourse, suggesting that priming does not only affect words but also constructions (cf. Gries 2005; Szmrecsanyi 2006).

This hypothesis has been confirmed by experimental evidence. For instance, in a seminal paper Kathryn Bock (1986) showed that speakers of English are much more likely to describe a ditransitive scene, i.e., a scene depicting an act of transfer, by the *to*-dative construction (rather than the ditransitive) if they had heard or used the *to*-dative construction prior to the experimental task. Parallel results were obtained for the active-passive alternation and other related clause types. Interestingly, while this type of priming is especially powerful if it involves the same sentence types (i.e., *to*-dative primes *to*-dative), Bock and Loebell (1990) showed that priming effects can also be observed between distinct grammatical patterns that share some of their structural properties. For instance, in one of their studies they found that an active sentence with a locative *by*-phrase can prime a passive sentence with an agentive *by*-phrase and vice versa (cf. 16–17).

(16) The 747 was landing by the airport's control tower.   [locative *by*-phrase]

(17) The 747 was alerted by the airport's control tower.   [passive *by*-phrase]

Since these priming effects occur even if prime and target have different meanings, Bock and colleagues dubbed this phenomenon "syntactic priming"; but later studies showed that priming also occurs with semantically related sentence types (e.g., Chang et al. 2003; Hare and Goldberg 2000). For instance, Hare and Goldberg (2000) showed that a sentence such *John provided Bill with news* primes a semantically related sentence such as *John gave the ball to Pete* although these sentences have very different structures. If there are priming effects between semantically or structurally related constructions, it is a plausible hypothesis that structures with similar forms and meanings are associated with each other like lexical expressions with similar phonetic and semantic features in the mental lexicon.

In accordance with this hypothesis, research on L1 acquisition has shown that grammatical development is crucially influenced by structural and semantic similarities between constructions (cf. Abott-Smith and Behrens 2006; Diessel 2004; Goldberg 2006). For instance, Diessel and Tomasello (2005) argued that the acquisition of relative clauses involves a piecemeal process whereby children gradually acquire various types of relative clauses based on their prior knowledge of simple sentences (i.e., main clauses). In English, the primary syntactic device to indicate the function of the head in the relative clause is word order. As can be seen in (18) to (21), the different structural types of relative clauses are differentiated by different word order patterns.

(18) The man who met Peter.   NP-*who*-V-NP   [subject RC]

(19) The man who Peter met.   NP-*who*-NP-V   [direct-object RC]

(20) The man who Peter sent   NP-*who*-NP-V-NP-P   [indirect-object RC]
     the letter to.

(21) The man who Peter went to.   NP-*who*-NP-V-P   [oblique RC]

German has the same range of relative clauses as English; but instead of word order, German uses relative pronouns to indicate the function of the head in the relative clause (cf. 22–25).

(22) Der Mann, der Peter getroffen hat.   *der*-NP ...   [subject RC]

(23) Der Mann, den Peter getroffen hat.   *den*-NP ...   [direct-object RC]

(24) Der Mann, dem Peter den Brief   *dem*-NP ...   [indirect-object RC]
     geschickt hat.

(25) Der Mann, zu dem Peter gegangen ist.   P-*dem*-NP ...   [oblique RC]

Using a sentence repetition task, Diessel and Tomasello (2005) found (in accordance with much previous research) that subject relatives cause fewer difficulties

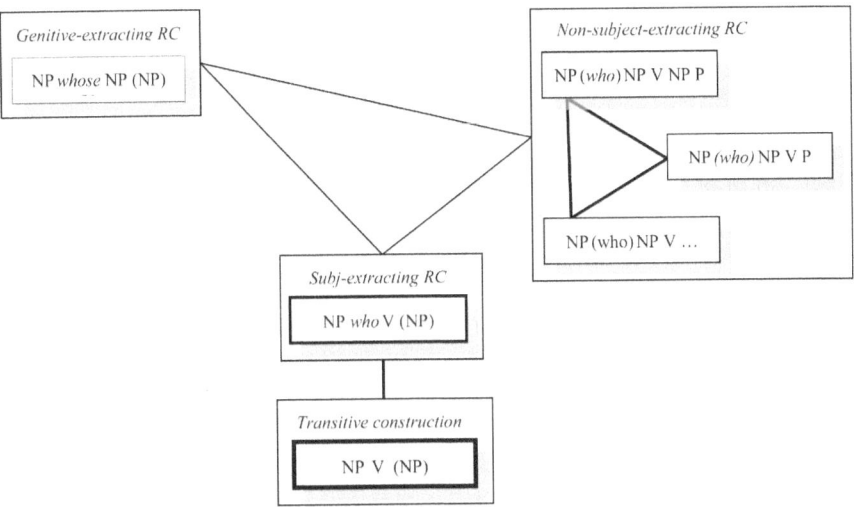

Fig. 3.8: Partial network of grammatical relations and constructions.

for preschool children than non-subject relatives. However, while the children's responses to subject relatives were very similar in the two languages, English- and German-speaking children produced strikingly different responses to the various types of non-subject relative clauses. In German, direct-object relatives (cf. 23) caused fewer difficulties than indirect-object relatives (cf. 24) and oblique relatives (cf. 25), which is consistent with the fact that direct-object relatives are much more frequent in the ambient language than the two other types of non-subject relatives. However, in the English study all non-subject relatives caused the same amount of errors despite the fact that direct-object relatives are much more frequent than indirect-object relatives and oblique relatives. But how then do we account for the English results and the differences between the English and German studies?

Diessel and Tomasello argue that direct-object relatives, indirect-object relatives, and oblique relatives caused the same amount of errors in the English study because these relative clauses involve the same general word order pattern, i.e., NP (*who*) NP V, which the children of their English study frequently converted to the order NP (*who*) V NP, as in example (26):

(26) a. TEST ITEM: This is the girl [who the boy teased at school].
     b. Child: This is the girl [who teased the boy at school].

Since non-subject relatives in German do not have a particular property in common (the relative clauses in 23 to 25 are marked by different relative pronouns), they were *not* treated as members of a common class, as indicated by the fact that in the German study direct-object relatives caused significantly fewer errors than indirect-object relatives and oblique relatives. Diessel and Tomasello take this as evidence for their hypothesis that similarity between constructions plays an important role in grammatical development (see Diessel 2009 for additional data and discussion). What children eventually learn is a network of interconnected relative clause constructions. The development starts with subject relatives involving the same sequence of nouns and verbs as simple main clauses and it ends with genitive relatives (e.g., *the man whose dog was barking*), which are structurally and semantically distinct from all other types of relative clauses (cf. Figure 3.8).

5 Constructions and syntactic categories [syntactic links]

The third type of link concerns the relationship between constructions and syntactic categories (e.g., grammatical relations and word classes). Most grammatical theories presuppose a set of syntactic categories prior to syntactic analysis; but in the usage-based approach syntactic categories are emergent from the language users' experience with constructions. This is most forcefully expressed in Radical Construction Grammar, a usage-based variety of construction grammar developed by Croft (2001).

The starting point of Croft's analysis is the observation that syntactic categories vary across constructions and across languages. Let us consider grammatical relations to illustrate this point.[2] Grammatical relations define the syntactic functions of words and phrases in verb-argument constructions. In formal syntactic theories, grammatical relations are commonly defined as primitive categories; but Croft argues that grammatical relations are derived from particular constructions. Consider, for instance, the notion of subject.

In English, the subject is commonly defined as the nominal that immediately precedes the (finite) verb. However, while this may hold for basic declarative sentences, it does not generally hold for other sentence types. In (non-subject) questions, for instance, the subject occurs only after the auxiliary (cf. 27), and in sentences with preposed quotative clauses the (main clause) subject can follow the quotative verb (cf. 28).

---

2 Traditionally, syntactic analysis involves two major types of categories: (i) grammatical relations (e.g., subject, object) and (ii) word classes (e.g., noun, verb). In addition, phrases (e.g., NP, VP) can be seen as syntactic categories (cf. Croft 2001); but in this chapter I treat phrases as constructions and keep them separate from syntactic categories because they evolve in different ways (see section 7).

(27) What did you say?

(28) "Good morning", said the young man with the red jacket.

In fact, even in simple declarative sentences, the subject does not always precede the verb. In the locative (inversion) construction, for instance, the position before the verb is occupied by an adverbial and the subject occurs only after the verb (cf. 29), and in constructions with negative inversion, the subject precedes the main verb and follows the auxiliary (cf. 30).

(29) Across the bridge lived an old man that was well-known in this region.

(30) Never would I talk to him about these things.

Another construction-particular property of grammatical relations is control. In complex sentences with non-finite complement clauses, for instance, the verb of the lower clause is usually controlled by the direct object of the higher clause (cf. 31); but if the main clause includes the verb *promise*, it is controlled by the matrix clause subject, i.e., the clause-initial NP (cf. 32).

(31) Peter convinced Sue to support his proposal.

(32) Peter promised Sue to support her proposal.

Similar construction-specific constraints have been observed in languages where grammatical relations are primarily expressed by morphological means, i.e., by case marking or agreement morphology (Croft 2001). In addition to such construction-particular properties, there are language-particular aspects of grammatical relations. Croft stresses that languages differ as to how they organize grammatical relations. There is an enormous amount of crosslinguistic variation in this domain, which typologists have analyzed in terms of three general semanto-syntactic roles: (i) the S role, which refers to the one participant that is entailed by an intransitive event, (ii) the A role, which refers to the most agent-like participant of a transitive event, and (iii) the P role, which refers to the most patient-like participant of a transitive event (e.g., Dixon 1994).

In English, the notion of subject subsumes the S and A roles, which are uniformly expressed by nominals that precede the finite verb (in basic declarative sentences); whereas the P role is encoded by a postverbal NP (cf. 33–34). Note, however, that in passive sentences the P role is promoted to subject and expressed by a preverbal nominal, whereas the A role is either omitted or demoted to an oblique (cf. 35).

(33) *The boy*$_{AG}$ kicked the ball$_{PA}$.

(34) *The man*$_{AG}$ is running.

(35) *The ball*$_{PA}$ was kicked (*by the boy*$_{AG}$).

Like English, many other languages encode S and A by the same word order or morphology; but this is not a universal strategy. It is well-known that in languages with ergative morphology, S and P are treated as a formal grammatical category (absolutive case) in contrast to A (ergative case), and that in languages with split-intransitive morphology the S role is divided into two categories: agent-like participants (e.g., *The man*$_{AG}$ is running) that are encoded in the same way as the A role of a transitive sentence, and patient-like participants (e.g., *The bomb*$_{PA}$ exploded) that are encoded in the same way as the P role. Moreover, there are languages in which the subject of a passive sentence occurs with the same case marker as the direct object (or an oblique), and there are other languages that differentiate between different P roles (see Bickel 2011 for a recent overview). Finally, the morphological marking of S, A and P does not always coincide with their syntactic functions. In fact, in most languages with ergative morphology, coordinate sentences and relative clauses are conjoined based on an S/A "pivot"; that is, most (morphological) ergative languages employ an S/A alignment pattern for the formation of complex sentences. Syntactic ergativity, i.e., occurrence of an S/P pivot, is a very rare phenomenon and always restricted to particular constructions (cf. Dixon 1994).

In general, there is an enormous amount of variation in the encoding of grammatical relations across languages and constructions. Most grammatical theories abstract away from this variation and define syntactic categories at a very high level of abstractness. In this approach, grammar includes a universal inventory of highly schematic categories that are defined prior to syntactic analysis. But this approach has been challenged by Croft (2001), who offers an alternative account in which syntactic categories are emergent from constructions:

> Constructions, not categories and relations, are the basic, primitive units of syntactic representation. (Croft 2001: 45–46)

Constructions are the basic units of grammar because in contrast to what is commonly assumed in linguistic theory, syntactic configurations are not derivable from atomic primitives. While Croft does not explicitly refer to usage and development, his analysis implies that syntactic categories are formed in the process of language acquisition and language change. On this view, syntactic

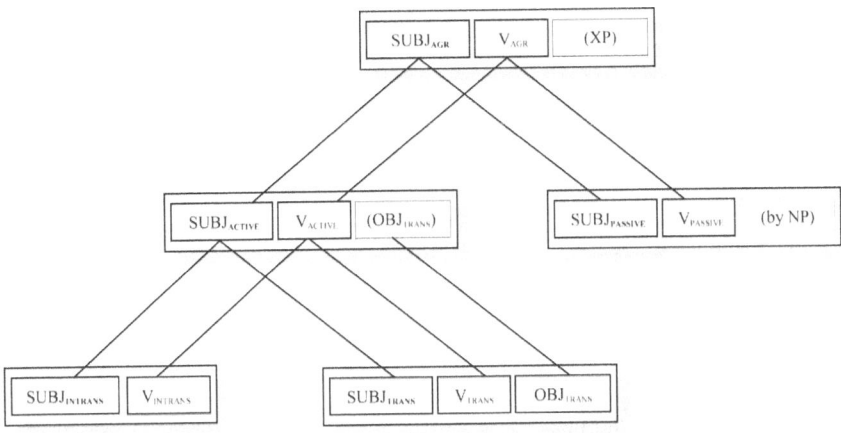

Fig. 3.9: Partial network of grammatical relations and constructions.

categories are emergent from the language user's (unconscious) analysis of particular constructions and are therefore subject to change.

The relationship between constructions and categories is similar to that between constructions at different levels of abstractness. Constructions are generalizations over concrete utterances, i.e., constructs, and categories are generalizations over recurrent parts of constructions. If we accept this comparison, we can think of grammatical relations (and word classes) as emergent categories of linguistic structure that children acquire through the analysis of constructions and that continue to be reinforced and adjusted throughout speakers' lives as they interact with each other. Like constructs and constructions, categories and constructions are related to each other by taxonomic links that are part of our grammatical knowledge (cf. Figure 3.9).

6 Constructions and lexemes [lexical links]

Finally, there are associative links between (schematic) constructions and (concrete) lexical expressions (see Geeraerts this volume). In structuralist and generative linguistics, individual words are irrelevant for grammatical analysis; but in the usage-based approach linguistic structure is fundamentally grounded in the language user's experience with concrete lexical expressions. In fact, constructions are often immediately associated with particular words (see Diessel 2016 for a review of the relevant literature). This is perhaps most obvious in the case of closed-class function words. The comparative correlative construction, for instance, includes two grammatical morphemes, i.e., two instances of *the*, which only occur in this particular pattern (cf. 36).

(36) The bigger the house, the smaller the garden.

Other constructions that are associated with particular function words are the passive construction (cf. 37), the nominal extraposition construction (cf. 38), the existential *there*-construction (cf. 39), the *way*-construction (cf. 40), and the hortative construction (cf. 41). In all of these sentence types, there are particular words that are so closely associated with the structural pattern that they can only be analyzed as an integral part of the construction.

(37) Peter was struck by lightening.

(38) It's unbelievable the amount of food that he can eat.

(39) There was an old man who lived in a house in the woods.

(40) John found his way out of business.

(41) Let's have a beer.

The relationship between constructions and content words is more variable. In fact, in the construction-based literature it is commonly assumed that construction include "open slots" for particular content words (see above); but these slots are usually associated with particular words by probabilistic links.

Stefanowitsch and Gries (2003) developed a corpus method, i.e., "collostructional analysis", to analyze the probabilistic links between lexemes and constructions. Let us consider the ditransitive construction to illustrate this approach. The ditransitive construction consists of a subject, a verb, and two noun phrases, which together denote an act of transfer between an actor and a recipient. The construction occurs with a wide range of verbs – *give, send, offer, show, teach*, to mention just a few. Most of these verbs can also appear in other grammatical contexts, in the *to*-dative, for instance, or in the transitive construction (cf. 42–44).

(42) Peter sent John a letter.

(43) Peter sent a letter to John.

(44) Peter sent a letter by mail.

What Stefanowitsch and Gries have shown is that individual lexemes are often more (or less) frequent in a particular construction than statistically expected if

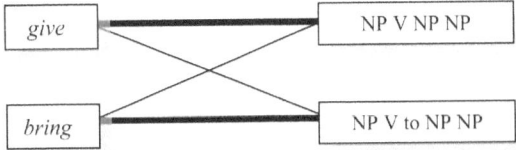

Fig. 3.10: The relationship between verbs and constructions.

the relationships between lexemes and constructions were random. The verb *give*, for instance, is strongly attracted by the ditransitive construction and appears less frequently than expected in the *to*-dative; and for the verb *bring* it is the other way around (cf. Figure 3.10) (cf. Gries and Stefanowitsch 2004).

Both the ditransitive and the *to*-dative denote an act of transfer, but have slightly different meanings. The *to*-dative implies a greater distance between actor and recipient than the ditransitive and is therefore more strongly associated with activities involving motion (cf. Thompson and Koide 1987). This explains why the verbs *bring* and *take* are particularly frequent in the *to*-dative construction, whereas verbs such as *give* and *tell* are proportionally more frequent in the ditransitive (cf. Gries and Stefanowitsch 2004). In other words, verbs and constructions seem to "attract" (or "repel") each other based on their meanings: there is a tendency to use verbs that are semantically compatible with the constructional meaning (Goldberg [1995: 50] calls this the "Semantic Coherence Principle"); but the semantic fit is not the only factor influencing the relationships between lexemes and constructions.

Consider, for instance, the verb *donate*, which is semantically very similar to the verbs of transfer that are commonly used in the ditransitive and *to*-dative constructions; however, although *donate* is semantically compatible with both constructions, it is exclusively found in the *to*-dative (cf. 45) (in American English).[3] For most speakers, *donate* is unacceptable in the ditransitive construction (cf. 46); but not because *donate* would not fit the constructional meaning, but simply because *donate* has never been experienced in the ditransitive construction.

(45) Peter donated money to the Red Cross.

(46) *Peter donated the Red Cross money.

---

[3] In British English, *donate* is sometimes used in the ditransitive construction (Ewa Dąbrowska p.c.).

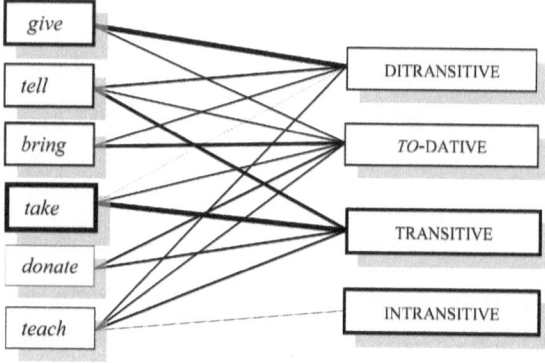

Fig. 3.11: Partial network of verbs and constructions.

Similar semantically unmotivated restrictions have been observed for other verbs and other constructions, suggesting that the associations between verbs and constructions are not fully predictable from semantic criteria. In addition to the semantic fit, it is the language user's experience with an established pattern that influences the associative links between lexemes and constructions. Of course, the semantic fit affects the language users' linguistic behaviour, which in turn determines their experience, so that the two factors are likely to reinforce each other over time; but, as we have seen in the case of *donate*, the language users' linguistic experience does not always reflect the semantic fit between lexemes and constructions, suggesting that the two factors, i.e., semantic fit and frequency/entrenchment, are in principle independent of each other (see Diessel 2016 for discussion of this point).

One can think of the relationship between lexemes and constructions as part of a probabilistic network shaped by language use. On this account, verbs (and other lexemes) and constructions are related to each other by connections with graded activation values that are determined by the combined effect of general semantic criteria and the language users' experience with particular lexical expressions and constructions (cf. Figure 3.11).

7 Phrase structure

To summarize the discussion thus far, we have looked at four different types of links between linguistic elements, namely the links between (i) constructions at different levels of abstractness (taxonomic links), (ii) constructions at the same level of abstractness (horizontal links), (iii) constructions and syntactic categories (syntactic links), and (iv) constructions and lexemes (lexical links).

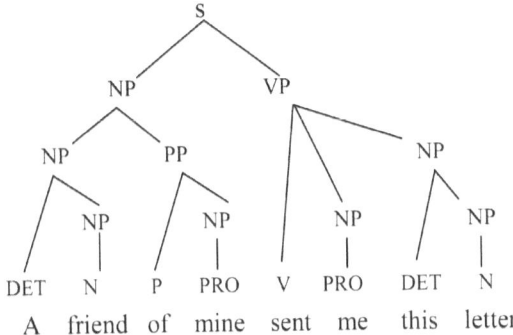

Fig. 3.12: Phrase structure graph.

What we have not yet considered is constituent structure, i.e., the hierarchical organization of clauses and phrases, which provides perhaps the best evidence for a compositional approach. In generative grammar, constituent structure is derived from a small inventory of discrete categories, e.g., NP, VP, PP, and S, that are combined to larger syntactic units by general phrase-structure rules (e.g., PP → P-NP). The resulting structures are commonly represented in phrase-structure graphs, as exemplified in Figure 3.12.

Obviously, this analysis is not consistent with the dynamic nature of grammar in the usage-approach. If grammar is grounded in experience, we have to ask where do these structures come from and how do they change?

There is not much research on constituent structure in the usage-based approach; but Bybee (2002) and Langacker (2008) have made some interesting suggestions as to how constituency can be analyzed from a usage-based perspective. Specifically, Bybee argues that phrases, or phrasal constructions, are "processing units" that have evolved from frequent strings of linguistic elements. The development of these units is driven by two general aspects of language use, namely (i) semantic coherence and (ii) automatization or chunking.

In accordance with much previous research, Bybee argues that there is a general tendency to place semantically related elements next to each other. An early statement of this is Behaghel's 'first law':

> *Geistig eng Zusammengehöriges wird auch eng zusammengestellt.* 'Conceptually related entities are placed close to each other.' (Behaghel 1932)

The second factor that influences the emergence of constituency is frequency (see Divjak and Caldwell-Harris volume 1). Specifically, Bybee argues that frequency is the driving force behind a cognitive mechanism which she calls

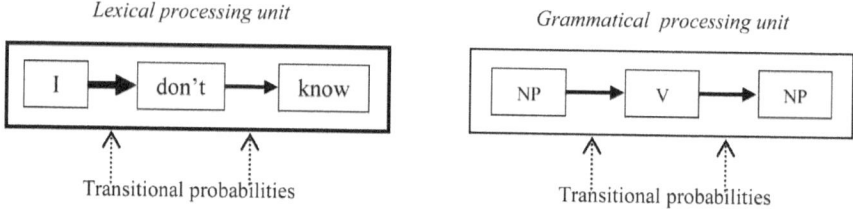

Fig. 3.13: Processing units.

"chunking", though "automatization" seems to be a better term, considering the way these terms, i.e., chunking and automatization, are used in cognitive psychology (see Diessel 2016 for discussion).

Automatization is a general psychological mechanism whereby controlled processes are transformed into automatic processes. Almost all sequential activities start off as controlled processes, but are then often transformed into automatic processes through repetition or practice. This is a very common cognitive phenomenon involved in many everyday tasks. Automatization enables people to perform complex sequential activities with little effort, but is also a common source for certain types of mistakes, i.e., slips, that occur for lack of attention or lack of conscious control (cf. Logan 1988; Schneider and Chein 2003).

Language is a sequential medium that is crucially influenced by automatization; but language unfolds in time. All linguistic elements, e.g., phonemes, morphemes, words, categories, and constructions, occur in sequence and are therefore subject to automatization. If we repeatedly process the same string of linguistic elements within a particular period of time, automatization creates associative links between them. This can involve either strings of (concrete) lexical expressions or strings of (abstract) categories. The strengths of the associative links can be expressed in terms of transitional probabilities or other statistical measures that have been explored in corpus and psycholinguistic studies (cf. Figure 3.13).

The cognitive result of this process is the emergence of an automated processing unit. Since automatization is a gradual process driven by frequency (or repetition) the units of speech vary on a continuum. Other things being equal, the more frequent a particular string of linguistic elements is processed, the stronger is the cohesion of the emerging processing unit; or as Bybee (2002: 220) put it: "the more often particular elements occur together, the tighter the constituent structure".

Since smaller units are usually more frequent than large ones, length and complexity vary with the degree of syntactic cohesion. As a consequence of this, more tightly organized processing units appear to be embedded in less

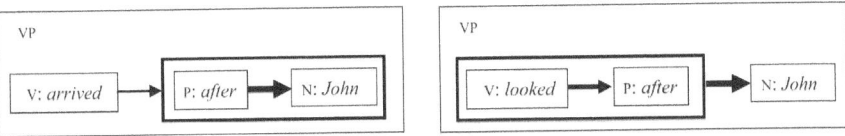

Fig. 3.14: Processing units.

automatized ones, creating a hierarchical organization of linguistic structure which one might analyze in terms of phrase structure trees. Note, however, that the resulting phrase structures are very different from traditional phrase structure representations. In generative grammar, syntactic phrase structure is analyzed by a set of discrete categories that are defined prior to syntactic analysis; but in the usage-based approach phrase structure is emergent and non-discrete. It is grounded in the language user's experience with strings of linguistic elements that are combined to fluid units. As a consequence of this, constituent structure is much more diverse and variable than in generative linguistics. Consider, for instance, a verb phrase such as *(She) arrived after John* (cf. Figure 3.14). In traditional phrase structure analysis, it is assumed that the VP consists of two immediate constituents, namely V and PP; but it is well-known that in a parallel structure such as *(She) looked after John* the preposition is more strongly associated with the verb than with the noun, creating a grouping of syntactic categories that is not consistent with general phrase-structure rules (i.e., [[V-P] NP]).

In the usage-based approach, this is readily explained by automatization or chunking. Since the sequence *look after* is much more frequent than *after John*, *look after* constitutes a chunk, i.e., an automated processing unit, that is largely independent of the general VP schema in which postverbal prepositions are associated with a subsequent noun, rather than with the verb. Other mismatches between traditional phrase structures and lexically specific chunks are described in Bybee and Scheibman (1999), Bybee (2002), and Beckner and Bybee (2009). Taken together these studies suggest that constituency is a gradient phenomenon emergent from concrete utterances of language use, just like any other aspect of grammar.

8 Conclusion

To conclude, this chapter has provided an overview of recent research on grammar in cognitive linguistics. The goal of this research is to develop a framework for the analysis of linguistic structure as it evolves from domain-general cognitive processes. In this approach, grammar is seen as a self-organizing system of emergent categories and fluid constructions that are in principle always changing, always in flux, under the influence of general cognitive mechanisms involved in language use such as analogy, categorization, and automatization (or chunking). There are two basic tenets that underlie the analysis of linguistic structure in this approach: First, linguistic structure consists of signs, i.e., constructions, and second constructions are associated with each other (and other linguistic signs) by various types of links creating an intricate system of interconnected elements that one might characterize as a dynamic network. The purpose of this chapter has been to elaborate the network metaphor of usage-based construction grammar, which had not yet been sufficiently described.

9 References

Abbott-Smith, Kirsten and Heike Behrens (2006): How known constructions influence the acquisition of other constructions: The German passive and future constructions. *Cognitive Science* 30: 995–1026.

Baayen, Harald and Michael Ramscar (volume 1): Abstraction, storage and naive discriminative learning. Berlin/Boston: De Gruyter Mouton.

Beckner, Clay and Joan Bybee (2009): A usage-based account of constituency and reanalysis. *Language Learning* 59: 27–46.

Behaghel, Otto (1932): *Deutsche Syntax. Eine geschichtliche Darstellung*. Vol. IV. *Wortstellung, Periodenbau*. Heidelberg: Winter.

Bever, Thomas G. (1970): The cognitive basis for linguistic structures. In: J. R. Hayes (ed.), *Cognition and Development of Language*, 279–352. New York: Wiley.

Bickel, Balthasar (2011): Grammatical relations typology. In: J. J. Song (ed.), *The Oxford Handbook of Linguistic Typology*, 399–444. Oxford: Oxford University Press.

Bock, Kathryn (1986): Syntactic persistence in language production. *Cognitive Psychology* 18: 355–387.

Bock, Kathryn and Helga Loebell (1990): Framing sentences. *Cognition* 35: 1–39.

Braine, Martin D. S. (1976): Children's first word combinations, *Monographs of the Society for Research in Child Development* 41.

Bybee, Joan (2002): Sequentiality as the basis of constituent structure. In: T. Givón and B. F. Malle (eds.) *The Evolution of Language out of Pre-Language*, 109–132. Amsterdam: John Benjamins.

Bybee, Joan (2007): *Frequency and the Organization of Language*. Oxford: Oxford University Press.

Bybee, Joan (2010): *Language, Usage, and Cognition*. Cambridge: Cambridge University Press.

Bybee, Joan and Joanne Scheibman (1999): The effect of usage on degrees of constituency: The reduction of *don't* in English. *Linguistics* 37: 575–596.

Chang, Franklin, Kathryn Bock, and Adele E. Goldberg (2003): Can thematic roles leave traces of their places? *Cognition* 90: 29–49.

Chomsky, Noam (1965): *Aspects of the Theory of Syntax*. Cambridge: MIT Press.

Chomsky, Noam (1995): *The Minimalist Program*. Cambridge: MIT Press.

Croft, William (2001): *Radical Construction Grammar: Syntactic Theory in Typological Perspective*. Oxford: Oxford University Press.
Croft, William (2007): Construction grammar. In: D. Geeraerts and H. Cuyckens. (eds.), *Handbook of Cognitive Linguistics*, 463–508. Oxford: Oxford University Press.
Croft, William and Alan Cruse (2004): *Cognitive Linguistics*. Cambridge: Cambridge University Press.
Dąbrowska, Ewa (2000): From formula to schema: the acquisition of English questions. *Cognitive Linguistics* 11: 83–102.
Dąbrowska, Ewa (2004): *Language, Mind and Brain: Some Psychological and Neurological Constraints on Theories of Grammar*. Edinburgh: Edinburgh University Press.
Dąbrowska, Ewa and Elena Lieven (2005): Towards a lexically-specific grammar of children's questions. *Cognitive Linguistics* 16: 437–474.
Deacon, Terrence (1997): *The Symbolic Species. The Co-Evolution of Language and the Brain*. New York: W.W. Norton & Company.
Diessel, Holger (1997): Verb-first constructions in German. In: M. Verspoor, L. K. Dong, and E. Sweetser (eds.), *Lexical and Syntactical Constructions and the Construction of Meaning*, 51–68. Amsterdam: John Benjamins.
Diessel, Holger (2004): *The Acquisition of Complex Sentences*. Cambridge: Cambridge University Press.
Diessel, Holger (2007): Frequency effects in language acquisition, language use, and diachronic change. *New Ideas in Psychology* 25: 108–127.
Diessel, Holger (2009): On the role of frequency and similarity in the acquisition of subject and non-subject relative clauses. In: T. Givón and M. Shibatani (eds.), *Syntactic Complexity*, 251–276. Amsterdam: John Benjamins.
Diessel, Holger (2011a): Review article of 'Language, Usage and Cognition' by Joan Bybee. *Language* 87: 830–844.
Diessel, Holger (2011b): Grammaticalization and Language Acquisition. In: B. Heine and H. Narrog (eds.), *Handbook of Grammaticalization*, 130–141. Oxford: Oxford University Press.
Diessel, Holger (2012): Language Change and Language Acquisition. In: A. Bergs and L. Brinton (eds.), *Historical Linguistics of English: An International Handbook*, Vol. 2, 1599–1613. Berlin: Mouton de Gruyter.
Diessel, Holger (2013): Construction Grammar and First Language Acquisition. In: G. Trousdale and T. Hoffmann (eds.), *The Oxford Handbook of Construction Grammar*, 347–364. Oxford: Oxford University Press.
Diessel, Holger (2016): Frequency and lexical specificity. A critical review. In: H. Behrens and S. Pfänder (eds.), *Experience Counts: Frequency Effects in Language*, pp 209–238. Berlin: Mouton de Gruyter.
Diessel, Holger and Michael Tomasello (2005): A new look at the acquisition of relative clauses. *Language* 81: 1–25.
Divjak, Dagmar and Catherine Caldwell-Harris (volume 1): Frequency and entrenchment. Berlin/Boston: De Gruyter Mouton.
Dixon, R. M. W. (1994): *Ergativity*. Cambridge: Cambridge University Press.
Elman, Jeffrey L. (1995): Language as a dynamical system. In: R. F. Port and T. van Gelder (eds.), *Minds as Motion, Explanations in the Dynamics of Cognition*, 195–225. Cambridge: MIT Press.
Ferreira, Fernanda (2003): The misinterpretation of noncanonical sentences. *Cognitive Psychology* 47: 164–203.

Fillmore, Charles J. and Paul Kay (1999): *Construction Grammar*. Berkeley: University of California.
Fillmore, Charles J., Paul Kay and Catherine O'Connor (1988): Regularity and idiomaticity in grammatical constructions: The case of *let alone*. *Language* 64: 501–538.
Fried, Mirjam (2010): Construction Grammar. In: A. Alexiadou and T. Kiss (eds.), *Handbook of Syntax*. Second edition. Berlin: Walter de Gruyter.
Geeraerts, Dirk (this volume): Lexical semantics. Berlin/Boston: De Gruyter Mouton.
Gerken, LouAnn (2006): Decisions, decisions: infant language learning when multiple generalizations are possible. *Cognition* 98: 67–74.
Goldberg, Adele E. (1995): *Constructions: A Construction Grammar Approach to Argument Structure*. Chicago: University of Chicago Press.
Goldberg, Adele E. (2006): *Constructions at Work. The Nature of Generalization in Language*. Oxford: Oxford University Press.
Gómez, Rebecca L. and Lou Ann Gerken (1999): Artificial grammar learning by 1-year-olds leads to specific abstract knowledge. *Cognition* 70: 109–135.
Gries, Stefan Th. (2005): Syntactic priming: A corpus-based approach. *Journal of Psycholinguistic Research* 34: 365–399.
Gries, Stefan Th. (volume 3): Polysemy. Berlin/Boston: De Gruyter Mouton.
Gries, Stefan Th. and Anatol Stefanowitsch (2004): Extending collexeme analysis. *International Journal of Corpus Linguistics* 9: 97–129.
Hare, Mary and Adele E. Goldberg (2000): Structural priming: purely syntactic? *Proceedings of the Twenty-first Annual Meeting of the Cognitive Science Society*, 208–211. Mahwah: Laurence Erlbaum.
Harley, Trevor (2001): *The Psychology of Language. From Data to Theory*. Second edition. Hove: Taylor and Francis.
Hilpert, Martin (2013): *Constructional Change in English: Developments in Allomorphy, Word-formation and Syntax*. Cambridge: Cambridge University Press.
Hilpert, Martin (2014): *Construction Grammar and its Application to English*. Edinburgh: Edinburgh University Press.
Hoffmann, Thomas and Graeme Trousdale (2013): *The Oxford Handbook of Construction Grammar*. Oxford: Oxford University Press.
Hopper, Paul (1987): Emergent Grammar. *Proceedings of the Thirteenth Annual Meeting of the Berkeley Linguistics Society*, 139–157. Berkeley.
Jackendoff, Ray (2002): *Foundations of Language. Brain, Meaning, Grammar, Evolution*. Oxford: Oxford University Press.
Langacker, Ronald W. (1982): Space Grammar, analysability, and the English passive. *Language* 58: 22–80.
Langacker, Ronald W. (1987): *Foundations of Cognitive Grammar*, Vol. 1, *Theoretical Prerequisites*. Stanford: Stanford University Press.
Langacker, Ronald W. (1988): A usage-based model. In: B. Rudzka-Ostyn (ed.), *Topics in Cognitive Linguistics*, 127–161. Amsterdam: John Benjamins.
Langacker, Ronald W. (1991): *Foundations of Cognitive Grammar*, Vol. 2, *Descriptive Application*. Stanford: Stanford University Press.
Langacker, Ronald W. (2000): A dynamic usage-based model. In: M. Barlow and S. Kemmer (eds.), *Usage-based Models of Language*, 24–63. Stanford: Stanford University Press.
Langacker, Ronald W. (2008): *Cognitive Grammar. A Basic Introduction*. Oxford: Oxford University Press.

Lieven, Elena V. M., Julian M. Pine, and Gillian Baldwin (1997): Lexically-based learning and early grammatical development. *Journal of Child Language* 24: 187–219.
Logan, Gordon D. (1988): Toward an instance theory of automatization. *Psychological Review* 95: 492–527.
Marcus, Gary, S. Vijayan, S. B. Rao, and P. M. Vishton (1999): Rule learning by seven-month-old infants. *Science* 283: 77–80.
Matthews, Danielle and Grzegorz Krajewski (this volume): First language acquisition. Berlin/Boston: De Gruyter Mouton.
McNamara, Timothy P. (2005): *Semantic Priming. Perspective from Memory and Word Recognition*. New York: Taylor & Francis.
Michaelis, Laura (2013): Sign-based construction grammar. In: G. Trousdale and T. Hoffmann (eds.), *The Oxford Handbook of Construction Grammar*, 133–152. Oxford: Oxford University Press.
Nunberg, Geoffrey, Ivan A. Sag, and Thomas Wasow (1994): Idioms. *Language* 70: 491–538.
Pinker, Steven and Ray Jackendoff (2005): The faculty of language: What's special about it? *Cognition* 95: 201–236.
Sag, Ivan A. (2012): Sign-based construction grammar: An informal synopsis. In: H. C. Boas and I. A. Sag (eds.), *Sign-Based Construction Grammar*, 39–170. Stanford: CSLI Publications.
Saussure, Ferdinand de ([1916] 1996): *Course in General Linguistics*. La Salle, Illinois: Open Court.
Schneider, Walter and Jason M. Chein (2003): Controlled and automatic processing: behavior, theory, and biological mechanisms. *Cognitive Science* 27: 525–559.
Searle, John R. (1979): *Expression and Meaning: Studies in the Theory of Speech Acts*. Cambridge: Cambridge University Press.
Slobin, Dan I. and Thomas G. Bever (1982): Children use canonical sentence schemas: A crosslinguistic study of word order and inflections. *Cognition* 12: 229–265.
Steels, Luc (ed.) (2011): *Design Patterns in Fluid Construction Grammar*. Amsterdam: John Benjamins.
Stefanowitsch, Anatol (2003): The English imperative. A construction-based approach. Unpublished manuscript. Universität Bremen.
Stefanowitsch, Anatol and Stefan Gries (2003): Collostructions: Investigating the interaction of words and constructions. *International Journal of Corpus Linguistics* 8: 209–243.
Szmrecsanyi, Benedikt (2006): *Morphosyntactic Persistence in Spoken English. A Corpus Study at the Intersection of Variationist Sociolinguistics, Psycholinguistics, and Discourse Analysis*. Berlin: Mouton de Gruyter.
Talmy, Leonard (1978): Figure and ground in complex sentences. In: J. H. Greenberg (ed.), *Universals of Human Language*, Vol. 4, 625–649. Stanford: Stanford University Press.
Talmy, Leonard (1988): The relation between grammar and cognition. In: B. Rudzka-Ostyn (ed.), *Topics in Cognitive Linguistics*, 165–205, Amsterdam: John Benjamins.
Thompson, Sandra A. and Yuka Koide (1987): Iconicity and 'indirect objects' in English. *Journal of Pragmatics* 11: 399–406.
Tomasello, Michael (1992): *First Verbs. A Case Study of Early Grammatical Development*. Cambridge: Cambridge University Press.
Tomasello, Michael (1999): *The Cultural Origins of Human Cognition*. Cambridge: Harvard University Press.
Tomasello, Michael (2000): Do young children have adult syntactic competence? *Cognition* 74: 209–253.

Tomasello, Michael (2003): *Constructing a Language. A Usage-Based Approach.* Cambridge: Harvard University Press.
Tooley, Kristen M. and Matthew J. Traxler (2010): Syntactic priming effects in comprehension: A critical review. *Language and Linguistics Compass* 4: 925–937.
Townsend, David J. and Thomas G. Bever (2001): *Sentence Comprehension. The Integration of Habits and Rules.* Cambridge: MIT Press.
Traugott, Elizabteh Closs and Graeme Trousdale (2013): *Constructionalization and Constructional Changes.* Oxford: Oxford University Press.
Weiner, Judith E. and William Labov (1983): Constraints on agentless passive. *Journal of Linguistics* 19: 29–58.

Christopher Hart
Chapter 4: Discourse

1 Introduction

In this chapter, I focus on discourse, understood as language in social practice. I focus specifically on media and political discourse to show how language can, through the patterns of conceptualisation it invokes, function ideologically. In doing so, I survey the most recent developments at the intersection between Cognitive Linguistics and Critical Discourse Analysis. This synergy represents both a social, or, more specifically, a critical, turn in Cognitive Linguistics as well as a cognitive turn in Critical Discourse Analysis, which has traditionally adopted more social science based methodologies. One site where these two perspectives have most successfully and most visibly converged is in the critical study of metaphor, which now constitutes one of the most productive and pervasive methodological approaches to ideological discourse research. More recently, however, the utility of combining Cognitive Linguistics and Critical Discourse Analysis has been expounded in relation to a wider range of linguistic and conceptual phenomena. In this chapter, then, I only very briefly touch up on critical metaphor studies and concentrate instead on some of the other ways in which Cognitive Linguistics and Critical Discourse Analysis can be usefully combined to shed light on the ideological properties of texts and conceptualisation. Rather than chronologically chart the development of this field, however, I offer an overview of the landscape from a contemporary vantage point which brings together several analytical strands inside a single, integrated framework.

2 Cognitive Linguistics and Critical Discourse Analysis: A useful synergy?

Critical Discourse Analysis (CDA) is a text-analytical tradition which studies the way language use encodes and enacts ideologies leading to social power abuse, dominance and inequality (Van Dijk 2001; Wodak 2001). Grounded in poststructuralist discourse analysis and Critical Theory, it comes with its own conceptualisation of the relationship between language and society in which language

---

Christopher Hart, Lancaster, United Kingdom

https://doi.org/10.1515/9783110626452-004

use, discourse, is seen as "socially constitutive as well as socially conditioned" (Fairclough and Wodak 1997: 258). That is, discourse exists in a dialectic with social situations and relations, both reflecting and reinforcing social structures. From a socio-cognitive rather than purely post-structuralist perspective, Van Dijk has argued that any cogent account of the relationship between discourse and social structure requires an explanation which first and foremost connects structures in text and talk with structures in the mind (e.g., Van Dijk 1998). The ideologies which support social action, he argues, consist in the socially shared "system of mental representations and processes of group members" (Van Dijk 1995: 18). To study the social action effects of language use, then, entails looking at the cognitive or conceptual effects of text and talk in social, economic and political contexts.

Cognitive Linguistics, of course, comes with its own explicitly theorised account of the relationship between language and conceptualisation (Langacker 1987, 1991; Talmy 2000). The incorporation of Cognitive Linguistics in CDA is therefore well motivated: Cognitive Linguistics offers CDA the "missing link" (cf. Chilton 2005) it needs to explain the relationship between discursive and social practices.[1] At the same time, CDA offers Cognitive Linguistics the opportunity to extend its analyses beyond linguistic and conceptual structure to include the constraints that these place on societal structure. This triangular relation is something which has always been alluded to in Cognitive Linguistics, as when, for example, Lakoff and Johnson (1980: 156) stated that "metaphors create realities for us, especially social realities. A metaphor may thus be a guide for future action, such actions will, of course, fit the metaphor". The body of work converging on a cognitive approach to language and ideology can therefore be seen to come from both cognitive linguists applying their theories in critical contexts and critical discourse analysts turning to Cognitive Linguistics for new methodologies.[2] Such work in the space between the two disciplines can, according to Dirven et al. (2003: 2), be seen as an invitation to CDA scholars not yet familiar with the tenets and analytic tools that Cognitive Linguistics has to offer to find out more about them as well as an invitation to cognitive linguists to look beyond the traditional areas of language structure to study the social belief and

---

[1] The mutual benefits that collaboration between CL and CDA brings and the extent to which they are compatible has been addressed in several works (including Dirven et al. 2007; Hart 2010, 2011b; Hart and Lukeš 2007; Koller 2014; Nuñez-Perucha 2011; Stockwell 1999).

[2] It is unfortunate that a significant body of the American Cognitive Linguistic work on ideology (e.g., Lakoff 1996) does not pay heed to the more European and Australian work in CDA or European "critical" social theorists like Bakhtin, Bourdieu, Foucault and Habermas who present detailed treatments of the instrumentality of language within the social structure.

value systems (ideologies) that linguistic structures serve to maintain and perpetuate.[3]

The principle aim of CDA is to bring to the surface for inspection the otherwise clandestine ideological properties of text and talk and in so doing to correct a widespread underestimation of the influence of language in shaping thought and action (Fairclough 1989; Fowler 1991: 89). The claim in CDA is that representation in discourse is "always representation from some ideological point of view" (Fowler 1991: 85). Such perspectivised representations, however, may have become normalised within a given Discourse[4] so that they are no longer recognised as ideological but are rather taken for granted as commonsensical. Thus, language is seen, in line with Systemic Functional Linguistics, not only as "a resource for reflecting on the world" (Halliday and Matthiessen 1999: 7) but as a refracting force which "lends structure to ... experience and helps determine ... way[s] of looking at things" (Halliday 1973: 106).

This relativist position, of course, is also assumed in Cognitive Semantics which, in opposition to structuralist and generativist semantics, has shown that the cognitive models, in the form of categories, frames and conceptual metaphors, which underpin lexical relations, coherence and metaphor in language, are subjective and culturally specific (Lakoff 1987). Like CDA, then, Cognitive Linguistics has revealed that the knowledge structures we take for granted as corresponding with reality in fact mediate and organise reality for us in ways which accord with our language habits. This is most clear in the case of metaphor. One of the fundamental findings of Cognitive Linguistics has been the extent to which complex and abstract knowledge domains are structured, metaphorically, by more basic, familiar domains of experience (Lakoff and Johnson 1980; Gibbs volume 1). Ontological correspondences in the source domain get mapped on to elements in the target domain to provide it with internal structure. This input, in turn, provides the basis for reason and inference within the target domain. These *conceptual* metaphors are evidenced by the systematic way that they are reflected in metaphorical *expressions*. Toward the more conventional end of the cline from novel to conventional metaphor, however, lan-

---

[3] The synergy between CL and CDA, then, which focuses more on functional variation in text and talk, is entirely in line with, and may be regarded as being part of, the movement toward a broader Cognitive Sociolinguistics (Dirven 2005; Kristiansen and Dirven 2008).

[4] Discourse in this more abstract sense is understood as a "regulated practice that accounts for a number of statements" (Foucault 1972: 80), including their lexical, grammatical, phonological, pragmatic and multimodal forms, within a given domain/genre. Discourses in this Foucauldian sense conceal ideology by "making what is social seem natural" (Kress 1989: 10). Following Gee (1990) we may use "(d)iscourse" to refer to language in use and "(D)iscourse" to refer to social practices that license and are licensed by language in use.

guage users are not aware that they are producing or processing metaphor.[5] Crucially, therefore, the "logic" in the target domain is not consciously experienced as derived and therefore mediated but is taken for granted as absolutely, objectively reflecting reality. There are obvious parallels here between conceptual metaphors and other forms of representation normalised inside a Discourse (see Hart 2010). More recently, experimental research on cross-linguistic differences has confirmed the effects of language on cognition in both basic and metaphorised domains of experience (Levinson 2003; Boroditsky 2001). The relativist argument is pursued in CDA, however, along the following lines: "differences of linguistic structure in the same variety of English (such as in different news reports) can cause readers to see the world being described in different ways" (O'Halloran 2003: 15). Metaphor is of particular significance here as alternative source domains are available to construe the same target domain in alternative terms, leading to different emotional reactions and "logical" conclusions. In so far as "ideology is made possible by the choices a language allows for representing the same material situation in different ways" (Haynes 1989: 119), then, metaphor in discourse is inherently ideological.[6] Consider a brief example:

(1) [A] largely peaceful demonstration **spilled over** into bloody violence in the centre of London ... Clashes later **erupted** at Mansion House Street and Queen Victoria Street near the Bank. (*Telegraph*, 1 April 2009)

(2) The G20 protests in central London turned violent today ahead of tomorrow's summit, with a **band of demonstrators** close to the Bank of England **storming** a Royal Bank of Scotland branch, and baton-wielding police **charging** a sit-down protest by students. (*Guardian*, 1 April 2009)

The contrast between (1) and (2) lies in the competing source domains recruited to conceptualise the same violent situation. In (1), the source domain is that of a VOLCANO. The image invoked is of a potentially dangerous liquid previously

---

5 As Shimko (1994: 657) states, "certain metaphors are so taken for granted that they usually slip into our thoughts and actions undetected and unrecognised".
6 Ideology in discourse is defined most broadly here as "a systematically organised presentation of reality" (Hodge and Kress 1993: 15). In the Socio-Cognitive Approach to CDA, Van Dijk (e.g., 1998) has attempted to articulate at a finer level of detail the properties of ideologies. Most basically, for Van Dijk, ideologies involve an Us/Them polarisation and, typically, positive beliefs about and attitudes toward Us and negative beliefs about and attitudes toward Them. For a further, more detailed, discussion of the contents, structure and format of ideologies from a Cognitive Linguistic perspective see Koller (2014).

contained "boiling up" and escaping from the container. Such a conceptualisation suggests the need to control the liquid which in the target domain equates to the controversial crowd control technique known, presumably by no coincidence, as "kettling". The construal invoked by (1) thus seems to disempower the protesters, reducing their actions to natural phenomena and thus removing their agency, whilst at the same time sanctioning police practices. The source domain in (2), by contrast, is that of WAR. According to Semino (2008: 100), war metaphors in political discourse "tend to dramatize the opposition between different participants ... who are constructed as enemies". Crucially, however, the use of such militarising metaphors in relation to both sides serves to empower protesters, presenting their actions as "fighting" for some cause. The use of *storm* in particular seems to have positive connotations of purpose and precision.

While metaphor is central in Cognitive Linguistic approaches to ideological discourse research, of equal importance is the relation between grammar and conceptualisation where, as Langacker puts it, "it is precisely because of their conceptual import – the contrasting images they impose – that alternative grammatical devices are commonly available to code the same situation" (1991: 295). Grammar, on this account, is inherently meaningful. Grammatical constructions impose a particular construal on the scene described. They guide attention along particular parameters where, analogous with visual processing, "what we actually see depends on how closely we examine it, what we choose to look at, which elements we pay most attention to, and where we view it from" (Langacker 2008: 55). Alongside what it has been able to reveal about semantic metaphor in discourse, then, another important contribution of Cognitive Linguistics in CDA has been to theorise in cognitively plausible terms the conceptual weight of grammatical metaphor (in the form of agentless passivisation and nominalisation), which, in specific discursive contexts, is also said to be ideologically load-bearing (Hart 2011b).

If linguistic (semantic or grammatical) structures have the facility, in specific contexts, to reproduce ideology, then language is not only an important instrument of power but, from a critical analytical perspective, it's operationalization in discourse is an important window on the ideologies of powerful speakers and the discourse communities over whom they have influence. It is in this sense that Cognitive Linguistics "offers analytic tools for the critical assessment of ideologies" (Dirven et al. 2007: 1236). It is a central tenet of Cognitive Linguistics that language reflects conceptual structures and processes, which are in turn grounded in more general cognitive abilities (Croft and Cruse 2004). And since "any ideology is a conceptual system of a particular kind" (Lakoff 1996: 37), it follows that language use affords access to ideologies. Linguistic analysis, and Cognitive Linguistic analysis in particular, is therefore an important tool in ideological research. Cognitive Linguistics addresses "the structuring within language of such basic conceptual categories as those of space and time, scenes and events, entities and processes, motion and location, and force and causation" (Talmy 2000: 3) – precisely the kind of transitivity phenomena that critical discourse analysts have been interested in. Cognitive Linguistics, then, is especially useful for CDA in so far as it can "lay bare the structuring of concepts and conceptions" (Dirven et al. 2003: 4) which constitute ideologies.[7] Cognitive Linguistics, in other words, can serve as an analytical lens through which the latent ideologies expressed in, and enacted through, discourse can be brought to critical consciousness.

In the following sections, I review some of the ways in which Cognitive Linguistics and CDA can be usefully combined in ideological discourse research.

3 The Cognitive Linguistic approach to CDA

Unsurprisingly given its centrality in the development of Cognitive Linguistics, the earliest and most influential combination of Cognitive Linguistics and CDA is in the guise of Critical Metaphor Analysis utilising Lakoff and Johnson's (1980) Conceptual Metaphor Theory (Chilton 1996; Santa Ana 2002; Wolf and Polzenhagen 2003; Musolff 2003, 2004; Charteris-Black 2004, 2006; Koller 2004; Maalej 2007; Goatly 2007). As readers of this handbook will know, however, there is much more to the Cognitive Linguistics bow than metaphor theory. Cognitive Linguistics offers a number of theories which have in common a specific set of assumptions including that linguistic (semantic and grammatical) structures are based on the same general cognitive abilities as other domains of cognition, that linguistic knowledge is conceptual in nature, that meaning is grounded in experience, and that words and constructions both construe experience. These theories address a range of linguistic/conceptual phenomena, including categorisation, schematisation, metaphor, salience, selection and perspectivisation (topics covered in volume 1; see chapters by Ramscar and Port; Baayen and Ramscar; Gibbs; Tomlin and Myachykov; and Langacker), all of which

---

[7] On this account, ideology is seen as "a system of beliefs and values based on a set of cognitive models" (Dirven et al. 2003: 1) and may thus be analysed in terms of categories, frames, conceptual metaphors and image schemas as well as the "online" conceptualisations which may become idealised in more stable "offline" conceptual structures (Hart 2010).

can be seen, in certain discursive contexts, to function ideologically.[8] The broader synergy between Cognitive Linguistics and CDA aims to account for the reproduction of ideology in discourse in terms of these conceptual operations. This synergy thus offers an explanatory framework in which the ideological dimensions of language are related to general conceptual principles (Dirven et al. 2007: 1236). Indeed, it is a particular strength of the Cognitive Linguistic Approach to CDA that a wide array of ideological phenomena in discourse, which may appear to be diverse, can be accounted for against a common theoretical backdrop (Dirven et al. 2007). Whilst metaphor studies have dominated Cognitive Linguistic investigations of ideology in CDA, then, other theories in Cognitive Linguistics have been applied, including prototype theory (O'Halloran 2003), force-dynamics (Hart 2011a) and various aspects of Cognitive Grammar (Marín Arrese 2011a; Hart 2013a, 2013b). Cognitively motivated theories of linguistic description and conceptual modelling have also been developed to account for ideology in longer stretches of discourse, most notably Chilton's (2004) Discourse Space Theory.

Based on Croft and Cruse's (2004) classification of construal operations, Hart (2011b, 2013a, 2013b) offers a taxonomy which attempts to locate these analytical strands inside a single coherent framework.[9] Here, construal operations are classified as instantiations of four general cognitive systems: Gestalt, Comparison, Attention, and Perspective.[10] Similarly, the ideological functions of these construal operations can be analysed in terms of their realisation of four "discursive strategies": Structural configuration, framing, identification, and positioning (see Figure 4.1).[11] Discursive strategies are understood here, following Reisigl and Wodak (2001), as more or less intentional/institutionalised plans of practices whose realisation achieves particular cognitive, emotive and/or social action effects. Realisation, in its cognitive dimension, is understood as constituting hearers' conceptions of the situations/events described. Construal operations invoked in the hearer are the site of this realisation and thus ideological reproduction.[12]

---

[8] It should be noted that various labels and classifications have been applied to these "construal operations" (cf. Croft and Cruse 2004; Verhagen 2010).
[9] This is not to say that all authors in this field would necessarily situate their work with respect to this taxonomy or the broader Cognitive Linguistic Approach envisaged here.
[10] See Langacker (volume 1) for an alternative classification.
[11] For alternative taxonomies of discursive strategies see Reisigl and Wodak (2001); Chilton and Schäffner (1997); Chilton (2004).
[12] I stop short of suggesting that discursive strategies force particular conceptualisations and inferences on the grounds that speakers are never in total control of hearer's cognitive processes. However, they can construct contexts and guide interpretation in such a way that certain conceptualisations and inferences are at least likely to be entertained. The extent to which

Strategy \ System	Gestalt	Comparison	Attention	Perspective
Structural Configuration	Schematization			
Framing		Categorization		
		Metaphor		
Identification			Profiling	
			Scanning	
			Scalar adjustment	
Positioning				Point of view
				Deixis

(Construal operations)

Fig. 4.1: Construal operations and discursive strategies.

In Figure 4.1 structural configuration strategies are realised through schematisation involving the imposition of a particular image-schematic representation which constitutes our most basic understanding of the object- or event-structure. Schematisation is based in the Gestalt system which enables conceptualisers to analyse complex scenes as holistic structures. Framing strategies concern the attribution of particular qualities to entities, actors, actions, relations and processes as alternative categories and metaphors are apprehended in their conceptualisation.[13] Identification strategies concern the salience with which social actors are represented in the conceptualisation and are realised through a number of construal operations including profiling, scanning and scalar adjustment. These construal operations are grounded in the system of attention. Positioning strategies can be spatial, temporal or modal. They relate to where, in space or time, we view a scene from and where we locate elements in the discourse relative to that "anchorage point". Modal positioning relates to where we locate propositions in the discourse relative to our own conceptions of real-

---

audiences are manipulated by language is a fundamental issue to CDA which has recently been revisited in light of developments in Cognitive Science (see Chilton 2005, 2011; Hart 2010, 2011c, 2013c; O'Halloran 2011; Oswald 2011; Maillat and Oswald 2011; Marín Arrese 2011b; de Saussure 2011).

13 It should be noted that whilst structural configuration and framing strategies can be separated for purposes of analysis they are rarely, if ever, separable in the practice of discourse. For example, categorization and metaphor may involve the imposition of particular schemas.

ity (epistemic) and morality (deontic).[14] Positioning strategies are grounded in our ability to conceive of a scene from different perspectives. They are realised in point of view and deixis.

The ideological functions of these construal operations have been analysed across a range of specific contexts including, *inter alia*, immigration (El Refaie 2001; Santa Ana 2002; Charteris-Black 2006; Hart 2010), urban planning (Todolí 2007), business (Koller 2004), European politics (Musolff 2004; Sing 2011; Nasti 2012), war (Chilton 1996, 2004; Maalej 2007; Marín Arrese 2011a), and political protests (Hart 2013a, 2013b). In what follows, I try to demonstrate how Cognitive Linguistic analyses of some of these conceptual parameters allow a handle on the ideological properties of text and talk. Sections are organised around the discursive strategies given in Figure 4.1. I leave out framing strategies realised in categorisation and metaphor due to limits on space and the availability of a now significant body of research in this area (see references herein). I illustrate these strategies and construal operations with data from across various social and political Discourses and genres.

4 Conceptual parameters for ideology

4.1 Structural configuration (Gestalt)

Structural configuration is a strategy by means of which speakers impose on the scene a particular image-schematic representation which constitutes our most basic understanding of the topological and relational structure of the complex under conception. Grounded in the Gestalt system, it relies on our ability to analyse multifaceted entities and events in terms of particular, holistic structures – image schemas. Image schemas are abstract Gestalt structures many of which emerge pre-linguistically from repeated patterns in embodied experience (Johnson 1987; Mandler 2004). They later come to form the meaningful basis of many lexical concepts as well as grammatical constructions and are thus invoked in discourse to construe experience in particular ways.

Various image schemas have been identified in Cognitive Linguistics. These can be catalogued in various ways (see, for example, Evans and Green 2006: 190). However, let us here mention four broad domains of image schemata: SPACE, MOTION, FORCE, and ACTION. SPACE schemas include a CONTAINER

---

[14] I would also be inclined to consider evaluations in the system of Appraisal as described by Martin and White (2007) as construal operations realising positioning strategies.

schema, a VERTICALITY schema, a NEAR-FAR schema, and a CONTACT schema. MOTION schemas include a SOURCE-PATH-GOAL schema and a MOMENTUM schema. FORCE schemas incorporate the various force-dynamic schemas which, as described by Talmy (2000), constitute concepts of CAUSATION and LETTING. Finally, ACTION schemas would include the canonical ACTION-CHAIN as described by Langacker (1991, 2002) as well as 'transformations' of that schema. In structural configuration strategies, speakers select from the set of available schemas to construe entities and events as being of a particular type and internal structure. Schematisation is ideological, then, because image schemas "constrain and limit meaning as well as patterns of inference in our reasoning" (Johnson 1987: 42). And, since different schemas have different topological and relational properties, giving rise to different entailments – defined as functional "implications of the internal structure of image schemata" (Johnson 1987: 22) – their particular selection in discourse may achieve different ideological effects.

Hart (2011a) has shown how immigration discourse makes use of force-dynamic schemas to construe the physical, political and legal dimensions of immigration. Consider the contrast between (3) and (4).

(3) It's estimated that between 1,000 and 1,200 asylum seekers are **coming into the country** every month. (*The Mirror*, 10 May 2002)

(4) Downing Street acknowledge that illegal immigration was an issue because of growing frustrations over the stream of people **getting into Britain** from France through the Channel tunnel. (*Daily Telegraph*, 21 May 2000)

In (3), the speaker selects a MOTION schema to construe the physical process of migration. This schema consists of a Trajector (TR) (immigrants) moving along a path of motion into a Landmark (LM) (Britain). By contrast, (4), as a function of the lexical semantics for *getting* in this context, encodes a force-dynamic construal. Here, immigrants are cast in the role of an AGONIST (AGO), defined in Talmy's terminology like a Trajector as an entity whose circumstance or location is at issue. However, there is a second active participant, an ANTAGONIST (ANT), defined as an entity whose relation with the AGONIST determines its circumstance or location. The ANTAGONIST can be construed as engaging with the AGONIST in various force-dynamic relations, including impingement as in (4). Here the ANTAGONIST is left implicit but can be read as physical barriers to immigration. The two alternative schemas invoked by (3) and (4) can be modelled as in Figures 4.2 and 4.3 respectively. The arrow in Figure 4.2 designates "free" motion. In Figure 4.3, by contrast, it represents the resultant of a force-interaction between two entities in which the ANTAGONIST attempts to restrict

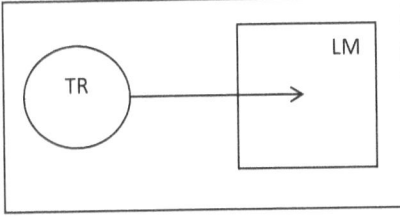
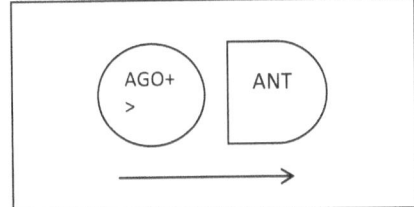

Fig. 4.2: MOTION schema.   **Fig. 4.3:** FORCE schema.

the movement of the AGONIST but, as the stronger entity (+), the AGONIST is able to overcome or avoid the constraints placed upon it.

Schematising the movement of people in force-dynamic terms constructs a binary opposition in which ANT and AGO are pitted against one another and thus contributes to an Us versus Them ideological structure. There is then a further ideological dimension in which particular role participants are cast (Wolf and Polzenhagen 2003: 265). Casting immigrants in the role of AGONIST with an intrinsic tendency toward action as in (4) depicts them as instigators of force interactions. The ANTAGONIST, on the other hand, is seen as simply maintaining the status quo. More rhetorically, a force-dynamic construal seems to presuppose that immigration ought to be prevented and that in overcoming or avoiding the impinging force of the ANTAGONIST immigrants are acting wrongfully.

Hart (2013a, 2013b) has similarly shown the ideological effects of schematisation in media representations of political protests. Here he shows that the "cognitive discourse grammar" for representing interactions between police and protestors provides recourse to ACTION, FORCE or MOTION schemas. Ideologically, these schemas mitigate the role of participants in the events described to differing degrees. Consider, for example, the contrast between (5) and (6).

(5) A number of police officers were injured after they **came under attack from** youths, some wearing scarves to hide their faces. (*Times*, 10 November 2010)

(6) Activists who had masked their faces with scarves **traded punches with** police. (*Guardian*, 10 November 2010)

In (5), at a discourse level, the interaction between participants is construed in terms of a canonical action chain in which there is a transfer of energy from an AGENT (A) 'upstream' in the energy flow to a PATIENT (P) 'downstream' in the energy flow. As with force-dynamic construals, there is an ideological dimen-

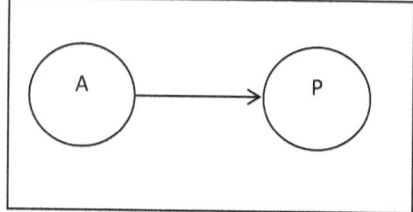
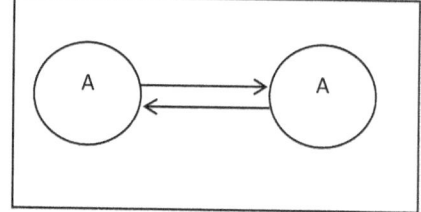

Fig. 4.4: ASYMMETRICAL ACTION schema.   **Fig. 4.5:** RECIPROCAL ACTION schema.

sion to the roles that participants are assigned. In a case study of online press reports of the UK Student Fees protests in 2010, Hart (2013b) found that protestors were significantly more likely to be represented as agents in a canonical action chain and police as patients than the other way around. When police were construed as agentive in an ACTION event, it was found, as in (6), that this was more likely to be in a RECIPROCAL rather than the canonical ASYMMETRICAL action chain (Hart 2013b). The alternative construals invoked by (5) and (6) can be modelled as in Figures 4.4 and 4.5 respectively. The arrow in Figure 4.4 indicates the transfer of energy from an AGENT (the source of the energy flow) to a PATIENT (the target of the energy flow). In Figure 4.5, however, the energy flow is bidirectional. Each participant is both a source and a target and so both are assigned agency. Ideologically, construing interactions between police and protestors in terms of a reciprocal action chain serves to mutually apportion responsibility for the violent encounter. Thus, when police are attributed agency in violent interactions their part is mitigated as a consequence of shared accountability.

In the same case study, it was further found that police agency was most likely to be construed in terms of FORCE or MOTION schemas, thus further legitimating or mitigating their part in the violence. Consider (7) and (8).

(7) The 20 officers lining the route at Millbank faced an impossible task of trying to **hold back** thousands of demonstrators (*Daily Mail*, 10 November 2010)

(8) About 50 riot police **moved in** just after 5 pm (*Independent*, 10 November 2010)

In (7), the speaker selects a force-dynamic schema casting police in the role of ANTAGONIST and protestors in the role of AGONIST. Notice, then, that this sets up an oppositional relation in which protestors are seen as being on the wrong side of the law and presented as instigators of force or violence who, if not held

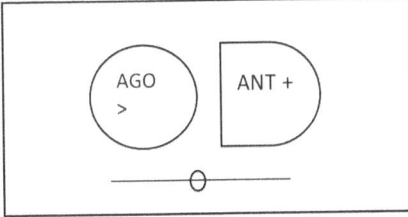

Fig. 4.6: FORCE schema.

back, will "take over". The police, by contrast, are presented in the valiant role of defenders of moral order. The schema invoked by (7) can be modelled as in Figures 4.6.

In this force-dynamic schema, the ANTAGONIST is the stronger entity (+) able to prevent the AGONIST from realising its intrinsic force tendency (>) resulting in a state of equilibrium (0). There is no transfer of energy from a source to a target but, rather, what is at stake is the balance of strength between the two participants. Compare this to (9) in which the police are agentive in a RETALIATORY ACTION schema:

(9) Rocks, wooden banners, eggs, rotten fruit and shards of glass were thrown at police officers trying to **beat back** the crowd with metal batons and riot shields. (*Telegraph*, 10 November 2010)

The schema invoked by (8) is the same as modelled in Figure 4.2. In this context, however, the construal serves euphemistically to present police action in terms of motion. The arrow denotes a path of motion rather than a transfer of energy with its terminus a location (GOAL) rather than a participant (PATIENT). The asymmetry in construal of agency between police and protestors contributes to a Discourse in which the current social order is legitimated and civil action is seen as deviant and therefore delegitimated.

Structural configuration strategies overlap with identification strategies as image schemata invoked in discourse are subject to various kinds of "focal adjustment" within the system of attention. We turn to identification strategies in the following section.

4.2 Identification (Attention)

Identification strategies concern the salience of social actors within the conceptual contents invoked by linguistic constructions. There is a significant amount

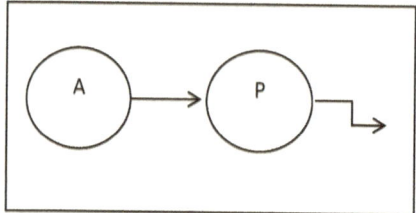

Fig. 4.7: ACTION schema (CHANGE OF STATE).

of work in CDA on the ideological potential of particular types of grammatical construction, including agentless passives, which are said to "enable speakers to conjure away responsible, involved or affected actors (whether victims or perpetrators), or to keep them in the semantic background" (Reisigl and Wodak 2001: 58). In Cognitive Grammar, the conceptual reflex of such grammatical devices and the psychological reality of "the semantic background" are accounted for in terms of profile/base distinctions grounded in the system of attention (Langacker 2002).

It is a fundamental feature of cognition that in perceiving any scene one entity stands out relative to another. Cognitive Linguists (e.g., Talmy 2000; Langacker 2002) recognise this phenomenon in language too. Words and constructions bring to prominence particular facets of a given conceptual structure, such as a frame or schema. In Cognitive Grammar, this construal operation is called "profiling". According to this framework, transactive processes invoke an ACTION schema such as modelled in Figure 4.7.[15] The straight arrow represents the transfer of energy between participants. The stepped arrow represents the resultant of this interaction on the PATIENT.

Depending on the grammatical realisation, however, different constructions, by linguistically encoding particular aspects of the whole event-structure, distribute attention across the model in different ways. A full transactive clause, for example, profiles the whole schema, where the profiled portion of the schema is that stretch downstream of the participant encoded as Subject. This is modelled in Figure 4.8. An agentless passive construction, by contrast, profiles only that portion of the schema downstream of the PATIENT, leaving the AGENT in the 'scope of attention' but cognitively and experientially backgrounded. As Langacker (2008: 384) puts it, "when one participant is left unspecified, the other becomes more salient just through the absence of competition. On the

---

[15] For present purposes, I am glossing over a third possible participant in the event-structure in the form of an INSTRUMENT or THEME.

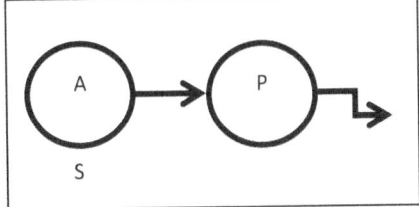
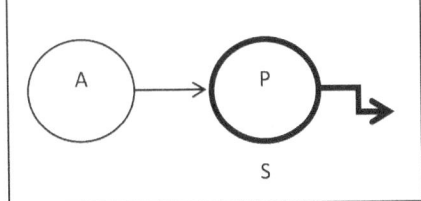

Fig. 4.8: Full profile.   **Fig. 4.9:** Partial profile.

other hand, augmenting the salience of one participant diminishes that of others (in relative terms)". Consider the following example.

(10) Seven **killed** in Afghanistan Koran burning protests [headline]
Seven people **were killed** today in clashes between Afghan security forces and protesters demonstrating against **the burning** of Muslim holy books at a NATO military base. (*Independent online,* 22 February 2012)

In (10), the agents of *killing* are not specified, either in the headline or the body of the article. The agentless passive construction invokes a conceptualisation as modelled in Figure 4.9. Such a construal, it would be argued in CDA, represents a "preferred model" (Van Dijk 1998) of the event in which agency in actions that are not consonant with dominant Discourses gets obfuscated (Toolan 1991). In this case, of course, the actions of Afghan security forces might be considered to destabilise the Discourse of democratization which sanctified intervention in Afghanistan.

Nominalisation can serve a similar ideological function in excluding agency from the lause (Fairclough 1989; Fowler 1991). The conceptual reflex of nominalisation is also grounded in the system of attention. In Cognitive Grammar it is said to involve a particular mode of "scanning". According to Cognitive Grammar we conceptualise events by mentally scanning the series of relations obtaining between participants at different (continuous) stages in the process that constitutes an event. There are two modes of scanning: sequential scanning and summary scanning. In sequential scanning, "the various phases of an evolving situation are examined serially, in noncumulative fashion" (Langacker 2002: 78–79). This is the mode of scanning invoked by a transactive clause where the relationships held between entities at different moments in the evolving event get profiled. However, as Langacker put is, "we nevertheless have the conceptual agility to construe an event by means of summary scanning" (2002: 79). In summary scanning, the various facets of an event are examined cumulatively so that the whole complex comes to cohere as a single gestalt (Langacker 2002).

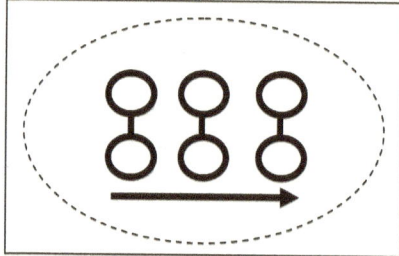 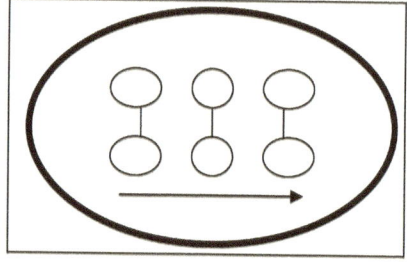

Fig. 4.10: Sequential scanning. **Fig. 4.11:** Summary scanning.

That is, we see an event as an OBJECT or THING rather than as a series of INTERACTIONS and PROCESSES. And since "things do not pertain to time, we do not scan their internal component states sequentially but see all of them accumulated" (Radden and Dirven 2007: 80). Through summary scanning, then, attention to internal event-structure, including participant roles, is occluded. In example (10) above, we see an instance of nominalisation in *the burning of Muslim holy books*. The nominalised verb profiles the reification and thus conceptually backgrounds agent-patient relations, again contributing to a preferred model of ideologically "awkward" events. The two modes of scanning are modelled in Figures 4.10 and 4.11.

The construal operations we have examined so far are semantically encoded. The final strategy we examine, in the next section, is positioning. Positioning strategies are more pragmatic in nature, directly anchored to the communicative context and more dependent on an intersubjective consensus of values.

4.3 Positioning (Perspective)

Positioning strategies in various (spatial, temporal and modal) guises have been studied from a broadly Cognitive Linguistic perspective (Bednarek 2006; Cap 2006, 2011; Marín Arrese 2011a). Positioning strategies pertain to the ontological relations between elements in a text, as well as epistemological/axiological relations between propositions and the speaker/hearer. They rely on our ability to "fix" conceptions relative to a particular perspective. Literally, this perspective is a VIEWPOINT (Langacker 1987) in space which is operationalised on two dimensions: the vertical or the horizontal. Langacker refers here to VANTAGE POINT and ORIENTATION respectively. The VIEWPOINT can, in turn, be construed at different DISTANCES from the scenes conceived. In Croft and Cruse's (2004) taxonomy of construal operations, deixis and Langacker's subjectivity/objectivity distinction are both also seen as instantiations of the PERSPECTIVE system.

Grounded in Mental Spaces Theory (Fauconnier 1994) and geometrical approaches to conceptualisation (Gärdenfors 2004), Chilton (2004) proposes an inherently deictic cognitive model of discourse coherence in which spatial representations metaphorically extend to account for social, temporal and modal "positioning". This framework, which Chilton refers to as Discourse Space Theory, has become an increasingly popular approach to conceptually modelling the interpersonal and affective dimensions of political discourse (see, for example, Cap 2013; Kaal 2012; Filardo Llamas 2013).

Discourse Space Theory is specifically designed to account for the conceptual structures built in "discourse beyond the sentence".[16] The claim is that during discourse hearers open a mental space in which the world described in the discourse is conceptually represented. The mental space, or discourse space, consists of three intersecting axes around which the discourse world is constructed. These axes are a socio-spatial axis (S), a temporal axis (T) and a modal axis (M). Each axis represents a scale of remoteness from a "deictic centre", which corresponds with the deictic reference points for the communicative event. Crucially, for the theory, this extends beyond the spatiotemporal "here" and "now" to include the social group "us" and shared evaluations of what is "right" both cognitively and morally. We can think of each axis as having polar reference points with various intermediate stations. For example, the S axis may be taken to represent an Us versus Them polarisation. The T axis represents a time line from "now" to "distant future" and "distant past". And the M axis represents a right-wrong scale.

The construction of discourse worlds involves the "plotting" of discourse elements within the three dimensional space relative to one and other and in relation to the topography of the basic model. The relative coordinates of these elements are indexed in text by linguistic representations and presupposed knowledge/value systems. Hearers are then invited to reconstruct this particular worldview. The basic architecture is seen in Figure 4.12.[17]

Crucially, the mapping out of elements inside the discourse space does not directly reflect reality but rather constructs it. The representation is thus subject to construal. Discourse elements can be proximised or distanced relative to the deictic centre. This deictic construal operation seems to be based on a CONTRACTION/PROTRACTION image schema. In the discourse space, this involves a shortening or lengthening of the distance between discourse elements and the deictic centre. Thus, as Chilton states, for many English speakers/hearers, Australia

---

16 In this way, the theory has much in common with Text World Theory (Werth 1999) which is often applied in Cognitive Poetics (see Stockwell this volume).
17 Note that the diagram is a two-dimensional representation of a three-dimensional space.

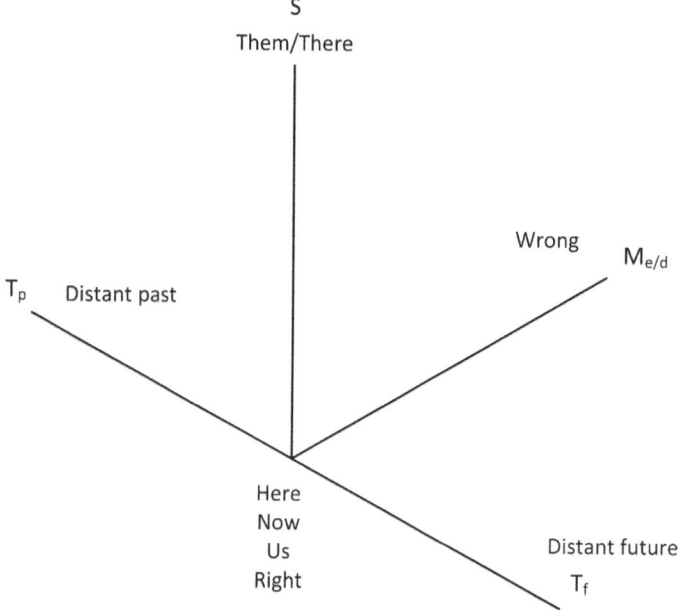

Fig. 4.12: Basic Discourse Space Model.

might be conceptualised as closer to the deictic centre along the socio-spatial axis than Albania. Evans (2004) shows that TIME too may be conceptualised as contracted or protracted.

Cap (2006) presents an elaborated theory of "proximisation" – a rhetorical strategy which works by "alerting the addressee to the proximity or imminence of phenomena which can be a 'threat' to the addressee and thus require immediate reaction" (2006: 4). Within the taxonomy presented in Figure 1, we can characterise proximisation as a deictic construal operation realising spatio-temporal positioning strategies. To illustrate how all of this works, consider first the following extract from Tony Blair's (the then British Prime Minister) foreword to the 24 September 2002 dossier outlining the case for war against Iraq:

(11) I am in no doubt that the threat is serious and current, that he has made progress on WMD, and that he has to be stopped. Saddam has used chemical weapons, not only against an enemy state, but against his own people. Intelligence reports make clear that he sees the building up of his WMD capability, and the belief overseas that he would use these weapons, as vital to his 3 strategic interests, and in particular his goal of regional domination. And the document discloses that his military

planning allows for some of the WMD to be ready within 45 minutes of an order to use them.

I am quite clear that Saddam will go to extreme lengths, indeed has already done so, to hide these weapons and avoid giving them up. In today's inter-dependent world, a major regional conflict does not stay confined to the region in question ...

The threat posed to international peace and security, when WMD are in the hands of a brutal and aggressive regime like Saddam's, is real. Unless we face up to the threat, not only do we risk undermining the authority of the UN, whose resolutions he defies, but more importantly and in the longer term, we place at risk the lives and prosperity of our own people.

The discourse world constructed by the text is (partially) modelled in Figure 4.13. Actors and locations are positioned along the S axis at relative distances from deictic centre, dependent on construed social distance. *Saddam Hussein* and his *regime* are constructed as Them and positioned at the extreme end of the S axis. Other participants are positioned between Them and the presupposed Us indexed in the text by *we*. The *United Nations* and the *international community* are construed as "closer" to Us than *Iraq* and the broader *region*.

The modal axis is simultaneously engaged in both a deontic and an epistemic capacity. In Figure 4.13 it is presented in its deontic guise where it stands as a scale of morality/immorality. Elements in the text like *brutal and aggressive*, *threat*, *WMD* and *regional domination*, based on an assumed shared value system, are associated with "immorality" and so positioned at the remote end of M_d. Elements along the different axes are linked by means of "connectors" which represent various kinds of relation including attribution, possession and intention. The zone around the deictic centre represents the extension of the conceptualiser's physical, social, moral and temporal ground.

The location of elements along S and M in the discourse space realise distancing positioning strategies. However, we can see both spatial and temporal proximisation where the *threat* posed by *Saddam Hussein* and his *WMD* is construed as (potentially) closer to or entering the conceptualiser's spatio-temporal ground. This construal operation is denoted in Figure 4.13 by the "vectors" pointing toward deictic centre along S and T_f. Spatial proximisation is indexed in the text by predicates which indicate (sometimes indirectly) that the range of the threat may extend to the conceptualiser's physical ground. These include:

- has **used** chemical weapons, not only **against an enemy state**, but **against his own people**
- does not **stay confined to the region in question**
- **place at risk** the lives and prosperity of **our own people**

Fig. 4.13: Spatial and Temporal Proximisation.

This proximisation, then, is built up in the text progressively as the threat is presented as extending from *enemy states* and *his own people* to the broader *region* and, finally, to *our own people*. Interestingly, this conceptual proximisation is also symbolically represented in the information sequence of the unfolding discourse. Temporal proximisation occurs where elements in the text position the reality of this threat as close to "now". Expressions of temporal proximisation include *current* and the now notorious *within 45 minutes*.

Operating over the other dimensions, we can identify epistemic proximisation as realising an epistemological positioning strategy (Hart 2014; see also Bednarek 2006). In the discourse space, the modal axis is also always engaged in an epistemic aspect representing a scale of reality/irreality. The discourse world for the text above, this time with the modal axis presented in its epistemic capacity, is shown in Figure 4.14. The zone around the deictic centre here represents the extension of the conceptualiser's epistemic ground, that is, what the conceptualiser takes to be "known reality" (Langacker 1991). Epistemic proximisation occurs as propositions embedded in the text, such as 'Saddam Hussein possesses WMD and poses a threat to the world which may be realised within

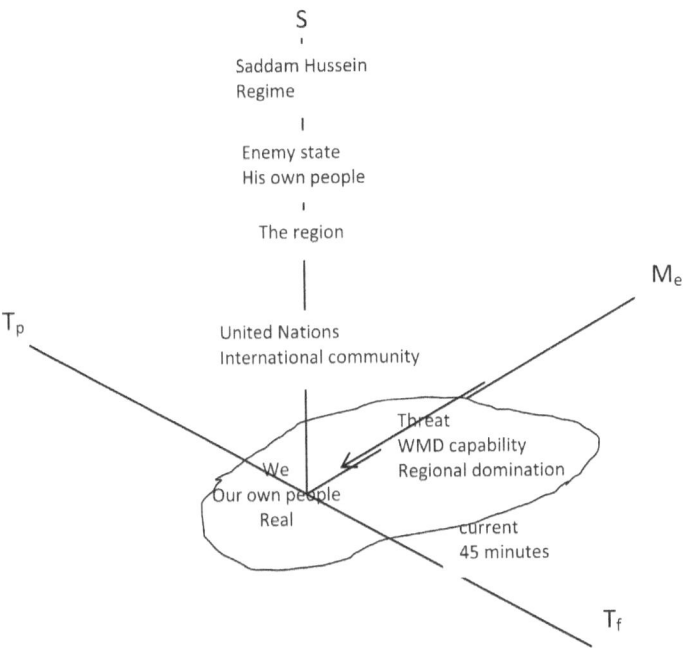

Fig. 4.14: Epistemic Proximisation.

45 minutes', represented in the discourse space by the connections between elements, are construed as part of known reality. Epistemic proximisation is indexed in text by expressions of epistemic modality and evidentiality, as well as existential presuppositions, which act as metaphorical "forces" (cf. Sweetser 1990; Talmy 2000) on the proposition propelling it toward the conceptutualiser's "right" at the deictic centre. In the text we find examples such as "I am in no doubt that", "is real", "intelligence reports make clear that" and *the document discloses that*.

One further, final, construal operation worth discussing in relation to modal positioning strategies is subjectivity/objectivity. This construal operation pertains to whether or not the speaker places themselves "onstage" as part of the object of conception (Langacker 1991) and, if so, whether this is alone or accompanied. According to Langacker, the speaker is objectified, made salient, if they are explicitly designated as the source of the predication. They are subjectified when they remain only implicitly the source of the predication. Since in both cases, the speaker rather than some third party is the source of the predication Langacker's subjectification and objectification both relate to notions of subjectivity as traditionally dealt with in the literature on stance and evaluation (e.g.,

Hunston and Thompson 2000; Englebretson 2007). Here, speakers may express either a subjective or an intersubjective stance on a given proposition. In Langacker's framework, a speaker may thus be subjectively or intersubjectively objectified.

Marín Arrese (2011a) discusses the ideological implications of subjectivity and, cutting across these notions, proposes a four-way classification of "epistemic stance-taking acts" as follows:
- Subjective Explicit (SE): the speaker is objectified as the sole evaluator
- Intersubjective Explicit (IE): the speaker and some other subject are together objectified as appraisers in agreement
- Subjective Implicit (SI): the speaker is subjectified but understood to be the sole evaluator
- Intersubjective Opaque (IO): the speaker is not identified as evaluator subjectively or objectively but rather evidence in favour of a particular evaluation is presented as (potentially) mutually accessible.

This "grammar" provides for ideologically motivated choices which depend on whether and to what extent of explicitness the speaker is prepared to claim sole responsibility for the assertion being made as in SE/SI, whether they wish to share in the evaluation either to stand behind an institution (*we the Government*) or to claim common ground with the audience (*we the speaker and addressee*) (IE), or whether the speaker needs to invoke external sources of support (IO). The expressions of epistemic proximisation in the text above are categorised in Marín Arrese's typology as follows:
- I am in no doubt that; I am clear that (SE)
- is real (SI)
- intelligence reports make clear that; the document discloses that (IO)

(SE) is a marked characteristic of Blair's rhetorical style (Marin Arrese 2011a). In effect, it asks the audience not just to believe the speaker but to believe *in* the speaker. It betrays a speaker confident in their own credibility. However, as Van Dijk (2011: 53) states, "speakers are more credible when they are able to attribute their knowledge or opinions to reliable sources, especially if some of the recipients may doubt whether they are well grounded". In order to convince audiences, therefore, political and media genres often require speakers to advance evidence for their assertions (Chilton 2004; Hart 2011c). Various types of evidence are available (see Bednarek 2006). However, particularly prominent in political discourse is the kind of "proof" invoked by Blair including "independent reports", "investigations", "studies" and "statistics".

5 Conclusion

In this chapter, I have tried to provide an overview of some of the ways in which Cognitive Linguistics and CDA can be combined to reveal ideological properties of text and conceptualisation. In doing so, I have surveyed a number of construal operations which, invoked by particular linguistic instantiations in discourse, may carry some ideological load. I have further attempted to systematise these inside a single, coherent theoretical framework relating construal operations to the domain-general cognitive systems on which they rely and to the discursive strategies which they potentially realise. Several construal operations have been identified as fulfilling an ideological potential in specific discursive contexts. Those discussed in this chapter should not be taken as an exhaustive set. Nearly all construal operations may be ideologically significant in certain contexts. They are, however, representative of those so far addressed within the body of work existing at the intersection between Cognitive Linguistics and CDA.

6 References

Baayen, Harald and Michael Ramscar (volume 1): Abstraction, storage and naive discriminative learning. Berlin/Boston: De Gruyter Mouton.
Bednarek, Monika (2006): Epistemological positioning and evidentiality in English news discourse: A text-driven approach. *Text and Talk* 26(6): 635–660.
Boroditsky, Lera (2001): Does language shape thought? English and Mandarin speakers' conceptions of time. *Cognitive Psychology* 43(1): 1–22.
Cap, Piotr (2006): *Legitimization in Political Discourse*. Newcastle: Cambridge Scholars Press.
Cap, Piotr (2011): Axiological proximisation. In: C. Hart (ed.), *Critical Discourse Studies in Context and Cognition*, 81–96. Amsterdam: John Benjamins.
Cap, Piotr (2013): *Proximization: The Pragmatics of Symbolic Distance Crossing*. Amsterdam: John Benjamins.
Charteris-Black, Jonathan (2004): *Corpus Approaches to Critical Metaphor Analysis*. Basingstoke: Palgrave Macmillan.
Charteris-Black, Jonathan (2006): Britain as a container: Immigration metaphors in the 2005 election campaign. *Discourse and Society* 17(6): 563–82.
Chilton, Paul A. (1996): *Security Metaphors: Cold War Discourse from Containment to Common House*. New York: Peter Lang.
Chilton, Paul A. (2004): *Analysing Political Discourse: Theory and Practice*. London: Routledge.
Chilton, Paul A. (2005): Missing links in mainstream CDA: Modules, blends and the critical instinct. In R. Wodak and P. Chilton (eds.), *A New Research Agenda in Critical Discourse Analysis: Theory and Interdisciplinarity*, 19–52. Amsterdam: John Benjamins.
Chilton, Paul A. (2011): Still something missing in CDA. *Discourse Studies* 13(6): 769–781.

Chilton, Paul A. and Christina. Schäffner (1997): Discourse and politics. In: T. A. van Dijk (ed.), *Discourse as Social Interaction*, 206–230. London: Sage.

Croft, William and D. Alan Cruse (2004): *Cognitive Linguistics*. Cambridge: Cambridge University Press.

de Saussure, Louis (2011): Discourse analysis, cognition and evidentials. *Discourse Studies* 13(6): 781–788.

Dirven, René, Roslyn M. Frank, and Martin Putz (2003): Introduction: Categories, cognitive models and ideologies. In: R. Dirven, R. Frank and M. Putz (eds.), *Cognitive Models in Language and Thought: Ideology, Metaphors and Meanings*, 1–24. Berlin: Mouton de Gruyter.

Dirven, René, Frank Polzenhagen, and Hanz-Georg Wolf (2007): Cognitive linguistics, ideology and critical discourse analysis. In: D. Geeraerts and H. Cuyckens (eds.), *The Oxford Handbook of Cognitive Linguistics*, 1222–1240. Oxford: Oxford University Press.

El Refaie, Elisabeth (2001): Metaphors we discriminate by: Naturalized themes in Austrian newspaper articles about asylum seekers. *Journal of Sociolinguistics* 5(3): 352–71.

Engelbretson, Robert (ed.) (2007): *Stancetaking in Discourse: Subjectivity, Evaluation, Interaction*. Amsterdam: John Benjamins.

Evans, Vyvyan (2004): *The Structure of Time: Language, Meaning and Temporal Cognition*. Amsterdam: John Benjamins.

Evans, Vyvyan and Melanie Green (2006): *Cognitive Linguistics: An Introduction*. Edinburgh: Edinburgh University Press.

Fairclough, Norman (1989): *Language and Power*. London: Longman.

Fairclough, Norman and Ruth Wodak (1997): Critical discourse analysis. In: T. A. van Dijk (ed.), *Discourse as Social Interaction. Discourse Studies: A Multidisciplinary Introduction* Vol. 2, 258–284. London: Sage.

Fauconnier, Gilles (1994): *Mental Spaces: Aspects of Meaning Construction in Natural Language* 2nd edn. Cambridge: Cambridge University Press.

Filardo Llamas, Laura (2013): 'Committed to the ideals of 1916': The language of paramilitary groups: the case of the Irish Republican Army. *Critical Discourse Studies* 10(1): 1–17.

Foucault, Michel (1972): *Archaeology of Knowledge*. London: Routledge.

Fowler, Roger (1991): *Language in the News: Discourse and Ideology in the Press*. London: Routledge.

Gärdenfors, Peter (2004): *Conceptual Spaces: The Geometry of Thought* 2nd edn. Bradford: Bradford Books.

Gee, James P. (1990): *Social Linguistics and Literacies: Ideology in Discourses*. London: Falmer Press.

Gibbs, Raymond W. Jr. (volume 1): Metaphor. Berlin/Boston: De Gruyter Mouton.

Goatly, Andrew (2007): *Washing the Brain: Metaphor and Hidden Ideology*. Amsterdam: John Benjamins.

Halliday, Michael A. K. (1973): *Explorations in the Functions of Language*. London: Edward Arnold.

Halliday, Michael A. K. and C. M. I. M. Matthiessen (1999): *Construing Experience Through Meaning: A Language-Based Approach to Cognition*. London: Continuum.

Hart, Christopher (2010): *Critical Discourse Analysis and Cognitive Science: New Perspectives on Immigration Discourse*. Basingstoke: Palgrave.

Hart, Christopher (2011a): Force-interactive patterns in immigration discourse: A Cognitive Linguistic approach to CDA. *Discourse and Society* 22(3): 269–286.

Hart, Christopher (2011b): Moving beyond metaphor in the Cognitive Linguistic approach to CDA: Construal operations in immigration discourse. In: C. Hart (ed.), *Critical Discourse Studies in Context and Cognition*, 171–192. Amsterdam: John Benjamins.

Hart, Christopher (2011c): Legitimising assertions and the logico-rhetorical module: Evidence and epistemic vigilance in media discourse on immigration. *Discourse Studies* 13(6): 751–769.

Hart, Christopher (2013a): Event-construal in press reports of violence in political protests: A Cognitive Linguistic Approach to CDA. *Journal of Language and Politics* 3: 159.

Hart, Christopher (2013b): Constructing contexts through grammar: Cognitive models and conceptualisation in British Newspaper reports of political protests. In: J. Flowerdew (ed.) *Discourse and Contexts*, 159–184. London: Continuum.

Hart, Christopher (2013c): Argumentation meets adapted cognition: Manipulation in media discourse on immigration. *Journal of Pragmatics* 59: 200–209.

Hart, Christopher (2014): *Discourse, Grammar and Ideology: Functional and Cognitive Perspectives*. London: Bloomsbury.

Hart, Christopher and Dominik Lukeš (eds.) (2007): *Cognitive Linguistics in Critical Discourse Analysis: Application and Theory*. Newcastle: Cambridge Scholars Publishing.

Haynes, John (1989): *Introducing Stylistics*. London: Hyman.

Hodge, Robert and Gunther Kress (1993): *Language as Ideology* 2nd edn. London: Routledge.

Hunston, Susan and Geoff Thompson (eds.) (2000): *Evaluation in Text: Authorial Stance and the Construction of Discourse*. Oxford: Oxford University Press.

Johnson, Mark (1987): *The Body in the Mind: The Bodily Basis of Meaning, Imagination, and Reason*. Chicago: University of Chicago Press.

Kaal, Bertie (2012): Worldviews: Spatial ground for political reasoning in Dutch Election manifestos. *Critical Approaches to Discourse Analysis across Disciplines* 6(1): 1–22.

Koller, Veronika (2004): *Metaphor and Gender in Business Media Discourse: A Critical Cognitive Study*. Basingstoke: Palgrave.

Koller, Veronika (2014): Cognitive Linguistics and ideology. In: J. R. Taylor and J. Littlemore (eds.), *Companion to Cognitive Linguistics*, 234–252. London: Continuum.

Kress, Gunther (1989): *Linguistic Processes in Sociocultural Practice* 2nd edn. Oxford: Oxford University Press.

Lakoff, George (1987): *Women, Fire, and Dangerous Things: What Categories Reveal about the Mind*. Chicago: University of Chicago Press.

Lakoff, George (1996): *Moral Politics: How Liberals and Conservatives Think*. Chicago: University of Chicago Press.

Lakoff, George and Mark Johnson (1980): *Metaphors We Live By*. Chicago: University of Chicago Press.

Langacker, Ronald W. (1987): *Foundations of Cognitive Grammar*, vol. I: *Theoretical Prerequisites*. Stanford: Stanford University Press.

Langacker, Ronald W. (1991): *Foundations of Cognitive Grammar*, vol. II: *Descriptive Application*. Stanford: Stanford University Press.

Langacker, Ronald W. (2002): *Concept, Image, and Symbol: The Cognitive Basis of Grammar*. 2nd edn. Berlin: Mouton de Gruyter.

Langacker, Ronald W. (2008): *Cognitive Grammar: A Basic Introduction*. Oxford: Oxford University Press.

Langacker, Ronald W. (volume 1): Construal. Berlin/Boston: De Gruyter Mouton.

Levinson, Stephen C. (2003): *Space in Language and Cognition: Explorations in Cognitive Diversity*. Cambridge: Cambridge University Press.

Maalej, Zouhair (2007): Doing critical discourse analysis with the contemporary theory of metaphor: Toward a discourse model of metaphor. In: C. Hart and D. Lukeš (eds.), *Cognitive Linguistics in Critical Discourse Analysis: Application and Theory*, 132–58. Newcastle: Cambridge Scholars Press.

Maillat, Didier and Steve Oswald (2011): Constraining context: A pragmatic account of cognitive manipulation. In: C. Hart (ed.), *Critical Discourse Studies in Context and Cognition*, 65–80. Amsterdam: John Benjamins.

Mandler, Jean M. (2004): *The Foundations of Mind: Origins of Conceptual Thought*. Oxford: Oxford University Press.

Marín Arrese, Juana (2011a): Effective vs. epistemic stance and subjectivity in political discourse: Legitimising strategies and mystification of responsibility. In: C. Hart (ed.), *Critical Discourse Studies in Context and Cognition*, 193–224. Amsterdam: John Benjamins.

Marín Arrese, Juana (2011b): Epistemic legitimizing strategies, commitment and accountability in discourse. *Discourse Studies* 13(6): 789–797.

Musolff, Andreas (2003): Ideological functions of metaphor: The conceptual metaphors of *health* and *illness* in public discourse. In: R. Dirven, R. Frank and M. Putz (eds.), *Cognitive Models in Language and Thought: Ideology, Metaphors and Meanings*, 327–352. Berlin: Mouton de Gruyter.

Musolff, Andreas (2004): *Metaphor and Political Discourse: Analogical Reasoning in Debates about Europe*. Basingstoke: Palgrave Macmillan.

Nasti, Chiara (2012): *Images of the Lisbon Treaty Debate in the British Press: A Corpus-Based Approach to Metaphor Analysis*. Newcastle: Cambridge Scholars Publishing.

Nuñez-Perucha, Begoña (2011): Critical Discourse Analysis and Cognitive Linguistics as tools for ideological research: A diachronic analysis of feminism. In: C. Hart (ed.), *Critical Discourse Studies in Context and Cognition* 97–118. Amsterdam: John Benjamins.

O'Halloran, Kieran (2003): *Critical Discourse Analysis and Language Cognition*. Edinburgh: Edinburgh University Press.

O'Halloran, Kieran (2011): Legitimations of the logico-rhetorical module: Inconsistency in argument, online discussion forums and electronic deconstruction. *Discourse Studies* 13(6): 797–806.

Oswald, Steve (2011): From interpretation to consent: Arguments, beliefs and meaning. *Discourse Studies* 13(6): 806–814.

Radden, Gunter and Rene Dirven (2007): *Cognitive English Grammar*. Amsterdam: John Benjamins.

Ramscar, Michael (volume 1): Categorization. Berlin/Boston: De Gruyter Mouton.

Reisigl, Martin and Ruth Wodak (2001): *Discourse and Discrimination: Rhetorics of Racism and Anti-Semitism*. London: Routledge.

Santa Ana, Otto (2002): *Brown Tide Rising: Metaphors of Latinos in Contemporary American Public Discourse*. Austin: University of Texas Press.

Semino, Elena (2008): *Metaphor in Discourse*. Cambridge: Cambridge University Press.

Shimko, Keith L. (1994): Metaphors and foreign policy decision making. *Political Psychology* 15(4): 655–671.

Sing, Christine (2011): The ideological construction of European identities: A critical discourse analysis of the linguistic representation of the old vs. new Europe debate. In C. Hart (ed.), *Critical Discourse Studies in Context and Cognition*, 143–170. Amsterdam: John Benjamins.

Stockwell, Peter (1999): Towards a critical cognitive linguistics. In: A. Combrink and I. Bierman (eds.), *Discourses of War and Conflict*, 510–528. Potchefstroom: Ptochefstroom University Press.
Stockwell, Peter (this volume): Poetics. Berlin/Boston: De Gruyter Mouton.
Sweetser, Eve (1990): *From Etymology to Pragmatics: Metaphorical and Cultural Aspects of Semantic Structure*. Cambridge: Cambridge University Press.
Talmy, Leonard (2000): *Toward a Cognitive Semantics*. Cambridge: MIT Press.
Todolí, Júlia (2007): Disease metaphors in urban planning. *Critical Approaches to Discourse Analysis across Disciplines* 1(2): 51–60.
Toolan, Michael J. (1991): *Narrative: A Critical Linguistic Introduction*. London: Routledge.
Tomlin, Russell and Andriy Myachykov (volume 1): Attention and salience. Berlin/Boston: De Gruyter Mouton.
van Dijk, Teun A. (1995): Discourse analysis as ideology analysis. In: C. Schäffner and A. I. Wenden (eds.), *Language and Peace*, 17–36. Amsterdam: Harwood Academic Publishers.
van Dijk, Teun A. (1998): *Ideology: A Multidisciplinary Approach*. London: Sage.
van Dijk, Teun A. (2001): Critical discourse analysis. In: D. Schiffrin, D. Tannen and H. E. Hamilton (eds.), *The Handbook of Discourse Analysis*, 352–371. Oxford: Blackwell.
van Dijk, Teun A. (2011): Discourse, knowledge, power and politics: Towards critical epistemic discourse analysis. In: C. Hart (ed.), *Critical Discourse Studies in Context and Cognition*, 27–64. Amsterdam: John Benjamins.
Verhagen, Arie (2010): Construal and perspectivisation. In: D. Geeraerts and H. Cuyckens (eds.), *The Oxford Handbook of Cognitive Linguistics*, 48–81. Oxford: Oxford University Press.
Werth, Paul (1999): *Text Worlds: Representing Conceptual Space in Discourse*. Harlow: Longman.
Wodak, Ruth (2001): What is CDA about: A summary of its history, important concepts and its developments. In: R. Wodak and M. Meyer (eds.), *Methods of Critical Discourse Analysis*, 1–13. London: Sage.
Wolf, Hans-Georg and Frank Polzenhagen (2003): Conceptual metaphor as ideological stylistic means: An exemplary analysis. In: R. Dirven, R. Frank and M. Putz (eds.), *Cognitive Models in Language and Thought: Ideology, Metaphors and Meanings*, 247–276. Berlin: Mouton de Gruyter.

Martin Hilpert
Chapter 5: Historical linguistics

1 Introduction

At first blush it may seem odd that researchers in Cognitive Linguistics should have an interest in the historical development of language. After all, analyzing the relationship between language and cognition seems a much more feasible task if there are speakers whose behavior can be observed in the here-and-now. This of course is not possible with languages or language varieties that are no longer spoken. To give just two examples, one cannot conduct a lexical decision task with speakers of Old English, nor is it possible to study the metaphorical underpinnings of gestures that accompanied conversations in Hittite. How can a cognitive approach to language history be anything but utter speculation? This chapter will make the case that looking at language change is not only perfectly in line with the cognitive linguistic enterprise, but that furthermore an understanding of how language change works is a necessary prerequisite for an adequate theory of how language and cognition are related in synchrony. The key idea underpinning this argument is the usage-based approach to language, that is, the hypothesis that language use shapes speakers' cognitive representation of language.

This argument will be made in five sections. The first section is a general presentation of the usage-based approach that Cognitive Linguistics brings to the study of language change (e.g., Langacker 1987; Bybee 2007, 2010). On this view, the major cause of language change is language use itself. Language change on a historical time-scale is viewed as the emergent outcome of speaker behavior in the here-and-now. This behavior, in turn, is governed by cognitive and social principles, which serve as explanations of why and how language changes. Grounding the study of language change in cognitively and socially motivated explanations can be seen as the main agenda of usage-based historical linguistics.

The introductory section sets the scene for four sections that illustrate different domains of language change. The first addresses lexical semantic change. The development of lexical meaning is inherently tied to the topics of conceptual metaphor and metonymy, polysemy, and prototype theory (Geeraerts 1997). The section will chart the semantic developments of selected lexical items and

Martin Hilpert, Neuchâtel, Switzerland

https://doi.org/10.1515/9783110626452-005

clarify the relation between historical change and synchronic polysemy. The next section discusses grammaticalization theory (Heine et al. 1991; Lehmann 1995; Hopper and Traugott 2003) and its relation to Cognitive Linguistics. The emergence of grammatical forms from lexical items yields evidence for conceptual and formal shifts that take place in highly similar ways across genetically unrelated languages; examples of such shifts will be presented. A third section will look at sociolinguistic change. A growing body of studies in Cognitive Linguistics acknowledges the importance of the social dimension of language and hence adopts a variationist framework (Geeraerts et al. 2010). It will be outlined how this work replaces the assumption of an idealized speaker-hearer with more realistic models of inter- and intraspeaker variation, and how it proceeds methodologically. The fourth section reports on work that applies the framework of Construction Grammar to the analysis of language change. Studies in Diachronic Construction Grammar (Noël 2007) analyze historical developments at the level of form-meaning pairings. This section discusses how such work differs from other approaches to the diachrony of language structure. A final section examines how these four domains of language change intersect and how they connect back to the usage-based approach of cognitive linguistics.

2 Language change and the usage-based model

There is ample theoretical motivation and empirical evidence that the synchronic structure of any human language is the emergent result of language use (Bybee and Hopper 2001; Barlow and Kemmer 2000). Grammatical structures are created through the social activity of human beings who engage in linguistic interaction, trying to "do things with words". As is discussed by Diessel (this volume), language use is dependent on several cognitive processes that are not in themselves linguistic. Amongst other things, the capacities for categorization, schematization, and analogy formation (cf. volume 1) are necessary cognitive prerequisites for language use. Similarly, language use is shaped by non-linguistic factors that are social in nature. These include the human inclination to cooperate (Grice 1975; Tomasello 2009), the ability to be polite, i.e., to respect the self-image of interlocutors in social interaction (Goffman 1955; Brown and Levinson 1987), and the disposition towards engaging in joint attention (Tomasello 1995), that is, "two people experiencing the same thing at the same time and knowing together that they are doing this" (Tomasello and Carpenter 2007: 121). A cornerstone of the usage-based model is hence the claim that language is grounded in domain-general socio-cognitive processes. The epithet domain-general indicates that these processes are active in basically all kinds of human cognition, not only cognition that relates to language.

A consequence of that claim is that it is impossible to separate the synchronic study of language from inherently dynamic issues, such as language acquisition and language change. Forming linguistic categories, constructional schemas, or analogies is not only what enables communication between human beings in the present, but these processes are also necessary for learning a first language (Matthews and Krajewski this volume), and the constant application of these processes by adult language users can be seen as the driving force behind language change: As particular forms of language are used again and again in linguistic interaction, routinization processes effectuate small steps of change in constructions' pronunciations, their meanings, their morpho-syntactic properties, etc. Frequency effects, together with the notion of entrenchment, are discussed in detail in Divjak and Caldwell-Harris (volume 1). Some effects of this kind are seen a result of speech production. For example, certain frequency effects come about as the consequences of repeated, routinized events of language production (Bybee and Thompson 1997). For instance, in the phrase *I don't know what you mean* the negated auxiliary is often heavily reduced and the final stop of *what* shows palatization. By comparison, these phenomena do not occur to the same extent in the phonologically similar but much less frequent phrase *I don't notice the dot you mean*. Other types of change are believed to result from language processing. Frequent processing of a linguistic form leads to "chunking", in which a complex sequence of items comes to be mentally represented as a holistic unit (Bybee and Scheibman 1999). The more often a string of elements is processed in sequence, the more likely hearers are to process this string as a single unit. An example for this would be the chunk *sitting and waiting*, which in some respects behaves like a single verb: In the question *What are you sitting and waiting for?* it is the prepositional object of the verb *waiting* that is questioned. Usually however, it is not possible in English to question constituents that are part of a coordinated phrase (Ross 1967: 89). An utterance such as *What are you whistling and waiting for?* sounds unidiomatic if not ungrammatical to most speakers. This is evidence that speakers reanalyzed the string *sitting and waiting* as a chunk, i.e., as a single verbal constituent. The presence of such frequency effects suggests that speakers' mental grammars undergo gradual changes that are driven by repetition and that only eventually result in categorical changes. The idea that one's mental representation of grammar may change during adulthood is very much at odds with the theory that first language acquisition is the only place where grammar change can occur (Lightfoot 1979). Instead of viewing language change as the result of compromised transmission between generations of speakers, the usage-based model offers a perspective in which language change happens gradually, with every usage event.

A notion that is central for this perspective is that speakers retain a large number of usage events in memory (Bybee 2010: ch. 2). Each token of linguistic usage is stored in a highly detailed fashion, so that even minute aspects of sound and meaning are registered and remembered. To stay with the example of *sitting and waiting*, the mental bookkeeping of speakers will include the rate with which *sitting* is realized with a final alveolar nasal, the rate with which the verbal complex *sitting and waiting* is used intransitively, and the rate with which it is followed by a phrase referring to a time span, amongst many other details. Of course, speakers' memories of linguistic usage events do not form an unstructured collection, but rather, each usage event is categorized as being more or less similar to previously encountered tokens. Speakers thus form generalizations over "clouds" of exemplar tokens. When speakers repeatedly experience tokens that are peripheral to an established cloud, eventually the shape of that cloud may change. It may become more diffuse or it may drift into one particular direction, or it may indeed develop into two separate clouds. The acceptability of *What are you sitting and waiting for?* suggests that in current usage, the chunk *sitting and waiting* forms an exemplar cloud of its own that is autonomous from the clouds of the form *sitting* and the form *waiting* respectively. As time progresses, this kind of emancipation may, but need not, become ever stronger. For example, the emerging modal verb *gonna* is fully emancipated from lexical uses of *going to*, as in *going to the beach*. Emancipation can result in complete dissociation, such that for instance the indefinite article *an* is no longer recognized by present-day speakers as deriving from the numeral *one*. In all three cases though (*sitting and waiting*, *gonna*, *an*), the process that has been at work is essentially the same: A peripheral group of uses in the original exemplar cloud becomes frequent enough to develop its own center of gravity, so that eventually there are two exemplar clouds, which may be partly overlapping at first, but nonetheless distinct.

Two points fall out of this exemplar-based view. First, it follows that even instances of completely regular patterns are redundantly stored as holistic forms. Speakers of English know that the plural of /kæt/ is formed through the addition of a voiceless dental fricative, but this does not keep them from memorizing /kæts/ as a pattern of usage in its own right. The division of linguistic knowledge into productive rules on the one hand and exceptions on the other in the interest of representational parsimony has been criticized by Langacker (1987: 29) as the rule/list fallacy: It is not necessary to settle for either one or the other, speakers demonstrably do both (Dąbrowska 2008). Second, the exemplar-based view suggests that linguistic categories are fuzzy and gradient

(Aarts 2007). Words, syntactic constructions, and also phonemes are represented as categories with substantial category-internal variation as well as overlap with other categories. In addition, exemplar-based categories may have one center of gravity, i.e., a single prototype (Rosch 1975), but they may also be pluricentric, so that there are several typical subcategories that are connected through family resemblances and together make up the structure of a superordinate category.

The exemplar-based view of variation that is built into the usage-based model of language holds a natural explanation for the fact that many linguistic forms develop multiple meanings over time, or may exhibit changes in their morphosyntactic behavior. What may start as a peripheral, context-dependent use of a form may eventually become a conventionalized pattern of usage. This insight is relevant for the study of lexical semantic change, where the development of polysemy can be observed. For instance, the English noun *paper* has, besides its sense of 'thin writing material', developed the senses of 'a piece of academic writing' and even 'an academic conference talk' (Nerlich and Clarke 2001). Hence, we find utterances such as *John gave an interesting paper*, which refer to the 'talk' sense, but not to any of the others.

Variation is furthermore important for the study of grammaticalization, where gradual changes in usage lead to what is called de-categorialization (Hopper 1991: 30), i.e., the development of discrete categorical differences between linguistic units. To illustrate, the English phrase *seeing as though* (Taylor and Pang 2008) has developed from a verbal complex into a clause connector in expressions such as *You should go and talk to him, seeing as though you're his only relative*. The meaning of the connector *seeing as though* can be circumscribed as 'considering that' or 'since'. It is clear enough that the clause connector goes back to a pattern that involves the lexical verb *seeing* in the sense of 'perceiving visually', but in several ways the form *seeing* that is part of the connector has become categorically different from its verbal source. First, unlike lexical *seeing*, the connector may not be used with a copula and an explicit subject (**I am seeing as though ...*). Second, lexical *seeing* can be negated or modified by an adverb, but this is not possible with the connector (**Clearly seeing as though ...*). Third, lexical *seeing* may be followed by a *that*-clause (*Seeing that John left ...*) or an accusative-cum-infinitive construction (*Seeing him leave ...*), but not by a canonical declarative clause (**Seeing John is leaving...*), which is the default choice for *seeing as though*.

An area of language study that has long been concerned with variation in usage is of course sociolinguistics (Labov 1994, 2001, 2010). The growing awareness that sociolinguistic work is of tremendous importance for the usage-based research program has been termed the social turn in Cognitive Linguistics

(Harder 2010). What this social turn boils down to is a more realistic notion of speakers' linguistic knowledge. The idea of an idealized speaker as a "brain in a vat" is no longer tenable if speakers are viewed as social agents that vary their language use according to the situational context. For instance, how speakers will formulate a request for someone to step aside will depend on a number of factors, including how well they know their interlocutor, how much the request interferes with their interlocutor's personal sphere, and how well the interlocutor can be assumed to anticipate the nature of the request (Brown and Levinson 1987). Likewise, in cases where there are different phonological realizations of a given form, such as for instance *running* with either a final [ŋ] or a final [n], speakers' choices will depend partly on their social allegiance with their interlocutor. Lastly, choices between alternative lexical expressions, such as *coat*, *jacket*, or *anorak*, are of course motivated by the prototypicality of the referent in question, but they also have a social dimension (Geeraerts et al. 1999; Grondelaers and Geeraerts 2003). Knowledge of language thus includes knowledge of how to say things in a certain situation, which is a conception of linguistic compentence that goes well beyond the ability to distinguish between sentences that are grammatical and ungrammatical respectively. As is pointed out by Geeraerts (2010: 238), a socially informed cognitive linguistics stands to gain a lot from engaging with the empirical methodologies of variationist sociolinguistics. These methods have been developed with the explicit goal of teasing apart which factors lead speakers to talk in a certain way in a certain situation, thus yielding small-scale models of what speakers must know in order to use a set of variant forms in appropriate ways. Thus far, most work in cognitive sociolinguistics has focused on issues in language synchrony (cf. Kristiansen and Dirven 2008; Geeraerts et al. 2010), but as language variation and change are inextricably interlinked, some research also has addressed cognitive aspects of variation in diachrony (Geeraerts et al. 1999; Gries and Hilpert 2010; Szmrecsanyi 2010, amongst others).

Finally, more and more studies that take a usage-based approach to language change adopt Construction Grammar (Goldberg 1995, 2006) as a theoretical framework (e.g., Israel 1996; Verhagen 2002; Bergs and Diewald 2008; Traugott and Trousdale 2010; Hilpert 2013; Traugott and Trousdale 2013). These studies investigate how the usage of symbolic form-meaning pairings shifts over time. Changes in usage patterns can be taken to reflect gradual differences in the corresponding generalizations that represent these constructions in speakers' minds. Present-day speakers of English thus cognitively represent a construction such as the *s*-genitive (*John's brother*) in a way that is different from how it used to be represented in the past (Szmrecsanyi 2010). Work in this area overlaps to a large extent with ongoing research into grammaticalization. However, the project of Diachronic Construction Grammar is broader in scope, as it not only comprises the development of grammaticalizing constructions, but also changes in constructions that are not readily defined as grammatical (Noël 2007). So while it might be a matter of debate whether or not a construction such as *What's X doing Y?* (Kay and Fillmore 1999) falls into the domain of grammatical markers, the emergence of this construction in English usage would definitely be a question of interest in Diachronic Construction Grammar. A second reason to treat the constructional perspective on language change as a subject of its own is that changes in constructions include processes that go beyond the kinds of developments that are recognized in grammaticalization. For instance, some definitions of grammaticalization exclude certain types of word order change (Hopper and Traugott 2003: 24) that would fall squarely into the domain of Diachronic Construction Grammar.

To sum up this section, the usage-based model of language is deeply interconnected with issues of language change that pertain to all levels of structure and meaning, i.e., everything from phonemes to syntactic constructions and further to discourse patterns, and everything from stable, conventionalized meanings to purely contextual and incidental meanings. The domain-general socio-cognitive processes that underlie language use in the present are also responsible for the fact that there is gradual change both in the patterns of usage and in the cognitive representations that speakers abstract away from those patterns. The following sections will return to the four aspects of language change that have been raised in this section, offering more examples and further motivating the claim that language change and human cognition are mutually interdependent.

3 Lexical semantic change

One of the key insights from work on cognitive lexical semantics (Geeraerts this volume; Gries volume 3) is that word meanings are multifaceted and flexible. Depending on the context of use, a word such as for example *book* may mean quite different things.

(1) a. That book is slightly damaged.
     b. That book is now a movie with Leonardo DiCaprio.
     c. That book has been translated into over thirty languages.

The above examples make reference to a book as a physical object, as a story, and as a written text that can be translated. To come to terms with such flexibility, Croft and Cruse speak of the meaning potential of a word, which they define as "a region in conceptual space" (2004: 109) that outlines the range of possible interpretations that a word may have. Contained in that region are one or more areas that speakers will consider as central. These areas represent prototypical meanings, which are those that speakers will learn early during first language acquisition, verify swiftly as category members, offer as examples when asked, and rate as highly typical in experimental settings (Croft and Cruse 2004: 78). Importantly, the meaning potential of a lexical item may change over time. The conceptual space covered by a word may grow to include new meanings, or it may in fact shrink, so that some meanings fall out of use. In any event, the semantic changes that can be observed with a given lexical item reflect conceptual associations that speakers would have made between related meanings. Particularly important kinds of associations in this regard are metonymy (Barcelona volume 1) and metaphor (Gibbs volume 1). Over time, repeated meaning extensions give rise to the development of polysemy (Gries volume 3), so that the meaning potential of a word is divided up into conceptual regions that are relatively distinct. Depending on how strong or weak the associations between these regions are, speakers may thus distinguish different word senses.

Nerlich and Clarke (2001: 261–263) discuss several examples of semantic change that involve metonymic reasoning, specifically conceptual associations between objects and related activities. The word *counter*, for instance, used to refer to an accountant's tool, an object made for counting. This meaning was extended to the accountant's desk, at which the counting was taking place. Eventually, the word *counter* was generalized to refer to any kind of desk in a commercial setting. As another example, the noun *toilet* entered the English language as a French loan word referring to a piece of cloth, which was used for wrapping clothes, and later also as a cover for one's shoulders while hairdressing, or for the covering of a dressing table. Through that association, *toilet* came to designate the things on the dressing table, the act of dressing itself, as well as the room in which the dressing took place. As dressing rooms were furnished with facilities for washing and performing bodily functions, *toilet* became a convenient euphemism for rooms of this kind, even when they did not have any dressing tables in them.

Whereas metonymic associations can go freely back and forth between objects, their parts and wholes, and related activities and persons, metaphorical association patterns are believed to be more constrained, insofar as changes tend to be unidirectional, going from a more concrete source domain to a more abstract target domain. For example, given that the word *fruit* synchronically has, amongst others, the senses 'edible product of a plant' and 'result', it would be a default assumption that the latter is a metaphorical extension of the former. It is however not always possible to exploit synchronic polysemy for the purpose of internal semantic reconstruction. Allan (2012: 32) presents the case of *dull*, which has the senses 'blunt', 'not clear or bright', 'stupid' and 'boring', amongst several others. Whereas it might be assumed that the senses denoting physical qualities are historically prior to the senses denoting mental and perceptual qualities, the historical record, in this particular case the Oxford English Dictionary, does not support that assumption. The historical sequence of metaphorically related word senses, though often in line with a development from more concrete to more abstract, can therefore not be inferred from general principles, but has to be determined on the basis of the empirical record. The hypothesis of unidirectionality in semantic change will be discussed further in the section on grammaticalization, where it is of central concern.

Besides metonymic and metaphorical shifts, lexical items also tend to undergo processes of narrowing and broadening. In such cases, the meaning of a word either comes to refer to only a subset of its erstwhile referents (e.g., English *deer* from Old English *dēor* 'animal') or, conversely, a word widens in its categorical scope (e.g., English *manage* from Early Modern English *manege* 'train/direct a horse'). Semantic shifts of this kind have sometimes been subsumed under the heading of metonymy (Seto 1999), but it may be useful to reserve separate labels for categorical relationships on the one hand, which concern the processes of narrowing and broadening, and contiguity relationships on the other, which concern metonymic extensions proper.

A final aspect of lexical semantic change to be discussed here is the fact that lexical items may undergo changes that do not affect their referential meaning, but rather their affective or evaluative meaning. A word that undergoes pejoration develops increasingly negative connotations, conversely, a word undergoing amelioration acquires more positive connotations. An example for the former would be the example of *toilet* that was already mentioned above. Initially, the word *toilet* functioned as a euphemism for 'a place where bodily functions are performed'. Over time however, euphemisms tend to wear out, so that they acquire the negative connotations that are associated with their referents. As a consequence, new euphemisms have to be invented to replace the old ones. Hence, present-day speakers prefer *bathroom* to *toilet* and *disabled* to *crippled*, and most nation states have a *ministry of defense* instead of a *ministry of war*. Keller (1994) explains the cyclic replacement of euphemisms in terms of an emergent process that he describes as the "invisible hand": Speakers aim to use socially acceptable expressions and thus will rather err on the side of caution, choosing a relatively more indirect term. As speech events of this kind repeat, an erstwhile euphemism comes to be regarded as the new default, whereas the old default term seems too direct and thus undergoes pejoration. The cognitive underpinnings of euphemistic speech include social awareness, i.e., speakers' ability to engage in mutual mind-reading, and an exemplar-based linguistic memory, which allows speakers to keep track of how often a phenomenon is labeled with one of several alternative expressions. Besides pejoration, there is also the converse development, amelioration. This process has been at work in examples such as *nice*, which used to mean 'ignorant, stupid', and *marshal*, which used to mean 'person who tends horses'. Both terms thus have meanings in Present-Day English that are more positive than their respective earlier meanings. Whereas pejoration is a process that can receive a principled socio-cognitive explanation, amelioration has to be seen as a relatively sporadic and circumstantial phenomenon.

Summing up this section, it can be stated that lexical semantic change reflects several domain-general socio-cognitive processes, such as reasoning in terms of metaphor and metonymy, categorization, social awareness, and exemplar-based memory. In their mutual combinations, these processes lead to different types of lexical semantic change. A typology of these kinds of change that further explains their respective cognitive motivations and thus expands on what is offered here can be found in Blank (1999).

4 Grammaticalization

Whereas the trajectories of change in the domain of lexis are relatively unconstrained and hence unpredictable, pervasive regularities have been documented in the domain of grammatical change. Studies in grammaticalization (Heine et al. 1991; Bybee et al. 1994; Heine and Kuteva 2002; Hopper and Traugott 2003; van der Auwera et al. volume 3) have established that across languages, grammatical forms come into being and develop in strikingly similar ways. In order to elaborate on this point, it is necessary to clarify briefly what is meant by the terms grammar and grammaticalization.

Grammar (Diessel this volume) has in generative traditions been defined as a system of rules allowing speakers to produce well-formed utterances. Accompanying such a rule system would be a lexicon supplementing the words that can be put together into sentences by means of those rules. In Cognitive Linguistics, this dichotomy of a grammar and a lexicon is replaced by an integrated model. Knowledge of language is viewed as a 'constructicon' (Goldberg 2006: 64), that is, a network of symbolic units that contains exemplar-based representations of both highly abstract syntactic constructions, semi-fixed phrases, morphological constructions, and also simplex lexical items. Grammar, in that view, refers to the relatively more abstract parts of such a network. This would include syntactic schemas for questions, ditransitives, or cleft sentences, but also morphological schemas that serve as templates for the usage of verbs in the past tense, nouns in the plural, or adjectives in the comparative. Further, elements such as determiners, pronouns, or clause linkers, which have highly schematic meanings and commonly project an adjacent linguistic structure, would also be located towards the grammatical end of the constructicon. The question of what counts as grammar would thus primarily be answered on the basis of semantic and structural schematicity: A linguistic form is to be viewed as grammatical if it is schematic in form and if it conveys a relatively abstract meaning that can be characterized as a grammatical function, i.e., tense, aspect, modality, number, gender, case, definiteness, comparison, subordination, or topicality, to name just a few. Conceived of in this way, a terminological opposition of grammar and lexis can be maintained despite the fact that no crisp categorical distinction is made between the two. Towards the lexical end of the continuum, constructions are fully specified with regard to form and highly specific in meaning. Towards the grammatical end of the continuum, constructions tend to be schematic in form, more abstract in meaning, and internally complex (cf. Langacker 2005: 108, Figure 3). Importantly, they are also relatively more frequent in usage (Bybee 2007: ch. 16).

As was pointed out in the introduction, the usage-based perspective on language is inherently dynamic. Understanding what grammar is hence depends to a large extent on an understanding of how this grammar came into being. This question is addressed in research on grammaticalization. Grammaticalization refers to "the change whereby lexical items and constructions come in certain contexts to serve grammatical functions, and, once grammaticalized, continue to develop new grammatical functions" (Hopper and Traugott 2003: xv). With regard to the definition of grammar that was offered above, this means that when a word or construction grammaticalizes, a part of the constructicon is re-structured so that form and meaning of the grammaticalizing unit increases in schematicity as it acquires a grammatical function. Typically, the grammaticalizing unit simultaneously undergoes changes in its combinatorics.

Regarding these aspects of change, Traugott (2010) distinguishes two main pathways of grammaticalization. In the first of these, grammaticalizing forms reduce in phonological substance and become increasingly dependent on a morpho-syntactic host structure. This pathway produces markers of grammatical categories such as tense, person, case, or voice, which many languages express as obligatory inflections on the verb. One example of this would be the Germanic weak past tense marker found in forms such as English *walk-ed* or German *sag-te* 'said', which derives historically from a formerly independent verb *dōn* 'do' that was postposed to the main predicate (Kiparsky 2009). Another example is the inflectional passive in the North Germanic languages (Heltoft 2006). The final alveolar fricative in Swedish examples such as *Ingenting hördes* 'Nothing was heard' or *Dörren öppnade-s* 'The door was opened' derives from a full reflexive pronoun *sik* 'self' that became attached to its verbal host. The formal and combinatory changes that occur in these and other similar cases have been summarized by Lehmann (1995) as parameters of increasing degrees of grammaticalization. As a form grammaticalizes, its relative placement becomes increasingly fixed, its presence is increasingly obligatory, its integrity as an independent word diminishes, it reduces its semantic scope to its host, it coalesces phonologically with the host, and it becomes part of a tightly organized paradigm of alternative forms, such as present vs. past or active vs. passive. Importantly, all of these changes can be interpreted as the result of increased frequency of usage. Through the repeated use of a certain sequence of linguistic units, routinization and chunking lead to fixation, semantic association, coalescence, reduction, and ultimately obligatorification. Whereas this pathway of morphologization arguably still represents the most widely shared definition of grammaticalization, inflectional morphology only comprises a subpart of the grammatical end of the constructicon. In particular, syntactic constructions and elements such as clause linkers or discourse markers are not accounted for in this pathway, and yet, their emergence would seem to constitute grammaticalization in a straight-forward interpretation of the term.

Traugott (2010: 274) therefore proposes a second pathway under the heading of grammaticalization as expansion. Expansion here refers to three separate processes that have been identified by Himmelmann (2004). The first of these is host-class expansion, which describes the fact that grammaticalizing units often do not reduce their combinatorial variability but conversely, are observed to expand the range of environments in which they can occur. An example of this would be the English *it*-cleft construction (Patten 2010). The construction initially just accommodated nominal elements in the focus phrase, as in *It was the butler that killed them*. In its later development, the construction expands to accommodate prepositional phrases (*It's in December that she's coming*) and even subordinate clauses (*It's because you cheated that you won*). The second type of expansion is syntactic expansion, which is the inverse process of Lehmann's parameter of scope decrease. Some grammaticalizing forms increase in syntactic scope. Notably, this applies to the development of discourse markers (Tabor and Traugott 1998) such as English *in fact*. As a discourse marker, it may take scope over an entire clause-level utterance (*In fact, why don't we ask John?*). As an adverbial, from which the discourse marker derives, it only takes scope over a phrase-level constituent (*If John in fact leaves the company, we'll hire Bob*). The third type of expansion is semantic and pragmatic expansion, which boils down to increasing schematicity in meaning of exactly the kind that was observed in the cases of morphologization that were discussed above. This third type of expansion hence works in parallel in both pathways of grammaticalization whereas the two other types of expansion are specific to the second pathway.

Grammaticalization as expansion shares a number of characteristics with lexical semantic change, in particular the processes of metonymic extension and semantic broadening. An example for this can be seen in the development of the degree modifier *a lot of* (Traugott 2008: 230). The lexical noun *lot* initially referred to a small wooden object that was used in the practice of selecting by chance. By metonymic extension, the noun came to refer to that which a person received if their lot was drawn, i.e., the allotment. Hence, the construction *a lot of* could develop a more general meaning equivalent to 'a certain quantity of something'. The meaning of 'a certain quantity' was then further extended to the present-day interpretation of 'a large quantity'. This change coincided with a syntactic reanalysis of the expression. Whereas in earlier usage, the noun *lot* constituted the head of an expression such as *a lot of books*, the copula in an utterance such as *A lot of books were on sale* agrees in number with *books*, indicating that reanalysis has taken place. As *a lot of* came to be conventionally associated with the meanings of 'many' and 'much', it became possible to use *a lot* as a degree modifier, as in *a lot faster* or *I enjoyed it a lot*. To summarize, this process of change shows host-class expansion, as *a lot* spreads to syntactic environments in which it was not found before; it shows syntactic expansion in examples such as *There was a lot of me and him not getting along*, with *a lot* taking scope over a clause rather than a nominal; and there is semantic and pragmatic expansion, which is evident in expressions such as *a lot faster*, in which *a lot* goes beyond specifying a quantity of physical things. It is especially the latter type of expansion that is also often found in lexical semantic change.

But despite such similarities with lexical semantic change, it was pointed out in the beginning of this section that processes of grammaticalization tend to be relatively more constrained and highly similar across genetically unrelated languages. Comparative research (Bybee et al. 1994; Heine and Kuteva 2002) has identified numerous semantic pathways that are cross-linguistically pervasive in the development of grammatical forms. For example, constructions with the grammatical function of future time reference tend to develop out of a small set of potential sources. Typologically common are lexical verbs of coming and going, verbs of obligation, and verbs of desiring. Another example can be seen in clause linkers with causal meaning, which often go back to elements that mean 'after' or 'since'. Yet another example would be markers of spatial relations, which in many languages exist in the form of adpositions or inflectional case affixes. Historically, these markers often derive from body part terms, so that there are etymological relations between expressions meaning 'face' and 'in front', 'back' and 'behind', or 'belly' and 'in'. These regularities in semantic change contrast sharply with the idiosyncratic trajectories in lexical semantic change. A semantic change such as the development of *nice* from 'stupid' to 'pleasant' is probably unique in the world's languages. By contrast, the development of *be going to* from 'movement' to 'future' represents a type of change that is highly common.

What explains the cross-linguistic regularities in grammaticalization is the fact that its semantic pathways are motivated by metonymic and metaphorical mappings that are widely shared across cultures. For instance, the grammaticalization of future markers from motion verbs draws on the conceptual metaphor TIME IS SPACE, which in turn is grounded in the repeated correlated experience of travelling through space and the passage of time. For the traveller, successive points in space correspond to successive points in time. Similarly, the development of causal meaning out of temporal meaning is grounded in the metonymic association of cause and effect. If two events are presented as happening in temporal sequence, as in *After Bob joined our team, things took a turn for the worse*, human conceptualizers have the tendency to view the two as causally related.

While developments in grammaticalization are arguably more strongly constrained than developments in lexical semantic change, it is disputed how regular grammaticalization really is. While grammaticalization is anything but deterministic – changes do not need to happen and may stop at any time – the claim has been made that when a form grammaticalizes, it undergoes a change that is in principle irreversible (Givón 1971; Lehmann 1995). This is the so-called unidirectionality hypothesis, which appears to hold true as a statistical tendency, but which also has to face a number of counterexamples (Janda 2001). While the validity of many such counterexamples is debated, one widely accepted case is the development of the enclitic *s*-genitive in English and the North Germanic languages out of a case ending, which thus reverses several of Lehmann's parameters (Norde 2009). The strong tendency of unidirectionality in grammatical change can again be explained with reference to frequency of usage (Bybee 2011: 77). Repeated use of a form leads to schematization in form and meaning, but once this has happened, not even subsequent decreases in frequency can restore the semantic or formal details that characterized the lexical source of the grammaticalized form.

In summary then, cognitive factors such as the ability to form schemas from repeated tokens of experience and the ability to form metaphorical and metonymic associations go a long way towards explaining the regularities that are observed in grammaticalization, notably the presence of cross-linguistically attested semantic pathways and the tendency of unidirectional change in both morphologization and grammaticalization as expansion. A factor that might explain why grammatical change is more regular than lexical semantic change is frequency. Grammatical forms tend to be relatively more frequent in usage. The powerful shaping force of repetition is thus much more at work in the emergence of grammar than it is in the expansion of the lexicon.

5 Historical sociolinguistics

It was discussed in the introduction to this chapter that there is a growing trend in cognitive linguistics towards a view of language as a socially embedded phenomenon (Kristiansen and Dirven 2008; Geeraerts et al. 2010; Harder 2010). In the usage-based model of language, social factors stand on an equal footing with cognitive factors, and many important concepts, as for instance joint attention or face work, indeed resist a categorization as either one or the other. The introduction also mentioned that most research that has been done to date under the heading of cognitive sociolinguistics has addressed issues in language synchrony. Nonetheless, there are a number of studies that illustrate the approach of a cognitively oriented historical sociolinguistics, which borrows not only theoretical concepts from sociolinguistics, but crucially also many methodological tools.

Geeraerts et al. (1999) study diachronic variation in the lexicon of Belgian and Netherlandic Dutch. Their main research question is whether the two standard varieties of Dutch become more or less similar over time. This question is investigated on the basis of lexical units for items of clothing and for terms in football, which are retrieved from texts that were written in the 1950s, 1970s, and 1990s respectively. What is investigated is in what ratios a concept such as 'tight-fitting trousers made of stretch fabric' is expressed by words such as *legging, leggings,* or *caleçon*, and whether these ratios become more or less similar in Belgian and Netherlandic Dutch as time goes on. Geeraerts et al. (1999) analyze the usage of multiple lexical items in the domains of clothing and football, finding that in both domains there is increasing convergence between the two standard varieties, and that it is specifically Belgian Dutch that develops a normative orientation towards the Netherlandic standard. The general conclusion from the study is that when speakers label an object with a linguistic form, that process is influenced by cognitive factors, such as categorization and assessment of prototypicality, but also by social factors, such as orientation towards a certain standard variety. Geeraerts et al. (1999) thus show that social factors are at work in onomasiological change. Beyond that, they are also involved in semasiological change.

Robinson (2012) analyzes semasiological change in the English adjective *skinny*. In order to do so, she uses the socio-linguistic concept of apparent time, i.e., differences between speakers of different age brackets with regard to a linguistic variable. The study prompts respondents from different age groups and socioeconomic backgrounds for the meaning of *skinny*. While the sense 'thin' comfortably accounts for the majority of responses across all groups, the results indicate that certain senses of *skinny* are only used by older cohorts of speakers, as for instance 'mean, stingy' or 'showing skin'. The analysis also shows that the recently developed sense of 'low-fat', as in *skinny latte* 'coffee with low-fat steamed milk', is restricted to respondents between 19 and 60 years of age. Furthermore, it emerges that not only age but also other social factors account for the distribution of the different senses. For instance, the sense 'mean, stingy' is offered as a response mostly by old respondents from a relatively low socioeconomic background. Robinson's study shows that lexical semantic change is not only a cognitive phenomenon that draws on processes such as metonymy and metaphor, but at the same time very much a social phenomenon, as new word senses propagate through networks of socially related speakers.

Of course, cognitive studies of sociolinguistic change have not been limited to developments in the lexicon. Socio-cognitive factors are also crucial for the study of grammatical change. Szmrecsanyi (2010) studies how the dynamics between the English *s*-genitive and the *of*-genitive has changed in recent British and American English across different text genres. As has been shown across many different studies, genitive choice in English depends on several factors relating to meaning and processing, such as the animacy of possessor and possessum and their length and thematicity. Several language-external factors have also been shown to matter to genitive choice. Specifically, the *s*-genitive is favored in informal genres, and it is more frequently used in American English. Given that a multitude of factors is at work, it is a non-trivial task to determine whether and how anything has changed in the ecology of factors that condition genitive choice in English. In order to analyze the interplay of cognitive and cultural factors as it unfolds over time, Szmrecsanyi (2010) compares how these factors govern genitive choice in ten different corpora, which differ with regard to modality (speech, writing), genre (conversation, reportage, editorial), variety (British, American), and time (1960s, 1990s). The main finding is that genitive choice is consistently governed by the same semantic and cognitive factors across the different corpora. For instance, speakers and writers of all corpora favor the *s*-genitive with animate possessors and when the possessum is long. However, the respective strengths of the factors are modulated by the language-external factors. The effect of priming for instance is more pronounced in the spoken corpora as compared to written corpora. Thematicity of the possessor favors the *s*-genitive, but only in writing, not in speech. The analysis also reveals several differences that concern the variable of time. For instance, genitive choice in British editorials becomes more colloquial between the 1960s and 1990s. The ecology of factors governing the choice between *s*-genitive and *of*-genitive thus increasingly resembles the pattern that is found in spoken data. Similarly, the gap between British and American press texts is widening over time, which is mainly due to American usage developing further away from older norms. On the whole then, the study shows that social factors are an indispensable complement to the cognitive factors that underlie probabilistic choices in grammar.

The examples of cognitively oriented historical sociolinguistics that this section has discussed present analyses of fairly recent and short-term changes. This reflects to a certain extent the focus on recent or on-going developments that characterizes the sociolinguistic mainstream. However, there are several strands of work that have established a wider temporal horizon in the sociolinguistic study of language change, addressing for instance Canadian French (Poplack and St-Amand 2007) or Early Modern English (Nevalainen and Raumolin-Brunberg 2003). Gries and Hilpert (2010) draw on the latter in a diachronic study of English present tense suffix *-(e)th*, which marks the third person singular. Between the early 15th century and the late 17th century, the interdental suffix that is seen in forms such as *giveth* gradually disappeared, and it was replaced with an alveolar fricative, as in *gives*. The overall phenomenon that is observed here is a case of variation in which one variant, in this case the Northern dialectal form *-(e)s*, gradually wins out over another one. This means that, similarly to the developments in genitive choice studied by Szmrecsanyi (2010), there are changes in the conditioning factors that govern the choice between *-(e)th* and *-(e)s*. In particular, it appears that those conditioning factors that once biased speakers towards the interdental variant are no longer at work: Speakers of Present-Day English invariably choose the alveolar variant. Among the factors that used to underlie the variation between the two variants, some concern language structure and some concern social factors. For instance, structural influences on the choice between the two include whether the verb stem ends in a sibilant, as in *wish*, or whether the following word begins with either an *s* or *th*. Social factors include the gender of author and intended recipient. Gries and Hilpert (2010) show that the observed variation is best explained by a dynamic interplay of structural and social factors. Crucially, some influences do not stay the same over time. For instance, verb-final sibilants matter, but only during one early period, after which the effect disappears. Similarly, the effect of writer gender is there, but it is transient. The study thus shows that there is not only a complex interplay of language-internal and language-external factors at work, but that this interplay is inherently dynamic and subject to change.

6 Diachronic Construction Grammar

The final avenue of research to be discussed in this chapter is the diachronic branch of Construction Grammar. Studies in Diachronic Construction Grammar focus on shifts in the usage of a particular conventionalized form-meaning pairing, i.e., a construction in the sense of Goldberg (2006: 5). These shifts may concern any aspect of a construction, notably its form and meaning, but also its text frequency, its productivity, or its dispersion across different types of writing or speech (Hilpert 2013: 16). In the well-worn example of English *be going to*, all of these aspects have undergone significant changes, but there are many cases of constructional change where only some of these aspects have been subject to change. For instance, the English *many a NOUN* construction, as exemplified by *many a day* or *many a mile*, has undergone recent changes in meaning and frequency, but not in form (Hilpert 2012).

Given that in Cognitive Linguistics knowledge of language is viewed as knowledge of constructions, it could be asked whether Diachronic Construction Grammar does not in fact subsume all phenomena of change that have been discussed in the previous three sections. In lexical semantic change, grammaticalization, as well as in sociolinguistic change, one can observe changes that pertain to individual form-meaning pairings, or to small sets of such symbolic units. It is certainly true that a constructional approach to language change largely converges in theory as well as in subject matter with the areas of research that were discussed above. The distinguishing mark of Diachronic Construction Grammar is that it maintains a focus on linguistic generalizations at the level of individual constructions. This is not necessarily so for the other approaches: Historical sociolinguistics might address issues such as systematic sound changes, which pertain to many lexical items at the same time. Similarly, research on lexical semantic change and grammaticalization aims to uncover the general pathways along which lexical items and grammatical formatives develop. The generalizations that come out of this kind of research span many constructions, often across many languages. The following paragraphs illustrate the approach of Diachronic Construction Grammar with a few examples.

A pioneering study of constructional change is Israel (1996). This study addresses the emergence of the English *way*-construction, as in *John cheated his way into law school*. The construction expresses the creation of a path through difficult terrain, often in a metaphorical interpretation. In accordance with this constructional meaning, the *way*-construction occurs in present-day usage with verbs denoting the manner of a movement, such as *crawl*, *wind*, or *stumble*, and with verbs such as *dig*, *cut*, or *force*, which can encode the means to create a path. Israel shows on the basis of data from the Oxford English Dictionary that both of these verb classes developed independently at first. Through repeated analogical formations, both the manner-thread and the means-thread occurred with an increasingly greater range of verbs, which eventually led to the formation of a single, overarching generalization, i.e., the modern *way*-construction. Israel observes that simultaneously to the increasing schematization of the constructional meaning, there is an increasing obligatorification of the path constituent of the construction. Whereas there are many examples without path constituents in earlier usage, such as *The moving legions speed their headlong way*, the modern *way*-construction requires the presence of a phrase such as *across the field* or *along the river*. In summary, the development of the *way*-construction is an example of a widening generalization: Speakers kept track of the verbs that they heard in the construction and kept producing analogical formations that widened the cloud of exemplar tokens that represented the construction in their minds.

Verhagen (2000) offers another early study of constructional change in which he analyzes the history of the Dutch analytic causative constructions with *doen* 'make' and *laten* 'let'. In Present-Day Dutch, the two constructions differ with regard to animacy and directness. Whereas *doen* primarily occurs with inanimate causers in contexts of direct causation, e.g., the sun causing temperatures to increase, *laten* favors animate causers and indirect causation, such as a writer causing a change of state in someone else's mind by means of written communication. Historically, Verhagen (2000) observes an apparent shift in usage. When speakers of Present-Day Dutch are confronted with some 18th century examples of causative *doen*, they can understand what is meant but would themselves use *laten* instead of *doen* in order not to sound old-fashioned. Verhagen (2000) goes on to show that the shift in usage has not been a mere replacement of *doen* with *laten*, the latter in fact does not increase in text frequency in the diachronic corpora that are consulted. Instead, what underlies the development is a more general change in the texts that are sampled. In earlier texts, causative *doen* is commonly used with causers that represent authorities such as kings, military officials, or doctors who prescribe treatments. Over time, the semantic category of authoritative causers drastically diminishes. This affects the usage of *doen*, whose meaning of direct causation is less and less suitable for the expression of causation between human beings. The usage of *laten*, on the other hand, is not affected much by this change. Verhagen (2000) further corroborates the idea of a cultural change with historical data of *doen* and *laten* that shows a gender asymmetry. Expectably, *doen* is used more often with male causers, whereas *laten* is more frequent with female causers. Typically, *doen* is used for the case of male causers acting on female causees. The intriguing idea of cultural change acting on usage is that the respective meanings and structures of constructions such as causative *doen* and *laten* may stay the same, and yet, there may be constructional change going on, insofar as there are changes in frequency and changes in the dispersion of the constructions across different text types.

Most studies in constructional change up to the present have addressed syntactic phenomena, but as Construction Grammar aims to be an all-encompassing theory of language, it stands to reason that also change at lower levels of linguistic organization should be of interest. Hilpert (2013) studies historical changes in the usage of the nominalizing morpheme *-ment*, which is found in nouns that encode actions (*development*), results (*settlement*), or means to an action (*refreshment*). The suffix tends to occur with verbal stems, but there are sporadic attestations of adjectival stems (*merriment*) and nominal stems (*scholarment*). Like Israel (1996), Hilpert (2013) uses data from the OED to analyze how the *ment*-construction developed over time. The dictionary entries suggest that an initial group of borrowed French forms served as a critical mass for the formation of a native productive schema. This schema is initially very closely modeled on existing loan words: Since the French loans typically involved transitive verbal stems and denoted actions (*punishment, judgment*, etc.), native formations followed this tendency. There are occasional departures from the mainstream, as is evidenced by forms such as *merriment* or *jolliment*, which are based on adjectives, but none of these departures gain enough momentum to become sustainably productive. In the 20th century, the construction is entirely unproductive, and the only forms with *-ment* that show up as new entries in the OED are in fact old formations with a new prefix, such as *malnourishment* or *noninvolvement*. The main result of the analysis is that the exemplar cloud of a construction may be pluricentric, such that there are particular subconstructions that can be productive at different points in time. Also, the analysis shows that Diachronic Construction Grammar is well-positioned to address issues of change in word formation.

7 Concluding remarks

The introduction of this chapter started with the question how issues of language change can possibly be relevant to Cognitive Linguistics. The preceding sections have tried to support the idea that the usage-based model that underlies synchronic research in Cognitive Linguistics is inherently dynamic, and hence not to be understood without reference to language change and language history. Any theory that aims to relate language and cognition thus needs to engage with issues of diachrony. By the same token, any theory of language change should be in accordance with what is known about language use and cognition in present-day speakers. Strengthening the on-going dialogue between historical linguistics and psycholinguistics will be a worthwhile challenge for Cognitive Linguistics in the coming years. A guiding question in this enterprise would be how the four areas of research that were discussed in this chapter can inform our understanding of how cognition and language change relate to one another. The existing research on lexical semantic change, grammaticalization, historical sociolinguistics, and Diachronic Construction Grammar needs to be mutually contextualized, and the usage-based model of Cognitive Linguistics provides the ideal conceptual bracket for this undertaking. If this path is followed, it just may turn out that the study of language change is not a marginal aspect of Cognitive Linguistics, but rather one of its central concerns.

8 References

Aarts, Bas (2007): *Syntactic Gradience: The Nature of Grammatical Indeterminacy*. Oxford: Oxford University Press.

Allan, Kathryn (2012): Using OED data as evidence. In: K. Allan and J. Robinson (eds.), *Current Methods in Historical Semantics* 17–40. Berlin: Mouton de Gruyter.

Barcelona, Antonio (volume 1): Metonymy. Berlin/Boston: De Gruyter Mouton.

Barlow, G. Michael and Suzanne E. Kemmer (eds.) (2000): *Usage-Based Models of Language*. Stanford: CSLI.

Bergs, Alexander and Gabriele Diewald (eds.) (2008): *Constructions and Language Change*. Berlin: Mouton de Gruyter.

Blank, Andreas (1999): Why do new meanings occur? A cognitive typology of the motivations for lexical semantic change. In: A. Blank and P. Koch (eds.), *Historical Semantics and Cognition*, 61–90. Berlin: Mouton de Gruyter.

Brown, Penelope and Stephen C. Levinson (1987): *Politeness: Some Universals in Language Usage*. Cambridge: Cambridge University Press.

Bybee, Joan (2007): *Frequency of use and the Organization of Language*. Oxford: Oxford University Press.

Bybee, Joan (2010): *Language, Usage and Cognition*. Cambridge: Cambridge University Press.

Bybee, Joan (2011): Usage-based theory and Grammaticalization. In: H. Narrog and B. Heine (eds.), *The Oxford Handbook of Grammaticalization*, 69–78. Oxford: Oxford University Press.

Bybee, Joan L., Revere D. Perkins, and William Pagliuca (1994): *The Evolution of Grammar: Tense, Aspect and Mood in the Languages of the World*. Chicago: University of Chicago Press.

Bybee, Joan and Sandra Thompson (1997): Three frequency effects in syntax. *Berkeley Linguistic Society* 23: 65–85.

Bybee, Joan and Joanne Scheibman (1999): The effect of usage on degrees of constituency: The reduction of *don't* in American English. *Linguistics* 37(4): 575–596.

Bybee, Joan L. and Paul J. Hopper (eds.) (2001): *Frequency and the Emergence of Language Structure*. Amsterdam: John Benjamins.

Croft, William and D. Alan Cruse (2004): *Cognitive Linguistics*. Cambridge: Cambridge University Press.

Dąbrowska, Ewa (2008): The effects of frequency and neighbourhood density on adult native speakers' productivity with Polish case inflections: An empirical test of usage-based approaches to morphology. *Journal of Memory and Language* 58: 931–951.

Diessel, Holger (this volume): Usage-based construction grammar. Berlin/Boston: De Gruyter Mouton.

Divjak, Dagmar and Catherine Cardwell-Harris (volume 1): Frequency and entrenchment. Berlin/Boston: De Gruyter Mouton.

Geeraerts, Dirk (1997): *Diachronic Prototype Semantics: A Contribution to Historical Lexicology*. Oxford: Clarendon Press.

Geeraerts, Dirk (2010): Schmidt redux: How systematic is the linguistic system if variation is rampant? In K. Boye and E. Engberg-Pedersen (eds.), *Language Usage and Language Structure*, 237–262. Berlin: Mouton de Gruyter.

Geeraerts, Dirk (this volume): Lexical semantics. Berlin/Boston: De Gruyter Mouton.

Geeraerts, Dirk, Stefan Grondelaers, and Dirk Speelman (1999): *Convergentie en divergentie in de Nederlandse woordenschat. Een onderzoek naar kleding- en voetbaltermen.* Amsterdam: Meertens Instituut.

Geeraerts, Dirk, Gitte Kristiansen, and Yves Peirsman (eds.) (2010): *Advances in Cognitive Sociolinguistics*. Berlin: De Gruyter Mouton.

Gibbs, Raymond W., Jr. (volume 1): Metaphor. Berlin/Boston: De Gruyter Mouton.

Givón, Talmy (1971): Historical syntax and synchronic morphology: An archaeologist's field trip. *Chicago Linguistic Society* 7: 394–415.

Goffman, Erving (1955): On Face-work: An analysis of ritual elements of social interaction. *Psychiatry: Journal for the Study of Interpersonal Processes* 18(3): 213–231.

Goldberg, Adele E. (1995): *Constructions: A Construction Grammar Approach to Argument Structure*. Chicago: University of Chicago Press.

Goldberg, Adele E. (2006): *Constructions at Work: The Nature of Generalization in Language*. Oxford: Oxford University Press.

Grice, H. Paul (1975): Logic and conversation. In: P. Cole and J. L. Morgan (eds.), *Syntax and Semantics*, Volume 3: *Speech Acts*, 41–58. New York: Academic Press.

Gries, Stefan Th. (volume 3): Polysemy. Berlin/Boston: De Gruyter Mouton.

Gries, Stefan Th. and Martin Hilpert (2010): Modeling diachronic change in the third person singular: A multifactorial, verb- and author-specific exploratory approach. *English Language and Linguistics* 14(3): 293–320.

Grondelaers, Stefan and Dirk Geeraerts (2003): Towards a pragmatic model of cognitive onomasiology. In: H. Cuyckens, R. Dirven & J. Taylor (eds.), *Cognitive Approaches to Lexical Semantics*, 67–92. Berlin: Mouton de Gruyter.

Harder, Peter (2010): *Meaning in Mind and Society: A Functional Contribution to the Social Turn in Cognitive Linguistics*. Berlin: Mouton de Gruyter.

Heine, Bernd, Ulrike Claudi, and Friederike Hünnemeyer (1991): *Grammaticalization: A conceptual framework*. Chicago: University of Chicago Press.

Heine, Bernd and Tania Kuteva (2002): *World Lexicon of Grammaticalization*. Cambridge: Cambridge University Press.

Heltoft, Lars (2006): Grammaticalisation as content reanalysis: The modal character of the Danish S-passive. In: O. Thomsen (ed.), *Competing Models of Linguistic Change: Evolution and Beyond*, 268–288. Amsterdam: John Benjamins.

Hilpert, Martin (2012): Diachronic collostructional analysis meets the noun phrase: Studying *many a noun* in COHA. In: T. Nevalainen & E. C. Traugott (eds.), *The Oxford Handbook of the History of English*, 233–244. Oxford: Oxford University Press.

Hilpert, Martin (2013): *Constructional Change in English: Developments in Allomorphy, Word Formation, and Syntax*. Cambridge: Cambridge University Press.

Himmelmann, Nikolaus P. (2004): Lexicalization and grammaticization: Opposite or orthogonal? In: W. Bisang, N. Himmelmann & B. Wiemer (eds.), *What makes Grammaticalization? A Look from Its Components and Its Fringes*, 21–42. Berlin: Mouton de Gruyter.

Hopper, Paul J. (1991): On some principles of grammaticalization. In: E. C. Traugott & B. Heine (eds.), *Approaches to Grammaticalization*, Volume 1, 17–35. Amsterdam: John Benjamins.

Hopper, Paul J. & Elizabeth C. Traugott (2003): *Grammaticalization*. 2nd edition. Cambridge: Cambridge University Press.

Israel, Michael (1996): The way constructions grow. In: A. Goldberg (ed.), *Conceptual Structure, Discourse and Language*, 217–230. Stanford: CSLI.

Janda, Richard D. (2001): Beyond 'pathways' and 'unidirectionality': On the discontinuity of language transmission and the counterability of grammaticalization. *Language Sciences* 23(2/3): 265–340.

Kay, Paul and Charles J. Fillmore (1999): Grammatical constructions and linguistic generalizations: The What's X doing Y? construction. *Language* 75(1): 1–33.

Keller, Rudi (1994): *On Language Change: The Invisible Hand in Language*. New York: Routledge.

Kiparsky, Paul (2009): The Germanic weak preterite. In: P. O. Steinkrüger & M. Krifka (eds.), *On Inflection*, 107–124. Berlin: Mouton de Gruyter.

Kristiansen, Gitte and René Dirven (eds.) (2008): *Cognitive Sociolinguistics: Language Variation, Cultural Models, Social Systems*. Berlin: Mouton de Gruyter.

Labov, William (1994): *Principles of Linguistic Change*, Volume 1: *Internal Factors*. Oxford: Blackwell.

Labov, William (2001): *Principles of Linguistic Change*, Volume 2: *Social Factors*. Oxford: Blackwell.

Labov, William (2010): *Principles of Linguistic Change*, Volume 3: *Cognitive and Cultural Factors*. Oxford: Blackwell.

Langacker, Ronald W. (1987): *Foundations of Cognitive Grammar*, Volume 1: *Theoretical Prerequisites*. Stanford: Stanford University Press.

Langacker, Ronald W. (2005): Construction grammars: Cognitive, radical, and less so. In: F. J. Ruiz de Mendoza Ibáñez and M. Sandra Peña Cervel (eds.), *Cognitive Linguistics: Internal Dynamics and Interdisciplinary Interaction*, 101–159. Berlin: Mouton de Gruyter.

Lehmann, Christian (1995): *Thoughts on Grammaticalization*. Munich: Lincom.

Lightfoot, David (1979): *Principles of Diachronic Syntax*. Cambridge: Cambridge University Press.
Matthews, Danielle and Grzegorz Krajewski (this volume): First language acquisition. Berlin/Boston: De Gruyter Mouton.
Nerlich, Brigitte and David Clarke (2001): Serial Metonymy: A study of reference based polysemisation. *Journal of Historical Pragmatics* 2(2): 245–272.
Nevalainen, Terttu and Helena Raumolin-Brunberg (2003): *Historical Sociolinguistics: Language Change in Tudor and Stuart England*. London: Pearson.
Noël, Dirk (2007): Diachronic construction grammar and grammaticalization theory. *Functions of Language* 14: 177–202.
Norde, Muriel (2009): *Degrammaticalization*. Oxford: Oxford University Press.
Patten, Amanda L. (2010): Grammaticalization and the *it*-cleft construction. In: E. C. Traugott and G. Trousdale (eds.), *Gradience, Gradualness and Grammaticalization*, 221–243. Amsterdam: John Benjamins.
Poplack, Shana and Anne St-Amand (2007): A real-time window on 19th century vernacular French: The Récits du français québécois d'autrefois. *Language in Society* 36(5): 707–734.
Robinson, Justyna (2012): A sociolinguistic perspective on semantic change. In: K. Allan and J. Robinson (eds.), *Current Methods in Historical Semantics*, 199–231. Berlin: Mouton de Gruyter.
Ross, John R. (1967): Constraints on Variables in Syntax. PhD Dissertation, MIT.
Rosch, Eleanor (1975): Cognitive Reference Points. *Cognitive Psychology* 7: 532–547.
Seto, Ken-ichi (1999): Distinguishing metonymy from synecdoche. In: K. Panther and G. Radden (eds.), *Metonymy in Language and Thought*, 77–120. Amsterdam: John Benjamins.
Szmrecsanyi, Benedikt (2010): The English genitive alternation in a cognitive sociolinguistics perspective. In: D. Geeraerts, G. Kristiansen and Y. Peirsman (eds), *Advances in Cognitive Sociolinguistics*, 141–166. Berlin: Mouton de Gruyter.
Tabor, Whitney and Elizabeth C. Traugott (1998): Structural scope expansion and grammaticalization. In: A. G. Ramat and P. Hopper (eds.), *The Limits of Grammaticalization*, 227–270. Amsterdam: Benjamins.
Taylor, John R. and Kam-Yiu S. Pang (2008): Seeing as though. *English Language and Linguistics* 12(1): 103–139.
Tomasello, Michael (1995): Joint attention as social cognition. In: C. Moore and P. Dunham (eds.), *Joint Attention: Its Origins and Role in Development*, 103–130. Hillsdale: Lawrence Erlbaum.
Tomasello, Michael (2009): *Why We Cooperate*. Cambridge: MIT Press.
Tomasello, Michael and Malinda Carpenter (2007): Shared Intentionality. *Developmental Science* 10(1): 121–125.
Traugott, Elizabeth C. (2008): Grammaticalization, constructions and the incremental development of language: Suggestions from the development of degree modifiers in English. In: R. Eckardt, G. Jäger, and T. Veenstra (eds.), *Variation, Selection, Development – Probing the Evolutionary Model of Language Change*, 219–250. Berlin: Mouton de Gruyter.
Traugott, Elizabeth C. (2010): Grammaticalization. In: S. Luraghi and V. Bubenik (eds.), *Continuum Companion to Historical Linguistics*, 269–283. London: Continuum Press.
Traugott, Elizabeth C. and Graeme Trousdale (eds.) (2010): *Gradience, Gradualness and Grammaticalization*. Amsterdam: John Benjamins.

Traugott, Elizabeth C. and Graeme Trousdale (2013): *Constructionalization and Constructional Changes*. Oxford: Oxford University Press.
van der Auwera, Johan, Daniël van Olmen and Denies du Mon (volume 3): Grammaticalization. Berlin/Boston: De Gruyter Mouton.
Verhagen, Arie (2000): Interpreting usage: Construing the history of Dutch causal verbs. In: M. Barlow and S. Kemmer (eds.), *Usage-Based Models of Language*, 261–286. Stanford: CSLI.
Verhagen, Arie (2002): From parts to wholes and back again. *Cognitive Linguistics* 13(4): 403–439.

Dirk Geeraerts and Gitte Kristiansen
Chapter 6: Variationist linguistics

1 Introduction

The past ten to fifteen years have witnessed a steady increase, within Cognitive Linguistics and other cognitively oriented approaches to language, of the interest in language variation in all its dimensions. Why is that and what type of studies fall within the scope of this development? In the present chapter (which is a revised and expanded version of Geeraerts and Kristiansen 2014), we will address these questions from a double perspective: what is the role of variationist linguistics within Cognitive Linguistics, and what does Cognitive Linguistics have to offer to variationist linguistics? As a first step, we will argue that studying cultural and lectal linguistic variation is an essential aspect of Cognitive Linguistics, for reasons relating to the historical position of Cognitive Linguistics in the development of contemporary linguistics. (We use the term *lectal* to refer to all types of language varieties or *lects*: dialects, regiolects, national varieties, registers, styles, idiolects etc.). Further, we will offer a brief survey of the state of the art in variationist Cognitive Linguistics, with a specific focus on the area of lectal variation (a field sometimes referred to as Cognitive Sociolinguistics). The chapter concludes with an overview of some of the challenges that a variationist approach to Cognitive Linguistics will have to meet.

To avoid misunderstandings about the scope of the chapter, three preliminary remarks are due. First, by "variationist approaches" in Cognitive Linguistics, we intend to refer to all kinds of research with an interest in the sociocultural aspects of linguistic variation, both from an intralingual and an interlingual perspective. To be sure, the interlingual, cross-linguistic perspective does not include the entire domain of linguistic typology: linguistic typology is interested in language variation, but not necessarily or predominantly from a social or cultural point of view. Second, a distinction needs to be made between variationist linguistics in the context of Cognitive Linguistics, and cognitive approaches to linguistic variation in a broader sense. In a general way, all approaches that combine psycholinguistic and sociolinguistic points of view are forms of "cognitive sociolinguistics", even if they do not specifically refer to theoretical concepts or descriptive practices that are typical for Cognitive Linguistics. In this sense,

Dirk Geeraerts, University of Leuven, Belgium
Gitte Kristiansen, Universidad Complutense de Madrid, Spain

we will have to ask ourselves to what extent, to put it simplistically, Cognitive Sociolinguistics contributes to sociolinguistics. The distinction is, however, not an easy one, and we will come back to it in the final section. Third, applied studies are not taken into account in the following pages. Questions of language variation may play an important role in the classroom, or in the context of language policies, but that is an area that we will not attempt to cover here.

2 Motivations for variationist Cognitive Linguistics

When we try to understand why the study of linguistic variation might be of specific interest to Cognitive Linguistics, we need to take into account two perspectives: a theoretical one and a methodological one. The first is to some extent the more important of the two, because the methodological reasons for paying attention to linguistic variation derive from the theoretical ones, as we shall see.

2.1 Theoretical motivations for variationist Cognitive Linguistics

To arrive at a clear understanding of the theoretical reasons for looking at language variation, we first need to understand the position of Cognitive Linguistics in the history of linguistics. We will argue that Cognitive Linguistics embodies a far-reaching paradigm shift in linguistics, and that the interest in interlinguistic and intralinguistic language variation constitutes the cornerstone of that paradigm shift. This is a bold statement that undoubtedly requires a longer and more detailed argumentation than we can offer in these pages, but we believe that we can bring across the bottom line of the argument if we concentrate on a few essential features of the development of linguistics in the course of the 20th and the early 21st century. That development is broadly characterized by a succession of three stages of theory formation: the structuralist one, the generative one, and the cognitive-functional one. The structuralist era symbolically took off with the publication of De Saussure's *Cours de linguistique générale* in 1916, and if we stay within such a symbolical framework, we can situate the beginning of the generativist stage in 1957 with the publication of Chomsky's *Syntactic Structures*, and the emergence of Cognitive Linguistics in 1987, a year that saw the landmark publication of both Lakoff's *Women, Fire and Dangerous Things* and Langacker's 1987 *Foundations of Cognitive Grammar*.

(We deliberately use the word 'emergence' to characterize the landmark year 1987, because the actual birth of Cognitive Linguistics should be situated about a decade earlier. See Geeraerts 2010a for details). Clearly, we are not suggesting that Cognitive Linguistics superseded generative grammar in the final quarter of the previous century in the same way in which the latter replaced structuralist linguistics in the third quarter: generative linguistics is still a strong tradition, but it now exists alongside a broad family of functional and cognitive approaches. That is a second point we have to emphasize: we focus on Cognitive Linguistics, but in the context of the history of linguistics, Cognitive Linguistics is just a member of a more extensive set of cognitive-functional approaches including approaches like Systemic Functional Grammar in the Hallidayan sense, the Amsterdam school of Functional Linguistics founded by Simon Dik, functional-typological approaches in the sense of Talmy Givón, and many others: see Nuyts (2007) for an insightful overview. Now, we do believe that Cognitive Linguistics is not just *a* member of that family of approaches, but that it actually is a *central* member – both in terms of the appeal that it exerts on large numbers of linguists and in terms of the quality and quantity of the conceptual and descriptive contributions that it renders. Again, this is a point that would have to be established at a more leisurely pace, but for now let us take it for granted that Cognitive Linguistics embodies, if not epitomizes, the post-generativist cognitive-functional approaches.

Crucially, these cognitive-functional approaches reverse the underlying drift of the development of linguistics in the two preceding stages of theory formation. As argued in Geeraerts (2010a), we may identify that trend as one of *decontextualization*: when linguistic theorizing reaches the generative stage, the core of linguistics (that subfield of linguistics that concentrates on what is considered essential to language) is conceived of as "autonomous syntax", i.e., the study of an innate and universal endowment for building formal syntactic structures. Disappearing from the centre of the attention are aspects of language like meaning and function (and the lexicon as a major repository of meaning), context of use, and social variation. In a more analytic fashion, we can identify three conceptual oppositions that were formulated in the successive stages of theory development, and that each contribute to the decontextualizing tendencies by the specific hierarchy of preferences that they are introduced with. First, structuralism introduces the distinction between language as system – *langue* – and language as usage – *parole*. *Langue* is defined as a social system, a set of collective conventions that constitutes a common code shared by a linguistic community. *Parole* on the other hand is an individual activity that takes the form of producing specific combinations from the elements that are present in the code. *Langue* is epistemologically prior to *parole*: the use of a semiotic code logically presupposes the existence of that code.

Second, generative grammar adds an emphasis on the universal aspects of language: in the opposition between the universal and the diverse, language variation is the losing party. Shifting the emphasis from language as a social code to language as a psychological phenomenon (and, in fact, largely ignoring the relevance of the social aspects of language), Chomsky emphasizes the innate, genetically given (and hence universal) aspects of language.

Third, generative grammar takes shape as a formal model of grammar, both in its adoption of symbolic formalization as the descriptive method of linguistics and its outspoken preference for form over function (or meaning) as the starting-point of linguistic analysis.

These three oppositions articulate the decontextualizing trend that leads from structuralism to generativism. The features of language that are deemed central to linguistic theorizing abstract away from meaning and function, from cultural and social diversity, from the actual contexts of language use in action and in interaction. We acknowledge that there might be other ways of spelling out the decontextualizing tendencies, but for our present purposes, these oppositions are particularly pertinent, because they help us to clarify how decontextualization implies a diminished relevance of – and focus on – the study of language variation. In particular, if the essence of language is genetically universal, the study of *interlinguistic* variation is not relevant per se, but only to the extent that it helps to determine what is typologically invariant in the diversity of languages. Similarly, when we think of languages as systems, such systems will have to be internally homogeneous, and *intralinguistic* variation takes the form of a network of dialects that are each (homogeneous) linguistic systems in their own right: the unit of variation, to the extent that variation is considered at all, is the homogeneous, self-contained linguistic system.

The three oppositions also help us to understand why we can think of Cognitive Linguistics as a recontextualizing approach to language. On each of the three counts, in fact, Cognitive Linguistics and functional approaches more generally take exactly the antithetical position from the structuralist and generativist tradition. Working through the three oppositions in reverse order, it hardly needs to be argued, first, that meaning and function take precedence over form in Cognitive Linguistics theorizing: if anything, Cognitive Linguistics is a systematic attempt to give meaning and function a central role in the description of natural language – by looking at language as a tool for categorization and cognitive construal. Second, Cognitive Linguistics embraces an experiential view of meaning. The meaning we construct in and through the language is not a separate and independent module of the mind, but it reflects our overall experience as human beings. There are at least two main aspects to this broader experiential grounding of linguistic meaning. On the one hand, we are embodied beings, not pure minds. Our organic nature influences our experience of the world, and this experience is reflected in the language we use. On the other hand, we are not just biological entities: we also have a cultural and social identity, and our language may reveal that identity (Kristiansen 2001, 2003), i.e., languages may embody the historical and cultural experience of groups of speakers (and individuals). What is interesting about language is then not just the universal features: the diversity of experience expressed in language matters at least as much.

Third, Cognitive Linguistics adopts a usage-based model of language, roughly in the sense that there is a dialectal relationship between structure and use: individual usage events are realizations of an existing systemic structure, but at the same time, it is only through the individual usage events that changes might be introduced into the structure. "System", in fact, is primarily an observable commonality in the behavior of language users, and as such, it is the result of social interaction. People influence each other's linguistic behavior, basically by co-operative imitation and adaptation, and in some cases by opposition and a desire for distinctiveness.

It follows from this radical reversal of the decontextualizing mainstream positions that the study of language variation is a compelling field of research for Cognitive Linguistics. The interest in experiential diversity that comes with the second assumption translates into an interest in interlinguistic variation: to what extent do different cultures express a different construal of the world in their language use (cf. Koptjevskaja-Tamm volume 3)? And the usage-based model certainly implies a concern with intralinguistic variation: "usage-based implies variational" (Geeraerts 2005). When we say that common linguistic behavior derives from the interaction between language users, it needs to be established just how common that behavior actually is, and how the existing variation is structured by social factors – precisely the kind of questions that are central within dialectology and sociolinguistics.

In other words, if Cognitive Linguistics is indeed a recontextualizing model of linguistics par excellence, and if that recontextualization involves reversing a number of preferences that seemed ingrained in mainstream 20th century linguistics – a preference for system over use, for universality over diversity, for form over function – then a thorough investigation of interlinguistic and intralinguistic variation is an integral part of the Cognitive Linguistics enterprise.

2.2 Methodological motivations for variationist Cognitive Linguistics

The usage-based nature of Cognitive Linguistics also implies that there are methodological reasons for taking into account variation (see also Tummers et al. 2005). If one believes in the existence of a homogeneous linguistic system, then there is at least some justification for the generativist preference for an introspective methodology: if all users of a given language have the same system in their heads, then any given language user constitutes a representative sample of the population – and which language user's internal grammar is more accessible than that of the linguists themselves? Condoning armchair linguistics, in other words, fits in with the assumptions of a "system before use" approach. As soon as that assumption is rejected, however, homogeneity can no longer be assumed, and armchair linguistics becomes anathema: there is no way in which the linguist could claim representativity for the linguistic population at large, and thus, data will have to be sampled in a way that ensures a broad coverage of the behavior in a linguistic community. This explains the rise of corpus linguistics in Cognitive Linguistics: as archives of non-elicited, spontaneous language behavior, text corpora constitute a suitable empirical basis for a usage-based linguistics. Similarly, there is a growing interest in experimental methods for studying the on-line aspects of language usage. Traditional variationist sociolinguistic methods such as surveys and ethnographic methods likewise aim to retrieve data that ultimately constitute a corpus.

More often than not, however, the corpus will not be internally homogeneous: because the texts collected for the corpus come from various sources, it will not be known in advance whether the variation that may be observed in the corpus is due to lectal factors or not. As such, determining the effects of such factors will be necessary for any cognitive linguistic attempt to analyse the usage data – even if the analysis is not a priori interested in lectal variation. That is to say, even if the analysis of lectal variation is not the primary concern of the investigation, filtering out lectal effects requires an analysis of variation. Methodologically speaking, an awareness of variation is thus indispensable for a data-oriented usage-based analysis.

3 Domains of investigation

Having established that an investigation of interlinguistic and intralinguistic variation should come naturally to Cognitive Linguistics, we may now address the question where the field actually stands. If we look back at the three oppositions with which we started, we may note that Cognitive Linguistics did not effectuate the reversal of the three perspectives at the same time. A shift from form to function and meaning has obviously been there all along; it was definitional for the Cognitive Linguistics theoretical framework from the very start. Rather, it is the other two oppositions that interest us more: we observe that the domain of interlinguistic and cultural variation is fairly well established, but that the study of intralinguistic and lectal variation has been slower to develop.

3.1 Interlinguistic and cultural variation

An interest in cultural effects at the level of interlinguistic variation existed from an early date in the history of Cognitive Linguistics. For instance, Rosch's research on prototype categorization (Rosch 1977), which had a major influence on theory formation in Cognitive Linguistics, is characterized by an anthropological background, just like Berlin's research on colour terms and ethnobiological classification from which it derived (Berlin and Kay 1969; Berlin et al. 1974). Questions of cultural relativity play a natural role in this kind of investigation, although the research endeavours are very much motivated by an interest in universal patterns of variation – we will come back to the point in a moment. The notion of "cultural model" (which invokes the notion of "frame" and "conceptual metaphor", that other pillar of semantics in Cognitive Linguistics, next to prototypicality) also made an early entrance: see Holland and Quinn (1987) for an influential early volume. Cross-cultural studies of metaphorical patterns and conceptual metaphors are by now an established line of research: for representative examples, see Dirven (1994), Yu (1998, 2009), Dirven, Frank, and Ilie (2001), Dirven, Hawkins, and Sandikcioglu (2001), Dirven et al. (2003), Boers (2003), Littlemore and Low (2006), Sharifian et al. (2008). The existence of a book series entitled *Cognitive Linguistic Studies in Cultural Contexts* (with Sharifian 2011 as its first volume) points in the same direction. A broadly anthropological view on cultural linguistics has been developed by Palmer (1996) and Kronenfeld (1996).

Three additional remarks may help to represent the field with a little more detail. In particular, we would like to draw the attention to a number of shifts that occurred in the course of the development of culture-related research in Cognitive Linguistics.

In the first place, the traditional preference for universality ("traditional" from the point of view of mainstream 20th century linguistics as represented by generative theory, that is) seems to some extent to have influenced the interest in cultural variation in the framework of Cognitive Linguistics. As we noted earlier, the experiential nature of a Cognitive Linguistic conception of semantics involves both a physiological and a cultural kind of experience: embodiment and socialization, so to speak. But the physiological perspective suggests a universality that the cultural perspective lacks. In some domains of enquiry both perspectives opposed each other. This applies specifically to the study of conceptual metaphors for the emotions, a field which has always been one of the main areas of attention of Conceptual Metaphor Theory. In contrast with the predominantly physiological explanation for "anger" metaphors suggested by Kövecses (1986), Geeraerts and Grondelaers (1995) drew the attention to the culture-specific background of at least some of the anger expressions, which turn out to have a historical background in the theory of humours that dominated Western medical and psychological thinking from antiquity to the early modern period. Although Lakoff and Kövecses (1987; Kövecses 1995), in line with the tradition, at first opposed the cultural interpretation in favour of a physiological one, more recent work shows a wholehearted acceptance of the cultural perspective; in particular see Kövecses (2005), a book heralding a "cultural turn" of metaphor studies. As the "anger" studies suggest, a consequence of this growing cultural sensitivity of Conceptual Metaphor Theory could well be an increase in diachronic metaphor studies. Cultural models, i.e., the more or less coherent sets of concepts that cultures use to structure experience and make sense of the world are not reinvented afresh with every new period in the culture's development. But if it is by definition part of their cultural nature that they have a historical dimension, it is only by investigating their historical origins and their gradual transformation that their contemporary form can be properly understood. Diachronic research into the history of metaphors (as in the work of Gevaert 2005 or Allan 2009) is however still a relatively underdeveloped area of cross-cultural work in Cognitive Linguistics.

In the second place, the classificatory combination we are making in the title of this section between "interlinguistic" and "cultural" is one of convenience only. Surely, there can be cultural differences within one language: Lakoff's (1996) analysis of the distinction between a "stern father" and a "nurturing parent" model of political organization would be a case in point. Lakoff argues that the cluster of values and beliefs held by liberals on the one hand and by conservatives on the other, derive their internal coherence from the different metaphorical models that both political (sub)cultures in the US entertain with regard to the role of the state. Here as in other areas of Cognitive Linguistics, corpus linguistics provides the basis for new studies. Ahrens (2011), for instance, examines lexical frequency patterns in U.S. presidential speeches as a corroboration of the Lakovian hypothesis about underlying cultural models of liberals and conservatives. For another example of such a corpus-based study into intralinguistic cultural differences, see Speelman et al. (2008) on different preferences for evaluative adjectives in Netherlandic Dutch and Belgian Dutch. Intralinguistic cultural differences of this kind belong together with what we will refer to in the following section as "variation of meaning" studies, i.e., studies that look into the lectal distribution of meaningful phenomena within a given language.

In the third place, investigations into the relation between language diversity and thought exhibit an increasing methodological sophistication, as in the experimental approaches illustrated by the work of Boroditsky (2001), Lucy and Gaskins (2003), and Levinson (2003). A naïve approach might assume that the presence of certain expressions in a given language suffices to establish a difference of semantic outlook between that language and others that display a different set of expressions. However, from a usage-based perspective, it needs to be established on independent grounds whether language indeed influences thought at the level of actual usage. The essential methodological step that is taken in recent research into linguistic relativity is to define non-verbal tasks for a given conceptual domain, and then show that speakers of different languages perform differently on such tasks in a way that corresponds to the structural characteristics of their language. For instance, in Levinson's research on spatial reference, languages turn out to have different spatial systems: not all languages have a spatial system like English (in which things are located relative to the observer or to another landmark), but some of them use an "absolute" system of reference, in which the position of anything may be given in terms of the cardinal directions. Experimental data show that speakers of a language with such an absolute system of spatial reference are better at performing some kinds of non-verbal tasks, such as identifying positions in open terrain, whereas speakers of languages like English perform better in tasks involving locating objects relative to the speaker. For a further overview of recent research into linguistic relativity and the interface between language and thought, we refer to Everett (2013).

3.2 Intralinguistic and lectal variation

Within Cognitive Linguistics, the first decade of the present century has seen a growing interest for language-internal variation in all its dimensions, as witnessed by several publications referring to "Cognitive Sociolinguistics" or "social cognitive linguistics" as the study of lectal variation in the context of Cognitive Linguistics: Kristiansen and Dirven (2008), Croft (2009), Geeraerts et al. (2010), Pütz et al. (2012), and Kristiansen and Geeraerts (2013). Cognitive Sociolinguistics as demarcated by these publications strives towards a convergence of the usage-based traditions of language studies, as represented by pragmatics and sociolinguistics, and the post-generative theories of grammar illustrated by Cognitive Linguistics. The field of intralinguistic variation studies in Cognitive Linguistics may be broadly divided into three areas of research.

While the first area is concerned with general theoretical models of the role of social factors in language, the other two areas cover the descriptive contributions of Cognitive Linguistics to the study of linguistic variation. Theoretical and programmatic studies falling within that first area of research analyze the way in which the emergence of language as such and the presence of specific features in a language can only be adequately conceived of if one takes into account the socially interactive nature of linguistic communication. Important representatives of this strand of research include Croft (2000) on a socio-evolutionary view of language, Sinha (2007, 2009) on language as an epigenetic system, Zlatev (2005) on situated embodiment, Itkonen (2003) on the social nature of the linguistic system, Verhagen (2005) on the central role of intersubjectivity in language, Harder (2003, 2010) on the socio-functional background of language, and Beckner et al. (2009) on language as a complex adaptive system. Regardless of their differences, these approaches share a foundational perspective: they present high-level models of the principled role of social factors and usage-based phenomena in language and linguistic evolution. (It may be useful to add that the various approaches are mentioned here with just a few representative reference publications. For all of the models mentioned in this brief list, more literature can readily be found).

While all of these approaches emphasize the importance of language as a social phenomenon, they do not all pay equal attention to the existence of language-internal variation, i.e., to variation of the kind that constitutes the focus of sociolinguistics, dialectology, stylistics and related disciplines. There are basically two different types of reasons for this relative neglect. The theoretical position taken by Itkonen, for instance, relies heavily on a view of language systems as (largely implicit) social norms. Such a view, resembling a Saussurean conception of the linguistic system as a set of shared conventions, seems to assume the internal homogeneity of lects, in contrast with a more radical view that considers lects themselves to exhibit prototype structure. In methodological terms, this is reflected in Itkonen's adherence to intuition rather than observation as the basic method in linguistics. (For a more extended discussion of Itkonen's views, their relationship to variationist linguistics, and their methodological consequences, see Geeraerts 2005, and compare Geeraerts 2010b on the pervasiveness of variation).

Conversely, some of the theoretical approaches mentioned here simply focus on other aspects of the social nature of language than its lectal structure, without theoretical implications with regard to the latter. Verhagen's work on intersubjectivity, for instance, has an essentially grammatical focus: he argues that in many cases the meaning of grammatical constructions has more to do with the human capacity for taking other people's points of view than with providing referential descriptions of the world. Specific expressions and constructions (like negation, or complementation, or connectives) are shown to have an interactive function rather than just a descriptive meaning.

Similarly, theorists propagating a view of language as a complex adaptive system, like Croft and Sinha, tend to focus on the emergence and development of language from an evolutionary perspective. This is a perspective that links up directly with the interdisciplinary field of evolutionary linguistics, as represented a. o. by Kirby (1999; Christiansen and Kirby 2003) or Steels (2002, 2011). Steels for instance investigates experimentally how, in a setting with robots as artificial agents, languages with naturalistic properties arise through a process of self-organizing communication. Like the views formulated by Beckner et al., this kind of research is based on the hypothesis that language is a complex adaptive system that emerges through interactive coordination between agents, and that further linguistic evolutions occur in response to changes in the environment or the needs of the agents.

Approaches such as the intersubjectivity model or the complex adaptive system view far from exclude a more lectal approach; their current focus just lies elsewhere. But if Cognitive Linguistics aims to contribute to variationist linguistics, it should also produce studies with the empirical detail and the methodological rigor that is customary in sociolinguistics and dialectology. This entails the question what Cognitive Linguistics may specifically have to offer to variationist linguistics: we may be convinced of the relevance of a social perspective for Cognitive Linguistics, but can the latter convince variationist linguistics of its specific relevance? Two specific perspectives come to mind, which we may refer to in a lapidary way as studies in the *variation of meaning* and studies in the *meaning of variation*.

The basic question for the *variation of meaning* approach will be obvious: how does language-internal variation affect the occurrence of linguistic phenomena that have the specific attention of Cognitive Linguistics, notably meaning, and more generally, conceptual construal by linguistic means? The question is relevant for variationist linguistics at large because meaning is probably the least studied aspect of language in mainstream sociolinguistics (which, like mainstream grammar studies, favours formal variables). Variationist studies within Cognitive Linguistics, then, involve issues such as the social distribution of prototype-based meaning extensions (Robinson 2010), the lectal productivity of metonymical patterns (Zhang et al. 2011), the variable use of metaphor in discourse (Semino 2008), lexical variation in pluricentric languages (Soares da Silva 2005; Glynn 2008), usage-based approaches to borrowing (Zenner et al. 2012), spatial semantics at dialect level (Berthele 2006), and lectal variation of constructions and constructional semantics (Grondelaers et al. 2002; Speelman and Geeraerts 2009; Colleman 2010; Szmrecsanyi 2010; Hollmann and Siewierska 2011; Hollmann 2013; Schönefeld 2013; Gries 2013). Studies of intralingual cultural differences of the type that we mentioned in section 2.1 also fall in this category.

We should note that the importance of meaning for sociolinguistics goes well beyond descriptive comprehensiveness, because questions of meaning implicitly lie at the heart of the sociolinguistic enterprise. Consider the concept of a "sociolinguistic variable" as a cornerstone of the standard methodology of socio-variationist research. Simply put, a sociolinguistic variable in the sense of contemporary variationist sociolinguistics is a set of alternative ways of expressing the same linguistic function or realizing the same linguistic element, where each of the alternatives has social significance: "Social and stylistic variation presuppose the option of saying 'the same thing' in several different ways: that is, the variants are identical in reference or truth value, but opposed in their social and/or stylistic significance" (Labov 1972: 271). Thus, according to a variationist Labovian perspective, a sociolinguistic variable is a linguistic element that is sensitive to a number of extralinguistic independent variables like social class, age, sex, geographical group location, ethnic group, or contextual style and register. This automatically raises the question of semantic equivalence: if we are interested in the contextual choice between synonymous (functionally equivalent) expressions as a reflection of sociolinguistic factors, we first need to control for meaning – but how? Within the field of sociolinguistics, the methodological problem of semantic equivalence was recognized early on by Beatriz Lavandera. She argued that "it is inadequate at the current state of sociolinguistic research to extend to other levels of analysis of variation the notion of sociolinguistic variable originally developed on the basis of phonological data. The quantitative studies of variation which deal with morphological, syntactic, and lexical alternation suffer from the lack of an articulated theory of meanings" (Lavandera 1978: 171). In the mainstream development of sociolinguistics, however, the question of semantic equivalence, as a methodological prerequisite for the sociovariationist study of lexis and grammar, was not systematically explored. An important issue for Cognitive Sociolinguistics, then, is a renewed look at Lavandera's question and the interplay between semantic and formal variation. In practice, this research line is primarily being pursued by Geeraerts and his associates, with a focus on onomasiological variation within the lexicon: see the long-term development going from Geeraerts et al. (1994) over Geeraerts et al. (1999), Speelman et al. (2003), to Heylen et al. (2008) and Ruette et al. (2011).

The third main area of investigation for Cognitive Sociolinguistics is concerned with what we have called the *meaning of variation*, that is to say, with the way in which language variation is perceived and categorized by the language user. This is a field of research that links up with perceptual dialectology and folk linguistics in the sense of Preston and Niedzielski (2000) and related work. Relevant questions about the processing and representation of linguistic variation include the following: how do language users perceive lectal differences, and how do they evaluate them attitudinally? What models do they use to categorize linguistic diversity? How does linguistic stereotyping work: how do language users categorize other groups of speakers? What is the role of subjective and objective linguistic distances: is there a correlation between objective linguistic distances, perceived distances, and language attitudes? Are there any cultural models of language diversity: what models of lectal variation, standardization, and language change do people work with? To what extent do attitudinal and perceptual factors have an influence on language change? How do language users acquire lectal competence, how is it stored mentally, and how does it work in language production?

Again, in the context of this overview, we particularly need to ask ourselves what the specific contribution of Cognitive Linguistics to the field could be. In general, if the cognitive representation of language variation by the language user is of the same type as other types of categorization, then the categorization phenomena that Cognitive Linguistics typically focuses on should also be relevant for an analysis of the way in which language users mentally represent linguistic variation – in other words, we expect phenomena like prototypicality, metaphor and metonymy to play a role in the cognitive representation of variation. In practice, two strands of research so far stand out, concentrating on prototypicality effects and metaphorical conceptualization.

To begin with the latter, metaphorical models of lectal structure are concerned with the question to what extent metaphors frame people's perception of language varieties. Work in this direction covers both high-level cultural models of language variation and normativity in general (Geeraerts 2003; Polzenhagen and Dirven 2008), and attitudinal metaphors involving specific dialect and standard language environments (Berthele 2008, 2010).

Prototype-based models of lectal structure (Kristiansen 2003) emphasize that lects are not internally homogeneous, but are rather characterized by centrality effects: some aspects have a more central role than others, and will be more saliently represented in the mind of the language users. These central features can be linguistic phenomena: some pronunciation habits, or elements of lexis and grammar, are more typical than others. But the typical aspects can also be speakers of a variety: in Kristiansen's (2010) research into the acquisition of accent recognition in children, familiarity with iconic speakers appears to play a decisive role: when comparing the age groups of 6, 8 and 12, an increase in accent recognition correlated significantly with knowledge of social paragons and the ability to describe salient speech-related features. Clark and Trousdale (2010) in turn demonstrate how the cognitive identification with a specific social group correlates with the realization of linguistic features expressing that identity. In line with these thoughts, Guy (2013) observes that linguistic variants are indexical of social traits and social identities and that every speech community has many sociolinguistic variables, and asks the question whether multiple variables cohere in forming sociolects: if each variable has a variant considered "working class", do working class speakers use all such variants simultaneously? Soukup (2013) in turn examines identity projection in an Austrian TV show and implements two empirical tests (a speech perception elicitation test and a speaker evaluation experiment) to derive evidence for the perception of linguistic cues associated with different social meanings.

This type of research opens up towards the interest that has been growing in sociolinguistics at large in the interactive and flexible use of social variables, as surveyed in Kristiansen (2008): whereas mainstream sociolinguistics of the Labovian type tends to focus on the more or less stable structural correspondences between social groups and linguistic variables, the so-called "third wave" of sociolinguistic studies (Eckert 2012) explores what individuals actively do with group-related variables in order to do meaningful things with variants. Traditional sociolinguistic variables such as gender, age, race, socio-economic status ultimately correspond to social identities, and when combined to multiple social identities that can be enacted through socially significant linguistic variables. Acts of identity (Le Page and Tabouret-Keller 1985) and proactive identity construal are key words in third wave sociolinguistics. Because this is a kind of variationist linguistics that is situated at usage level, interactional sociolinguistics is of specific interest to Cognitive Linguistics, all the more so since, up to a point, it combines the "variation of meaning" and "meaning of variation" perspectives: social variation of language that is perceived as meaningful by the language users is itself used in a situationally variable process of expressing and creating social meaning. In more technical terms, if lectal varieties and social identities form prototype categories that relate to one another through a metonymic link, perceptually salient group-related variants may be used to index existing identities or set up new, local schemas (Kristiansen 2003, 2006). The awareness and acquisition of socially related linguistic schemata is an experientially grounded process that emerges during the first ten years of life (Kristiansen 2010). These processes are crucial in the dialectic relationship of structure and use: if linguistic structure emerges from language use, socially structured language use will result in lectal subsystems – but once set up, these structured sets of choices become available to the individual user for imitation or for creative modulation. In spite of the overall relevance, though, the interactional perspective is not yet strongly represented in the actual descriptive practice of Cognitive Sociolinguistics. See Soukup (2013), Zenner et al. (2009) and Zenner et al. (2012) for a few representative examples.

The approaches described above are in consonance with the principles of frequency-based and exemplar-based approaches to language variation and change (Bybee 2006; Bod et al. 2003; Kretzschmar 2009). In exemplar-based models, as applied to e.g., phonetics, phonology, semantics or language acquisition, schematic mental representations emerge over usage-based events, defined by a rich inventory of tokens, or "exemplars", which are stored in long-term memory (cf. Ramscar and Port volume 1 on categorization and Baayen and Ramscar on analogy and schematization). By contrast, the generative conception of representation maintains that stored knowledge of a particular word consists of a minimal, abstract sequence of symbolic elements. In exemplar based-models, not only is language acquisition experientially grounded, but what children acquire are not a set of rules but a collection of fully specified examples that gradually result in generalisations and patterns (Abbot-Smith and Tomasello 2006; see also Matthews and Krajewski this volume). Thus, phonetic detail, for instance, is not discarded but plays an important role in the representation of lexical items (Bybee 2001; Pierrehumbert 2002), just as it does in the gradual acquisition of distinct lectal schemata. For a recent paper describing the importance of exemplar-based models for second dialect acquisition see Nycz (2013). Nycz first defines the predictions of two prominent models of phonological representation (generative phonology and usage-based phonology) regarding how specific types of second dialect features are acquired, and then she evaluates these predictions against the results of a sociolinguistic study of native adult speakers of Canadian English who moved to the New York region. More information on the role of experience in the usage-based approach can be found in Divjak and Caldwell-Harris (volume 1).

4 Challenges

We have shown that the study of cultural and lectal linguistic variation is an essential aspect of Cognitive Linguistics, for reasons deriving from the historical position of Cognitive Linguistics in the development of contemporary linguistics: as a usage-based, recontextualizing model of linguistics, interlinguistic and intralinguistic variation are a crucial element of the theory. With an emphasis on what the specific contribution of Cognitive Linguistics consists of, we have offered a survey of the field of variationist studies in Cognitive Linguistics by distinguishing four domains of enquiry: cross-cultural variation of meaning, general models of the socially mediated dialectic relationship between system and use, the study of "variation of meaning", and the study of the "meaning of variation".

The interest in variationist phenomena, specifically to the extent that they involve intralingual variation, is a relatively recent trend within Cognitive Linguistics, but as we have argued, this social turn is inextricably wound up with the very nature of Cognitive Linguistics as a usage-based approach. Given its recent character, the approach is not stabilized: it would be stretching the truth to claim that – beyond the shared interest in the social nature of language and language variation – a common framework of concepts and practices unites the approaches that we have presented in the previous pages. To complete the overview, it therefore seems fitting to attempt to identify the main challenges that the emerging field of variationist studies in Cognitive Linguistics will have to meet. We would like to suggest that there are fundamentally speaking two different types: a theoretical one, and a methodological one.

The theoretical challenge involves the relationship between variationist Cognitive Linguistics and the broader field of language variation studies. The approaches that we have introduced in these pages emerge, by and large, from cognitive linguists who recognize the importance of including social and lectal factors into the cognitive linguistic models. To be successful, then, these approaches will have to interact intensively with existing variationist linguistics, and defend the specific contribution of Cognitive (Socio)linguistics in that context. More specifically, as we mentioned in the introduction to this chapter, Cognitive Sociolinguistics will have to stake out its specific position within the context of cognitive sociolinguistics. The latter phrase may be used to identify any attempt to combine the traditionally distinct lines of variationist, sociolinguistic and cognitive, psycholinguistic research into the use of language. Cognitive Sociolinguistics is one such attempt, but it is important to observe that the convergence of perspectives is currently happening on a broader scale than what is happening within the confines of Cognitive Linguistics (and in fact, some of the authors that we referred to above would not necessarily consider themselves to be cognitive linguists). Without trying to be exhaustive, it may be useful to indicate and briefly illustrate the two main research lines that contribute to the convergence. They are, in a sense, each other's converse. On the one hand, starting from the psychological end, the question arises how sociolinguistic variation (and language variation at large) is cognitively represented and processed. On the other hand, starting from the sociolinguistic end, the question is how factors relating to cognitive processing and storage influence language variation.

To illustrate the first perspective, we can primarily refer to the well-established fields of perceptual dialectology and attitude research that were already mentioned. In addition, there is a somewhat younger line of research investigating how language variation influences speech perception (see Drager 2010 for a review) or lexical processing (see e.g., Clopper 2012), and a growing interest in individual differences in the mental representation of grammar (Dąbrowska 2012; see also Dąbrowska volume 3). In language acquisition research as well there is a lively interest in sociophonetic variation, see Butler et al. (2011), Floccia et al. (2012), and Schmale et al. (2012) for a few examples of early accent recognition studies in infants. For the evolution of accent recognition across different age groups in early childhood see e.g., Floccia et al. (2009) and Kristiansen (2010).

To illustrate the second perspective, various types of work can be mentioned. In a very direct way, psycholinguistic factors can be among the features that describe the distribution of an expression or construction. A clear case in point is Szmrecsanyi (2009), who includes on-line processing factors next to structural and variational factors in a statistical model of morphosyntactic persistence. Similar "multivariate grammar" studies including psychological factors along variational ones among the explanatory variables are Grondelaers et al. (2008), and De Sutter et al. (2008). A second type of work links language variation to specific models of acquisition. Probably the best known example here is Labov's (2010) view that the transmission of speech patterns within a community is dependent on child language acquisition, whereas diffusion across communities is dependent on adult learning. A third type of work involves the different models that try to describe the mutual adaptation of interacting interlocutors, from older models like the accommodation theory of Giles and Powesland (1975), which sees linguistic convergence as reducing social distance, to newer models like the interactive alignment approach of Pickering and Garrod (2004), which assumes that persistent priming effects ensure an alignment of cognitive representations between interlocutors.

An important theoretical challenge for Cognitive Sociolinguistics, then, is to take into account the rich tradition of sociolinguistics, and specifically also those approaches that combine psycholinguistic and sociolinguistic perspectives, and to situate its specific contributions against that background. Interestingly, the double perspective that we displayed to introduce "cognitive sociolinguistics" in the broader sense is typical for the second major challenge that we would like to evoke. On the one hand, taking a psychological point of departure, we mentioned studies that introduce sociolinguistic variables into psychological research lines. On the other hand, taking a sociolinguistic point of departure, we found studies that introduce psycholinguistic variables into sociological research lines. When we cast the net a bit more widely, we can notice that that pattern occurs on a more systematic basis in the field that we are exploring here: sociolinguistic variation can be both the output and the input of the investigation. Consider what we said about semantics. On the one hand,

Cognitive Sociolinguistics is interested in the way in which social factors influence the presence or emergence of meaning. On the other hand, when we try to define sociolinguistic variables, we try to keep meaning or function constant and see how social structure is present in or emerges from variation in the expression of that constant. Or think about the way in which constructions are studied. In "multivariate grammar" studies of the type referred to above, the occurrence of a construction α is modeled in terms of a variety of factors: semantic, structural, discursive, processing-related – and lectal, in the sense that the frequency of the construction in language variety A or language variety B, in the broadest possible reading of "language variety", plays a role in the analysis. According to this perspective, the existence of A or B is taken for granted in the analysis. But conversely, the very existence of A or B as separate varieties needs to be established – and that can be done by exploring, in aggregate studies, whether construction α systematically co-occurs with other linguistic phenomena in the context of external variables (geography for dialects, nations for natiolects, social features for sociolects etc.).

The Janus-headed nature of Cognitive Sociolinguistics also shows up on the methodological level. The incorporation of meaningfulness into variationist studies raises the methodological bar: what methods are most appropriate for throwing light on the interaction between language-internal linguistic variation, language-external social factors, and cognitive aspects of variation? It is testimonial to the dynamism of Cognitive Sociolinguistics that scholars working in that direction may often be found at the forefront of methodological innovation in linguistics. On an initial level, this may be illustrated by the various distributional methods for identifying meanings in corpus data, from collocational methods (Stefanowitsch and Gries 2003) over "behavioral profiles" (Gries 2010) to vector space models (Heylen et al. 2012). If we go beyond that initial level and look at the way lectal factors are incorporated into the analysis, we can discern two methodological lines that correspond neatly with the two perspectives that we pointed at. On the one hand, when social factors are part of the input, the preference is for regression analyses modelling the distribution of linguistic variables: see the dissertations of Grondelaers (2000) and Gries (2003) for pioneering examples, and Gries (2013) or Zenner et al. (2012) for the current state of development, involving mixed effects regression models. By way of example, Gries discusses three case studies which showcase how contextual as well as cognitive or psycholinguistic language-internal and sociolinguistic language-external factors interact. The many variables under scrutiny in the three case studies (the first two of which investigate syntactic priming effects in constructional alternations and the third diachronic morphological change) were successfully analysed by logistic regression and mixed-effects models that offer an "elegant treatment of interactions with and across internal and external factors" (Gries 2013: 14).

On the other hand, when social structure emerges from the analysis, the methodological focus lies on methods of aggregate analysis of the type illustrated by Geeraerts et al. (1999) and similar later work (see above). It will be appreciated that both methodological lines (both of which are young and in full development) mirror each other in the same way as the descriptive perspectives: either you investigate how lectal structure influences the behavior of linguistic variables, or you investigate how the joint behavior of linguistic variables establishes lectal structure.

The co-existence of these descriptive and methodological switches of perspective is typical for a usage-based view of language as a complex adaptive system. Common trends and patterns of linguistic behavior (the clusters of phenomena that we tend to refer to as dialects, natiolects, sociolects etc.) emerge from separate communicative events. But at the same time, once it has emerged, the transmission of such a lectal structure feeds the trends and patterns back to the level of usage. The two perspectives that we observed constitute the two sides of this complex adaptive coin, but then the methodological challenge will be to integrate the two viewpoints, which now mostly exist alongside each other, into a single comprehensive model. Thinking about language as a complex adaptive system has its own methodological complexities – but linguists will adapt ...

Acknowledgement

Financial support for the second author's contribution to this paper was provided by the Spanish Ministry of Science and Innovation (Research Project FFI2010-19395).

5 References

Abbot-Smith, Kirsten and Michael Tomasello (2006): Exemplar-learning and schematization in a usage-based account of syntactic acquisition. *The Linguistic Review* 23: 275–290.
Ahrens, Kathleen (2011): Examining conceptual metaphor models through lexical frequency patterns: A case study of U. S. presidential speeches. In: S. Handl and H.-J. Schmid (eds.), *Windows to the Mind. Metaphor, Metonymy and Conceptual Blending*, 167–184. Berlin: De Gruyter Mouton.
Allan, Kathryn (2009): *Metaphor and Metonymy. A Diachronic Approach*. London: Wiley-Blackwell.
Baayen, Harald and Michael Ramscar (volume 1) Abstraction, storage and naive discriminative learning. Berlin/Boston: De Gruyter Mouton.

Beckner, Clay, Richard Blythe, Joan L. Bybee, Morten H. Christiansen, William Croft, Nick C. Ellis, John Holland, Jinyun Ke, Diane Larsen-Freeman, and Tom Schoenemann (2009): Language is a complex adaptive system. *Language Learning* 59: 1–26.

Berlin, Brent, Dennis E. Breedlove, and Peter H. Raven (1974): *Principles of Tzeltal Plant Classification: An Introduction to the Botanical Ethnography of a Mayan-speaking People of Highland Chiapas*. New York: Academic Press.

Berlin, Brent and Paul Kay (1969): *Basic Color Terms. Their Universality and Evolution*. Berkeley: University of California Press.

Berthele, Raphael (2006): *Ort und Weg. Die sprachliche Raumreferenz in Varietäten des Deutschen, Rätoromanischen und Französischen*. Berlin/New York: Walter de Gruyter.

Berthele, Raphael (2008): A nation is a territory with one culture and one language: The role of metaphorical folk models in language policy debates. In: G. Kristiansen and R. Dirven (eds.), *Cognitive Sociolinguistics. Language Variation, Cultural Models, Social Systems*, 301–331. Berlin/New York: Mouton de Gruyter.

Berthele, Raphael (2010): Investigations into the folk's mental models of linguistic varieties. In: D. Geeraerts, G. Kristiansen and Y. Peirsman (eds.), *Advances in Cognitive Sociolinguistics*, 265–290. Berlin/New York: De Gruyter Mouton.

Bod, Rens, Jennifer Hay, and Stefanie Jannedy (eds.) (2003): *Probabilistic Linguistics*. Cambridge: MIT Press.

Boers, Frank (2003): Applied linguistics perspectives on cross-cultural variation in conceptual metaphor. *Metaphor and Symbol* 18: 231–238.

Boroditsky, Lera (2001): Does language shape thought? Mandarin and English speakers' conceptions of time. *Cognitive Psychology* 43: 1–22.

Butler, Joseph, Caroline Floccia, Jeremy Goslin, and Robin Panneton (2011): Infants' discrimination of familiar and unfamiliar accents in speech. *Infancy* 16(4): 392–417.

Bybee, Joan L. (2001): *Phonology and Language Use*. Cambridge: Cambridge University Press.

Bybee, Joan L. (2006): *Frequency of Use and the Organization of Language*. Oxford: Oxford University Press.

Chomsky, Noam (1957): *Syntactic Structures*. The Hague: Mouton.

Christiansen, Morten H. and Simon Kirby (eds.) (2003): *Language Evolution*. Oxford: Oxford University Press.

Clark, Lynn and Graeme Trousdale (2010): A cognitive approach to quantitative sociolinguistic variation: Evidence from th-fronting in Central Scotland. In: D. Geeraerts, G. Kristiansen and Y. Peirsman (eds.), *Advances in Cognitive Sociolinguistics*, 291–321. Berlin/New York: De Gruyter Mouton.

Clopper, Cynthia G. (2012): Effects of dialect variation on the semantic predictability benefit. *Language and Cognitive Processes* 27: 1002–1020.

Colleman, Timothy (2010): Lectal variation in constructional semantics: 'Benefactive' ditransitives in Dutch. In: D. Geeraerts, G. Kristiansen and Y. Peirsman (eds.), *Advances in Cognitive Sociolinguistics*, 191–221. Berlin/New York: De Gruyter Mouton.

Croft, William (2000): *Explaining Language Change: An Evolutionary Approach*. Harlow: Longman.

Croft, William (2009): Towards a social cognitive linguistics. In: V. Evans and S. Pourcel (eds.), *New Directions in Cognitive Linguistics*, 395–420. Amsterdam: John Benjamins.

Dąbrowska, Ewa (2012): Different speakers, different grammars: Individual differences in native language attainment. *Linguistic Approaches to Bilingualism* 2: 219–253.

Dąbrowska, Ewa (volume 3): Individual differences in grammatical knowledge. Berlin/Boston: De Gruyter Mouton.
De Saussure, Ferdinand (1916): *Cours de linguistique générale*. Paris: Payot.
De Sutter, Gert, Dirk Speelman, and Dirk Geeraerts (2008): Prosodic and syntactic-pragmatic mechanisms of grammatical variation: the impact of a postverbal constituent on the word order in Dutch clause final verb clusters. *International Journal of Corpus Linguistics* 13: 194–224.
Dirven, René (1994): *Metaphor and Nation: Metaphors Afrikaners Live by*. Frankfurt: Peter Lang.
Dirven, René, Roslyn Frank, and Cornelia Ilie (eds.) (2001): *Language and Ideology 2. Descriptive Cognitive Approaches*. Amsterdam: John Benjamins.
Dirven, René, Roslyn Frank, and Martin Pütz (eds.) (2003): *Cognitive Models in Language and Thought. Ideology, Metaphors and Meanings*. Berlin/New York: Mouton de Gruyter.
Dirven, René, Bruce Hawkins, and Esra Sandikcioglu (eds.) (2001): *Language and Ideology 1. Theoretical Cognitive Approaches*. Amsterdam: John Benjamins Publishing Company.
Divjak, Dagmar and Catherine Caldwell-Harris (volume 1): Frequency and entrenchment. Berlin/Boston: De Gruyter Mouton.
Drager, Katie (2010): Sociophonetic variation in speech perception. *Language and Linguistics Compass* 4: 473–480.
Eckert, Penelope (2012): Three waves of variation study: The emergence of meaning in the study of variation. *Annual Review of Anthropology* 41: 87–100.
Everett, Caleb (2013): *Linguistic Relativity. Evidence Across Languages and Cognitive Domains*. Applications of Cognitive Linguistics 25. Berlin/New York: Mouton de Gruyter.
Floccia, Caroline, Joseph Butler, Frédérique Girard, and Jeremy Goslin (2009): Categorization of regional and foreign accent in 5- to 7-year-old British children. *International Journal of Behavioral Development* 33: 366–375.
Floccia, Caroline, Claire Delle Luche, Samantha Durrant, Joseph Butler, and Jeremy Goslin (2012): Parent or community: Where do 20-month-olds exposed to two accents acquire their representation of words? *Cognition* 124(1): 95–100.
Geeraerts, Dirk (2003): Cultural models of linguistic standardization. In: R. Dirven, R. Frank and M. Pütz (eds.), *Cognitive Models in Language and Thought. Ideology, Metaphors and Meanings*, 25–68. Berlin/New York: Mouton de Gruyter.
Geeraerts, Dirk (2005): Lectal variation and empirical data in Cognitive Linguistics. In: F. Ruiz de Mendoza Ibáñez and S. Peña Cervel (eds.), *Cognitive Linguistics. Internal Dynamics and Interdisciplinary Interactions*, 163–189. Berlin/New York: Mouton de Gruyter.
Geeraerts, Dirk (2010a): Recontextualizing grammar: Underlying trends in thirty years of Cognitive Linguistics. In: E. Tabakowska, M. Choinski and Ł. Wiraszka (eds.), *Cognitive Linguistics in Action: From Theory to Application and Back*, 71–102. Berlin/New York: De Gruyter Mouton.
Geeraerts, Dirk (2010b): Schmidt redux: How systematic is the linguistic system if variation is rampant? In: K. Boye and E. Engberg-Pedersen (eds.), *Language Usage and Language Structure*, 237–262. Berlin/New York: De Gruyter Mouton.
Geeraerts, Dirk and Stefan Grondelaers (1995): Looking back at anger: Cultural traditions and looking back at anger: Cultural traditions and metaphorical patterns. In: J. R. Taylor and R. E. MacLaury (eds.), *Language and the Cognitive Construal of the World*, 153–179. Berlin/New York: Mouton de Gruyter.
Geeraerts, Dirk, Stefan Grondelaers, and Peter Bakema (1994): *The Structure of Lexical Variation. Meaning, Naming, and Context*. Berlin/New York: Mouton de Gruyter.

Geeraerts, Dirk, Stefan Grondelaers, and Dirk Speelman (1999): *Convergentie en divergentie in de Nederlandse woordenschat. Een onderzoek naar kleding- en voetbaltermen*. Amsterdam: Meertens Instituut.

Geeraerts, Dirk and Gitte Kristiansen (2014): Cognitive linguistics and linguistic variation. In: J. Littlemore and J. Taylor (eds.), *The Bloomsbury Companion to Cognitive Linguistics*, 202–217. London: Continuum Publishing.

Geeraerts, Dirk, Gitte Kristiansen, and Yves Peirsman (eds.) (2010): *Advances in Cognitive Sociolinguistics*. Berlin/New York: De Gruyter Mouton.

Gevaert, Caroline (2005): The anger is heat question: Detecting cultural influence on the conceptualisation of anger through diachronic corpus analysis. In: N. Delbecque, J. van der Auwera and D. Geeraerts (eds.), *Perspectives on Variation. Sociolinguistic, Historical, Comparative*, 195–208. Berlin: Mouton de Gruyter.

Giles, Howard and Peter F. Powesland (1975): *Speech, Style and Social Evaluation*. London: Academic Press.

Glynn, Dylan (2008): *Mapping meaning. Towards a usage-based methodology in cognitive semantics*. PhD Thesis, University of Leuven.

Gries, Stefan Th. (2003): *Multifactorial Analysis in Corpus Linguistics: A Study of Particle Placement*. London/New York: Continuum Press.

Gries, Stefan Th. (2010): Behavioral profiles: A fine-grained and quantitative approach in corpus-based lexical semantics. *The Mental Lexicon* 5(3): 323–346.

Gries, Stefan Th. (2013): Sources of variability relevant to the cognitive sociolinguist, and corpus- as well as psycholinguistic methods and notions to handle them. In: G. Kristiansen and D. Geeraerts (eds.), *Contexts of Use in Cognitive Sociolinguistics*. Special Issue. *Journal of Pragmatics* 52: 5–16.

Grondelaers, Stefan (2000): *De distributie van niet-anaforisch er buiten de eerste zinplaats: Sociolexicologische, functionele en psycholinguïstische aspecten van er's status als presentatief signaal*. PhD dissertation, KU Leuven.

Grondelaers, Stefan, Marc Brysbaert, Dirk Speelman, and Dirk Geeraerts (2002): 'Er' als accessibility marker: on- en offline evidentie voor een procedurele interpretatie van presentatieve zinnen. *Gramma/TTT* 9: 1–22.

Grondelaers, Stefan, Dirk Speelman, and Dirk Geeraerts (2008): National variation in the use of er "there". Regional and diachronic constraints on cognitive explanations. In: G. Kristiansen and R. Dirven (eds.), *Cognitive Sociolinguistics. Language Variation, Cultural Models, Social Systems*, 153–203. Berlin/New York: Mouton de Gruyter.

Guy, Gregory R. (2013): The cognitive coherence of sociolects: How do speakers handle multiple sociolinguistic variables? In: G. Kristiansen and D. Geeraerts (eds.), *Contexts of Use in Cognitive Sociolinguistics*. Special Issue. *Journal of Pragmatics* 52: 63–71.

Harder, Peter (2003): The status of linguistic facts: Rethinking the relation between cognition, social institution and utterance from a functional point of view. *Mind and Language* 18: 52–76.

Harder, Peter (2010): *Meaning in Mind and Society. A Functional Contribution to the Social Turn in Cognitive Linguistics*. Berlin/New York: De Gruyter Mouton.

Heylen, Kris, Yves Peirsman, and Dirk Geeraerts (2008): Automatic synonymy extraction. In: S. Verberne, H. van Halteren and P.-A. Coppen (eds.), *Computational Linguistics in the Netherlands 2007*, 101–116. Amsterdam: Rodopi.

Heylen, Kris, Dirk Speelman, and Dirk Geeraerts (2012): Looking at word meaning. An interactive visualization of Semantic Vector Spaces for Dutch synsets. In: M. Butt, S. Carpendale, G. Penn, J. Prokic and M. Cysouw (eds.), *Visualization of Language*

Patters and Uncovering Language History from Multilingual Resources. Proceedings of the EACL-2012 Joint Workshop of LINGVIS and UNCLH, 16–24. Avignon: Association for Computational Linguistics.

Holland, Dorothy and Naomi Quinn (eds.) (1987): *Cultural Models in Language and Thought*. Cambridge: Cambridge University Press.

Hollmann, Willem (2013): Constructions in cognitive sociolinguistics. In: T. Hoffmann and G. Trousdale (eds.), *The Oxford Handbook of Construction Grammar*, 491–509. Oxford: Oxford University Press.

Hollmann, Willem and Anna Siewierska (2011): The status of frequency, schemas, and identity in Cognitive Sociolinguistics: A case study on definite article reduction. *Cognitive Linguistics* 22: 25–54.

Itkonen, Esa (2003): *What is Language? A Study in the Philosophy of Linguistics*. Turku: Åbo Akademis tryckeri.

Kirby, Simon (1999): *Function, Selection and Innateness: The Emergence of Language Universals*. Oxford: Oxford University Press.

Koptjevskaja-Tamm, Maria (volume 3): Semantic typology. Berlin/Boston: De Gruyter Mouton.

Kövecses, Zoltán (1986): *Metaphors of Anger, Pride and Love: A Lexical Approach to the Structure of Concepts*. Amsterdam/Philadelphia: John Benjamins.

Kövecses, Zoltán (1995): Anger: Its language, conceptualization, and physiology in the light of cross-cultural evidence. In: J. R. Taylor and R. E. MacLaury (eds.), *Language and the Cognitive Construal of the World*, 181–196. Berlin: Mouton de Gruyter.

Kövecses, Zoltán (2005): *Metaphor in Culture. Universality and Variation*. Oxford: Oxford University Press.

Kretzschmar, William A. (2009): *The Linguistics of Speech*. Cambridge: Cambridge University Press.

Kristiansen, Gitte (2001): Social and linguistic stereotyping: A cognitive approach to accents. *Estudios Ingleses de la Universidad Complutense* 9: 129–145.

Kristiansen, Gitte (2003): How to do things with allophones: Linguistic stereotypes as cognitive reference points in social cognition. In: R. Dirven, R. Frank and M. Pütz (eds.), *Cognitive Models in Language and Thought: Ideologies, Metaphors, and Meanings*, 69–120. Berlin/New York: Mouton de Gruyter.

Kristiansen, Gitte (2006): Towards a usage-based cognitive phonology. *International Journal of English Studies* 6(2): 107–140.

Kristiansen, Gitte (2008): Style-shifting and shifting styles: A socio-cognitive approach to lectal variation. In: G. Kristiansen and R. Dirven (eds.), *Cognitive Sociolinguistics*, 45–88. Berlin/New York: Mouton de Gruyter.

Kristiansen, Gitte (2010): Lectal acquisition and linguistic stereotype formation. In: D. Geeraerts, G. Kristiansen and Y. Peirsman (eds.), *Advances in Cognitive Sociolinguistics*, 225–264. Berlin/New York: De Gruyter Mouton.

Kristiansen, Gitte and René Dirven (eds.) (2008): *Cognitive Sociolinguistics: Language Variation, Cultural Models, Social Systems*. Berlin/New York: Mouton de Gruyter.

Kristiansen, Gitte and Dirk Geeraerts (eds.) (2013): *Contexts of Use in Cognitive Sociolinguistics*. Special issue. *Journal of Pragmatics* 52: 1–104.

Kronenfeld, David B. (1996): *Plastic Glasses and Church Fathers. Semantic Extension from the Ethnoscience Tradition*. New York: Oxford University Press.

Labov, William (1972): *Sociolinguistic Patterns*. Philadelphia: University of Pennsylvania Press.

Labov, William (2010): *Principles of Linguistic Change* III. *Cognitive and Cultural Factors.* London: Wiley-Blackwell.

Lakoff, George (1987): *Women, Fire and Dangerous Things. What Categories Reveal About the Mind.* Chicago: University of Chicago Press.

Lakoff, George (1996): *Moral Politics: What Conservatives Know that Liberals Don't.* Chicago: University of Chicago Press.

Lakoff, George and Zoltán Kövecses (1987): The cognitive model of anger inherent in American English. In: D. Holland and N. Quinn (eds.), *Cultural Models in Language and Thought*, 195–221. Cambridge: Cambridge University Press.

Langacker, Ronald W. (1987): *Foundations of Cognitive Grammar 1. Theoretical Prerequisites.* Stanford: Stanford University Press.

Lavandera, Beatriz (1978): Where does the sociolinguistic variable stop? *Language in Society* 7: 171–183.

Le Page, Robert Brock and Andrée Tabouret-Keller (1985): *Acts of Identity: Creole-Based Approaches to Language and Ethnicity.* Cambridge: Cambridge University Press.

Levinson, Stephen C. (2003): *Space in Language and Cognition. Explorations in Cognitive Diversity.* Cambridge: Cambridge University Press.

Littlemore, Jeannette and Graham Low (2006): *Figurative Thinking and Foreign Language Learning.* Basingstoke: Palgrave MacMillan.

Lucy, John and Suzanne Gaskins (2003): Interaction of language type and referent type in the development of nonverbal classification preferences. In: D. Gentner and S. Goldin-Meadow (eds.), *Language in Mind: Advances in the Study of Language and Thought*, 465–492. Cambridge: MIT Press.

Nycz, Jennifer (2013): Changing words or changing rules? Second dialect acquisition and phonological representation. In: G. Kristiansen and D. Geeraerts (eds.), *Contexts of Use in Cognitive Sociolinguistics.* Special Issue. *Journal of Pragmatics* 52: 49–62.

Nuyts, Jan (2007): Cognitive linguistics and functional linguistics. In: D. Geeraerts and H. Cuyckens (eds.), *The Oxford Handbook of Cognitive Linguistics*, 543–565. New York: Oxford University Press.

Palmer, Gary B. (1996): *Toward a Theory of Cultural Linguistics.* Austin: University of Texas Press.

Pickering, Martin and Simon Garrod (2004): Toward a mechanistic psychology of dialogue. *Behavioral and Brain Sciences* 27: 169–190.

Pierrehumbert, Janet (2002): Word-specific phonetics. In: C. Gussenhoven and N. Warner (eds.), *Laboratory Phonology* VII, 101–140. Berlin/New York: Mouton de Gruyter.

Polzenhagen, Frank and René Dirven (2008): Rationalist and romantic models in globalisation. In: G. Kristiansen and R. Dirven (eds.), *Cognitive Sociolinguistics. Language Variation, Cultural Models, Social Systems*, 237–299. Berlin/New York: Mouton de Gruyter.

Preston, Dennis and Nancy Niedzielski (2000): *Folk Linguistics.* Berlin/New York: Mouton de Gruyter.

Pütz, Martin, Justyna A. Robinson, and Monika Reif (eds.) (2012): *Cognitive Sociolinguistics: Social and Cultural Variation in Cognition and Language Use (Thematic issue of the Review of Cognitive Linguistics).* Amsterdam: John Benjamins.

Ramscar, Michael (volume 1): Categorization. Berlin/Boston: De Gruyter Mouton.

Robinson, Justyna A. (2010): Awesome insights into semantic variation. In: D. Geeraerts, G. Kristiansen and Y. Peirsman (eds.), *Advances in Cognitive Sociolinguistics*, 85–110. Berlin/New York: De Gruyter Mouton.

Rosch, Eleanor (1977): Human categorization. In: N. Warren (ed.), *Studies in Cross-Cultural Psychology*. 1–49. New York/London: Academic Press.

Ruette, Tom, Dirk Speelman, and Dirk Geeraerts (2011): Measuring the lexical distance between registers in national varieties of Dutch. In: A. Soares da Silva, A. Torres and M. Gonçalves (eds.), *Línguas Pluricêntricas. Variação Linguística e Dimensões Sociocognitivas*, 541–554. Braga: Publicações da Faculdade de Filosofia, Universidade Católica Portuguesa.

Schmale, Rachel, Alejandrina Cristia, and Amanda Seidl (2012): Toddlers recognize words in an unfamiliar accent after brief exposure. *Developmental Science* 15(6): 732–738.

Schönefeld, Doris (2013): It is ... quite common for theoretical predictions to go untested. A register-specific analysis of the English go un-V-en construction. *Contexts of Use in Cognitive Sociolinguistics*. Special issue. *Journal of Pragmatics* 52: 17–33.

Semino, Elena (2008): *Metaphor in Discourse*. Cambridge: Cambridge University Press.

Sharifian, Farzad (2011): *Cultural Conceptualisations and Language: Theoretical Framework and Applications*. Amsterdam: John Benjamins.

Sharifian, Farzad, René Dirven, Ning Yu, and Susanne Niemeier (eds.) (2008): *Culture, Body, and Language. Conceptualizations of Internal Body Organs across Cultures and Languages*. Berlin/New York: Mouton de Gruyter.

Sinha, Chris (2007): Cognitive linguistics, psychology and cognitive science. In: D. Geeraerts and H. Cuyckens (eds.), *The Oxford Handbook of Cognitive Linguistics*, 1266–1294. New York: Oxford University Press.

Sinha, Chris (2009): Language as a biocultural niche and social institution. In: V. Evans and S. Pourcel (eds.), *New Directions in Cognitive Linguistics*, 289–309. Amsterdam: John Benjamins.

Soares da Silva, Augusto (2005): Para o estudo das relações lexicais entre o Português Europeu e o Português do Brasil: Elementos de sociolexicologia cognitiva e quantitativa do Português. In: I. Duarte and I. Leiria (eds.), *Actas do XX Encontro Nacional da Associação Portuguesa de Lingüística*, 211–226. Lisboa: Associação Portuguesa de Linguística.

Soukup, Barbara (2013): Austrian dialect as a metonymic device: A cognitive sociolinguistic investigation of Speaker Design and its perceptual implications. In: G. Kristiansen and D. Geeraerts (eds.), *Contexts of Use in Cognitive Sociolinguistics*. Special Issue. *Journal of Pragmatics* 52: 72–82.

Speelman, Dirk and Dirk Geeraerts (2009): Causes for causatives: the case of Dutch 'doen' and 'laten'. In: T. Sanders and E. Sweetser (eds.), *Causal Categories in Discourse and Cognition*, 173–204. Berlin: Mouton de Gruyter.

Speelman, Dirk, Stefan Grondelaers, and Dirk Geeraerts (2003): Profile-based linguistic uniformity as a generic method for comparing language varieties. *Computers and the Humanities* 37: 317–337.

Speelman, Dirk, Stefan Grondelaers, and Dirk Geeraerts (2008): Variation in the choice of adjectives in the two main national varieties of Dutch. In: G. Kristiansen and R. Dirven (eds.), *Cognitive Sociolinguistics. Language Variation, Cultural Models, Social Systems*, 205–233. Berlin/New York: Mouton de Gruyter.

Steels, Luc (2002): Language as a complex adaptive system. In: F. Brisard and T. Mortelmans (eds.), *Language and Evolution*, 79–88. Antwerp: University of Antwerp.

Steels, Luc (2011): *Design Patterns in Fluid Construction Grammar*. Amsterdam: John Benjamins Publishing Company.

Stefanowitsch, Anatol and Stefan Th. Gries (2003): Collostructions: Investigating the interaction of words and constructions. *International Journal of Corpus Linguistics* 8(2): 209–243.

Szmrecsanyi, Benedikt (2009): *Morphosyntactic Persistence in Spoken English. A Corpus Study at the Intersection of Variationist Sociolinguistics, Psycholinguistics, and Discourse Analysis.* Berlin/New York: Mouton de Gruyter.

Szmrecsanyi, Benedikt (2010): The English genitive alternation in a cognitive sociolinguistics perspective. In: D. Geeraerts, G. Kristiansen and Y. Peirsman (eds.), *Advances in Cognitive Sociolinguistics*, 141–166. Berlin/New York: De Gruyter Mouton.

Tummers, José, Kris Heylen, and Dirk Geeraerts (2005): Usage-based approaches in Cognitive Linguistics: A technical state of the art. *Corpus Linguistics and Linguistic Theory* 1: 225–261.

Verhagen, Arie (2005): *Constructions of Intersubjectivity: Discourse, Syntax, and Cognition.* Oxford: Oxford University Press.

Yu, Ning (1998): *The Contemporary Theory of Metaphor. A Perspective from Chinese.* Amsterdam: John Benjamins Publishing Company.

Yu, Ning (2009): *The Chinese Heart in a Cognitive Perspective. Culture, Body, and Language.* Berlin/New York: Mouton De Gruyter.

Zenner, Eline, Dirk Geeraerts, and Dirk Speelman (2009): Expeditie tussentaal: leeftijd, identiteit en context in "Expeditie Robinson". *Nederlandse Taalkunde* 14(1): 26–44.

Zenner, Eline, Dirk Speelman, and Dirk Geeraerts (2012): Cognitive Sociolinguistics meets loanword research: Measuring variation in the success of anglicisms in Dutch. *Cognitive Linguistics* 23: 749–792.

Zhang, Weiwei, Dirk Speelman, and Dirk Geeraerts (2011): Variation in the (non)metonymic capital names in mainland Chinese and Taiwan Chinese. *Metaphor and the Social World* 1: 90–112.

Zlatev, Jordan (2005): What's in a schema? Bodily mimesis and the grounding of language. In: B. Hampe (ed.), *From Perception to Meaning: Image Schemas in Cognitive Linguistics*, 313–342. Berlin/New York: Mouton de Gruyter.

Danielle Matthews and Grzegorz Krajewski
Chapter 7: First language acquisition

1 Introduction

With every year of a child's early life come remarkable bounds in language ability. In this chapter, we will cover some of the major linguistic abilities acquired by children under the age of five. Starting in infancy, we will consider how infants become able to direct others' attention and start to break into conventional language by learning first words. We will then discuss how children refine their word knowledge, building an ever more adult-like lexicon. Next, we briefly describe the transition to combinatorial speech, which brings with it the possibility of grammar. On this topic, we first consider syntax and then inflectional morphology. Finally, we consider some pragmatic skills by focussing on the ability to refer to things effectively. Where appropriate, we will link findings in developmental psycholinguistics to Cognitive Linguistics as a theoretical framework. This framework has been popular with child language researchers for a number of quite different reasons. First, it recognises that natural languages reflect the ways humans perceive and conceptualise their environment. By virtue of viewing the world through roughly the same cognitive lens, so to speak, infants are in a good position to start acquiring the linguistic conventions of their community. Second, it is a usage-based framework, which sees developing linguistic systems as shaped by the utterances children have actually heard or produced themselves. Seen this way, language is not a given but has formed historically to meet the communicative needs of a speech community. Children need to learn conventions that have evolved over historical time. Third, it proposes that usage events are stored "redundantly", even if they could, in principle, be decomposed and stored as separate words and rules. Learning and processing can take advantage of this redundancy. Fourth, it is non-reductionist (utterances are understood in terms of complex wholes, within which constituents are identified). Thus, the same processes that allow children to identify words in the speech stream could simultaneously help identify the structures into which the atomic elements of language can enter (Langacker 2000). All of these properties of Cognitive Linguistic theories have been called upon to explain a broad set of phenomena in first language acquisition. This

---

Danielle Matthews, Sheffield, United Kingdom
Grzegorz Krajewski, Warsaw, Poland

https://doi.org/10.1515/9783110626452-007

chapter will review but a few illustrative cases of the kinds of things children learn as they become native speakers of their language(s). For broader reviews of child language acquisition, see Ambridge and Lieven (2011), Clark (2003), or Tomasello (2003).

2 Communication before words

Infants communicate with their caregivers from the word go. They love to make eye contact, to hear "motherese" and to engage in exquisitely timed dyadic exchanges of cooing and smiles, so much so that they will actively reengage a lapsing communicative partner (see Stephens and Matthews 2014 for a recent review). Over the first year of life, the ability to regulate interaction develops, so that infants become able to make the external world the topic of conversation with others. Thus, around 11 months, infants begin to point to things with the intention of directing their caregiver's attention to a referent. In doing so, they demonstrate some of the most fundamental psychological abilities and motivations that underpin all of language and communication (Bates 1976; Eilan 2005; Tomasello et al. 2007). Critically, around this point in development, infants are able to engage in *joint attention* (where the infant and caregiver both attend to the same thing and are mutually aware they are doing so) and they are motivated to share psychological states with others. Thus, they can both *follow* others' attention (e.g., they can follow an adults' gaze to an object located at a 90 degree angle to their line of vision) and *direct* the attention of others' (with pointing or with vocalisation and eye gaze). While all these social developments are taking place, infants are also getting to know more about the world and becoming adept in regulating their own attention to interesting new objects and events (Mandler 2004). Consequently, it comes naturally to them to communicate about things that have captured their attention, to set them as the topic to be talked about and commented on. Indeed, in her seminal 1976 book, Bates argued that it is the coming together of these two lines of development, contemplation of the external world and engaging of a caregiver, that sets the stage for the topic-comment structure of language (Bates 1976).

At the same time as discovering how to engage others in conversation, infants are tuning into the sounds of their language such that their perception, and to some degree their production, of speech sounds reflects the properties of the language(s) they have been exposed to (Jusczyk 2000; Vihman 1996). Whereas a new-born can perceive all the speech sounds of the entire world's languages (about 600 consonants and 200 vowels), a one-year-old will have lost the ability to tell apart many sounds that are not used contrastively in their native language. So, for example, a child exposed to English loses the ability to perceive the difference between a dental /t/ and a retroflex /t/, whereas a child exposed to Hindi or Urdu would retain this ability as the differences in sounds are used to mark differences in meaning in those languages (Werker and Lalonde 1988). When it comes to producing speech sounds, infants begin to engage in canonical babble (e.g., "dadada") around 6 months and by around 10 months the syllables infants produce reflect those most frequently found in the language the infant is learning (de Boysson-Bardies 1993; Oller and Eilers 1988). Indeed, this period of babble can be seen as an important precursor of language development, with the number of consonants an infant produces across this period having been found to correlate with their later ability to refer to things with words (McCune and Vihman 2001).

Another important process that infants engage involves segmenting the speech stream into units such as words. For an adult reader, it can be easy to forget that human speech does not come neatly separated into words by blanks in the way that written text is. Rather, listening to speech is rather like reading would be without spaces: onewordmergesintothenextwithonlytheoccasional pauseatcertainboundaries. There has been substantial research into how children could break into continuous speech in order to be able to identify units (word forms), such that they could subsequently learn what these forms are used to mean (e.g., Monaghan and Christiansen 2010; Saffran et al. 1996). Infants could potentially use a variety of cues to segment the speech stream (e.g., statistical information about the transitional probabilities between syllables, prosodic cues, allophonic cues, and phonotactic constraints). Interestingly, when making use of these sources of information to segment speech, far more is likely to emerge from the process than simply a list of candidate words. Indeed, it has recently be proposed that the way children chunk the speech stream into units would also be helpful for the development of grammar (Bannard and Matthews 2008), which we will come to later in the chapter.

In sum, during the first year of life, infants set the foundations for language by learning how to engage others in conversation and by learning about the speech sounds of their language(s). They are also making first passes at the next critical steps: identifying linguistic units in the speech stream (words and constructions) and learning how they can be used as conventions to convey thoughts and intentions. Indeed, this transition to conventional language is predicted by an infant's earlier developmental achievements such that infants who are early to follow eye gaze, point and babble are generally also quick to learn words (R. Brooks and Meltzoff 2008; Colonnesi et al. 2010; McGillion et al. 2017).

3 Developing a lexicon

Gauging when a child has first learnt to understand or say a word is a tricky business. It has recently been found that when infants between 6 and 9 months old are presented with a word they have heard frequently before and are shown two images, one corresponding to the word and another familiar distracter, they tend to look at the corresponding image slightly longer (Bergelson and Swingley 2012). Thus it seems that some aspects of word learning get going very early on in life, even while understanding of the sounds structure of language and its social function are still developing. However, associating a sound with an image is not all there is to word learning. As Tomasello argues, mere association "does not constitute an intersubjectively understood linguistic symbol used to direct and share attention with other persons – so it is not word learning" (Tomasello 2001: 1120). This difference between association and the awareness of the communicative function of words was illustrated in a recent study that compared the contexts in which infants were willing to use word knowledge gained in different settings (Bannard and Tomasello 2012 based on Baldwin et al. 1996). In the "coupled" setting, infants saw a novel object on a screen while sitting with an experimenter who labelled it with novel a name. In the "decoupled" setting, infants also saw a novel object while sitting with an experimenter, but this time another experimenter, who was on the other side of the room talking on the telephone (and completely unengaged with the infant), produced the novel names apparently as part of her phone conversation that was nothing to do with the images on the screen. In both conditions, infants came to associate the novel name with the novel image such that, when they heard the word, they would look preferentially to the correct image. However, when asked to point to the right object, infants only tended to do so if they had learnt the word in the coupled condition. Thus, making associations is one thing but understanding that and how a word can be used (with the goal of directing another's attention) is subtly but importantly different. Following Wittgenstein (1958), then, we can say that knowing the meaning of a word is knowing its use.

Social-pragmatic theories of word learning emphasise the idea that words are culturally created conventions and learning is all about figuring out how to use these conventions in the same way that everyone else does. On such accounts, children learn to talk by participating in interaction, often as part of familiar daily routines, using their skills of *joint attention* and *intention reading* (Tomasello 2003). A child and caregiver are in *joint attention* when they are attending to the same thing and are mutually aware that they are doing so. When in this attentional frame, it is especially easy for children to infer what a caregiver is talking about and to learn new words as a consequence. Early in development, an infant's ability to engage in joint attention is fragile and word learning tends to work best when the caregiver scaffolds learning by talking about what the infant is already attending to, a process called *following in* or *contingent talk* (Carpenter et al. 1998; McGillion et al. 2013). From around 18-months, infants become more adept at regulating joint attention themselves. For example, they can monitor a speaker's eye gaze and use this to infer what she must be talking about (Baldwin 1991; Nurmsoo and Bloom 2008). From about the first birthday infants also use their understanding of others intentions' to interpret communicative acts. For example, if an experimenter tells an 18-month-old that she is going to try to find *a toma* and then she proceeds to search through a number of buckets, looking at and rejecting the objects in them until one seems to meet her search (whereupon she stops searching with satisfaction) then the infant is likely to infer that the novel word refers to this final object (Tomasello 2003; Tomasello and Barton 1994).

Overall, there are a whole host of experiments that demonstrate how infants use pragmatic information about others' attention and intentions for word learning (see Grassmann 2014 for a review). It should be noted, however, that not all theories put pragmatics at the centre of word learning. Indeed, occasionally the same behaviour is assumed by some to be an illustration of a pragmatic inference and by others to demonstrate the application of a hard-wired lexical rule. Mutual exclusivity phenomena are perhaps the best example of this. In the standard mutual exclusivity test, a child is introduced to two objects, one that is familiar to them (e.g., an apple) and one that is not (i.e., a novel object). They are then asked to pick up something referred to with a novel word, e.g., *the modi*. Under such circumstances 18-month-olds will readily pick up the novel object (Markman and Wachtel 1988). By 24 months of age, children can succeed in a version of the test that controls for the possibility that children were simply drawn to the novel object. This time, the child is presented with two different novel objects. One is played with and labelled as, for example, *the toma* and the other is played with for the same length of time but not labelled. When the experimenter now asks for *the modi*, 24-month-olds will pick up the unlabelled novel object (Diesendruck and Markson 2001). On some accounts, these results demonstrate the application of a lexical principle that children bring with them to word learning (Markman 1991). On other, social-pragmatic accounts, these finding reflect children's application of the Principles of Contrast and Convention (Clark 1987, 2007), which state that children assume that speakers will use the same linguistic form to convey the same meaning across time and that any departure from this consistency marks a change in intended meaning. So, for this example, a child would reason along the following lines:

"if the experimenter had wanted to refer to the object she just labelled as *a toma* then she should ask for *the toma*. But she asked for *the modi* and therefore she must mean the other object we played with". There has long been debate about which type of account, lexical principles or pragmatic inferences, can best explain mutual exclusivity and related findings. Recent observations of children with Autism seem to suggest there are multiple routes to mutual exclusivity inferences (de Marchena et al. 2011; Preissler and Carey 2005). Furthermore, work investigating the type of language children hear when they are young, suggests that children may *learn* a mutual exclusivity principle, since parents tend to stick to a one-word-one-meaning pattern in their speech to young children (Callanan and Sabbagh 2004; Callanan et al. 2007; Callanan and Siegel 2014). That assumptions of mutual exclusivity may be learned is supported by evidence that bilingual and trilingual children (who frequently hear more than one word for the same object) demonstrate these effects to a lesser degree than monolinguals (Byers-Heinlein and Werker 2009).

4 Grammar

Infants tend to produce their first words around their first birthdays and then spend several months producing single words or at least single unit expressions that are referred to as *holophrases* (e.g., *allgone* produced as if it were one word). Once children have about 100 single words in their lexicon, they generally start to combine these words into short phrases like *more juice* (Bates et al. 1995). In doing so, they take their first steps towards using grammar, i.e., organising words into larger structures. Interestingly, this 100 word transition point seems to hold regardless of the age of the child. In a study of adopted children, Snedeker et al. (2012) asked American parents to report the language abilities of children whom they had adopted from China/Russia either when they were infants or when they were pre-schoolers. The children had heard no English before arriving in the US and only English thereafter. Following adoption, the pre-schoolers learnt English words faster than the infants. However, no matter how fast they learnt single words, parental reports indicated that both the infants and the pre-schoolers began occasionally producing word combinations when they had about 80 words in their lexicon and they both began producing combinations regularly when they had learned about 230 words. This is a close match to non-adopted infants (Bates et al. 1995) and suggests a fundamental link between the development of the lexicon and grammar.

Traditionally, grammar has been seen as a system of abstract rules which govern the way whole sentences can be built from single words (much like algebraic formulas or programming language rules). This view of grammar has serious drawbacks though. First is that it does poorly with exceptions and anyone who has taken foreign language classes knows that most grammatical rules taught in the class is accompanied by a list of exceptions one has to memorise. Second is that conceptualising grammar as an abstract rule system makes the learning task very difficult for children. In fact, it has been claimed that the system is too complicated and the input children have available is not sufficient to figure it out and hence our linguistic competence must have some specific innate basis and language acquisition is more about maturation than about learning (Chomsky 1965, 1981, 1995). This is only an illusory solution, though, as it is not clear how the same innate basis could accommodate all the varied languages of the world and it is not clear how children could map what they hear and learn from the input onto this innate knowledge.

The Cognitive Linguistic approach offers an alternative solution to grammar and its learnability problem. The key concept of this solution is the *construction* (Croft 2001; Diessel this volume; Goldberg 1995). A construction can be any piece of linguistic material paired with its meaning. It can be a single word or a whole sentence, or just a fragment; it can be concrete (*The fox pushed the bear*) or somewhat schematic (*X pushed Y*), or even highly schematic (*Subject Verb Object*). There is no clear-cut distinction between the lexicon (the set of words) of a given language and the grammar of that language. Children start with learning whole concrete constructions that they have memorised verbatim (e.g., *more juice* or *a bowl of cornflakes*), just like they learn single words and their meanings. Once children have heard many similar sentences (e.g., *more cookies, more milk, a bowl of soup, a bowl of water*) and can draw analogies across them, they gradually build more schematic constructions (e.g., *more X, a bowl of X*). We will describe in greater detail what one such process of gradual schematisation might look like when we discuss inflections later in this chapter. For now, we can think of the language system as a structured inventory of constructions (Langacker 1987). This inventory is basically a representation of all the language children have ever heard, organised such that similar forms overlap and naturally form abstractions. A tiny corner of such an inventory is given by way of example in figure 7.1. The phrases at the bottom of the diagram are concrete examples of speech directed to young children learning English. The generalisations at each level above are possible abstractions a child could arrive at on the basis of what they've heard. Precisely how children make these generalisations, and how they constrain them so they do not over-generalise their grammar, is an empirical question that is hard to solve. In recent years substantial progress has been made by building computational models that simulate what kinds of grammars might emerge from the language children hear around them (Bannard et al. 2009; Freudenthal et al. 2010).

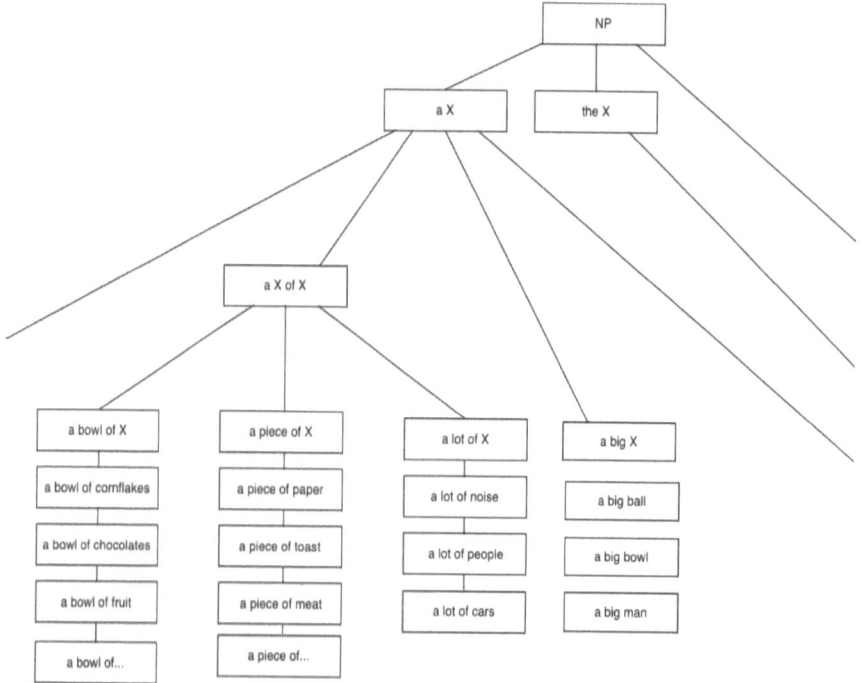

Fig. 7.1: Schematic diagram of part of a structured inventory of constructions. Concrete instances of child directed speech are presented at the bottom, with potential generalisations posited at higher levels.

One assumption of a Cognitive Linguistic approach to first language acquisition is that the language children hear, the so called *Child Directed Speech* (CDS), or the "input", is repetitive and formulaic, offering ample opportunity to break into grammar. This has been shown to be the case with corpus studies, i.e., analyses of written transcripts of the spontaneous conversations that occur between young children and their caregivers. Indeed, Cameron-Faulkner et al. (2003) analysed the CDS addressed to 12 English speaking children (aged 2;0–3;0) and found out that 51 % of all utterances in the corpus shared the first 1–3 words and that 45 % of all utterances began with one of only 17 words! This means that the majority of utterances children hear can be accounted for by highly repetitive item-based frames. Stoll et al. (2009) report similar findings for other languages.

One prediction of this account of learning, then, would be that children's own utterances, even if they look fully mature and adult-like, should be highly repetitive themselves. Lieven et al. (2003) used corpus data to show that immediate repetitions and imitations of the mother as well as the exact repetitions of what the child had said in the previous six weeks of recording accounted for 63% of all the multi-word utterances in an hour-long recording session. 74% of the remaining utterances could be "traced back" to previous utterances by simple substitutions, deletions etc. (see also Bannard et al. 2009; Dąbrowska and Lieven 2005).

Another prediction is that we should be able to find evidence of children storing whole sequences of words. Bannard and Matthews (2008) used CDS corpora to identify frequent multi-word sequences (e.g., *sit in your chair*) and to match them to infrequent sequences differing only by the final word (e.g., *sit in your truck*). They then run an experiment showing that children were more accurate at repeating the frequent sequences. Since the final words of sequences were matched for frequency (e.g., the number of occurrences of *chair* and *truck* in the corpus was more or less the same), the results suggest that children do store whole chunks of linguistic material. A further study suggested that children are able to generalise abstract grammatical patterns from this learned material (Matthews and Bannard 2010).

While some usage-based accounts may assume specific learned word sequences to be at the heart of language use right up to adulthood, once the complexity of the generalisations being made reaches a certain degree, it is standard to talk about them in terms of more abstract grammatical "cues". These cues play a variety of functions. Perhaps most importantly, they are used to mark "who did what to whom" or agent-patient relations (for example in the sentence *the fox pushed the bear* the order of the words tells us that the fox did the pushing and the bear was pushed). There are two main grammatical cues that perform this function: word order and case marking. We will focus on each in separate sections. The first section will discuss word order in transitive sentences such as *The fox pushed the bear* and *The bear pushed the fox*. The second section will discuss morphology, which is the branch of grammar dealing with word structure. In this chapter, we focus on inflectional morphology, which is used to modulate word meaning and mark case on words (e.g., adding the plural inflection – s to the word *dog* makes *dogs*, and changing *he* to *him* changes the case of the word from nominative to accusative: *He likes me* but *I like him*). Finally, we will discuss how word order and case marking can be put together in a coherent theoretical model.

On a Cognitive Linguistic account, children learn their grammar from what they hear (and use themselves) without relying on some innate linguistic biases. Hence much of the research conducted within this framework, and the empirical studies we discuss in the following sections, has focused on one of two issues. One is the evidence of gradual (rather than instantaneous) development of abstract grammatical knowledge; the other one is the effect of characteristics of the language children hear (and cross-linguistic differences) on the acquisition process; and both are taken as evidence in favour of the hypothesis that children learn grammar from the input.

4.1 Word order

In many languages, including English, the ordering of words in larger structures, particularly sentences, plays an important role in marking *who did what to whom*, which usually is what children want to talk about with others when discovering the world around them and when engaging in their first joined communicative behaviours with other people. Although children tend to produce correct English word order from the start, it appears to take quite some time for them to learn its function. This is to say, it is some time before children know that in the sentence *The goat pushed the cow*, the goat is the *agent* (the pusher) since it comes before the verb and the cow is the *patient* (the pushee) since it comes after the verb. Since marking agent-patient relations is one of the key functions of grammar, considerable research has been dedicated to investigating how children make this discovery.

The main question of interest with respect to the development of word order has been how *productive* or abstract children's knowledge is. A child can be said to have fully productive knowledge of word order if they understand its function regardless of the particular words in the sentence. Whilst a child might know how to understand a transitive construction when it comes to sentences containing words they have frequently heard before (that is they may know that in the example *He pushed the cow* that the cow was pushed and not the pusher), they may not know that, in general, in transitive structures like this the first noun phrase typically corresponds to the agent. To test for truly productive knowledge, many studies have used novel (invented) verbs that the child could not possibly have heard before. So if, for example, children hear the sentence *Big bird chammed Cookie monster*, and assume that Big Bird did something (whatever that may be) to Cookie Monster, then they must be doing so on the basis a fairly abstract understanding of the function of word order.

Studies have used a variety of methods to test for productive knowledge of word order, with findings varying according to the precise test used. In a series of experiments, Tomasello and colleagues (Akhtar and Tomasello 1997; P. J. Brooks and Tomasello 1999) taught children novel verbs (e.g., by introducing the verb *chamming* while showing a familiar character, Big Bird, jumping on a curved platform and catapulting another familiar character, Cookie Monster). They then tested the children's comprehension of word order by asking them 1) to describe similar scenes with different characters (e.g., where Ernie chammed, Bert) and 2) to "act out" the appropriate actions, for example, to *make Kermit cham Elmo*. Their results suggest that only around the age of three do children start to show productive understanding of the transitive construction.

In contrast, experiments that use the preferential looking paradigm, a less demanding test of young children's comprehension than the "act-out" method, find sensitivity to word order at a younger age (e.g., Fisher 2002; Naigles 1990). In these experiments children hear an utterance, for example *the duck is gorping the bunny*, while simultaneously being presented with two video clips: one showing a duck doing something to the rabbit, and the other showing the duck and the rabbit each doing something alone. The length of the children's looking time to each video is compared, with the assumption that if a child understands the transitive sentence they should look more to the scene where the duck is doing something to the rabbit. Results of these studies suggest that two-year-old children can correctly interpret transitive sentences with novel verbs. There is thus some evidence of abstract knowledge at this stage, although it takes time before it can fully manifest itself in a wide variety of tasks. The question, of course, is whether it is plausible that one could learn this by the age of two based on hearing one's native language everyday.

4.2 Inflectional morphology

While in English, word order is the primary tool for marking who-did-what-to-whom, in many other languages, inflections (different endings on words) are more important. For example, in Polish the sentence *The goat pushed the cow* is *Koza pchnęła krowę*. Critically, although it would be more typical to have the words in SVO order, it is perfectly possible to change the order of the words in this language (*Krowę pchnęła koza*) and for the sentence to mean the same thing since word order is not marking who did what to whom. Instead this work is being done by the case markers (-*a* is in the nominative form on *koza* ['goat'] and -*ę* in the accusative form on *krowę* ['cow']). To change the meaning of the sentences such that the cow is the agent, one would need to change the case of the noun to the nominative (from *krowę* to *krowa*). In languages like Polish, then, the order of constituents is usually less important and adult speakers know that if the first noun phrase in a sentence is marked as accusative and the second as nominative they should follow case marking to arrive at the meaning of the sentence. Children learning such languages have to master their inflectional systems in order to become fully productive with their grammar.

Even in languages with relatively simple morphological systems, like English, inflections are used to modulate the meanings of words, for example, to mark plurality (dog + s > dogs), the past tense (walk + ed > walked) or person

(1st person: *I sleep*; 3rd person: *She sleeps*). Inflectional systems in any language tend to form recurring, albeit not perfectly systematic, patterns which children have to notice and generalise. Clear evidence of a child having noticed an inflectional pattern comes when they *overgeneralise* the inflection and apply it to irregular words, saying things like *mouses* instead of *mice*, for example. When a child is able to add an inflection onto new words, we say that they can use it *productively*.

A classic experiment in the field of developmental psycholinguistics, the *wug test*, was developed to test children's productive knowledge of inflections (Berko 1958). In this test, a child is shown a drawing presenting a funny creature and given the novel name for that creature (*This is a wug*). The next drawing shows two such creatures and the child is encouraged to use the name in the plural form (*Now there is another one. There are two of them. There are two ...*). The use of novel words when performing such a test is critical: with familiar words (e.g., *One bird, two ...*) we could not be sure whether the child used the correct plural (*birds*) because they had already learnt the general pattern or simply because they remembered the plural form of that particular word. In the wug test, if the child says *wugs*, s/he necessarily has productive knowledge of the inflectional pattern. Indeed, as we have seen in the previous section on syntax, the use of novel words is a helpful tool when studying all sort of aspects of the development of grammar.

In the previous section we mentioned the great debate regarding the learnability of grammar. Those who think grammar is (at least to some extent) innate will posit a clear distinction between grammar and lexicon (since words are clearly something children have to learn from the input), and the grammar will be conceptualised as a set of abstract rules one has to apply to words in order to inflect and use them when building sentences. Such a *words and rules* approach to language (Pinker 1999) has been proposed to account for the acquisition and use of English inflections as well. In English, compared to most other languages, inflections are generally few and simple (e.g., adding *–s* to mark number). Whenever a single pattern cannot account for inflecting all words (e.g., *house* > *houses* but *mouse* > *mice*), there is nevertheless a fairly clear-cut distinction between the *regular* pattern and *irregular* exceptions. Seen from the words and rules perspective, children produce regular forms by applying a rule but they memorise irregular forms as separate words (just as they store any other words in the lexicon). In this approach, productive use of an inflection involves applying its rule to a given word and overgeneralisation indicates failure to retrieve a correct irregular from memory. As noted though, English is not the most typical language when it comes to morphology and the words and rules approach struggles with more complex inflectional systems, where a sin-

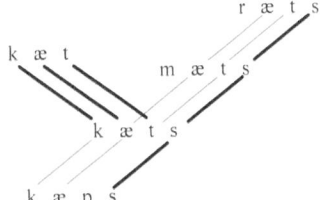

Fig. 7.2: An example of how word forms are stored in the mental lexicon according to the Network Model (from Bybee, 1995).

gle word can have many different forms, without there being a clear rule to tell which form is correct and when. Alternative accounts, routed in the tradition of Cognitive Linguistics, appear better able handle these cases where there is no clear cut between the grammar (rules) and the lexicon (words).

The most prominent model of inflectional morphology in this tradition is Bybee's Network Model (Bybee 1985, 1995), which offers a unified account of its acquisition, processing in adults, and diachronic change (i.e., language change over historical time). According to this model, all word forms, whether we call them regular or irregular, can be stored in your mental lexicon, as long as you have encountered them before (which seems sensible, since the mental lexicon is part of memory, and it does not seem reasonable that we keep some word forms in memory and discard others, based purely on some regularity criterion). Importantly, the mental lexicon is not just a loose bag of words. Rather, all words are stored in shared representational space such that they are interconnected based on their similarity: the more two items are similar to each other the stronger the connection between them. Words can be similar in their *phonological form* (what they sound like) and in their *meaning*. If the two types of similarity go together, a morphological *schema* can emerge (e.g., if a number of verb forms share the *-ed* ending and they are all associated with the meaning of "past" then we have the basis for a past tense schema).

At first sight, a fully emerged schema does not look very different from a traditional morphological rule. However, there are differences between the two and, crucially, these differences have implications for the acquisition process. Most importantly, the Network Model explains how schemas emerge in child language based on what a given child has heard (the *input*). There are two broadly defined input factors that affect the learning process. One is the above-mentioned similarity of formii and meaning: the more similar lexical items are to each other, the faster a schema based on them will emerge, and the more similar an item is to an existing schema, the more likely the schema will be applied to it. The other factor is frequency, which can be further divided into two. The greater the number of different types of word types (e.g., *jumped, hopped, skipped, bounced* ...) serving as a base for the schema generalisation (i.e., the greater its *type frequency*), the faster the schema will emerge and the easier it will be to apply it to novel items. On the other hand, the more often you hear a particular word form (i.e., the higher its *token frequency*), the stronger its representation, so the easier it will be to retrieve it from memory but at the same time the less "willing" it will be to participate in a schema generalisation.

Grounding the development of morphology in the actual language children hear, the model can explain some phenomena concerning English verbs that escape an easy explanation if one posits a clear-cut distinction between "regular" and "irregular" parts of the system. For example, there is some degree of productivity in children's use of "irregular" patterns on the one hand (e.g., *swung, clung, flung*) and there are effects of frequency and phonological similarity even for "regular" forms (Ambridge 2010; Bybee and Slobin 1982; Dąbrowska and Szczerbiński 2006; Köpcke 1998; Krajewski et al. 2011; Marchman 1997; Matthews and Theakston 2006).

Another important feature of inflectional schemas is their gradual development. Since children generalise schemas based on what they hear and already store in their memory, the learning process takes some time and, furthermore, early schemas will be limited in use (the more different word forms children know, the more open, i.e., easily applied to other items, their schemas will become). In fact, over-regularisation errors are not quite as common in morphological development as has been assumed. Even in English, a closer examination reveals that some words are far more prone to error than others and this difference is largely due to word frequency (Maslen et al. 2004). What turns out to be typical for the development of morphology across languages is the fact that early use of inflections is, at first, highly restricted in terms of different words an inflection will be used with. That is, children are actually quite conservative in the way they use their first inflections (Aguado-Orea 2004; Mueller Gathercole et al. 2002; Pine et al. 1998; Pizzuto and Caselli 1992).

This approach to morphological development receives further support from connectionist models, which are computational simulations of how people learn and represent knowledge (e.g., Cottrell and Plunkett 1994; Rumelhart and McClelland 1986; Westermann 1998). Connectionism became popular in cognitive psychology in the 1980's and one of the first things researchers tried their models on was the acquisition of English past tense. Results of these simulations replicate various experimental findings and strongly suggest that the learning is indeed possible without resorting to separate regular and irregular mechanisms.

In sum, Bybee's Network Model, as an example of the Cognitive Linguistics approach to grammar, radically rejects the traditional words and rules view of language. Instead it proposes that inflectional morphology develops gradually, without clear detachment from the lexicon, depends on input characteristics, and is prone to individual differences.

4.3 Combining word order and morphology to mark agent-patient relations: The cue competition model

While the above sections have illustrated how word order or inflectional morphology can be used to mark who did what to whom, it is worth noting that most languages actually use a combination of both types of marker. This can make learning grammar a little tricky for children and indeed some languages are easier to figure out in this respect than others. To account for all such cross-linguistic differences, Bates and MacWhinney (1989) proposed the Cue Competition Model. A cue can be any linguistic property (e.g., word order, inflections) that systematically co-occurs with a given function (e.g., marking agent-patient relations). The model makes predictions about the importance of a given cue in a given input language, taking into account how often a given cue is present when its function is present (*cue availability*; e.g., case marking is more available in Polish than in English) and how often a given function is present when the cue is present (*cue reliability*; word order is more reliable in English than in Polish). Many studies have tested this model and evidence suggests that the characteristics of the language children hear indeed affect how they learn various grammatical markers. The first studies of this type date back to the 1980's (MacWhinney et al. 1985; Sokolov 1988; Weist 1983) and in recent years new studies appeared, which use novel verbs and thus allow a better test of children's ability to use abstract transitive patterns (e.g., Dittmar et al. 2008). We know that in Turkish, which only minimally depends on word order for marking agent and patient, children do not pay much attention to it but are quick to learn to rely on inflections. In Serbo-Croatian, on the other hand, just like in Polish, younger children depend on word order heavily, even if it conflicts with inflections, perhaps because the latter form a complex and ambiguous system (Krajewski and Lieven 2014; Slobin and Bever 1982). We also know that children across languages find it more difficult to understand sentences with inanimate agents and animate patients (e.g., *The telephone meeks the horse* is more difficult than *The horse meeks the telephone*), which further confirms that learning is grounded in children's experience (Chan et al. 2009). All in all, studies on different languages and using different methods bring the same picture of development that is gradual and depends heavily on how easy it is for the learner to detect a grammatical marker and establish what it is used for.

5 Pragmatic skills: The case of reference

At the start of this chapter we noted how skilled infants are at engaging others in communicative exchanges. This can be considered a pragmatic skill, one which involves effective and appropriate use of language such that it is adapted to context and, particularly, the person we are speaking with. In this section, we will consider a number of other skills that are often described as pragmatic, although we should start by noting that this term is notoriously difficult to define (Ninio and Snow 1996). There are a whole host of pragmatic skills, such as engaging turn taking, using non-literal language (jokes, irony, metaphor), understanding implicatures (e.g., knowing that when I say *I ate some of the biscuits* it can be taken to mean I didn't eat them all) and being able to talk and write in an appropriate register (see Matthews 2014). We will focus here on a very restricted set of pragmatic skills, namely those required to refer to things effectively.

Learning how to refer to things is perhaps more difficult that one might initially expect since referring expressions (e.g., *my sister*, *she*, or *the girl over there with the blond hair*) convey meaning about how the speaker and addressee perceive the people and things they are talking about (Clark 1997). That is, they tell us about the perspective the speaker has or wants to confer upon the referent. Indeed, when speaking, even the apparently simple case of referring to tangible entities requires more than just matching up words to things. It requires choosing just those referring expressions that a co-operative listener could reasonably understand in a given context. For example, if a child in a crowded playground has her toy snatched from her and runs up to the teacher exclaiming *She took it off me!* then the teacher is unlikely to know who has taken what or to be able to do anything about it. This child has not yet learnt that you only use pronouns like *she* and *it* to refer to things the addressee already knows about or has direct perceptual access to.

The child in the playground is not alone in struggling to grapple with reference. The fact that different forms can refer to the same thing but to differing effect has long caused problems in the philosophy of language (Frege [1892] 1997) and has ultimately driven us to consider the meaning of an utterance as defined by use rather than the things words stand for (Wittgenstein 1958). In the field of linguistics, the differing functions of referring expressions have also been a major topic of discussion (Ariel 1988, 1990; Givón 1983; Gundel et al. 1993). When it comes to child language research, recent studies have shown that children gradually build up very detailed expectations regarding the expressions others will use, taking into account factors such as what can be seen in common ground, what has previously been talked about and the similarity of potential referents. Thus for example, children learn that it is fine to use pronouns (like *it*) if the thing being referred to is highly accessible to the interlocutor either because they are looking at it, or because it has recently been mentioned (Matthews et al. 2006). This view is compatible with Cognitive Linguistic accounts of pronoun use (van Hoek 1997; Matthews et al. 2009).

An important question concerns the type of experiences that are necessary for children to develop this knowledge of referring expressions. Although the many studies demonstrate some very early knowledge in this domain, it remains the case that fully mastering reference takes several years and children aged between 2 and 4 years have been shown to avoid linguistic reference altogether and to rely on pointing to refer to objects even in contexts where such gestures are extremely ambiguous (perhaps to spread the load of communication across the dyad). A recent series of training studies (Matthews et al. 2012; Matthews et al. 2006; Sarilar et al. 2013) demonstrated that actively engaging in conversations and needing to repair unsuccessful attempts at reference can help children to become more effective communicators. Indeed, by hearing specific options when being asked to clarify what they mean (e.g., *do you want the one who's skating or the one who's jumping*), they rapidly learn to use difficult-to-master constructions (such as relative clauses) very early on. Thus, when the pragmatic function of a given referring expression is made clear, young children readily learn to use this form in the future.

We assume, then, that over the course of countless conversations in the preschool years, children gradually build up very detailed expectations regarding how different types of referring expressions can be used, taking into account factors such as what can be seen in common ground and the similarity of potential referents. It appears that children play an active role in testing these expectations out, and propel along their learning in doing so (Morisseau et al. 2013).

6 Summary

We have seen that acquiring a language involves solving multiple interconnected challenges. In the first year of life, children discover that language can be used to regulate interaction and direct others' attention. They start to tune into the sounds of the ambient language and to segment the speech stream into meaningful units including words. In the second year, they learn the functions of hundreds of these words and start to understand how they can be combined to express a whole range of meanings. Over the following years, they develop a productive grasp on the grammar of their language, and gain all the expressive power this permits. In general, we can see the learning process as one of constant refinement: every experience of language leads to an ever more accurate grasp on the subtle differences that contrasting linguistic forms can mark. Sometimes these differences are important for marking semantic contrasts (e.g., the subtle difference in meaning between, *pull* and *tug*, for example) and other times they mark a pragmatic contrast (e.g., the difference between saying *she* or *my sister*). Children propel this process of refinement along themselves, actively seeking out information when their expectations about language use are not met.

7 References

Aguado-Orea, Javier (2004): *The acquisition of morpho-syntax in Spanish: Implications for current theories of development.* Unpublished PhD, University of Nottingham.

Ambridge, Ben (2010): Children's judgments of regular and irregular novel past tense forms: New data on the dual- versus single-route debate. *Developmental Psychology* 46(6): 1497–1504.

Ambridge, Ben and Elena V. M. Lieven (2011): *Child Language Acquisition: Contrasting Theoretical Approaches.* Cambridge: Cambridge University Press.

Akhtar, Nameera and Michael Tomasello (1997): Young children's productivity with word order and verb morphology. *Developmental Psychology* 33(6): 952–965.

Ariel, Mira (1988): Referring and accessibility. *Journal of Linguistics* 24: 65–87.

Ariel, Mira (1990): *Anaphoric Antecedents.* London: Croom Helm.

Baldwin, Dare A. (1991): Infants' contribution to the achievement of joint reference. *Child Development* 62: 875–890.

Baldwin, Dare A., Ellen M. Markman, Brigitte Bill, Renee N. Desjardins, Jane M. Irwin, and Glynnis Tidball (1996): Infants' reliance on a social criterion for establishing word-object relations. *Child Development* 67(6): 3135–3153.

Bannard, Colin, Elena V. M. Lieven, and Michael Tomasello (2009): Modeling children's early grammatical knowledge. *Proceedings of the National Academy of Sciences* 106(41): 17284–17289.

Bannard, Colin and Danielle E. Matthews (2008): Stored word sequences in language learning: The effect of familiarity of children's repetition of four-word combinations. *Psychological Science*, 19/3, 241–248.

Bannard, Colin and Michael Tomasello (2012): Can we dissociate contingency learning from social learning in word acquisition by 24-month-olds? *PLoS ONE* 7(11): e49881.

Bates, Elizabeth (1976): *Language and Context: The Acquisition of Pragmatics.* New York: Academic Press.

Bates, Elizabeth, Philip Dale, and Donna Thal (1995): Individual differences and their implications for theories of language development. *The Handbook of Child Language*, 96–151. Oxford: Basil Blackwell.

Bates, Elizabeth and Brian MacWhinney (1989): *The Cross-Linguistic Study of Sentence Processing.* Cambridge: Cambridge University Press.

Bergelson, Elika and Daniel Swingley (2012): At 6–9 months, human infants know the meanings of many common nouns. *Proceedings of the National Academy of Sciences* 109(9): 3253–3258.

Berko, Jean (1958): The child's learning of English morphology. *Word* 14: 150–177.
Brooks, Patricia J. and Michael Tomasello (1999): How children constrain their argument structure constructions. *Language* 75: 720–738.
Brooks, Rechele and Andrew N. Meltzoff (2008): Infant gaze following and pointing predict accelerated vocabulary growth through two years of age: a longitudinal, growth curve modeling study. *Journal of Child Language* 35(1): 207–220.
Bybee, Joan (1985): *Morphology: A Study of the Relation Between Meaning and Form.* Amsterdam: John Benjamins.
Bybee, Joan (1995): egular morphology and the lexicon. *Language and Cognitive Processes* 10(5): 425–455.
Bybee, Joan and Dan I. Slobin (1982): Rules and schemas in the development and use of the English past tense. *Language* 58: 265–289.
Byers-Heinlein, Krista and Janet F. Werker (2009): Monolingual, bilingual, trilingual: Infants' language experience influences the development of a word-learning heuristic. *Developmental Science* 12: 815–823.
Callanan, Maureen A. and Mark A. Sabbagh (2004): Multiple labels for objects in coversations with young children: Parents' language and children's developing expectations about word meanings. *Developmental Psychology* 40(5): 746–763.
Callanan, Maureen A., Deborah R. Siegel, and Megan R. Luce (2007): Conventionality in family conversations about everyday objects. *New Directions for Child and Adolescent Development* 115: 83–97.
Callanan, Maureen A. and Deborah R. Siegel (2014): Learning conventions and conventionality through conversation. In: D. Matthews (ed.), *Pragmatic Development in First Language Acquisition*. Amsterdam: John Benjamins.
Cameron-Faulkner, Thea, Elena V. M. Lieven, and Michael Tomasello (2003): A construction based analysis of child directed speech. *Cognitive Science* 27(6): 843–873.
Carpenter, Malinda, Katherine Nagell, and Michael Tomasello (1998): Social cognition, joint attention, and communicative competence from 9 to 15 months of age. *Monographs of the Society for Research in Child Development* 63(4): i–vi, 1–143.
Chan, Angel, Elena V. M. Lieven, and Michael Tomasello (2009): Children's understanding of the agent-patient relations in the transitive construction: Cross-linguistic comparisons between Cantonese, German, and English. *Cognitive Linguistics* 20(2): 267–300.
Chomsky, Noam (1965): *Aspects of the Theory of Syntax*. Cambridge: MIT Press.
Chomsky, Noam (1981): *Lectures on Government and Binding*. Dordrecht: Forris.
Chomsky, Noam (1995): *The Minimalist Program*. Cambridge: MIT Press.
Clark, Eve V. (1987): The principle of contrast: A constraint on language acquisition. In: B. MacWhinney (ed.), *Mechanisms of Language Acquisition*, 1–33. Hillsdale: Erlbaum.
Clark, Eve V. (1997): Conceptual perspective and lexical choice in acquisition. *Cognition* 64(1): 1–37.
Clark, Eve V. (2003): *First Language Acquisition*. Cambridge: Cambridge University Press.
Clark, Eve V. (2007): Conventionality and contrast in language and language acquisition. *New Directions for Child and Adolescent Development* 115: 11–23.
Colonnesi, Cristina, Geert J. J. M. Stams, Irene Koster, and Marc J. Noom (2010): The relation between pointing and language development: A meta-analysis. *Developmental Review* 30(4): 352–366.
Cottrell, Garrison W. and Kim Plunkett (1994): Acquiring the mapping from meanings to sounds. *Connection Science* 6(4): 379–412.

Croft, William (2001): *Radical Construction Grammar: Syntactic Theory in Typological Perspective*. Oxford: Oxford University Press.

Dąbrowska, Ewa and Elena V. M. Lieven (2005): Towards a lexically specific grammar of children's question constructions. *Cognitive Linguistics* 16(3): 437–474.

Dąbrowska, Ewa and Marcin Szczerbiński (2006): Polish children's productivity with case marking: the role of regularity, type frequency and phonological diversity. *Journal of Child Language* 33(3): 559–597.

de Boysson-Bardies, Bénédicte (1993): *Ontogeny of Language-Specific Syllabic Productions*. Springer.

de Marchena, Ashley, Inge-Marie Eigsti, Amanda Worek, Kim E. Ono, and Jesse Snedeker (2011): Mutual exclusivity in autism spectrum disorders: Testing the pragmatic hypothesis. *Cognition* 119(1): 96–113.

Diesendruck, Gil and Lori Markson (2001): Children's avoidance of lexical overlap: a pragmatic account. *Developmental Psychology* 37(5): 630.

Diessel, Holger (this volume): Usage-based construction grammar. Berlin/Boston: De Gruyter Mouton.

Dittmar, Miriam, Kirsten Abbot-Smith, Elena V. M. Lieven, and Michael Tomasello (2008): Young German children's early syntactic competence: A preferential looking study. *Developmental Science* 11(4): 575–582.

Eilan, Naomi (2005): Joint attention, communication and mind. In: N. Eilan, C. Hoerl, T. McCormack and J. Roessler (eds.), *Joint Attention: Communication and Other Minds*, 1–33. Oxford: Oxford University Press.

Fisher, Cynthia (2002): The role of abstract syntactic knowlegde in language acquisition: a reply to Tomasello (2000). *Cognition* 82: 259–278.

Frege, Gottlob (1997): On Sinn and Bedeutung. In: M. Beaney (ed.), *The Frege Reader*. Oxford: Blackwell.

Freudenthal, Daniel, Julian Pine, and Fernand Gobet (2010): Explaining quantitative variation in the rate of Optional Infinitive errors across languages: A comparison of MOSAIC and the Variational Learning Model. *Journal of Child Language* 37(3): 643–669.

Givón, Talmy (1983): *Topic Continuity in Discourse: A Quantitative Crosslanguage Study*. Amsterdam: John Benjamins.

Goldberg, Adele E. (1995): *Constructions: A Construction Grammar Approach to Argument Structure*. Chicago: University of Chicago Press.

Grassmann, Susanne (2014): The pragmatics of word learning. In: D. Matthews (ed.), *Pragmatic Development in First Language Acquisition*. Amsterdam: John Benjamins.

Gundel, Jeanette K., Nancy Hedberg, and Ron Zacharski (1993): Cognitive status and the form of referring expressions in discourse. *Language* 69: 274–307.

Jusczyk, Peter (2000): *The Discovery of Spoken Language*. Cambridge: MIT Press.

Köpcke, Klaus-Michael (1998): The acquisition of plural marking in English and German revisited: schemata versus rules. *Journal of Child Language* 25(2): 293–319.

Krajewski, Grzegorz and Elena V. M. Lieven (2014): Competing cues in early syntactic development. In: B. MacWhinney, A. Malchukov, and E. A. Moravcsik (eds.), *Competing Motivations in Grammar and Usage*. Oxford: Oxford University Press.

Krajewski, Grzegorz, Anna L. Theakston, Elena V. M. Lieven, and Michael Tomasello (2011): How Polish children switch from one case to another when using novel nouns: Challenges for models of inflectional morphology. *Language and Cognitive Processes* 26(4/6): 830–861.

Langacker, Ronald W. (1987): *Foundations of Cognitive Grammar* Vol. 1, *Theoretical Prerequisites*. Stanford: Stanford University Press.

Langacker, Ronald W. (2000): A dynamic usage-based model. In: S. Kemmer and M. Barlow (eds.), *Usage Based Models of Language*. Stanford: CSLI.

Lieven, Elena V. M., Heike Behrens, Jennifer Spears, and Michael Tomasello (2003): Early syntactic creativity: A usage-based approach. *Journal of Child Language* 30(2): 333–370.

MacWhinney, Brian, Csaba Pleh, and Elizabeth Bates (1985): The development of sentence interpretation in Hungarian. *Cognitive Psychology* 17(2): 178–209.

Mandler, Jean (2004): *The Foundations of Mind: Origins of Conceptual Thought*. Oxford: Oxford University Press.

Marchman, Virginia (1997): Children's productivity in the English past tense: The role of frequency, phonology and neighborhood structure. *Cognitive Science* 21(3): 283–304.

Markman, Ellen M. (1991): The whole-object, taxonomic and mutual exclusivity assumptions as initial constraints on word meanings. In: S. A. Gelman and J. P. Byrnes (eds.), *Perspectives on Language and Thought: Interrelations in Development*, 72–106. Cambridge: Cambridge University Press.

Markman, Ellen M. and Gwyn F. Wachtel (1988): Children's use of mutual exclusivity to constrain the meanings of words. *Cognitive Psychology* 20(2): 121–157.

Maslen, Robert, Anna L. Theakston, Elena V. M. Lieven, and Michael Tomasello (2004): A dense corpus study of past tense and plural overgeneralization in English. *Journal of Speech Language and Hearing Research* 47: 1319–1333.

Matthews, Danielle E. (ed.). (2014): *Pragmatic Development in First Language Acquisition*. Amsterdam: John Benjamins.

Matthews, Danielle E. and Colin Bannard (2010): Children's production of unfamiliar word sequences is predicted by positional variability and latent classes in a large sample of child-directed speech. *Cognitive Science* 34(3): 465–488.

Matthews, Danielle E., Jessica Butcher, Elena V. M. Lieven, and Michael Tomasello (2012): Two- and four-year-olds learn to adapt referring expressions to context: Effects of distracters and feedback on referential communication. *Topics in Cognitive Science* 4(2): 184–210.

Matthews, Danielle E. and Anna L. Theakston (2006): Errors of omission in English-speaking children's production of plurals and the past tense: The effects of frequency, phonology and competition. *Cognitive Science* 30(6): 1027–1052.

Matthews, Danielle E., Anna L. Theakston, Elena V. M. Lieven, and Michael Tomasello (2006): The effect of perceptual availability and prior discourse on young children's use of referring expressions. *Applied Psycholinguistics* 27: 403–422.

Matthews, Danielle E., Elena V. M. Lieven, Anna L. Theakston, and Michael Tomasello (2009): Pronoun co-referencing errors: challenges for generativist and usage-based accounts. *Cognitive Linguistics* 20(3): 599–626.

McCune, Lorraine and Marilyn M. Vihman (2001): Early phonetic and lexical development: A productivity approach. *Journal of Speech, Language and Hearing Research* 44(3): 670–684.

McGillion, Michelle L., Jane S. Herbert, Julian Pine, Tamar Keren-Portnoy, Marilyn Vihman, and Danielle E. Matthews (2013): Supporting early vocabulary development: What sort of responsiveness matters? *Autonomous Mental Development, IEEE Transactions on* 5(3): 240–248.

McGillion, Michelle L., Jane S. Herbert, Julian Pine. Marilyn Vihman, Rory DePaolis, Tamar Keren-Portnoy, and Danielle E. Matthews (2017): What paves the way to conventional language? The predictive value of babble, pointing, and socioeconomic status. *Child Development*, 88(1), 156–166.

Monaghan, Padraic and Morten H. Christiansen (2010): Words in puddles of sound: modelling psycholinguistic effects in speech segmentation. *Journal of Child Language* 37(3): 545–564.

Morisseau, Tiffany, Catherine Davies, and Danielle E. Matthews (2013): How do 3-and 5-year-olds respond to under-and over-informative utterances? *Journal of Pragmatics* 59: 26–39.

Mueller Gathercole, Virginia. C., Eugenia Sebastián, and Pilar Soto (2002): The emergence of linguistic person in Spanish-speaking children. *Language Learning* 52(4): 679–722.

Naigles, Letitia (1990): Children use syntax to learn verb meanings. *Journal of Child Language* 17: 357–374.

Ninio, Anat and Catherine E. Snow (1996): *Pragmatic Development*. Boulder: Westview Press.

Nurmsoo, Erika and Paul Bloom (2008): Preschoolers' perspective taking in word learning. *Psychological Science* 19(3): 211–215.

Oller, D. Kimbrough and Rebecca E. Eilers (1988): The role of audition in infant babbling. *Child Development* 59(2): 441–449.

Pine, Julian M., Elena V. M. Lieven, and Caroline F. Rowland (1998): Comparing different models of the development of the English verb category. *Linguistics* 36: 807–830.

Pinker, Steven (1999): *Words and Rules: The Ingredients of Language*. New York: Harper Collins.

Pizzuto, Elena and Maria C. Caselli (1992): The acquisition of Italian morphology: Implications for models of language development. *Journal of Child Language* 19(3): 491–557.

Preissler, Melissa A. and Susan Carey (2005): The role of inferences about referential intent in word learning: Evidence from autism. *Cognition* 97(1): B13–B23.

Rumelhart, David E. and James L. McClelland (1986): On learning the past tenses of English verbs. In: D. Rumelhart, J. McClelland and T. P. Group (eds.), *Parallel Distributed Processing: Explorations in the Microstructure of Cognition*. Cambridge: MIT Press.

Saffran, Jenny R., Richard N. Aslin, and Elissa L. Newport (1996): Statistical learning by 8-month-old infants. *Science* 274(5294), 1926–1928.

Sarilar, Ayşe, Danielle E. Matthews, and Aylin C. Küntay (2013): Hearing relative clauses boosts relative clause usage (and referential clarity) in young Turkish language learners. *Applied Psycholinguistics* FirstView, 1–28.

Slobin, Dan I. and Thomas G. Bever (1982): Children use canonical sentence schemas: A cross-linguistic study of word order and inflections. *Cognition* 12: 229–265.

Snedeker, Jesse, Joy Geren, and Carissa L. Shafto (2012): Disentangling the effects of cognitive development and linguistic expertise: A longitudinal study of the acquisition of English in internationally-adopted children. *Cognitive Psychology* 65(1): 39–76.

Sokolov, Jeffrey L. (1988): Cue validity in Hebrew sentence comprehension. *Journal of Child Language* 15(1): 129–155.

Stephens, Gemma and Matthews, D. (2014): The communicative infant from 0–18 months: The social-cognitive foundations of pragmatic development. In: D. Matthews (ed.), *Pragmatic Development in First Language Acquisition*. Amsterdam: John Benjamins.

Stoll, Sabine, Kirsten Abbot-Smith, and Elena V. M. Lieven (2009): Lexically restricted utterances in Russian, German, and English child-directed speech. *Cognitive Science* 33(1): 75–103.

Tomasello, Michael (2001): Could we please lose the mapping metaphor, please? *Behavioral and Brain Sciences* 24(6): 1119–1120.

Tomasello, Michael (2003): *Constructing a Language: A Usage-Based Theory of Language Acquisition*. Cambridge: Harvard University Press.
Tomasello, Michael and Michelle Barton (1994): Learning words in non-ostensive contexts. *Developmental Psychology* 30(5): 639–650.
Tomasello, Michael, Malinda Carpenter, and Ulf Liszkowski (2007): A new look at infant pointing. *Child Development* 78(3): 705–722.
Van Hoek, Karen (1997): *Anaphora and Conceptual Structure*. Chicago: University of Chicago Press.
Vihman, Marilyn M. (1996): *Phonological Development*. Oxford: Blackwells.
Weist, Richard M. (1983): Prefix versus suffix information processing in the comprehension of tense and aspect. *Journal of Child Language* 10(1): 85–96.
Werker, Janet F. and Chris E. Lalonde (1988): Cross-language speech perception: initial capabilities and developmental change. *Developmental Psychology* 24(5): 672.
Westermann, Gert (1998): Emergent modularity and U-shaped learning in a constructivist neural network learning the English past tense. Paper presented at the Proceedings of the 20th Annual Meeting of the Cognitive Science Society.
Wittgenstein, Ludwig (1958): *Philosophical Investigations*. (trans. G. E. M. Anscombe). Oxford: Blackwell.

Nick C. Ellis and Stefanie Wulff
Chapter 8: Second language acquisition

1 Introduction

This chapter introduces a cognitive-linguistic perspective on second language acquisition (L2A).[1] Over the last 15 or so years, various aspects of L2 acquisition have been examined through a cognitive-linguistic lens, including phonology, morpho-syntax, lexis, syntax, and pragmatics. Likewise, various cognitive-linguistic frameworks including cognitive grammar, metaphor theory, and conceptual blending have been employed in L2 acquisition and teaching research. This chapter deliberately focuses on a construction grammar perspective on L2 acquisition. Robinson and Ellis (2008b), Littlemore (2009), and Tyler (2012) give broader overviews of cognitive-linguistic L2 learning and teaching research.

In traditional generative approaches, language is understood as a modular system: phonology, morphology, syntax, and semantics (and, in some versions of generative grammar, also pragmatics) are distinct subsystems. These modules are largely independent in structure and functioning from other human cognitive processes, and largely uninfluenced by the ways in which humans interact with the world. This view of language as a largely autonomous system comprised of largely autonomous subsystems has stipulated the assumption of a *narrow language faculty* (or *Universal Grammar*) and a *broad language faculty* (Hauser et al. 2002). The broad language faculty comprises cognitive abilities that are required for and assist in, but are not exclusive to, language acquisition and processing, such as the human auditory, motor, and vocal systems, short- and long-term memory, and (joint) attention, among others (Jackendoff 2011).

Cognitive linguistics, in contrast, adopts a non-modular approach to language: language is seen as part of human cognition, with language and cognition being systematically intertwined. Consequently, the focus in cognitive linguistics is on how general human cognitive abilities are manifest in language, and how general cognitive abilities impact language form, change, processing, and acquisition. Similarly, cognitive linguistics is non-modular in the sense that the idea of distinct linguistic subsystems is discarded, including the long-stand-

---

[1] Throughout this chapter, we use the terms *acquisition*, *learning*, and *development* interchangeably.

Nick C. Ellis, Michigan, USA
Stefanie Wulff, Florida, USA

ing distinction between words (the lexicon) and the rules that combine them (grammar). Instead, mastery of a language entails knowing constructions at different levels of complexity and schematization, as well as knowledge of the probabilistic (as opposed to rigid) tendencies underlying their combination. In the following, we outline the implications of these working assumptions of cognitive linguistics for L2A.

In section 2, we provide a summary of how research on multi-word units in language learning and processing calls for a revised understanding of linguistic competence, and how a construction grammar perspective answers that call by shifting the focus to constructions and how they are learnable by both L1 and L2 speakers. In section 3, we outline the components of a constructionist model of language learning. Section 4 briefly discusses the observable differences between first and second language learning, and how a constructionist perspective accounts for them. Section 5 closes with suggestions for future research.

2 Constructions in first and second language acquisition

There is copious evidence from psycholinguistics, corpus linguistics, and cognitive linguistics that language users have rich knowledge of the frequencies of forms and of their sequential dependencies in their native language. Ellis (2002) reviewed evidence that language processing is sensitive to the sequential probabilities of linguistic elements at all levels from phonemes to phrases, and in comprehension as well as in fluency and idiomaticity of speech production. He argued that this sensitivity to sequence information in language processing is evidence of learners' implicit knowledge of memorized sequences of language, and that this knowledge in itself serves as the basis for linguistic systematicity and creativity. The last ten years has seen substantial research confirming native language users' implicit knowledge of the constructions of their language and their probabilities of usage. This is not the place to review this research, instead see Rebuschat and Williams (2012), Ellis (2012a), Trousdale and Hoffman (2013), and chapters by Tremblay and by Divjak and Caldwell-Harris (volume 1).

2.1 Do L2 learners have constructions too?

Such demonstrations of the psychological reality of constructions in native speakers' language raise the question if, and to what extent, constructions also underpin L2 learners' linguistic competence, and whether L2 learners implicitly "tally" and tune their constructional knowledge to construction-specific preferences in terms of the words that preferably occur in those constructions. There is mounting evidence that this is the case, as the following brief review of recent studies illustrates.

Jiang and Nekrasova (2007) examined the representation and processing of formulaic sequences using online grammaticality judgment tasks. L2 English and native English speakers were tested with formulaic and non-formulaic phrases matched for word length and frequency (e.g., *to tell the truth* vs. *to tell the price*). Both native and nonnative speakers responded to the formulaic sequences significantly faster and with fewer errors than they did to nonformulaic sequences. Similarly, Conklin and Schmitt (2007) measured reading times for formulaic sequences versus matched nonformulaic phrases in native and nonnative speakers. The formulaic sequences were read more quickly than the non-formulaic phrases by both groups of participants.

Ellis and Simpson-Vlach (2009) and Ellis et al. Maynard (2008) used four experimental procedures to determine how the corpus-linguistic metrics of frequency and mutual information (MI, a statistical measure of the coherence of strings) are represented implicitly in native and non-native speakers, thus to affect their accuracy and fluency of processing of the formulas of the Academic Formulas List (AFL; Simpson-Vlach and Ellis 2010). The language processing tasks in these experiments were selected to sample an ecologically valid range of language processing skills: spoken and written, production and comprehension, form-focused and meaning-focused. They were: (1) speed of reading and acceptance in a grammaticality judgment task, where half of the items were real phrases in English and half were not; (2) rate of reading and rate of spoken articulation; (3) binding and primed pronunciation – the degree to which reading the beginning of the formula primed recognition of its final word; and (4) speed of comprehension and acceptance of the formula as being appropriate in a meaningful context. Processing in all experiments was affected by various corpus-derived metrics: length, frequency, and mutual information (MI). Frequency was the major determinant for non-native speakers, whereas for native speakers it was predominantly the MI of the formula that determined processability.

Gries and Wulff (2005) showed that advanced German learners of English showed syntactic priming for ditransitive (e.g., *The racing driver showed the helpful mechanic* ...) and prepositional dative (e.g., *The racing driver showed the torn overall* ...) argument structure constructions in an English sentence completion task. Furthermore, they showed that learners' semantic knowledge of argument structure constructions affected their grouping of sentences in a sorting task. More specifically, learners' priming effects closely resembled those of native speakers of English in that they were highly correlated with native speakers' verbal subcategorization preferences whilst uncorrelated with the subcategorization preferences of the German translation equivalents of these verbs. Gries and Wulff (2009) found similar results for gerundial and infinitival complement constructions, and several other studies have demonstrated similar L2 syntactic priming effects (McDonough 2006; McDonough and Mackey 2006; McDonough and Trofimovich 2008). Liang (2002) replicated the semantic sorting experiment with three groups of Chinese learners of English at beginning, intermediate, and advanced proficiency levels, and found a significant positive correlation between the tendency to sort by construction and general proficiency.

Ellis and Ferreira-Junior (2009a, 2009b) analyzed longitudinal data for naturalistic L2 English learners in the *European Science Foundation* corpus (Klein and Perdue 1992; Perdue 1993) to show that naturalistic adult L2 learners used the same verbs in frequent verb argument constructions as are found in their input experience. Indeed, the relative ordering of the types in the input predicted uptake with correlations in excess of $r = 0.90$.

Taken together, these findings argue that grammatical and lexical knowledge are not stored or processed in different mental modules, but rather form a continuum from heavily entrenched and conventionalized formulaic units (unique patterns of high token frequency) to loosely connected but collaborative elements (patterns of high type frequency) (Bybee 2010; Ellis 2008c; Ellis and Larsen-Freeman 2009a, 2009b; Robinson and Ellis 2008a, 2008b). Accordingly, Wulff and Gries propose a constructionist definition of L2 accuracy as "the selection of a construction (in the Goldbergian sense of the term) in its preferred context within a particular target variety and genre" (2011: 70).

Thus, in both L1 and L2, learners are sensitive to the frequencies of occurrence of constructions and their transitional probabilities, and this suggests that they learn these statistics from usage, tallying them implicitly during each processing episode. Linguistic structure *emerges* from the conspiracy of these experiences (Ellis 1998, 2011). "The linguist's task is in fact to study the whole range of repetition in discourse, and in doing so to seek out those regularities which promise interest as incipient sub-systems. Structure, then, in this view is not an overarching set of abstract principles, but more a question of a spreading of systematicity from individual words, phrases, and small sets." (Hopper 1987: 143).

2.2 The role of formulaic language in L1 acquisition (L1A)

Demonstrating skilled language users' knowledge of formulaic language and other constructions is a separate but related matter from demonstrating that formulaic language plays a role in acquisition. It remains contentious in child language research whether children's early language (i) makes use of abstract categories and principles for composing sentences by combining those categories in ordered sequences, or whether it (ii) consists of a repertoire of more concrete constructions or formulas, many based on particular lexical items (e.g., *jump*, *put*, and *give*) rather than abstract syntactic categories like *Verb*. The corresponding theoretical positions are that (i) children don't need to learn grammar because the principles and categories of grammar are innate, requiring only minimal exposure to the language to be 'triggered', or that (ii) the process of syntactic development consists of acquiring a large repertoire of constructions and formulas by statistically inducing increasingly abstract categories on the basis of experience of the types of items that occupy their component parts. The last 20 years has seen considerable research that points to the second alternative. We have neither space nor remit here to dispute the case, and gladly defer to the chapters by Matthews and Krajewski (this volume) as well as other recent reviews (Ambridge and Lieven 2011; Behrens 2009; Dąbrowska 2004; Diessel 2013; Lieven et al. 2003; Tomasello 1992, 2003).

One important evidential source has been dense longitudinal corpora of naturalistic language development that capture perhaps 10 % of children's speech and the input they are exposed to, collected from 2–4 years of age when children are undergoing maximal language development (Behrens 2008; Maslen et al. 2004). Without such dense sampling, it is difficult if not impossible to clearly identify sequences of development of linguistic items of relatively low frequency as they unfold over time (Tomasello and Stahl 2004).

Using dense corpora, Lieven and colleagues have used the 'traceback' method (Dąbrowska and Lieven 2005) of analyzing adult-child conversation to show that very often when a child produces what seems to be a novel utterance, the ingredients for that utterance are to be found earlier in the transcript. That is, the novel utterance has not been generated from scratch but rather a previous sentence has been manipulated, replacing one content word. Even when children are more productive than that, the data-dependent nature of children's underlying knowledge is evidenced in the relations between the frequency of structures in the input and the frequency of children's production of those structures. Children are initially conservative in their language in that their production is more formulaic than openly combinatorial. These are the essential observations for the developmental sequence from formula to limited-scope pattern to creative construction in L1A (Lieven et al. 2003; Tomasello 2000, 2003).

2.3 The role of formulaic language in L2 acquisition

2.3.1 A review of the research

What about when learners *re*construct an L2? The field of SLA showed early interest in multi-word sequences and their potential role in language development. Corder (1973) coined the term *holophrase*, and, in similar spirit, Brown (1973) defined prefabricated routines as unanalyzed multi-word sequences associated with a particular pragmatic function. One of the main research questions for SLA researchers at the time was: do prefabricated routines pose a challenge to the traditional view of language learning as a process by which children start out with small units (morphemes and words) and then gradually combine them into more complex structures? Do children alternatively and/or additionally start out from large(r) chunks of language which they then gradually break down into their component parts? Early studies did not yield conclusive results (a good discussion can be found in Krashen and Scarcella 1978). For example, Hatch (1972) found evidence for both learning strategies in the English production data of a 4-year old Chinese boy. Hakuta (1974, 1976), based on data from a 5-year-old Japanese learner of English, argued in favor of a more fine-grained distinction between prefabricated routines and prefabricated patterns, that is, low-scope patterns that have at least one variable slot. Wong-Fillmore's (1976) dissertation project was one of the first to track more than one child over a longer period of time; her analysis suggested that children do in fact start out with prefabricated patterns which they gradually break down into their component parts in search for the rules governing their L2, which, in turn, ultimately enables them to use language creatively.

There were only a few early studies on adult L2 learners (Wray 2002: 172–198 provides a detailed overview). The general consensus, however, was that while adult L2 learners may occasionally employ prefabricated language, there was less evidence than in children's data that knowledge of prefabricated language would foster grammatical development in adult L2A. Hanania and Gradman (1977), for instance, studied Fatmah, a native speaker of Arabic. Fatmah was 19 years old at the time of the study, and she had received only little formal education in her native language. When speaking English, Fatmah used several routines that were tied to specific pragmatic situations; however, the researchers found her largely unable to analyze these routines into their component parts. Similarly, Schumann (1978), who investigated data from several adult L2 learners with different native language backgrounds, found only little evidence in favor of prefabricated language use in the first place, or any positive effect of prefabricated language knowledge on language development for that matter.

A slightly different picture emerged in Schmidt's (1983) well-known research on Wes, a native speaker of Japanese who immigrated to Hawaii in his early thirties. Wes seemed to make extensive use of prefabricated routines. However, while this significantly boosted Wes' fluency, his grammatical competence remained low. Ellis (1984), looking at the use of prefabricated language in an instructional setting, suggested that there is considerable individual variation in learners' ability to make the leap from prefabricated routines to the underlying grammatical rules they exemplify. Krashen and Scarcella (1978) were outright pessimistic regarding adult learners' ability to even retain prefabricated routines, and cautioned against focusing adult learners' attention on prefabricated language because "[t]he outside world for adults is nowhere near as predictable as the linguistic environment around Fillmore's children was" (Krashen and Scarcella 1978: 298).

In the light of developments in child language acquisition, Ellis (1996, 2002) revisited the issue, asking whether a common pattern of developmental sequence in both L1A and L2A might be from formulaic phrases to limited scope slot-and-frame patterns to fully productive schematic patterns. Ellis (2003) phrased the argument in terms of constructions rather than formulas. There are subsequent longitudinal studies in support of this sequence in L2A, though the available corpora are far from dense.

In an extensive study of secondary school pupils learning French as a foreign language in England, Myles (2004; Myles et al. 1999) analyzed longitudinal corpora of oral language in 16 beginning learners ([11–14 years old], tracked over the first 2 years, using 13 oral tasks) and 60 intermediate learners (20 classroom learners in each of years 9, 10 and 11 studied cross-sectionally using four oral tasks). These data showed that multimorphemic sequences, which go well beyond learners' grammatical competence, are very common in early L2 production. Notwithstanding that these sequences contain such forms as finite verbs, wh-questions and clitics, Myles denied this as evidence for functional projections from the start of L2A because these properties are not initially present outside of chunks. Analyses of inflected verb forms suggested that early productions containing them were formulaic chunks. These structures, sometimes syntactically highly complex (e.g., in the case of interrogatives), cohabited for extended periods of time with very simple sentences, usually verbless, or when a verb was present, this was normally untensed. Likewise, clitics first appeared in chunks containing tensed verbs, suggesting that it is through these chunks that learners acquire them. Myles characterizes these early grammars as consisting of lexical projections and formulaic sequences, showing no evidence of functional categories. "Chunks do not become discarded; they remain grammatically advanced until the grammar catches up, and it is this process of resolving the tension between these grammatically advanced chunks and the current grammar which drives the learning process forward" (Myles 2004: 152). The study also investigated the development of chunks within individual learners over time, showing a clear correlation between chunk use and linguistic development:

> In the beginners' corpus, at one extreme, we had learners who failed to memorize chunks after the first round of elicitation; these were also the learners whose interlanguage remained primarily verbless, and who needed extensive help in carrying out the tasks. At the other extreme, we had learners whose linguistic development was most advanced by the end of the study. These were also the learners who, far from discarding chunks, were seen to be actively working on them throughout the data-collection period. These chunks seem to provide these learners with a databank of complex structures beyond their current grammar, which they keep working on until they can make their current generative grammar compatible with them. (Myles 2004: 153)

Eskildsen and Cadierno (2007) investigated the development of *do*-negation by a Mexican learner of English. *Do*-negation learning was found to be initially reliant on one specific instantiation of the pattern *I don't know*, which thereafter gradually expanded to be used with other verbs and pronouns as the underlying knowledge seemed to become increasingly abstract, as reflected in token and type frequencies.

Mellow (2008) describes a longitudinal case study of a 12-year-old Spanish learner of English, Ana, who wrote stories describing 15 different wordless picture books during a 201-day period. The findings indicate that Ana began by producing only a few types of complex constructions that were lexically-selected by a small set of verbs which gradually seeded a growing range of constructions.

Sugaya and Shirai (2009) describe the acquisition of Japanese tense-aspect morphology in L1 Russian learner Alla. In her ten-month longitudinal data, some verbs (e.g., *siru* 'come to know,' *tuku* 'be attached') were produced exclusively with the imperfective aspect marker -*te i-(ru)*, while other verbs (e.g., *iku* 'go,' *tigau* 'differ') were rarely used with -*te i-(ru)*. Even though these verbs can be used in any of the four basic forms, Alla demonstrated a very strong verb-specific preference. Sugaya and Shirai followed this up with a larger cross-sectional study of 61 intermediate and advanced learners (based on the ACTFL scale), who were divided into 34 lower and 27 higher proficiency groups using grammaticality judgment tasks. The lower proficiency learners used the individual verbs in verb-specific ways, and this tendency was stronger for the verbs denoting resultative state meaning with -*te i-(ru)* (e.g., achievement verbs) than the verbs denoting progressive meaning with -*te i-(ru)* (e.g., activity, accomplishment, and semelfactive verbs). Sugaya and Shirai concluded that the intermediate learners begin with item-based learning and low scope patterns and that these formulas allow them to gradually gain control over tense-aspect.

Nevertheless, they also considered how memory-based and rule-based processes might co-exist for particular linguistic forms, and that linguistic knowledge should be considered a "formulaic-creative continuum".

On the other hand, there are studies of L2 that have set out to look for this sequence and found less compelling evidence.

Bardovi-Harlig (2002) studied the emergence of future expression involving *will* and *going to* in a longitudinal study of 16 adult L2 English learners (mean length of observation 11.5 months; 1,576 written texts, mainly journal entries, and 175 oral texts, either guided conversational interviews or elicited narratives based on silent films). The data showed that future *will* emerges first and greatly outnumbers the use of tokens of *going to*. Bardovi-Harlig described how the rapid spread of *will* to a variety of verbs suggests that, "for most learners, there is either little initial formulaic use of *will* or that it is so brief that it cannot be detected in this corpus" (Bardovi-Harlig 2002: 192). There was some evidence of formulaicity in early use of *going to*: "For 5 of the 16 learners, the use of *I am going to write* stands out. Their production over the months of observation show that the formula breaks down into smaller parts, from the full *I am going to write about* to the core *going to* where not only the verb but also person and number vary. This seems to be an example of learner production moving along the formulaic-creative continuum" (Bardovi-Harlig 2002: 197). But other learners showed greater variety of use of *going to*, with different verbs and different person-number forms, from its earliest appearance in the diary. Bardovi-Harlig concludes that "although the use of formulaic language seems to play a limited role in the expression of future, its influence is noteworthy" (Bardovi-Harlig 2002: 198).

Eskildsen (2009) analyzed longitudinal oral L2 classroom interaction for the use of *can* by one student, Carlo. *Can* first appeared in the data in the formula *I can write*. But Eskildsen noted how formulas are interactionally and locally contextualized, which means that they may possibly be transitory in nature, their deployment over time being occasioned by specific recurring usage events.

2.3.2 Methodological considerations

The outcome of such studies searching for developmental sequences seeded by use of formulaic patterns rests on a range of factors:

Firstly, regarding methodology, data has to be dense enough to identify repeated uses at the time of emergence (Tomasello and Stahl 2004). The use of formulas and constructions are determined by context, function, genre and register. If the elicitation tasks vary, the chance of sampling the same formula and its potential variants diminishes accordingly.

Secondly, they may vary as a function of L1A vs. L2A. L1A may indeed be more formulaic than L2 acquisition. When child learners are learning about language from formulaic frames (Ambridge and Lieven 2011; Mintz 2003; Tomasello 2003) and the analysis of sequences of words (Elman 1990; Kiss 1973; Redington and Chater 1998), they are learning from scratch about more abstract categories such as verb, pronoun, preposition, noun, transitive frame, etc. It is debatable whether the units of early L1A are words at all (Peters 1983). Adult L2 learners already know about the existence of these units, categories, and linguistic structures. They expect that there will be words and constructions in the L2 which correspond to such word classes and frames. Once they have identified them, or even, once they have searched them out and actively learned such key vocabulary, they are more likely therefore to attempt creative construction, swopping these elements into corresponding slots in frames.

Thirdly, as in all other areas of language processing, recognition of formulas is easier than production. As described in section 2.1, Ellis and Ferreira-Junior (2009a, 2009b) showed that naturalistic adult L2 learners used the same verbs in frequent verb argument constructions as are found in their input experience, with the relative ordering of the types in the input predicting uptake with correlations in excess of $r = 0.90$. Nevertheless, while they would accurately produce short simple formulaic sequences such as *come in* or *I went to the shop*, structurally more complex constructions were often produced in the simplified form of the Basic Variety (Klein and Perdue 1992; Perdue 1993) which involves a pragmatic topic-comment word ordering, where old information goes first and new information follows.

Fourthly, transfer from the L1 is also likely to affect the process (Granger 2001). The more learners attempt word-by-word translation from their L1, the more they deviate from L2 idiomaticity.

Finally, amount and type of exposure is bound to play a role. Children are naturalistic language learners from thousands of hours of interaction and input. While some adults learn naturalistically, others take grammar-rich courses. Dictionaries and grammar books do not provide naturalistic input, nor do they encourage fluent idiomatic expression of formulaic speech. Nevertheless, Myles (2004) demonstrates the viability of this sequence of acquisition even for classroom foreign language acquisition.

2.3.3 Caveat and conclusion

A common misunderstanding about the role of formulaic sequences in language acquisition warrants a caveat here. The fact that formulaic sequences play roles in the development of more creative competence does not imply that all apparently formulaic strings so serve. Far from it: Some formulaic sequences are readily learnable by dint of being highly frequent and prototypical in their functionality – *how are you?*, *it's lunch time*, *I don't know*, *I am going to write about*, and the like. These are likely candidates as construction seeds.

Other formulaic sequences are not readily learnable – these are of low frequency, often indeed rare, and many are non-transparent and idiomatic in their interpretation (e.g., *once in a blue moon*). As idioms they must be learned as such. However, learners require considerable language experience before they encounter these once, never mind sufficient times to commit them to memory (Ellis 2008b). This is why learners typically do not achieve nativelike idiomaticity (Granger 2001; Pawley and Syder 1983). These low frequency, low transparency formulas are targets for learning rather than seeds of learning. Hence the observations that learner language is often light in frequency of formulaic language compared to native norms (Granger 2001) and that acquisition of nativelike targets can be challenging (Pawley and Syder 1983).

Is the notion of language acquisition being seeded by formulaic phrases and yet learner language being formula-light 'having your cake and eating it too'? Pawley and Syder (1983) thought not. While much of their classic article concentrated on the difficulty L2 learners had in achieving nativelike formulaic selection and nativelike fluency, they nevertheless state "Indeed, we believe that memorized sentences are the normal building blocks of fluent spoken discourse, and at the same time, that they provide models for the creation of many (partly) new sequences which are memorable and in their turn enter into the stock of familiar uses" (1983: 208). Ellis (2012b) further examines this apparent paradox whereby large-scale analyses of learner corpora show that L2 learners typically do not achieve nativelike formulaicity and idiomaticity (Granger 2001; Pawley and Syder 1983) while, at the same time, formulas can provide learners with a databank of complex structures beyond their current grammar which can drive the learning process forward.

The most balanced conclusion is that linguistic knowledge is a formulaic-creative continuum. In this light, how are constructions acquired?

3 Components of a constructionist model of language learning

Constructionist accounts of language acquisition involve the distributional analysis of the language stream and the parallel analysis of contingent perceptual activity, with abstract constructions being learned from the conspiracy of concrete exemplars of usage following statistical learning mechanisms (Rebuschat and Williams 2012) relating input and learner cognition. Psychological analyses of this learning of constructions as form-meaning pairs is informed by the literature on the associative learning of cue-outcome contingencies where the usual determinants include: factors relating to the form such as frequency and salience; factors relating to the interpretation such as significance in the comprehension of the overall utterance, prototypicality, generality, redundancy, and surprise value; factors relating to the contingency of form and function; and factors relating to learner attention, such as automaticity, transfer, overshadowing, and blocking (Ellis 2002, 2003, 2006, 2008a, 2008b). These various psycholinguistic factors conspire in the acquisition and use of any linguistic construction. This section briefly considers each in turn.

3.1 Frequency of construction in the input

According to usage-based approaches to language, frequency of exposure promotes learning and cognitive entrenchment. Type and token frequency play different roles. Token frequency is the frequency with which a particular construction (i.e., a particular phonotactic sequence, morpheme, or syntactic frame) occurs in the input. Type frequency, in contrast, refers to the number of distinct realizations of a given construction. For example, the English past tense morpheme – *ed* has a very high type frequency: in any sizeable data sample of English, it occurs with thousands of different verbs. Irregular past tense forms as in *blew*, *sang*, or *rode*, on the contrary, have low type frequency: they occur only with a comparatively restricted number of verbs. Type frequency is one indicator of the productivity of a construction because high type frequency allows the hearer to parse the construction in question and results in a stronger schematic representation of the form, which in turn renders it more available not only for reuse, but also novel uses (Bybee and Hopper 2001). Bybee (2006: 15) provides the following example:

> If *happiness* is learned by someone who knows no related words, there is no way to infer that it has two morphemes. If *happy* is also learned, then the learner could hypothesize that – *ness* is a suffix, but only if it occurs on other adjectives would its status as a suffix become established. Thus a certain degree of type frequency is needed to uncover the structure of words and phrases.

High token frequency may in fact yield the opposite effect by promoting the conservation of specific realizations of a construction (see Bybee 2006 for a detailed discussion of the conserving, form-reducing, and autonomy-stipulating effects of high token frequency).

3.2 Distribution of construction in the input

In accordance with Goldberg et al. (2004), research suggests that acquisition benefits from initial exposure to massive, low-variance input that is centered around prototypical realizations (or exemplars) of the target construction (Elio and Anderson 1981, 1984). This focused and stereotypical input allows the learner to induce what accounts for the majority of the category members; continuing exposure to the full breadth of exemplar types later defines category boundaries (Nosofsky 1988). Both childrens' input and output in Goldberg et al. (2004) reflected a Zipfian distribution. According to Zipf's Law (Zipf 1935), in natural language, the frequency of a word is inversely proportional to its rank in a frequency table: the most frequent word occurs about twice as often as the second most frequent word, three times as often as the third most frequent word, and so on. Importantly, Goldberg et al. (2004) showed that Zipf's Law does not only hold when counting words in a given sample of naturalistic speech – it also seems to hold for verbs *within* a given construction. According to Goldberg et al., this Zipfian distribution of the childrens' input plays a significant role in acquisition: one specific typical verb is made salient by being extremely frequent in the input and serves as the "pathbreaking verb" in the process of category formation (see also Ninio 1999, 2006). Ellis and Ferreira-Junior (2009a, 2009b) examined a corpus of naturalistic L2A and likewise confirmed that the type/token ratio of the verbs in argument structure constructions is Zipfian. Furthermore, they were able to show that, as Tomasello (2003) has argued for L1A, the most frequent and prototypical verbs seem to act as "verb islands" around which the verb argument construction is gradually built up. Ellis and O'Donnell (2012) and Römer, O'Donnell, and Ellis (2015) confirm the Zipfian distribution of verb argument constructions in large-scale analyses of English language usage.

3.3 Recency of construction in the input

Research in cognitive psychology has taught us that three key factors influence the activation of memory schemata: frequency, recency, and context (Anderson 1989; Anderson and Schooler 2000). Recency, also referred to as priming or persistence, is an implicit memory effect: exposure to a stimulus affects a response to a later stimulus. Recency has been shown to impact processing at the level of phonology, conceptual representation, lexical choice, and syntax

(McDonough 2006; McDonough and Mackey 2006; McDonough and Trofimovich 2008).

3.4 Salience, redundancy, and perception of form of the construction

The general perceived strength of a stimulus is referred to as its salience. As the Rescorla-Wagner (1972) model of associative learning encapsulates, the amount of learning induced from an experience of a cue-outcome association depends crucially upon the salience of the cue and the importance of the outcome: low salience cues are less readily learned. Many grammatical functors in English have low salience in the input, for example, inflections like the third person singular – *s* morpheme. It is not surprising, then, that it is these grammatical symbols in particular that L2 learners tend to have most difficulty with.

The Rescorla-Wagner (1972) model also accounts for the fact that redundant cues tend not to be acquired. Many grammatical constructions are not only low in salience, but also are redundant in the listener's understanding of an utterance in that they compete with more salient psychophysical forms. For example, third person singular – *s* marks present tense, but *today* is more salient in the input and effectively overshadows and blocks acquisition of the morpheme (Ellis 2006, 2008b; Ellis and Sagarra 2010b, Goldschneider and DeKeyser 2001). Generally, inflectional case markings such as tense are often accompanied by (more salient) adverbs that indicate temporal reference. Accordingly, L2 learners typically prefer adverbial over inflectional cues to tense, a phenomenon that has been well-documented in longitudinal studies of naturalistic L2A (Dietrich et al. 1995; Bardovi-Harlig 2000), training experiments (Ellis and Sagarra 2010b, 2011), and studies of L2 language processing (VanPatten 2006; Ellis and Sagarra 2010a).

3.5 Prototypicality of function

Categories have graded structure: some members are better exemplars of the category than others. In Prototype Theory (Rosch and Mervis 1975; Rosch et al. 1976), the prototype of a category is defined as an idealized mental representation of the best example of that category in the sense of encapsulating the most representative features of that category. The prototype serves as the gold standard against which exemplars are classified as more or less central members of the category. For example, people readily classify sparrows as birds: sparrows are good examples of the category BIRD because they incorporate various representative attributes (they are average in size, beak size, color, etc.). In contrast, people take considerably longer to confirm that albatrosses are birds too. Prototypical exemplars are judged faster and more accurately even upon first encounter (Posner and Keele 1970) – a sparrow will be instantly recognized as a bird even by a person who has never seen a sparrow before. Prototypicality and token frequency interact: the higher the token frequency of an exemplar, the higher the likelihood of this exemplar becoming the prototype. Accordingly, Goldberg et al. (2004) showed that in L1A, children's first uses of verbs, in particular verb-argument constructions, are often semantically typical generic verb types that are at the center of the construction meaning (*go* for verb-locative, *put* for verb-object-locative, and *give* for the ditransitive). Likewise for L2A, Ellis and Ferreira-Junior (2009a) showed that the verbs first used by L2 learners are prototypical and generic in function: *go* dominates in the verb-locative construction (*She went home*), *put* in the verb-object-locative construction (*She put the groceries in the bag*), and *give* in the verb-object-object construction (*He gave her a flower*).

3.6 Contingency of form-function mapping

Psychological research on associative learning has long recognized that next to the form and the function of a given exemplar to be categorized and learned, the contingency of the form-function mapping plays a role as well (Shanks 1995). Let us return to the example of the category BIRD. All birds have eyes and wings, and so we encounter these features equally frequently. However, while many other animals have eyes, only birds have wings. That renders wings a much more reliable (or *distinctive*) cue to membership in the category BIRD than eyes. In other words, whether or not a given exemplar qualifies as a bird is much more contingent on its having the features "wings" than the feature "eyes". Such form-function mapping contingency is the driving force of all associative learning, which is often correspondingly referred to as *contingency learning*. One early powerful demonstration of contingency learning was Rescorla's (1968) classic conditioning study with rats. Rescorla found that if one removed the contingency between the conditioned stimulus and the unconditioned stimulus by preserving the temporal pairing between the two, yet adding trials where the unconditioned stimulus appeared on its own, the animals did not develop a conditioned response to the conditioned stimulus. Contingency, and its associated aspects of predictive value, information gain, and statistical association, have been at the core of learning theory ever since, including theories of L2A such as MacWhinney's *Competition Model* (MacWhinney 1987a, 1987b, 1997, 2001). Current research in cognitive and corpus linguistics focuses on the question which specific association measures are most predictive of linguistic representation, acquisition, and processing (Divjak and Gries 2012; Gries and Divjak 2012). Several studies have applied a Fisher Yates exact test as a measure of contingency of verb-complement construction pairings (Gries and Wulff 2009) and verb-tense/aspect morphology associations in learner data (Wulff et al. 2009); Ellis and Ferreira-Junior (2009b) used a directional association measure, DeltaP, to demonstrate effects of form-function contingency on the L2 acquisition of verb argument constructions (see Ellis 2006 for the use of this measure in research in human associative learning, Schmid 2010 supporting its use as a proxy for cognitive entrenchment, and Gries 2013 for its applications in collocation research); Boyd and Goldberg (2009) used conditional probabilities to analyze contingency effects in their L1A data of verb argument constructions. For a comprehensive contrastive analysis of corpus-based association measures and their correlation with behavioral data, see Wiechmann (2008).

4 First vs. second language learning: (re-)constructing a language

Countless studies in cognitive linguistics have demonstrated that language is grounded in our experience and our physical embodiment (Langacker 1987, 2000; Taylor 2002; Croft and Cruse 2004; Robinson and Ellis 2008b). The meaning of words in a given language, and how speakers combine them, depends on speakers' perception and categorization of, and interaction with, the real world around them. How speakers perceive, categorize, and interact with their environment is in turn a function of the human cognitive apparatus and bodily make-up. For example, the meaning of verbs like *push*, *poke*, *pull*, *hold* and so on, can only be fully distinguished if the sensori-motor features they encode, like hand posture, hand motions, force, aspect, and goals are taken into consideration (Bailey et al. 1997; Bergen and Chang 2005; Lakoff and Johnson 1999; Feldman 2006). Similarly, spatial language understanding is firmly grounded in our visual processing system as it relates to motor action (Regier and Carlson 2002; Conventry and Garrod 2004), multiple constraints relating to our knowledge about objects, dynamic-kinematic routines, and functional geometric analyses. What prepositions like *under*, *over*, *in*, or *on* mean is not fixed and steady, but dynamically construed on-line (Elman 2004; Spivey 2006; McRae et al. 2006). How exactly a given meaning is construed depends in large parts on where the language user's attention is being directed. Talmy (2000a, 2000b) describes the building blocks of the attentional system of language; each of around 50 building blocks, or factors, involves a particular linguistic mechanism that increases or decreases attention of a certain type of linguistic entity. Learning a language, then, means learning these various attention-directing mechanisms, which requires L1 learners to develop an attentional system in the first place, and L2 learners to reconfigure the attentional biases of having acquired their first language. In consequence, language cannot be taught through rules or rote-learning alone – ideally, it is learned in situated action.

Languages lead their speakers to experience different 'thinking for speaking' and thus to construe experience in different ways (Slobin 1996). Cross-linguistic research shows how different languages lead speakers to prioritize different aspects of events in narrative discourse (Berman and Slobin 1994). Because languages achieve these attention-directing outcomes in different ways, learning another language involves learning how to construe the world like natives of the L2, i.e., learning alternative ways of thinking for speaking (Cadierno 2008; Brown and Gullberg 2008, 2010) or 'rethinking for speaking' (Ellis and Cadierno 2009; Robinson and Ellis 2008a). Transfer theories such as the Contrastive Analysis Hypothesis (Lado 1957, 1964; James 1980; Gass and Selinker 1983) hold that L2A can be easier where languages use these attention-directing devices in the same way, and more difficult when they use them differently. To the extent that the constructions in L2 are similar to those of L1, L1 constructions can serve as the basis for the L2 constructions, but, because even similar constructions across languages differ in detail, the complete acquisition of the L2 pattern is hindered by the L1 pattern (Odlin 1989, 2008).

As Slobin (1993: 242) notes, "For the child, the construction of the grammar and the construction of semantic/pragmatic concepts go hand-in-hand. For the adult, construction of the grammar often requires a revision of semantic/pragmatic concepts, along with what may well be a more difficult task of perceptual identification of the relevant morphological elements". The human mind is built to integrate new information in a way that is maximally compatible with established knowledge – consequently, L1-attuned expectations and selective attention bias L2 acquisition.

5 Future priorities

Robinson and Ellis (2008b) provide a detailed list of issues in cognitive linguistics and L2 acquisition; we highlight just a few here.

A constructionist perspective, in particular, calls for thorough empirical analysis of language usage. This is the evidence from which learners induce how language works. We need to understand its latent structures. O'Donnell and Ellis (2010) and Römer et al. (2013) outline a proposal to describe a usage-based verbal grammar of English, to analyze the ways verb argument constructions map form and meaning, and to provide an inventory of the verbs that exemplify constructions, their lexical constituency, and their frequencies.

A constructionist perspective also calls for thorough empirical analysis of the syntactic and semantic bootstrapping of constructions. Given the demonstrated value of longitudinal corpus research in child language acquisition, corresponding corpora of L2A are needed that allow researchers to empirically investigate the adult L2A comprehensively, longitudinally, and cross-linguistically (Ortega and Iberri-Shea 2005; Collins and Ellis 2009).

The cognitive commitment we emphasize throughout this chapter demands converging evidence from corpus data and behavioral data (Ellis 2012a; Gries 2012). Only in combination will we be able to fully understand the interplay of input and cognition in shaping L2A. This holds in particular for recent discussions of the nature and relevance of frequency and form-function contingency effects in language acquisition.

Cognitive linguistics emphasizes how multiple factors at different scales jointly affect L2 acquisition: cognition, consciousness, experience, embodiment, brain, self, human interaction, society, culture, and history are all inextricably intertwined in rich, complex, and dynamic ways. Researching how these diverse factors interact dynamically in the emergence of linguistic structure will remain a priority and a challenge for some time to come. Ellis and Larsen-Freeman (2009a) provide an illustration of how computer simulations can inform this question for argument structure constructions. More generally, emergentism, complex adaptive systems theory, dynamic systems theory, exemplar theory, and related approaches provide means for modeling language development and language as a complex adaptive system (Ellis and Larsen-Freeman 2006a, 2006b, 2009b; Ellis 2008a; Beckner et al. 2009). Cognitive-linguistic and broader usage-based approaches have done much to inform our understanding of L2A. Nevertheless, the research agenda is long. Much remains to be done, both locally and within the still broader family of the cognitive sciences.

6 References

Ambridge, Ben and Elena Lieven (2011): *Child Language Acquisition: Contrasting Theoretical Approaches*. Cambridge: Cambridge University Press.

Anderson, John R. (1989): A rational analysis of human memory. In: E. Tulving, H. L. Roediger and F. I. M. Craik (eds.), *Varieties of Memory and Consciousness: Essays in Honour of Endel Tulving*, 195–210. Hillsdale: Lawrence Erlbaum.

Anderson, John R. and Lael J. Schooler (2000): The adaptive nature of memory. In: E. Tulving and F. I. M. Craik (eds.), *The Oxford Handbook of Memory*, 557–570. London: Oxford University Press.

Bailey, David, Jerome Feldman, Srini Narayanan, and George Lakoff (1997): Modelling embodied lexical development. *Chicago Linguistics Society* 19: 19–24.

Bardovi-Harlig, Kathleen (2000): *Tense and Aspect in Second Language Acquisition: Form, Meaning, and Use*. Oxford: Blackwell.

Bardovi-Harlig, Kathleen (2002): A new starting point? *Studies in Second Language Acquisition* 24: 189–198.

Beckner, Clay, Richard Blythe, Joan Bybee, Morton H. Christiansen, William Croft, Nick C. Ellis, John Holland, Jinyun Ke, Diane Larsen-Freeman, and Thomas Schoenemann (2009): Language is a complex adaptive system. *Language Learning* 59: 1–26.

Behrens, Heike (ed.) (2008): *Corpora in Language Acquisition Research: Finding Structure in Data*. Amsterdam: John Benjamins.

Behrens, Heike (2009): Usage-based and emergentist approaches to language acquisition. *Linguistics* 47: 383–411.

Bergen, Benjamin and Nancy Chang (2005): Embodied construction grammar in simulation-based language understanding. In: J. Östman and M. Fried (eds.), *Construction Grammars: Cognitive Grounding and Theoretical Extensions*, 147–190. Amsterdam: John Benjamins.

Berman, Ruth A. and Dan I. Slobin (eds.) (1994): *Relating Events in Narrative: A Cross-linguistic Developmental Study*. Hillsdale: Lawrence Erlbaum.

Boyd, Jeremy K. and Adele E. Goldberg (2009): Input effects within a constructionist framework. *Modern Language Journal* 93: 418–429.

Brown, Amanda and Marianne Gullberg (2010): Changes in encoding of path of motion after acquisition of a second language. *Cognitive Linguistics* 21: 263–286.

Brown, Amanda and Marianne Gullberg (2008): Bidirectional crosslinguistic influence in L1-L2 encoding of manner in speech and gesture. *Studies in Second Language Acquisition* 30: 225–251.

Brown, Roger (1973): *A First Language*. Cambridge: Harvard University Press.

Bybee, Joan (2006): *Frequency of Use and the Organization of Language*. Oxford: Oxford University Press.

Bybee, Joan and Paul Hopper (eds.) (2001): *Frequency and the Emergence of Linguistic Structure*. Amsterdam: John Benjamins.

Bybee, Joan (2010): *Language, Usage, and Cognition*. Cambridge: Cambridge University Press.

Cadierno, Teresa (2008): Learning to talk about motion in a foreign language. In: P. Robinson and N. C. Ellis (eds.), *Handbook of Cognitive Linguistics and Second Language Acquisition*, 239–275. London: Routledge.

Collins, Laura and Nick. C. Ellis (eds.) (2009): Input and second language construction learning: Frequency, form, and function. *Modern Language Journal* 93.

Conklin, Kathy and Norbert Schmitt (2007): Formulaic sequences: Are they processed more quickly than nonformulaic language by native and nonnative speakers? *Applied Linguistics* 28: 1–18.

Corder, S. Pit (1973): *Introducing Applied Linguistics*. New York: Penguin.

Coventry, Kenny R. and Simon C. Garrod (2004): *Saying, Seeing and Acting: The Psychological Semantics of Spatial Prepositions*. Hove/New York: Psychology Press.

Croft, William and Alan D. Cruse (2004): *Cognitive Linguistics*. Cambridge: Cambridge University Press.

Dąbrowska, Ewa (2004): *Language, Mind and Brain: Some Psychological and Neurological Constraints on Theories of Grammar*. Edinburgh: Edinburgh University Press.

Dąbrowska, Ewa and Elena Lieven (2005): Towards a lexically specific grammar of children's question constructions. *Cognitive Linguistics* 16: 437–474.

Diessel, Holger (2013): Construction grammar and first language acquisition. In G. Trousdale and T. Hoffmann (eds.), *The Oxford Handbook of Construction Grammar*, 347–364. Oxford: Oxford University Press.

Dietrich, Rainer, Wolfgang Klein, and Colette Noyau (eds.) (1995): *The Acquisition of Temporality in a Second Language*. Amsterdam: John Benjamins.

Divjak, Dagmar and Catherine Cardwell-Harris (volume 1): Frequency and entrenchment. Berlin/Boston: De Gruyter Mouton.

Divjak, Dagmar S. and Stefan Th. Gries (eds.) (2012): *Frequency Effects in Language Representation*. Berlin/New York: Mouton de Gruyter.

Elio, Renee and John R. Anderson (1981): The effects of category generalizations and instance similarity on schema abstraction. *Journal of Experimental Psychology: Human Learning and Memory* 7: 397–417.

Elio, Renee and John R. Anderson (1984): The effects of information order and learning mode on schema abstraction. *Memory and Cognition* 12: 20–30.

Ellis, Nick C. (1996): Sequencing in SLA: Phonological memory, chunking, and points of order. *Studies in Second Language Acquisition* 18: 91–126.

Ellis, Nick C. (1998): Emergentism, connectionism and language learning. *Language Learning* 48: 631–664.

Ellis, Nick C. (2002): Frequency effects in language processing: A review with implications for theories of implicit and explicit language acquisition. *Studies in Second Language Acquisition* 24: 143–188.

Ellis, Nick C. (2003): Constructions, chunking, and connectionism: The emergence of second language structure. In: C. J. Doughty and M. H. Long (eds.), *Handbook of Second Language Acquisition*, 33–68. Oxford: Blackwell.

Ellis, Nick C. (2006): Language acquisition as rational contingency learning. *Applied Linguistics* 27: 1–24.

Ellis, Nick C. (2008a): Usage-based and form-focused language acquisition: The associative learning of constructions, learned-attention, and the limited L2 endstate. In: P. Robinson and N. C. Ellis (eds.), *Handbook of Cognitive Linguistics and Second Language Acquisition*, 372–405. London: Routledge.

Ellis, Nick C. (2008b): Optimizing the input: Frequency and sampling in usage-based and form-focussed learning. In: M. H. Long and C. J. Doughty (eds.), *Handbook of Second and Foreign Language Teaching*, 139–158. Oxford: Blackwell.

Ellis, Nick C. (2008c): Phraseology: The periphery and the heart of language. In: F. Meunier and S. Granger (eds.), *Phraseology in Language Learning and Teaching*, 1–13. Amsterdam: John Benjamins.

Ellis, Nick C. (2011): The emergence of language as a complex adaptive system. In: J. Simpson (ed.), *Handbook of Applied Linguistics*, 666–679. London: Routledge/Taylor Francis.

Ellis, Nick C. (2012a): Formulaic language and second language acquisition: Zipf and the phrasal teddy bear. *Annual Review of Applied Linguistics* 32: 17–44.

Ellis, Nick C. (2012b): What can we count in language, and what counts in language acquisition, cognition, and use? In: S. Th. Gries and D. S. Divjak (eds.), *Frequency Effects in Language Learning and Processing*, 7–34. Berlin: Mouton de Gruyter.

Ellis, Nick C. and Diane Larsen Freeman (eds.) (2006a): Language emergence: Implications for Applied Linguistics. *Applied Linguistics* 27.

Ellis, Nick C. and Diane Larsen Freeman (2006b): Language emergence: Implications for Applied Linguistics (Introduction to the Special Issue). *Applied Linguistics* 27: 558–589.

Ellis, Nick C. and Diane Larsen-Freeman (2009a): Constructing a second language: Analyses and computational simulations of the emergence of linguistic constructions from usage. *Language Learning* 59: 93–128.

Ellis, Nick C. and Diane Larsen Freeman (eds.) (2009b): Language as a complex adaptive system. *Language Learning* 59.

Ellis, Nick C. and Fernando Ferreira-Junior (2009a): Construction learning as a function of frequency, frequency distribution, and function. *Modern Language Journal* 93: 370–386.

Ellis, Nick C. and Fernando Ferreira-Junior (2009b): Constructions and their acquisition: Islands and the distinctiveness of their occupancy. *Annual Review of Cognitive Linguistics* 7: 188–221.

Ellis, Nick C. and Matthew B. O'Donnell (2012): Statistical construction learning: Does a Zipfian problem space ensure robust language learning? In P. Rebuschat and J. N. Williams (eds.), *Statistical Learning and Language Acquisition*, 265–304. Berlin: Mouton de Gruyter.

Ellis, Nick C. and Nuria Sagarra (2010a): Learned attention effects in L2 temporal reference: The first hour and the next eight semesters. *Language Learning* 60: 85–108.

Ellis, Nick C. and Nuria Sagarra (2010b): The bounds of adult language acquisition: Blocking and learned attention. *Studies in Second Language Acquisition* 32: 1–28.

Ellis, Nick C. and Nuria Sagarra (2011): Blocking and learned attention in adult language acquisition: A replication and generalization study and meta-analysis. *Studies in Second Language Acquisition* 33: 589–624.

Ellis, Nick C. and Rita Simpson-Vlach (2009): Formulaic language in native speakers: Triangulating psycholinguistics, corpus linguistics, and education. *Corpus Linguistics and Linguistic Theory* 5: 61–78.

Ellis, Nick C., Rita Simpson-Vlach, and Carson Maynard (2008): Formulaic language in native and second-language speakers: Psycholinguistics, corpus linguistics, and TESOL. *TESOL Quarterly* 42: 375–396.

Ellis, Nick C. and Teresa Cadierno (eds.) (2009): Constructing a second language. Special section. *Annual Review of Cognitive Linguistics* 7: 111–290.

Ellis, Rod (1984): *Classroom Second Language Development*. Oxford: Pergamon.

Elman, Jeffrey L. (1990): Finding structure in time. *Cognitive Science* 14: 179–211.

Elman, Jeffrey L. (2004): An alternative view of the mental lexicon. *Trends in Cognitive Science* 8: 301–306.

Eskildsen, Søren W. (2009): Constructing another language – usage-based linguistics in second language acquisition. *Applied Linguistics* 30: 335–357.

Eskildsen, Søren W. and Teresa Cadierno (2007): Are recurring multi-word expressions really syntactic freezes? Second language acquisition from the perspective of usage-based linguistics. In: M. Nenonen and S. Niemi (eds.), *Collocations and Idioms 1: Papers from the First Nordic Conference on Syntactic Freezes*, 86–99. Joensuu: Joensuu University Press.

Feldman, Jerome A. (2006): *From Molecule to Metaphor: A Neural Theory of Language*. Boston: MIT Press.

Gass, Susan M. and Larry Selinker (eds.) (1983): *Language Transfer in Language Learning*. Rowley: Newbury House.

Goldberg, Adele E., Devin M. Casenhiser and Nitya Sethuraman (2004): Learning argument structure generalizations. *Cognitive Linguistics* 15: 289–316.

Goldschneider, Jennifer M. and Robert DeKeyser (2001): Explaining the "natural order of L2 morpheme acquisition" in English: A meta-analysis of multiple determinants. *Language Learning* 51: 1–50.

Granger, Sylviane (2001): Prefabricated patterns in Advanced EFL writing: Collocations and formulae. In: A. P. Cowie (ed.), *Phraseology: Theory, Analysis, and Applications*, 145–160. Oxford: Oxford University Press.

Gries, Stefan Th. (2012): Corpus linguistics, theoretical linguistics, and cognitive/psycholinguistics: Towards more and more fruitful exchanges. In: J. Mukherjee and M. Huber (eds.), *Corpus Linguistics and Variation in English: Theory and Description*, 41–63. Amsterdam: Rodopi.

Gries, Stefan Th. (2013): 50-something years of work on collocations: What is or should be next. *International Journal of Corpus Linguistics* 18(1): 137–165.

Gries, Stefan Th. and Dagmar S. Divjak (eds.) (2012): *Frequency Effects in Language Learning and Processing*. Berlin/New York: Mouton de Gruyter.

Gries, Stefan Th. and Stefanie Wulff (2005): Do foreign language learners also have constructions? Evidence from priming, sorting, and corpora. *Annual Review of Cognitive Linguistics* 3: 182–200.

Gries, Stefan Th. and Stefanie Wulff (2009): Psycholinguistic and corpus linguistic evidence for L2 constructions. *Annual Review of Cognitive Linguistics* 7: 163–186.

Hakuta, Kenji (1974): Prefabricated patterns and the emergence of structure in second language acquisition. *Language Learning* 24: 287–97.

Hakuta, Kenji (1976): A case study of a Japanese child learning English. *Language Learning* 26: 321–51.

Hanania, Edith A. S. and Harry L. Gradman (1977): Acquisition of English structures: A case study of an adult native speaker of Arabic in an English-speaking environment. *Language Learning* 27: 75–91.

Hatch, Evelyn (1972): Some studies in language learning. *UCLA Working Papers in Teaching English as a Second Language* 6: 29–36.

Hauser, Marc D., Noam A. Chomsky and W. Tecumseh Fitch (2002): The faculty of language: What is it, who has it, and how did it evolve? *Science* 298: 1569–1579.

Hopper, Paul J. (1987): Emergent grammar. *Berkeley Linguistics Society* 13: 139–157.

Jackendoff, Ray (2011): What is the human language faculty? *Language* 87: 587–624.

James, Carl (1980): *Contrastive Analysis*. London: Longman.

Jiang, Nan A. N., and Tatiana M. Nekrasova (2007): The Processing of formulaic sequences by second language speakers. *The Modern Language Journal* 91: 433–445.

Kiss, George R. (1973): Grammatical word classes: A learning process and its simulation. *The Psychology of Learning and Motivation* 7: 1–41.

Klein, Wolfgang and Clive Perdue (1992): *Utterance Structure: Developing Grammars Again*. Amsterdam: John Benjamins.

Krashen, Stephen and Robin C. Scarcella (1978): On routines and patterns in language acquisition and performance. *Language Learning* 28: 283–300.

Lado, Robert (1957): *Linguistics Across Cultures: Applied Linguistics for Language Teachers*. Ann Arbor: University of Michigan Press.

Lado, Robert (1964): *Language Teaching: A Scientific Approach*. New York: McGraw-Hill.

Lakoff, George and Mark Johnson (1999): *Philosophy in the Flesh: The Embodied Mind and Its Challenge to Western Thought*. New York: Basic Books.

Langacker, Ronald W. (1987): *Foundations of Cognitive Grammar*, Volume 1: *Theoretical Prerequisites*. Stanford: Stanford University Press.

Langacker, Ronald W. (2000): A dynamic usage-based model. In: M. Barlow and S. Kemmer (eds.), *Usage-based Models of Language*, 1–63. Stanford: CSLI Publications.

Liang, John (2002): Sentence comprehension by Chinese Learners of English: Verb centered or construction-based. M.A. dissertation, Guangdong University of Foreign Studies.

Lieven, Elena V. M., Heike Behrens, Jennifer Speares, and Michael Tomasello (2003): Early syntactic creativity: A usage based approach. *Journal of Child Language* 30: 333–370.

Littlemore, Jeanette (2009): *Applying Cognitive Linguistics to Second Language Learning and Teaching*. Basingstoke/New York: Palgrave Macmillan.

MacWhinney, Brian (1987a): Applying the Competition Model to bilingualism. *Applied Psycholinguistics* 8: 315–327.

MacWhinney, Brian (1987b): The Competition Model. In: B. MacWhinney (ed.), *Mechanisms of Language Acquisition*, 249–308. Hillsdale: Lawrence Erlbaum.

MacWhinney, Brian (1997): Second language acquisition and the Competition Model. In: A. M. B. de Groot and J. F. Kroll (eds.), *Tutorials in Bilingualism: Psycholinguistic Perspectives*, 113–142. Mahwah: Lawrence Erlbaum Associates.

MacWhinney, Brian (2001): The competition model: The input, the context, and the brain. In: P. Robinson (ed.), *Cognition and Second language Instruction*, 69–90. New York: Cambridge University Press.

Maslen, Robert, Anna L. Theakston, Elena V. M. Lieven, and Michael Tomasello (2004): A dense corpus study of past tense and plural overgeneralizations in English. *Journal of Speech, Language, and Hearing Research* 47: 1319–1333.

Matthews, Danielle and Grzegorz Krajewski (this volume): First language acquisition.

McDonough, Kim (2006): Interaction and syntactic priming: English L2 speakers' production of dative constructions. *Studies in Second Language Acquisition* 28: 179–207.

McDonough, Kim and Alison Mackey (2006): Responses to recasts: Repetitions, primed production and linguistic development. *Language Learning* 56: 693–720.

McDonough, Kim and Pavel Trofimovich (2008): *Using Priming Methods in Second Language Research*. London: Routledge.

McRae, Ken, Mary Hare, Jeffrey L. Elman and Todd Ferretti (2006): A basis for generating expectancies for verbs from nouns. *Memory and Cognition* 33: 1174–1184.

Mellow, J. Dean (2008): The emergence of complex syntax: A longitudinal case study of the ESL development of dependency resolution. *Lingua* 118: 499–521.

Mintz, Tobias (2003): Frequent frames as a cue for grammatical categories in child directed speech. *Cognition* 90: 91–117.

Myles, Florence (2004): From data to theory: The over-representation of linguistic knowledge in SLA. *Transactions of the Philological Society* 102: 139–168.

Myles, Florence, Mitchell, Rosamond, and Janet Hooper (1999): Interrogative chunks in French L2: A basis for creative construction. *Studies in Second Language Acquisition* 21: 49–80.

Ninio, Anat (1999): Pathbreaking verbs in syntactic development and the question of prototypical transitivity. *Journal of Child Language* 26: 619–653.

Ninio, Anat (2006): *Language and the Learning Curve: A New Theory of Syntactic Development*. Oxford: Oxford University Press.

Nosofsky, Robert M. (1988): Similarity, frequency, and category representations. *Journal of Experimental Psychology: Learning, Memory, and Cognition* 14: 54–65.

O'Donnell, Matt and Nick C. Ellis (2010): Towards an inventory of English verb argument constructions. *Proceedings of the NAACL HLT Workshop on Extracting and Using Constructions in Computational Linguistics*: 9–16.

Odlin, Terence (1989): *Language Transfer*. New York: Cambridge University Press.

Odlin, Terence (2008): Conceptual transfer and meaning extensions. In: P. Robinson and N. C. Ellis (eds.), *Handbook of Cognitive Linguistics and Second Language Acquisition*, 306–340. Ellis. London: Routledge.

Ortega, Lourdes and Gina Iberri-Shea (2005): Longitudinal research in second language acquisition: Recent trends and future directions. *Annual Review of Applied Linguistics* 25: 26–45.

Pawley, Andrew and Frances H. Syder (1983): Two puzzles for linguistic theory: Native-like selection and native-like fluency. In: J. C. Richards and R. W. Schmidt (eds.), *Language and Communication*, 191–226. New York: Longman.

Perdue, Clive (ed.) (1993): *Adult Language Acquisition: Cross-linguistic Perspectives*. Cambridge: Cambridge University Press.

Peters, Anne M. (1983): *The Units of Language Acquisition*. New York: Cambridge University Press.

Posner, Michael I. and Steven W. Keele (1970): Retention of abstract ideas. *Journal of Experimental Psychology* 83: 304–308.

Rebuschat, Patrick and John N. Williams (eds.) (2012): *Statistical Learning and Language Acquisition*. Berlin: Mouton de Gruyter.

Redington, Martin and Nick Chater (1998): Connectionist and statistical approaches to language acquisition: A distributional perspective. *Language and Cognitive Processes* 13: 129–192.

Regier, Terry and Laura Carlson (2002): Spatial language: Perceptual constraints and linguistic variation. In: J. Matter Mandler, P. J. Bauer and M. Rabinowitz (eds.), *Representation, Memory, and Development: Essays in Honor of Jean Mandler*, 199–221. Mahwah, NJ: Lawrence Erlbaum.

Rescorla, Robert A. (1968): Probability of shock in the presence and absence of CS in fear conditioning. *Journal of Comparative and Physiological Psychology* 66: 1–5.

Rescorla, Robert A. and Allen R. Wagner (1972): A theory of Pavlovian conditioning: Variations in the effectiveness of reinforcement and nonreinforcement. In: A. H. Black and W. F. Prokasy (eds.), *Classical Conditioning II: Current Theory and Research*, 64–99. New York: Appleton-Century-Crofts.

Robinson, Peter and Nick C. Ellis (2008a): Conclusion: Cognitive linguistics, second language acquisition and L2 instruction – issues for research. In: P. Robinson and N. C. Ellis (eds.), *Handbook of Cognitive Linguistics and Second Language Acquisition*, 489–546. London: Routledge.

Robinson, Peter and Nick C. Ellis (eds.) (2008b): *Handbook of Cognitive Linguistics and Second Language Acquisition*. London: Routledge.

Römer, Ute, Matthew B. O'Donnell, and Nick C. Ellis (2015): Using COBUILD grammar patterns for a large-scale analysis of verb-argument constructions: Exploring corpus data and speaker knowledge. In: M. Charles, N. Groom and S. John (eds.), *Corpora, Grammar, Text and Discourse: In Honour of Susan Hunston*. Amsterdam: John Benjamins.

Rosch, Eleanor and Carolyn B. Mervis (1975): Cognitive representations of semantic categories. *Journal of Experimental Psychology: General* 104: 192–233.

Rosch, Eleanor, Carolyn B. Mervis, Wayne D. Gray, David M. Johnson, and Penny Boyes-Braem (1976): Basic objects in natural categories. *Cognitive Psychology* 8: 382–439.

Schmid, Hans-Jörg (2010): Does frequency in text instantiate entrenchment in the cognitive system? In: D. Glynn and K. Fischer (eds.), *Quantitative Methods in Cognitive Semantics: Corpus-Driven Approaches*, 101–133. Berlin/New York: Mouton de Gruyter.

Schmidt, Richard W. (1983): Interaction, acculturation, and the acquisition of communicative competence: A case study of an adult. In: N. Wolfson and E. Judd (eds.), *Sociolinguistics and Language Acquisition*, 137–174. Rowley: Newbury House.

Schumann, John H. (1978): Second language acquisition: the pidginization hypothesis. In: E. M. Hatch (ed.), *Second Language Acquisition: A Book of Readings*, 256–271. Rowley: Newbury House.

Shanks, David R. (1995): *The Psychology of Associative Learning*. New York: Cambridge University Press.

Simpson-Vlach, Rita and Nick C. Ellis (2010): An Academic Formulas List (AFL). *Applied Linguistics* 31: 487–512.

Slobin, Dan I. (1993): Adult language acquisition: A view from child language study. In: C. Perdue (ed.), *Adult Language Acquisition: Cross-Linguistic Perspectives*, 239–252. Cambridge: Cambridge University Press.

Slobin, Dan I. (1996): From "thought and language" to "thinking for speaking". In: J. J. Gumperz and S. C. Levinson (eds.), *Rethinking Linguistic Relativity*, 70–96. Cambridge: Cambridge University Press.

Spivey, Michael (2006): *The Continuity of Mind*. Oxford: Oxford University Press.

Sugaya, N. and Yas Shirai (2009): Can L2 learners productively use Japanese tense-aspect markers? A usage-based approach. In: R. Corrigan, E. A. Moravcsik, H. Ouali and K. M. Wheatley (eds.), *Formulaic language*, Volume 2: *Acquisition, Loss, Psychological Reality, Functional Applications*, 423–444. Amsterdam: John Benjamins.

Talmy, Leonard (2000a): *Toward a Cognitive Semantics: Concept Structuring Systems*. Cambridge: MIT Press.

Talmy, Leonard (2000b): *Toward a Cognitive Semantics: Typology and Process in Concept Structuring*. Cambridge: MIT Press.

Taylor, John. R. (2002): *Cognitive Grammar*. Oxford: Oxford University Press.

Tomasello, Michael (1992): *First Verbs: A Case Study of Early Grammatical Development*. New York: Cambridge University Press.

Tomasello, Michael (2000): The item based nature of children's early syntactic development. *Trends in Cognitive Sciences* 4: 156–163.

Tomasello, Michael (2003): *Constructing a Language*. Boston: Harvard University Press.

Tomasello, Michael and Daniel Stahl (2004): Sampling children's spontaneous speech: How much is enough? *Journal of Child Language* 31: 101–121.

Trousdale, Graeme and Thomas Hoffmann (eds.) (2013): *Oxford Handbook of Construction Grammar*. Oxford: Oxford University Press.

Tyler, Andrea (2012): *Cognitive Linguistics and Second Language Learning*. London: Routledge.

VanPatten, Bill (2006): Input processing in adult SLA. In: B. VanPatten and J. Williams (eds.), *Theories in Second Language Acquisition: An Introduction*, 115–135. Mahwah: Lawrence Erlbaum.

Wiechmann, Daniel (2008): On the computation of collostruction strength. *Corpus Linguistics and Linguistic Theory* 4: 253–290.
Wong-Fillmore, Lilly (1976): *The second time around*: Cognitive and social strategies in second language acquisition. PhD dissertation, Stanford University.
Wray, Alison (2002): *Formulaic Language and the Lexicon*. Cambridge: Cambridge University Press.
Wulff, Stefanie and Stefan Th. Gries (2011): Corpus-driven methods for assessing accuracy in learner production. In: P. Robinson (ed.), *Second Language Task Complexity: Researching the Cognition Hypothesis of Language Learning and Performance*, 61–88. Amsterdam/Philadelphia: John Benjamins.
Wulff, Stefanie, Nick C. Ellis, Ute Römer, Kathleen Bardovi-Harlig, and Chelsea LeBlanc (2009): The acquisition of tense-aspect: Converging evidence from corpora, cognition, and learner constructions. *Modern Language Journal* 93: 354–369.
Zipf, George K. (1935): *The Psycho-Biology of Language*: An Introduction to Dynamic Philology. Cambridge: MIT Press.

Peter Stockwell
Chapter 9: Poetics

1 Linguistics and literature

The study of literature and culture has often proceeded in philosophical or thematic terms, influenced at different moments in history by an emphasis on sociology, anthropology or history itself. Currently in most university and college departments of literature across the world, the paradigm of discussion falls within a broad cultural studies, and we live in these early decades of the 21st century in one of the periodic moments in which the fact that literary texts are written in language is a relatively neglected notion. However, there has always been a thread running consistently through human intellectual development which has explored the workings of language both in its outward or recorded form (speech, writing, screen text) and in its inward manifestation (introspection, cognition and neuroscience). Most recently, this thread of interest in language has been finding expression once again in the study of literature, in a form variously known as *cognitive poetics*, *cognitive stylistics* or a generally *cognitive approach to literature*.

Literature is the most culturally highly valued form of language. It is usually regarded as being fixed in form as writing or public inscription, though there is a closely associated performative aspect that allows drama, theatre and readings aloud of poetry and prose to be encompassed within the notion of the literary. Hybrid forms blending poetry and graphic art, recitation and dance, and even quotation within architecture and horticulture can be regarded as even less prototypical examples. However, the normative historical perception of literature as writing on paper has encouraged a view of literary analysis in mainly formalist terms, whenever over time literature has been discussed for its language. The parameters of *language*, in other words, have been restricted to the boundaries of the physical text in most linguistic traditions of literary analysis. Aspects of language that a non-formalist might consider inherently part of the language system would include both the immediate and general social and ideological context, creative authorial perception and motivation, and the processes and predilections of a reader or reading community.

In the most famous statement of formalist literary analysis, Wimsatt and Beardsley (1954a, 1954b) set prescriptions against discussions of authorial intention on the one hand and against the psychology of the reader on the other. It must be borne in mind that Wimsatt and Beardsley and the whole New Critical movement of which they were a part were reacting to the worst sort of loose biographical musing and flowery speculation on readers and reading that served for much literary "debate" and "analysis" in those days. And the absurd and groundless treatments of literary authors in terms of their imagined psychoanalytical motivations or their assumed experiences and memories remain unfortunately a feature of the contemporary literary critical scene even today. However, the reaction against the extreme nonsense of the 1930s and '40s produced its own extremism: a bar on any consideration of psychology even when discussing readerly reactions; an assumption that aesthetic effects and meanings were purely the preserve of a text without reference to its reader; a literary work divorced from the integral culture of its language and the cognitive models and schemas that informed it.

Where much literary criticism in the latter part of the 20th century – especially in the US – headed off into abstraction and generalisation about language, other, more linguistically-focused traditions such as *stylistics* retained a formalist approach overall. Stylistics (arising mainly in France as *stylistique*, Germany as *stilistik*, and in Britain within applied linguistics) took a firmly delimited approach from linguistics to literary texts. It seems likely that this self-imposed constraint not to consider context alongside text was a contrastive reaction to literary critical theory's evasion of textuality altogether. The prohibitions of New Criticism still weighed heavily for stylisticians. And the nature of the linguistic toolkit available at the time led perhaps inevitably towards a focus on aspects of language up the rank-scale towards but not really including text linguistics and discourse analysis. For some, "linguistics" itself was a term that dealt only and single-mindedly with the rank-structure from phonology and phonetics and morphology and lexicology to semantics and syntax; even pragmatics, not to mention text and textuality, discourse and sociolinguistic matters, were regarded as extra-linguistic areas.

As stylistics evolved in the European tradition, the nature of its development has been a steady re-engagement with context, framed within a similarly rigorous and systematic methodology. Models from pragmatics, insights from sociolinguistics and discourse analysis, and the most recent advances in computerised corpus linguistics have enriched stylistics over the past few decades. The cognitive turn in the arts and humanities has been especially influential in stylistics, where there is no question it has been the main conduit for insights from cognitive science into literary studies. Today, the enrichment of literary studies by a cognitive poetics is a feature of literary research internationally. There are several different strands within this emerging but increasingly influential tradition, and several different angles on cognitive science that are taken by different areas of literary studies for different purposes, but it is becoming apparent that many of the concerns that literary critics and commentators have struggled to express inarticulately and in an ill-disciplined way are amenable to a rigorous cognitive poetics. In this chapter I will set out some of this variety, while also arguing for the sort of necessary focus on language textuality and texture that has served stylistics so well.

The study of literature is an important area within cognitive science. Literature is the most prestigious form of language in use. It is both highly culturally valued (as "Literature") and widely influential (as "literature" in all the demotic forms of popular lyrics and verses, formula fiction, trashy novels, soap operas, favourite good-reads and personal self-published stories and poetry blogs). Literary analysis reaches from the considered and disciplined work of professional literary critics and commentators in scholarly articles and the literary press right into the online reviews of books and reading groups, lists of favourites and all manner of informal observations on literature through the ages. Literary analysis, in short, has often been the territory on which more general discussions of language forms and effects have been conducted. Literary works themselves often incorporate particularly subtle features of everyday discourse, as well as features at the experimental edges of what is possible in language; the proper study of literary language – in all its fully contextualised diversity – offers the opportunity for cognitive scientists to understand human communication properly as well.

2 Precursors to a cognitive poetics

Poetics – the explicit statement and exploration of the theory of literary works – has an ancient history, and though some modern cognitive linguists point to the disjunctive revolutionary advances in the current discipline (see Lakoff and Johnson 1999), there are aspects of contemporary cognitive poetics that address directly concerns of human culture and expression that are centuries and millennia old. The earliest comprehensive theory of literary forms and effects was produced by Aristotle in around 330 BC as the *Poetics* (which mainly dealt with drama) and the *Rhetoric* (which, over three books, addressed poetry, persuasive speech and non-literary forms such as witness-statements, narrative accounts and the discourse of legal interrogation). While of course the ancient Greeks did not have access to neurological techniques nor what we might recognise as a modern scientific view of mind, their great innovation in intellectual human development was to bring an empirical sense to argumentation. Words of speech could be recorded in writing and examined for their forms; and the tangible effects of that language when performed could be observed in the audience, listener or court-room.

Crucially in Aristotle's work (and in that of other early theorists of poetics and rhetoric such as his precursors Plato and Isocrates, and later Roman writers such as Cicero and Quintilian, and for St Augustine in the 4th century AD), classical and early medieval Western rhetorical studies did not separate out the different facets of discourse: memory, knowledge, textual arrangement, word-choice and syntactic sequence, style of delivery, ideological intention, the immediate environment of the forum or culture of utterance, and the emotional, ethical and persuasive effects on the audience were all considered of a piece. The continuities between mind and body, embodiment and culture, and shared idealised cognitive models, frames and schemas that are at the heart of modern cognitive linguistics can all be discerned in these classical continuities.

For example, both classical poetics and rhetoric were concerned as much with performance and effect as with the structural content of the discourse. Aristotle (in the *Rhetoric*) arranges the nature of communication into three "appeals" rather than into formally-designated categories such as, perhaps, poetry, prose and drama, or fictional narrative and natural narrative, or political, romantic and pastoral topics, and so on. These "appeals" are meaning and informativity (*logos*), performative empathetic delivery (*pathos*), and the authority and moral credibility of the speaker (*ethos*). Cockcroft (2002) demonstrates how this Aristotelian scheme can be read through the lens of recent schema theory (from Schank and Abelson 1977 to G. Cook 1994), and he uses the cognitive scientific understanding of the classical scheme as an analytical tool for the exploration of writing in the English 16th century renaissance.

In the classical tradition, invention, text, and readerly effects were inextricably bound up with one another. However, as the study of rhetoric became instrumentalised by becoming a central part of European schooling in the later middle ages, the nature of human communication was partitioned. Informativity became the focus of study, for example in the five "canons" of rhetoric developed influentially by the 16th century writer Peter Ramus (also known as Pierre de la Ramée): *inventio, memoria, pronuntiatio, dispositio* and *elocutio*. These categories of invention, recall of facts, accuracy of pronunciation, the topical organisation of ideas and, lastly, lexicogrammatical style shift the focus onto meaningful content in a performative frame, with the relative demotion of explicit matters of emotion or ethics. Ong ([1958] 2004), writing in the 1950s, argues that the rise of print after 1500 and the spread of mass literacy across Europe and the US in the 19th century (see also Ong 1982) also served to diminish the emphasis on the performative aspects of discourse. We arrive in the middle of the 20th century with literary scholarship constrained by the New Critical formalism that was outlined at the beginning of this chapter.

More generally, it can be argued that the last five centuries encompassing the Enlightenment and the rise of analytical and empirical science have mainly founded our intellectual achievements on a necessary partitioning of human experience and the natural world. The principle within the scientific method of experimentally investigating a feature by observing a contrastive "control" requires the object under investigation to be delineated, isolated from other objects and defined exclusively. Crucially, the object and its interrelation with other objects needs to be detached from the observing consciousness. The central expression of this lies in the Cartesian dualities that separate mind from body, reason from perception, logical deduction from intuition, artificial from natural, and human consciousness and experience from the rest of the world and universe (see Descartes 1985).

All of this has created a good science that has led to advances in almost every aspect of human life, but we are now in a position of requiring a better science that remembers that objects and consciousnesses that have been artificially though necessarily separated are in actual fact part of a natural and holistic continuum. The 5th century BC precursor of the Aristotelian philosophers, Heraclitus (see 2001) originally characterised nature as flux, but contemporary cognitive science is establishing the demonstrable reality that mind is embodied, experience is situated, rational decisions are embedded within emotional decisions, and humans are connected by sharing common frames of knowledge and patterns of mind-modelling.

It is commonplace to mark the origins of recent cognitive poetics in the last two decades of the 20th century, with Tsur's (1992) coining of the phrase providing a home for several strands of work which brought together literary studies on the one hand and cognitive linguistics, cognitive psychology and neuroscience on the other. Pioneering studies of metaphor and conceptualisation (Lakoff and Johnson 1980; Lakoff 1987; Fauconnier and Turner 2003) often featured literary examples. Cognitively-informed accounts of narrative, such as Rumelhart's (1975, 1977) story-grammars and Schank and Abelson's (1977; Schank 1982) schema theory were adapted for application to literary narratives (for example by Cockcroft 2002; G. Cook 1994; and Culpeper 2001).

Cognitive poetics as a defined field and roughly common set of concerns and methods coalesced during the last decade of the 20th century. The polemical and demonstrative work of Turner (1991, 1996) in particular was instrumental in bringing the insights of cognitive science to the study of literature. Other key work from this period includes Spolsky (1993), Gerrig (1993), Fludernik (1996), Tsur (1992) and the work of Donald and Margaret Freeman (1995 and 2002, respectively). An influential textbook (Stockwell 2002) with companion volume (Gavins and Steen 2003), and a collection of papers (Semino and Culpeper 2002) served to bring the discipline to a wider and younger audience, and established it as a college and university course.

Though this work drew on the rapidly emerging insights from empirical cognitive science, West (2012) has recently pointed out that many of the concerns of modern cognitive poetics can also be discerned precursively in earlier work such as that of the English literary critic I. A. Richards. West argues that Richards was aiming at a science of criticism in much the same way as contemporary researchers in cognitive poetics. Of course, Richards did not have access to the recent insights into the mind that cognitive science is opening up today; he was scornful of the "monstrosities" of contemporary psychoanalysis (see West 2012: 8), but was enthusiastic about more empirical psychology such as that being developed at the time in Germany by the *gestalt* psychologists.

Similar arguments for precursors of modern cognitive poetics can be made for the work of Mikhail Bakhtin, Jan Mukařovský, and even F. R. Leavis. Though much of the writing of these scholars is cast in the register of their own times and can thus appear dogmatic and merely opinionated to our eyes, nevertheless Bakhtin was at pains to describe the inter-relations of textuality, culture and readerly cognition (see Keunen 2000); Mukařovský placed the effects of foregrounding at the centre of his understanding of literary reading (see van Peer 1986); and Leavis' notion of "enactment" in literature, whereby formal patterning is assigned a contextual significance by readers, is recognisable to modern cognitive poetics as literary iconicity (see Fischer 2014).

The main difference between these early precursors and modern cognitive poetics lies in the empirical basis of the disciplines of cognitive psychology and linguistics, which were not available in earlier ages. Modern practitioners of cognitive poetics are also conscious of the movements in literary theory which have swept across the field over the last few decades. While some of the positions argued and adopted in critical theory are proving to be at odds with the insights of cognitive science, other aspects of their thinking can be understood more clearly with reference to the rational evidence offered within cognitive poetics. In philosophical terms, cognitive poetics represents a form of experiential realism in the sense that most researchers assume a tangible set of data is available for investigation (authorial choices, textual patterns and readerly organisation), but that reality is only accessible through perceptual and cognitive mechanisms which represent it in particular though describable ways.

3 Cognition and literature

The study of literature comprises several different aspects, and the cognitive turn in arts and humanities affects all of them radically. The dominant paradigm in current literary scholarship is concerned with contextual matters of authorial creativity, the history of different edited versions of the literary work, the cultural environment at the text's initial publication, and the relationship of the literary work to parallel or similar philosophical or theoretical arguments. Historiography and critical theory, in other words, continue to dominate scholarly practice. While it is obvious that the close stylistic analysis of literary texts would be informed by cognitive linguistics, it is becoming apparent that cognitive scientific insights and methods can also inform historiography. Sotirova's (2013) work on manuscript versions of D. H. Lawrence's prose fiction is a case in point.

However, the current flight to historicism – or the "history of the book" – can be seen as the literary establishment's attempt to find something new "after Theory" (Eagleton 2003). Where it might be said that the literary work itself (its textuality and texture) was often overlooked in much recent critical-theoretical discussion, the new historicism placed the text at the centre of things once again, but mainly as an opportunity for exploring the culture of production. Textual versions and the history of editing became a prime concern, and so readerly reception and impact became relatively devalued once again. One of the key scholars of literary historicism, and also a highly influential literary-critical figure, Stephen Greenblatt (see 1992) has also argued for a refocus of attention in literary scholarship on the practice of teaching literature, as a means of reconnecting the profession of literary scholarship with public understanding.

All of these moves are interesting from the standpoint of anyone working in a stylistics, discourse analytical, or reception-theory tradition. Textual analysis in particular comes out of an applied linguistics field in which pedagogic practice was often the driving motivation behind the close attention to textual detail: stylistics has always been strongly teaching-focused. Much of the original drive towards atextual Theory and subsequent cultural poetics (Greenblatt 1989) originated in a desire to move away from the New Critical sense of a text integral to itself; so the focus (in historiography or text-editing theory) on the literary work as an artefact is ironic – where stylistic variation is not explored for its effect on meaning or aesthetic response but only for its value in what it tells us about its cultural origins.

In any case, the most recent work in cognitive poetics (see section 4 below) is in the process of demonstrating that even research into cultural production and reception, variants of editions, authorial choice and creativity are all amenable to and improvable by some attention to cognitive science.

All aspects of literary scholarship can (and should) be evaluated and defined with regard to the way they treat evidence. However, the definition and treatment of evidence when it comes to the practice of literary reading can have various aspects and outcomes. These are closely aligned with the methodology adopted in each case, as outlined below. The point I will emphasise throughout this brief survey is that the cognitive turn in poetics has affected each of these approaches.

3.1 Reader-control

In general, the "empirical approach to literature" has a strong German and Dutch tradition (see Schmidt 1982 and Ibsch et al. 1991), and has been promoted particularly by the journal *Poetics* and by the learned society *IGEL* (Internationale Gesellschaft für Empirische Literaturwissenschaft – Society for the Empirical Study of Literature and the Media). Here, the definition of empiricism is largely drawn from a social science perspective; where, in philosophy, rationalism and empiricism are regarded as being in dispute with each other (Morton 2004), in social science research, rational argument on extant phenomena and the experiential sense of those phenomena are regarded as complementary.

The core "IGEL" approach might be characterised as "hard empiricism", in which particular aspects of reading are controlled as rigorously as possible in order to discover measurable facts about the reading process and experience. This approach is very closely linked with the discipline of psychology, and indeed many of the studies in this tradition are undertaken by or in collaboration with psychologists (see, for example, Miall et al. 2004, or Bortolussi and Dixon 2003, or Louwerse and van Peer 2009). There is no question that this form of empirical investigation has yielded a host of valuable insights into literary reading, summarised most clearly by Miall (2012). Key questions concern the nature of literariness (what makes literary discourse singular), the nature of absorption (the extent to which readers feel themselves immersed in a literary work), and the nature of iconicity (the extent to which a literary text conveys patterns that also seem to embody or represent their meanings symbolically).

As mentioned, much of the methodology of this form of empirical poetics is drawn from psychology. So, typically, small groups of college students will be divided into a control and a variable group, given a task that corresponds to a literary reading experience, and then either observed for particular effects or questioned in the form of a variety of elicitation techniques. The advantage of this approach is that it isolates particular features of literary reading and renders largely measurable, statistically validatable results. The findings can be published with a high degree of confidence in their generalisability to the reading community at large.

Of course, there are also disadvantages to the approach. Often, groups which would be considered of an appropriate size for a psychological study (generally numbering in single-figures or tens) might be considered inadequately small from a sociolinguistic perspective. Often the objective of the approach is to discover generalisable facts about readers and the reading process, rather than particular facts or phenomena about the singular literary work that serves as a stimulus in the investigation. Many studies in this tradition therefore feature white middle-class young-adult college students as informants, which means at the very least that this socio-ethnic group is over-represented in the findings. Finally, of course, there is an inevitable privileging given to studies and phenomena that are easily (or even possibly) measurable, and less emphasis on those aspects of literary reading that are extremely subtle, transient or idiosyncratic, but which many might consider to be essential elements in the literary experience.

3.2 Reader-response

It should be said that many of the practitioners of "reader-control" empirical poetics are aware of these potential limitations, and often work hard to mitigate them. Miall (2005, 2006), in particular, blends the strongly quantitative psychology-leaning research with other, more qualitative techniques. Reader questionnaires, reading task protocols, thinking aloud techniques and other methods are designed to avoid the "lab-effect" of strongly reader-controlled experiments and aim more towards the exploration of a naturalistic reading experience. At the same time, experiments have been conducted in which readers are given real literary works instead of carefully controlled texts invented by the analysts, or complete texts rather than extracts and decontextualised sentences or "textoids" (Vipond and Hunt 1989; Gerrig 1993). Inevitably these sorts of approaches make it more difficult to control for precise textual or psychological features or effects, which is the cost of a more naturalistic and holistic set of data.

Moving even further away from the psychological method paradigm, several researchers within cognitive poetics have adopted more sociological methods in order to investigate the natural processes of reading. A common technique here is to use either the recorded notes and articulations of non-professional book-groups, blogs and discussions that are already available, or to engage in fieldwork data collection with these groups (see Whiteley 2011; Peplow 2011; Swann and Allington 2009). One advantage of these approaches is that the reading experiences that are being explored are not those of professional literary critics but often of a wider population of literary readers.

The results of the research might involve analytical frameworks that have a strong tradition in sociolinguistics (such as discourse analysis or accommodation theory) or alternatively the readers' responses can be analysed using models derived from cognitive linguistics or cognitive psychology (such as text worlds or schema theory). Often these sorts of studies are thoroughly qualitative, and are more particularly tied to the specific literary work in hand. This means of course that they gain as a democratic form of literary criticism, though there is perhaps less generalisability in terms of psychological process. And, of course, there are many examples of cognitive poetics (see section 3.5 below) in which a close cognitive poetic textual analysis is presented either to elaborate or interrogate a set of professional published literary critical responses. After all, literary critics are readers too, and their articulated responses are appropriate examples of data available for systematic analysis.

3.3 Computational and corpus stylistics

Both the quantitative and qualitative forms of readerly empiricism outlined above aim to avoid or mitigate the effects of the *reader's paradox* (Stockwell 2012a), a form of the *observer's paradox* familiar in sociolinguistic research. The latter recognises that investigators are likely to affect by their presence or intervention the data or informants they are researching. In the field of literary reading, the reader's paradox is even more intractable, because reading itself is a form of consciousness, and so even the slightest form of awareness or direct consideration will cause the experience to be different from the ordinary process of natural reading.

The great developments in computational corpus linguistics and concordance techniques over the last few decades offer possibilities for empirical poetics that minimise the effects of the reader's paradox in research. As Stubbs (2005, 2014) points out, features and effects that are distributed across a literary work can be explicitly apparent and measurable only by a software program, but they can reasonably be adduced as evidence for the generation of particular effects in literary readers. It may be that many literary effects operate at the level of sub-conscious processing, and their effects are only felt cumulatively or when several features are aligned for a particular thematic effect. In these cases, there is little point looking for the articulation of such effects with any degree of precision in the mainly intuitive and impressionistic discourse of literary criticism, nor in the discussions of non-professional readers. Nor is it useful to use the sort of quantitative empirical methods referenced in 3.1 and 3.2

above, because the effects that we are interested in might be too subtle or rarefied for accessible measurement. Instead, features that are distributed and diffused across a large expanse of literary text might cumulatively have a very subtle effect that is only measurable or even detectable objectively with the aid of a computer program and corpus stylistic technique.

Most corpus stylistics is not primarily cognitive poetic in design nor intention, but the method is adaptable enough to operate in the service of a cognitively-informed poetics. There have been explicit polemical arguments in this direction (O'Halloran 2007), and an increasing recognition that corpus linguistics has much empirical validation to offer cognitive linguistics (Gries and Stefanowitsch 2007; Arppe et al. 2010), and therefore to cognitive poetics (see 4.4 below).

3.4 Textual analysis

It has long been argued from within the discipline of stylistics that rigorous and systematic textual analysis itself is a form of empiricism. This argument rests on the assertion that textual and stylistic facts that are describable about a literary work are undeniably evidence for a particular reading or interpretation of that text. The commitment to clear description and openness of method in stylistic practice sets out the fruits of analysis for verification, adjustment or falsifiability by other readers. Aside from the reliance on textual evidence, this too represents a commitment to the empiricism of method.

Furthermore, there is a more indirect claim to evidential value in stylistic analysis, in the sense that the (usually) linguistic framework or insight that is deployed in the analysis at hand has almost always been tested and validated in another domain. So, for example, if a stylistician explores the effects of semantic prototypicality in a reading of a poem, the fact that there is a huge amount of evidence to suggest that semantic prototypicality is currently a reasonably safe hypothesis about language in general helps to underpin and validate indirectly the use of that model in the literary analysis. Of course, this indirect validation rests on the assumption that literary language is continuous with language in general, rather than being in itself formally different or special – most stylisticians today accept this fact: literary language is literary because of the deployment and framing, rather than for any inherent, essential properties of the text itself. It is this far that stylistics has moved from New Criticism.

Literary stylistics has been the discipline that has most enthusiastically embraced cognitive linguistics as a source for analytical frameworks. An early collection of articles (Semino and Culpeper 2002) was even entitled *cognitive stylis-*

tics, and in general the most active part of literary analysis for the last couple of decades has been characterised by close textual attention. Sometimes this has involved radical reshaping of existing notions in stylistics; at other times, it might have seemed as if existing notions were simply being given a cognitivist gloss (see Tsur's 2008 criticism of Stockwell 2002 in this regard). However, it is important to recognise that both aspects of the revaluation were necessary, in order to establish a coherent single discipline and understand in a consistent terminology and mindset where stylistics could make its greatest contribution – as well as those areas in which it lacked adequate concepts.

The field of narratology has been a particularly vibrant area of revitalised research, with a postclassical or *cognitive narratology* now largely treated as mainstream in that field (see Bundgard et al. 2012, Herman 2000, 2003, 2009). Narratology draws more on cognitive psychology than linguistics, exploring such notions as the creation of storyworlds, the nature and representation of consciousness, and the literary deployment, codification and recreation of emotion, for example. It can be regarded as empirical in the same sense as stylistics above, though of course there are similar problems of definition. Sternberg (2003) has argued, for example, that cognitive narratology needs to decide whether to adopt a social science methodology and ethos or an approach more suited to the humanities. It seems to me, again, that the use and status of evidence is at the heart of this distinction, and in fact I have argued elsewhere (Stockwell 2012b) for a characterisation of the ethos of cognitive poetics as an "artful science". This is because in literary reading we are dealing not only with the quantifiable and measurable effects of textuality and cognition, but also with experiences that are delicate, difficult to articulate, subjective and perhaps only precisely accessible by introspection.

3.5 Introspection

Introspection is not a form of perception (nor even analogous to it); it is a form of peculiar (that is, particular) self-knowledge (Byrne 2005). It thus has more to do with belief than with perception, but this formulation makes it more, rather than less, amenable to a cognitive scientific account. With the rise of behaviourism through the 20th century, the use of introspection as a scientific method became devalued (Lyons 1986), since it is by definition subjective and idiosyncratic. However, even the most highly-controlled reader experiments in cognitive psychology have often relied on informants' self-report of their own reactions, and introspective report, for all its flaws, remains the only direct access to consciousness.

Most recently, Jack and Roepstorff (2003, 2004) argued for a revaluation of introspection in the scientific method. In relation to literary reading and literary analysis, I have argued (Stockwell 2013) that it is impossible to read and simultaneously to watch and reflect on your reading, for good psychological and perceptual reasons concerning figure and ground differentiation. It is of course possible to reflect backwards on a prior reading experience, so introspection is apparently retrospection, but as Overgaard (2006) points out, this means that you are having a memory of something that was at the time unconscious. Instead, introspection seems more like a rationalization of your consciousness. This is philosophically complex but in literary terms relatively simple: it means that the articulated recount of a reading experience equates to the reader's belief about that experience. This is a combination of both aware and sub-conscious factors, but since the introspective recount is the only product of the experience, then that is to all practical purposes the reading in hand. On this argument, introspection remains a valid form of evidence, perhaps in fact the only direct form of evidence of literary reading, and therefore introspection can be included in a list of types of empiricism.

In practice, several cognitive poetic analyses (including many of my own) rely on an introspective sense of a key effect or feature in a literary text and reading that is then pinpointed for systematic linguistic exploration. Furthermore, the analysis is presented in as transparent and principled a way as possible, and comparison with other readers' introspective experiences is invited. This procedure certainly relies on subjectivity and self-consciousness, but it also maintains contact with the sorts of external empiricism outlined in sections 3.1 to 3.4 above.

Finally, of course, the most common pattern of cognitive poetic analysis involves a combination of several of these empirical methods. The consequence is a sort of triangulation of approaches in order to arrive at an account of literary reading that would remain otherwise ineffable.

4 Developments in cognitive poetics

Over the last two decades, work that has fallen under the term "cognitive poetics" has diversified a great deal. As Louwerse and van Peer (2009) point out, surprisingly most examples of cognitive poetics over this period have drawn more on cognitive psychology rather than linguistics, though of course the two are not entirely distinct in cognitive literary analysis. Popular areas include explorations of conceptual metaphor, the worlds of literary fiction, schemas of contextual knowledge, how elements of literary texts are foregrounded and thematised, how genre is delineated, and how blending and compression work to create connections between literature and life.

The first of these – the exploration of conceptual metaphor – arises from the earliest work of Lakoff and Johnson (1980), and studies on this topic remain popular. Identifying conceptual metaphors that underlie literary works, especially plays and novels, can reveal extended tropes and themes across large bodies of text. Any particular idealised conceptual metaphor can be linguistically realised in a variety of ways, of course, and the most convincing work focused on this stylistic variation (see, for example, D. C. Freeman 1995, and the articles collected in Gavins and Steen 2003, and Semino and Culpeper 2002). The least convincing work simply listed the conceptual metaphors that featured in the text, falling into the old trap of neglecting to link the textual description to the interpretative level of significance. Another common flaw in some of these studies lies in analysing conceptual metaphors in a particular literary work that in fact are simply common conventional metaphors in the language system of English generally: so, for example, finding lots of LIFE IS A JOURNEY or IDEAS ARE CONTAINERS metaphors in a literary text is often not particularly significant for the text as literature. Mistakes such as this were often what motivated some literary critics to dismiss cognitive poetics as reductive or only interested in universals, rather than in the particularity or singularity of the literary work.

Many literary scholars have drawn with interest on the ways that cognitive psychology has accounted for mental representations, schemas, mental models and conceptual worlds. This tradition has become particularly strong in the area of cognitive narratology (see 3.4 above), which has essentially become paradigmatic in what Herman (2000) calls "post-classical narratology". Interest in the "storyworlds" that authors construct in texts for readers to re-imagine has drawn substantially on cognitive psychological frameworks. Again, though, much of this research is conceptual and thematic in nature. An exception is the work which has been undertaken in *text world theory* (Werth 1999, Gavins 2007), which marries up a contextualised model of world-building with a close linguistic analysis of discourse. The most useful aspect of the approach, for literary critical purposes, is the convincing way in which the model accounts for attentional and deictic "world-switches" caused by metaphor, temporal disjunctions, embedded beliefs, wishes and other modalisations, and other unrealised possibilities.

A third major trend within cognitive poetics has been the way in which scholars have revisited the key research questions of past literary theory with new tools from the cognitive revolution. So, for example, the defamiliarising or estranging effects of literature, or literariness itself, or the functioning of foregrounding as a literary mechanism, have all been freshly addressed with the benefit of the empirical grounding of cognitive science (see, for example, van Peer 1986, van Peer and Louwerse 2003).

Overall, the history of cognitive poetics over the last two decades has been to complete one of the main objectives of stylistics, which was to offer a persuasive rational account of the generation of meaningfulness in literary texts. Though this work is of course ongoing, the systematic account of context, framing and readerliness that recent advances have provided has been striking. Furthermore, we have witnessed a principled reintegration – thanks to cognitive poetics – of aesthetics and ethics (*pathos* and *ethos*, see section 2 above) into the analytical study of literature. Now in the second decade of the 21st century, it is becoming apparent that cognitive poetics is becoming prominent as an influence in literary studies in general. Under a more broad *cognitive literary studies* heading, literary scholars are increasingly turning their attention to insights appearing across the range of cognitive science disciplines. This includes not only cognitive psychology and cognitive linguistics, but neuroscience, consciousness studies, and evolutionary theory. While this is welcome in general, there is a risk (it seems to me) that once again the linguistic texture of the literary work is in danger of being overlooked. Literary scholars often do not seem to realise that cognitive poetics is not simply the latest critical theory, but is a scientific method with empirical roots.

4.1 The return to linguistics

Having said that cognitive literary studies risks neglecting the stylistic dimension, it is worth observing that one of the current emerging projects within cognitive poetics proper is a return to cognitive linguistics proper. For most of its history, stylistics has drawn on a systemic-functional linguistic tradition for its close textual analysis. Given the emphasis on meaning and its interpretative effects, this is not surprising. It is also perhaps to be expected that a grammatical model most popular outside the US would be preferred in the discipline of stylistics within its European and British Commonwealth context. Moreover, the various generative grammars emerging in the US at the time were not usable for the stylistic analysis of "surface structure" or actual linguistic surface realisation.

Most recently, however, several varieties of cognitive and construction grammars have emerged, perhaps most comprehensively Langacker's (2008) Cognitive Grammar. These provide a means of parsing and accounting for matters of transitivity and participant roles in a similar way as Halliday's (and Matthiessen 2004) systemic-functional grammar, and are at least as effective in this dimension. Additionally, of course, these cognitive grammars have the advantage of being rooted in psychological plausibility, either by empirical testing or indirectly by sharing a set of basic paradigmatic principles in cognitive science. This makes them potentially very attractive to stylisticians of literary works.

As yet, the number of applications of cognitive grammar to literature has been fairly limited. Hamilton (2003) offers an account of a Wilfred Owen war poem in order to explain the depth of its poignancy. There is an account of the shifting strength and weakness of characters in a battle scene in *The Lord of the Rings* (in Stockwell 2009), and an analysis of apocalyptic science-fiction narratives to focus on human helplessness (in Stockwell 2010). What is noticeable about these applications is that their main concern is not meaning but emotional effect. The collected analyses in Harrison et al. (2013) all draw on Cognitive Grammar to account for a range of effects across literary works.

4.2 Enactment and dramatisation

Another recent trend in cognitive poetics develops the fundamental cognitivist principle of embodiment in order to revisit the iconicity effect of literary enactment. So, for example, the prototypicality scaling of phonetic features is used to identify sounds in a 19th century seduction poem by Robert Bowning – sounds that make readers reading aloud form kisses with their mouths (Stockwell 2009). Many psychological studies report the empathetic effects on reading narratives of physical states: drinking from a warm cup makes you feel more warmly to a fictional character, sitting on a hard chair makes you feel less empathy, and so on (see Gibbs 2006, 2012), and readers report and are observed writhing uncomfortably in their own clothes while reading the passages in Dickens' *David Copperfield* that feature the slimy, squirming character Uriah Heep. Embodiment and readerly relationships with literary characters is a strongly emerging interest in research in the field (see Vermeule 2010).

Similarly of literary critical interest is the notion of *simulation* that appears in both Cognitive Grammar and in neurological research. In the former, Langacker (2008) points out that every linguistic utterance is a representation that is attenuated to a greater or lesser degree from the actual experience; every piece of language helps to create a simulation in the user's mind that operates as a heuristic for understanding. Simulation at a global level is also important in empathetic relationships, feelings and the creation of a "Theory of Mind" (see Zunshine 2006 and Keen 2007 for literary applications). These slightly different instantiations of the notion of simulation promise a great deal of insight into the ways in which readers feel they are transported, immersed or absorbed by a literary fictional world.

Prose fiction and dramatic monologue in poetry are obvious places for an application of simulation to be researched. However, this work also suggests new avenues for study in relation to dramatic performance (traditionally an area of complexity for a text-based stylistics): see McConachie and Hart (2006) and A. Cook (2010).

4.3 Singularity and situatedness

One of the accusations levelled traditionally at both stylistics and cognitive poetics has been that they are interested in general patterns of readerly behaviour, language universals and overall principles and patterns. While perhaps overstated in the best work, it is important to recognise that a particular literary text – while having generic connections with other works by the same author, in the same genre or mode, from the same period, or on the same theme – is unique to itself. Attridge (2004) calls this the *singularity* of the text, and it is a common feature of a sense of literariness. Reducing a literary work to patterns and generalities risks neglecting this centrally important feature for literature.

As an antidote to the universalising tendency, the cognitivist notion of *situatedness* offers a useful corrective (see Barsalou 2008, 2009). A concept is understood as a set of particular instantiations which might share some aspects but are fundamentally dependent on the uniquely experienced situation at hand. Instead of pulling down a schematic template or idealised model for a particular concept or experience, these concepts and linguistic articulations are "soft-assembled" (Gibbs 2006) for the case in hand. The notion of situatedness neatly captures both the singularity and genre-definitions of literature. This is a promising route for cognitive poetics research; what is less clear is how the notion of situatedness in literary reading can be operationalised to produce accounts that are recognisable as literary criticism.

Until these ideas are fully worked out, my contention remains the traditional stylistic position that the leaning towards universalising reductivism can be successfully mitigated by a constant emphasis that ties literary analysis down to the linguistic specifics of the text. Ultimately, the text that readers share remains the source of evidential value.

4.4 Subtlety

The greatest difficulty for a discipline founded on precise analysis and evidential value lies in those aspects of literary reading that are at or below the level of measurement. It is relatively easy to conduct a psychological or a cognitive poetic experiment to discover literary texts that generate empathetic grief, sadness, laugh-out-loud comedy, and so on. These effects are either easily physically observable or are clearcut examples that can be intuited and reported in a carefully designed protocol. But more subtle aesthetic reactions (wry melancholy, poignant nostalgia, perhaps?) are more difficult to articulate, define and explore systematically. And yet these are exactly the sort of rich effects that characterise literary reading, and that feature particularly in the writing of literary critics. It seems to me desirable and possible for cognitive poetics to address issues like these of subtlety, delicacy and bareness, where the experienced effect that is reported by readers is rarefied, barely conscious or so highly diffused in the experience that it is difficult to articulate in conventional descriptive terms.

For a simple, as yet unexplored example, I have recently been trying to account for the notion of *aura* in literary text (Stockwell 2014). This is the atmospheric or tonal sense of a vague association, often reported by readers and usually described by literary critics in poetic terms themselves. For example, in Philip Larkin's (1974) poem "The Explosion", a mining accident is described is highly subdued terms. The features of the industrial landscape and nature are given agency and animation, while the miners are described by their bodies and clothing, chasing rabbits, collecting lark's eggs. The underground explosion itself is narrated simply as "a tremor" that disturbed the cows grazing above. The poem ends with an imagined scene in which the wives of the men see them again, brightly walking towards them, still alive:

> for a second
> Wives saw men of the explosion
>
> Larger than in life they managed –
> Gold as on a coin, or walking
> Somehow from the sun towards them,
>
> One showing the eggs unbroken.
> Philip Larkin (1974: 42)

Almost all readers – both professional literary critics and others who have read the whole poem – report the poignancy in this closing passage. Part of this effect, it seems to me, arises from the echoic value of elements that recur throughout the text. These repetitions are not simply examples of lexical or semantic cohesion, but are more subtle and delicate. Features from domains that are not usually linked (clothing, faces, the natural landscape, and industry) are placed in close proximity, and weave between each other.

I have had some success in using Langacker's (2008) notion of *dominion* and Evans' (2009) work on *lexical concepts and conceptual models* to understand how words and phrases in the first part of the poem generate a set of expectations and associations in the minds of readers, only some of which are lexicalised again later on. The unrealised associations, it seems plausible to me, constitute a set of non-instantiated but fleeting meanings and feelings that pervade the rest of the text on the border of conscious awareness. This is where the subtle effects that readers report in the poem are located.

It would be very difficult to devise a controlled experiment to verify these ideas (though of course probably not impossible). However, triangulating a finding like this in any literary text can be effective. In corpus linguistics, the notion of *semantic prosody* (Louw and Milojkovic 2014) captures the shading or mood (in the non-linguistic, emotional sense) that is inherent in particular collocations and larger structures: certain phrases are always used negatively, for example, regardless of their semantic or dictionary content traditionally conceived – this is their semantic prosody characteristic. It strikes me that this sort of diffused semantic analysis (which in corpus linguistics can be measured) is a useful way of trying to pin down the same sorts of subtle effects that are captured in the cognitive grammatical account. This loose example is a preliminary illustration of the necessary triangulation that will be needed to catch such notions.

5 Futures

Cognitive poetics is inherently interdisciplinary, with researchers typically possessing a high awareness of both the scientific method and the state of current scholarship in social science. However, the natural home of cognitive poetics is clearly in arts and humanities, and an assertive emphasis on integrated linguistic form and effect offers discipline, rigour and insight where these have traditionally been rather neglected. A study of literature that is informed by cognitive linguistics seeks to broaden the potential of the cognitive revolution by encompassing the most culturally-valued form of language in use, and finally refuting the claim that cognitive linguistics is insufficiently social or critically aware in its practices.

On the other side, literary texts, literary readings, and poetics offer a great deal to cognitive science in general and cognitive linguistics in particular. Cognitive poetic analyses are always founded on whole texts in context, rather than isolated or invented fragments of language; the concerns that interest researchers in cognitive poetics serve as a reminder of the social world in which minds and bodies operate, and offer demonstrations in practice for how an extended embodied cognition works.

Finally, the field itself embodies a return to a time when a scholar could be interested professionally both in an engagement in the arts and a commitment to science and rational thinking. Cognitive poetics offers a practical means of achieving this integration.

6 References

Aristotle ([1991]): *The Art of Rhetoric*. Harmondsworth: Penguin.
Aristotle ([1996]): *Poetics*. Harmondsworth: Penguin.
Arppe, Antti, Gaëtanelle Gilquin, Dylan Glynn, Martin Hilpert, and Arne Zeschel (2010): Cognitive corpus linguistics: five points of debate on current theory and methodology. *Corpora* 5: 1–27.
Attridge, Derek (2004): *The Singularity of Literature*. London: Routledge.
Barsalou, Lawrence (2008): Grounded cognition. *Annual Review of Psychology* 59: 617–665.
Barsalou, Lawrence (2009): Simulation, situated conceptualization and prediction. *Philosophical Transactions of the Royal Society* 364: 1281–1289.
Bortolussi, Marisa and Peter Dixon (2003): *Psychonarratology: Foundations for the Empirical Study of Literary Response*. Cambridge: Cambridge University Press.
Bundgaard, Per, Frederik Stjernfelt, and Henrik Skov Nielsen (eds.) (2012): *Narrative Theories and Poetics: 5 Questions*. Copenhagen: Automatic Press.
Byrne, Alex (2005): Introspection. *Philosophical Topics* 33(1): 79–104.
Cockcroft, Robert (2002): *Renaissance Rhetoric: Reconsidered Passion – The Interpretation of Affect in Early Modern Writing*. London: Palgrave.
Cook, Amy (2010): *Shakespearean Neuroplay: Reinvigorating the Study of Dramatic Texts and Performance Through Cognitive Science*. New York: Palgrave Macmillan.
Cook, Guy (1994): *Discourse and Literature*. Oxford: Oxford University Press.
Culpeper, Jonathan (2001): *Language and Characterisation: People in Plays and other Texts*. Harlow: Longman.
Descartes, René ([1985]): *The Philosophical Writings of Descartes*: 2 volumes [trans.] J. Cottingham, R. Stoothoff, D. Murdoch]. Cambridge: Cambridge University Press.
Eagleton, Terry (2003): *After Theory*. New York: Basic Books.
Evans, Vyvyan (2009): *How Words Mean: Lexical Concepts, Cognitive Models and Meaning Construction*. Oxford: Oxford University Press.
Fauconnier, Gilles and Mark Turner (2003): *The Way We Think: Conceptual Blending and the Mind's Hidden Complexities*. New York: Basic Books.
Fischer, Olga (2014): Iconicity. In: P. Stockwell and S. Whiteley (eds.), *The Handbook of Stylistics*, 377–392. Cambridge: Cambridge University Press.
Fludernik, Monika (1996): *Towards a "Natural" Narratology*. London: Routledge.
Freeman, Donald C. (1995): "Catch[ing] the nearest way": *Macbeth* and cognitive metaphor. *Journal of Pragmatics* 24: 689–708.
Freeman, Margaret H. (2002): Cognitive mapping in literary analysis. *Style* 36: 466–483.
Gavins, Joanna (2007): *Text World Theory*. Edinburgh: Edinburgh University Press.
Gavins, Joanna and Gerard Steen (eds.) (2003): *Cognitive Poetics in Practice*. London: Routledge.

Gerrig, Richard J. (1993): *Experiencing Narrative Worlds: On the Psychological Activities of Reading*. New Haven: Yale University Press.
Gibbs, Raymond W. (2006): *Embodiment and Cognitive Science*. New York: Cambridge University Press.
Gibbs, Raymond W. (2012): Walking the walk while thinking about the talk: embodied interpretation of metaphorical narratives. *Journal of Psycholinguistic Research* 42(4): 363–378.
Greenblatt, Stephen (1989): Towards a poetics of culture. In: H. Aram Veeser (ed.), *The New Historicism*, 1–14. London: Routledge.
Greenblatt, Stephen (ed.) (1992): *Redrawing the Boundaries: The Transformation of English and American Literary Studies*. New York: Modern Language Association of America.
Gries, Stephan Th. and Anatol Stefanowitsch (eds.) (2007): *Corpora in Cognitive Linguistics: Corpus-Based Approaches to Syntax and Lexis*. Berlin: Mouton.
Halliday, Michael A. K. and Christian Matthiessen (2004): *An Introduction to Functional Grammar*. London: Hodder.
Hamilton, Craig (2003): A cognitive grammar of "Hospital Barge" by Wilfred Owen. In: J. Gavins and G. Steen (eds.), *Cognitive Poetics in Practice*, 55–65. London: Routledge.
Harrison, Chloe, Louise Nuttall, Peter Stockwell, and Wenjuan Yuan (eds.) (2013): *Cognitive Grammar in Literature*. Amsterdam: Benjamins.
Heraclitus ([2001]): *Fragments: The Collected Wisdom of Heraclitus* [trans. B. Haxton]. New York: Viking.
Herman, David (2000): Narratology as a cognitive science. *Image and Narrative* 1. http://www.imageandnarrative.be/inarchive/narratology/davidherman.htm
Herman, David (ed.) (2003): *Narrative Theory and the Cognitive Sciences*. Stanford: CSLI.
Herman, David (2009): Cognitive narratology. In: P. Hühn, J. Pier, W. Schmid and J. Schönert (eds.), *Handbook of Narratology*, 30–43. Berlin: de Gruyter.
Ibsch, Elrud, Dick Schram, and Gerard Steen (eds.) (1991): *Empirical Studies of Literature*. Amsterdam: Rodopi.
Jack, Anthony I. and Andreas Roepstorff (2003): Trusting the subject I. *Journal of Consciousness Studies* 10: 9–10.
Jack, Anthony I. and Andreas Roepstorff (2004): Trusting the subject II. *Journal of Consciousness Studies* 11: 7–8.
Keen, Suzanne (2007): *Empathy and the Novel*. New York: Oxford University Press.
Keunen, Bart (2000): Bakhtin, genre formation, and the cognitive turn: Chronotopes as memory schemata. *CLCWeb: Comparative Literature and Culture* 2(2). http://docs.lib.purdue.edu/clcweb/vol2/iss2/2
Lakoff, George (1987): *Women, Fire and Dangerous Things: What Categories Reveal About the Mind*. Chicago: University of Chicago Press.
Lakoff, George and Mark Johnson (1980): *Metaphors We Live By*. Chicago: University of Chicago Press.
Lakoff, George and Mark Johnson (1999): *Philosophy in the Flesh*. Chicago: University of Chicago Press.
Langacker, Ronald (2008): *Cognitive Grammar: A Basic Introduction*. New York: Oxford University Press.
Larkin, Philip (1974): *High Windows*. London: Faber.
Louw, Bill and Marijka Milojkovic (2014): Semantic prosody. In: P. Stockwell and S. Whiteley (eds.), *The Handbook of Stylistics*, 263–280. Cambridge: Cambridge University Press.

Louwerse, Max M. and Willie van Peer (2009): How cognitive is cognitive poetics? The interaction between symbolic and embodied cognition. In: G. Brône and J. Vandaele (eds.), *Cognitive Poetics: Goals, Gains and Gaps*, 423–444. Berlin: de Gruyter.

Lyons, William (1986): *The Disappearance of Introspection*. Cambridge: MIT Press.

McConachie, Bruce A. and F. Elizabeth Hart (2006): *Performance and Cognition: Theatre Studies and the Cognitive Turn*. London: Taylor and Francis.

Miall, David S. (2005): Beyond interpretation: the cognitive significance of reading. In: H. Veivo, B. Pettersson and M. Polvinen (eds.), *Cognition and Literary Interpretation in Practice*, 129–156. Helsinki: University of Helsinki Press.

Miall, David S. (2006): *Literary Reading: Empirical and Theoretical Studies*. New York: Peter Lang.

Miall, David S. (2012): In pursuit of literariness: emotional and empirical perspectives. Paper presented at PALA conference, University of Malta, 16–18 July 2012.

Miall, David S., Don Kuiken, and Shelley Sikora (2004): Forms of self-implication in literary reading. *Poetics Today* 25(2): 171–203.

Morton, Adam (2004): *Philosophy in Practice: An Introduction to the Main Questions*. Oxford: Blackwell.

O'Halloran, Kieran A. (2007): Critical discourse analysis and the corpus-informed interpretation of metaphor at the register level. *Applied Linguistics* 28(1): 1–24.

Ong, Walter J. (1982): *Orality and Literacy: The Technologizing of the Word*. New York: Methuen.

Ong, Walter J. ([1958] 2004): *Ramus, Method, and the Decay of Dialogue: From the Art of Discourse to the Art of Reason*, second edn. Cambridge: Harvard University Press.

Overgaard, Morten (2006): Introspection in science. *Consciousness and Cognition* 15: 629–633.

Peplow, David (2011): "Oh, I've known a lot of Irish people". Reading groups and the negotiation of literary interpretation. *Language and Literature* 20(4): 295–315.

Rumelhart, David E. (1975): Notes on a schema for stories. In: D. G. Bobrow and A. Collins (eds.), *Representation and Understanding*, 211–236. New York: Academic Press.

Rumelhart, David E. (1977): Understanding and summarizing brief stories. In: D. LaBerge and S. J. Samuels (eds.), *Basic Processes in Reading: Perception and Comprehension*, 265–303. Hillsdale: Lawrence Erlbaum.

Schank, Robert C. (1982): *Dynamic Memory: A Theory of Reminding and Learning in Computers and People*. Cambridge: Cambridge University Press.

Schank, Robert C. and Roger Abelson (1977): *Scripts, Plans, Goals and Understanding*, Hillsdale: Lawrence Erlbaum.

Schmidt, Siegfried J. (1982): *Foundation for the Empirical Study of Literature: The Components of a Basic Theory* [trans. R. de Beaugrande]. Hamburg: Helmut Buske.

Semino, Elena and Jonathan Culpeper (eds.) (2002): *Cognitive Stylistics*. Amsterdam: John Benjamins.

Sotirova, Violeta (2013): *Consciousness in Modernist Fiction: A Stylistic Study*. London: Palgrave.

Spolsky, Ellen (1993): *Gaps in Nature: Literary Interpretation and the Modular Mind*. New York: SUNY Press.

Sternberg, Meir (ed.) (2003): *The Cognitive Turn?: A Debate on Interdisciplinarity*. Special issue of *Poetics Today* 24(2).

Stockwell, Peter (2002): *Cognitive Poetics: An Introduction*. London: Routledge.

Stockwell, Peter (2009): *Texture: A Cognitive Aesthetics of Reading*. Edinburgh: Edinburgh University Press.
Stockwell, Peter (2010): The eleventh checksheet of the apocalypse. In: B. Busse and D. McIntyre (eds.) *Language and Style*, 419–432. London: Palgrave.
Stockwell, Peter (2012a): The reader's paradox. In: M. Burke, S. Csabi, L. Week, and J. Zerkowitz (eds.), *Pedagogical Stylistics*, 45–57. London: Continuum.
Stockwell, Peter (2012b): The artful science of literary study [original in Chinese, translated by Juling Ma]. *Journal of Foreign Language and Literature* (Sichuan).
Stockwell, Peter (2013): The positioned reader. *Language and Literature* 22(3): 263–277.
Stockwell, Peter (2014): Atmosphere and tone. In: P. Stockwell and S. Whiteley (eds.) *The Handbook of Stylistics*, 360–374. Cambridge: Cambridge University Press.
Stubbs, Michael (2005): Conrad in the computer: examples of quantitative stylistic methods. *Language and Literature* 14(1): 5–24.
Stubbs, Michael (2014): Quantitative methods in literary linguistics. In: P. Stockwell and S. Whiteley (eds.), *The Handbook of Stylistics*, 46–62. Cambridge: Cambridge University Press.
Swann, Joan and Daniel Allington (2009): Reading groups and the language of literary texts: a case study in social reading. *Language and Literature* 18(3): 247–264.
Tsur, Reuven (1992): *Toward a Theory of Cognitive Poetics*. Amsterdam: Elsevier.
Tsur, Reuven (2008): Deixis in literature – what *isn't* Cognitive Poetics? *Pragmatics and Cognition* 16(1): 123–154.
Turner, Mark (1991): *Reading Minds: The Study of English in the Age of Cognitive Science*. Princeton: Princeton University Press.
Turner, Mark (1996): *The Literary Mind*. New York: Oxford University Press.
van Peer, Willie (1986): *Stylistics and Psychology: Investigations of Foregrounding*. London: Croom Helm.
van Peer, Willie and Max Louwerse (eds.) (2003): *Thematics. Interdisciplinary Studies*. Amsterdam/Philadelphia: John Benjamins.
Vermeule, Blakey (2010): *Why Do We Care about Literary Characters?* Baltimore: Johns Hopkins University Press.
Vipond, Doug and Russell A. Hunt (1989): Literary processing and response as transaction: evidence for the contribution of readers, texts and situations. In: D. Meutsch and R. Viehoff (eds.), *Comprehension of Literary Discourse: Results and Problems of Interdisciplinary Approaches*, 155–174. Berlin: de Gruyter.
Werth, Paul (1999): *Text Worlds*. Harlow: Longman.
West, David (2012): *I. A. Richards and the Rise of Cognitive Stylistics*. London: Bloomsbury.
Whiteley, Sara (2011): Text World Theory, real readers and emotional responses to *The Remains of the Day*. *Language and Literature* 20(1): 23–41.
Wimsatt, W. K. and Monroe C. Beardsley (1954a): The intentional fallacy. In: *The Verbal Icon: Studies in the Meaning of Poetry*, 3–18. Lexington: University of Kentucky Press. First published in *Sewanee Review* 54: 468–488.
Wimsatt, W. K. and Monroe C. Beardsley (1954b): The affective fallacy. In: *The Verbal Icon: Studies in the Meaning of Poetry*, 21–39. Lexington: University of Kentucky Press. First published in *Sewanee Review* 57(1): 31–p55.
Zunshine, Lisa (2006): *Why We Read Fiction: Theory of Mind and the Novel*. Columbus: Ohio State University Press.

Index

References such as '178–9' indicate (not necessarily continuous) discussion of a topic across a range of pages. Wherever possible in the case of topics with many references, these have either been divided into sub-topics or only the most significant discussions of the topic are listed. Because the entire work is about 'cognitive linguistics', the use of this term (and certain others which occur constantly throughout the book) as an entry point has been minimised. Information will be found under the corresponding detailed topics.

Abelson, R. 211–12
abstract categories 53, 60, 186, 191
abstract rules 164–5, 170
abstraction 6, 12, 165, 209
abstractness, levels of 59, 62–3, 69, 72
accent recognition 145, 149
accents 14, 16, 19
acceptability 32, 111
accommodation theory 149, 217
accuracy 184–5, 211
acquisition 19, 51, 145–6, 182, 185–7, 189, 191–4, 197–9
– first language see *first language acquisition*
– second dialect 147
– second language see *second language acquisition*
action schemas 90, 94
active sentences 57, 63
acts of transfer 63, 70–1
addressees 98, 102, 174
adult L2 learners 185, 187, 190–1
adult-like lexicon 159
age 33, 123, 144–6, 149, 163–4, 169, 210, 213
agency 85, 92–3, 95
agent-patient relations 96, 167–8, 173
agents 55, 91–2, 94–5, 143, 168–9
agonists 90–3
agreement morphology 67
Allan, K. 34, 116, 140
allophones 3, 5, 8–13
allophonic cues 161
allophony 3, 13
amelioration 116–17
American English 3, 7–10, 71, 123
analysis, empirical 198–9
antagonists 90–3

archi-phonemes 4
argument structure constructions 184, 194, 199
arguments 12–13, 33, 108, 134, 188, 213, 218, 220
– theoretical 214
armchair linguistics 138
articulation 15–16, 184, 216–17
artificial agents 143
aspirated stops 3, 8, 14
associations 72, 115, 162, 225–6
– metonymic 115, 121
associative learning 193, 195–7
associative links 63, 69, 72, 74
atomic primitives 54–5, 68
attention 18–19, 34, 36, 85, 139–40, 159–60, 162–3, 214–15
– close 214, 219
– joint 109, 122, 160, 162–3
– scope of 94
– system 88, 93–5, 197–8
attributes 26–8, 54, 102, 196
authorial choices 213, 215
automatization 73–6
auxiliaries 55–6, 62, 66–7, 110

Baayen, H. 11, 59, 86, 147
babble 161
Baldwin, D. A. 162–3
Bannard, C. 161–2, 165, 167
Bardovi-Harlig, K. 190, 195
basic declarative sentences 56, 66–7
Bates, E. 160, 164, 173
Beckner, C. 75, 142–3, 199
Behaghel, O. 73
behavior 108, 137–8, 151
– linguistic 20, 72, 137, 151
behavioral data 197, 199

Berlin, B. 26, 38, 139
Bever, T. G. 57, 173
Blair, Tony 98, 102
Bloomfield, L. 5–6
Bock, K. 63
bodily functions 115–16
British English 71
Brugman, C. 1, 31
Bybee, J. L. 6, 13, 51, 53, 73–5, 108–11, 171–2, 193
by-phrases 55, 63

Cadierno, T. 189, 198
Caldwell-Harris, C. 40, 73, 110, 147, 183
Canadian English 147
Cap, P. 98
caregivers 160, 162–3, 166
categories 10, 26–9, 39–40, 68–9, 74, 112, 186, 195
- abstract 53, 60, 186, 191
- emergent 51, 69, 76
- exemplar-based 6, 112
- grammatical 50, 118
- natural 27
- primitive 51, 57, 66
- radial prototype 6, 8, 10
- syntactic 59, 66, 68, 72, 75
categorization 2, 5–6, 38–9, 86, 88–9, 122, 145, 147
- alternative views 11–12
- phenomena 27, 145
- prototype 139
- theory 10
causal meaning 120–1
causative doen 126–7
causative events 55–6
CDA (Critical Discourse Analysis) 82–8, 94–5, 103
- cognitive linguistic approach 86–9
- synergy with cognitive linguistics 81–6
CDS (child directed speech) 166–7
center of gravity 111–12
CG see Cognitive Grammar
change
- and flexibility 32–4
- language 51, 68, 108–11, 113–14, 124–5, 127–8, 145, 171

- lexical semantic 108, 112, 114–17, 120–3, 125, 128
- morphological 150
- phonological 20
- semantic see *semantic change*
- sociolinguistic 109, 123, 125
- sound 7, 125
child directed speech (CDS) 166–7
children 8–9, 14, 16–17, 59–62, 64–6, 159–70, 172–6, 186–7
- young 164, 166, 173, 175
Chilton, P. A. 82, 86–9, 97, 102
Chomsky, N. 1, 5, 54–5, 134, 136, 165
chunking 73–6, 110, 119
chunks 75, 110–11, 161, 167, 187–9
classical poetics 211
classifications 36, 39, 87, 102, 139
clause connectors 112
clause linkers 118–20
clause types 54–7, 63
clause-initial NP 55–6, 67
clauses 67, 73, 120
- declarative 112
- main 64, 66–7
- relative 54, 57, 64–6, 68, 175
- subordinate 119
- transactive 94–5
- transitive 54, 57
cleft sentences 57, 118
clitics 188
close attention 214, 219
closed syllables 3
clusters 4, 8, 12, 29–30, 140, 151
- polysemous 31–2
Cockcroft, R. 211–12
cognition 84, 86, 94, 108, 110, 128, 199, 208
- and literature 214–20
cognitive approaches 25, 50, 56, 82, 108, 133, 135, 208
cognitive construal 136
cognitive entrenchment 193, 197
Cognitive Grammar (CG) 2, 5, 8, 11, 15, 20, 94–5, 222–3
cognitive linguistics see *Introductory Note and detailed entries*
cognitive models 83, 86, 97, 209, 211
cognitive narratology 219, 221

cognitive phenomena 35, 50, 74, 123
cognitive poetics 97, 208–10, 212–14, 216–27
– developments 220–6
– enactment and dramatisation 223–4
– futures 226–7
– precursors 210–13
– return to linguistics 222–3
– singularity and situatedness 224
– subtlety 224–6
cognitive processes 50, 87, 109, 182
– domain-general 51, 75, 103
cognitive psychology 74, 172, 194, 212–13, 217, 219–22
cognitive representations 108, 114, 145, 149
cognitive science 58, 88, 199, 209–10, 212–13, 215, 222–3, 226
cognitive semantics 31–5, 83
Cognitive Sociolinguistics 41, 113, 122, 133–4, 141, 144, 146, 148–50
cognitive stylistics 208, 218
cognitive turn 81, 209, 214–15
cognitive-functional approaches 135
coherence, semantic 71, 73
colour terms 26, 139
commands 53–4
commercial transaction scene 37–8
common ground 102, 174–5
communication, before words 160–1
comparative correlative construction 56, 69
competence 50–1, 53
– creative 192
– lectal 145
– linguistic 165, 183–4
complex sentences 50, 67–8
complex structures 187, 189, 192
compositional approach 54–5, 73
computational stylistics, and corpus stylistics 217–18
conceptual construal 143
conceptual metaphors 34–6, 83–4, 86, 108, 121, 139–40, 220–1
conceptual metonymy 34, 36–7
conceptual models 37, 225
conceptual onomasiological variation 40–1
conceptual primitives 50
conceptual proximisation 100
conceptual structures 50, 82, 85–6, 94, 97

conceptualisation 81–2, 84–5, 87–8, 95, 97, 103, 159, 212
conceptualisers 88, 99–100, 121
concrete lexical expressions 59, 69
concrete utterances 59, 69, 75
configuration, structural 87–93
connectors, clause 112
consciousness 86, 199, 212, 217, 219–20, 222
consonants 5, 7, 9–10, 16–17, 95, 160–1
constituency 19, 73, 75
– lexical 199
constituent structure 73–5
constituents 19, 75, 110, 119, 126, 159, 169
construal 85, 92–3, 95, 97, 137
– cognitive 136
– conceptual 143
– force-dynamic 90–1
– operations 87–9, 94, 96–9, 101, 103
– and discursive strategies 88
– proactive identity 146
constructicon 117–19
construction grammar 52–4, 56–7, 66, 109, 113, 125, 127, 182
– usage-based 50–76
constructional priming 63
constructional schemas 53, 55, 60, 62, 110
constructional semantics 143
constructionist model of language learning 183, 192–7
constructionist perspective 183, 198–9
construction-particular properties 55, 67
constructions 51–60, 63–72, 113–14, 118–20, 125–7, 183–6, 188–95, 198–9
– comparative correlative 56, 69
– complex 189, 191
– concrete 165, 186
– and constructs 59
– creative 186, 191
– at different levels of abstractness 59–62
– ditransitive 70–1
– in first and second language acquisition 183–92
– general aspects 54–6
– grammatical 63, 85, 89, 94, 142, 195
– grammaticalizing 114
– imperative 53
– importance 52, 54

– and L2 learners 183–5
– and lexemes 54, 69–72
– morphological 54, 117
– passive 55–7, 63, 67–8, 70, 94–5, 119
– at same level of abstractness 63–6
– structured inventory 165–6
– syntactic 112, 114, 119
– and syntactic categories 66–9
– to-dative 63, 70–1
– transitive 57, 70, 168–9
– verb argument 61, 66, 185, 191, 194, 196–7, 199
constructs 59, 69, 91, 97
content words 70, 186
contexts 32–4, 85, 87, 89–90, 133–6, 148, 174–5, 209
– discursive 85, 87, 103
– monosemic 26
– polysemic 26, 30
contextual dynamics and polysemy 32–4
contingency 193, 196–7, 199
– form-function 196–7, 199
Contrastive Analysis Hypothesis 198
control 19, 37, 67, 85, 144, 189, 212, 215–16
– conscious 74
conversations 20, 108, 123, 160–2, 166, 175
– adult-child 186
corpora 42, 74, 123–4, 138, 166–7, 188–90, 194, 199
corpus data 42, 150, 166, 199
corpus linguistics 138, 140, 183–4, 196, 209, 217–18, 226
corpus stylistics, and computational stylistics 217–18
corpus-based approaches 34, 42
count nouns 50
creative competence 192
Critical Discourse Analysis see CDA
Critical Metaphor Analysis 86
Croft, W. 34, 36, 52–4, 66–8, 85, 87, 115, 141–3
cross-linguistic differences 84, 168, 173
cross-linguistic regularities 121
Cruse, D. A. 33–4, 37, 54, 85, 87, 96, 115, 197
cue competition model 173
cues 4, 57, 161, 167, 173, 195–6
– grammatical 167
– inflectional 195

cultural models 35, 139–40, 145
cultural perspective 139–40
cultures 4, 121, 137, 140, 199, 208, 211, 213–14
Cutler, A. 14
Cuyckens, H. 31

data
– behavioral 197, 199
– corpus 42, 150, 166, 199
– longitudinal 185, 189
– usage 42, 138
de Courtenay, B. 1, 4–5, 13
Deane, P. D. 31
de-categorialization 112
declarative sentences, basic 56, 66–7
decontextualization 135–6
Dekeyser, X. 34, 195
deletions 13, 167
description 29, 31–2, 36–9, 136
– semantic 25, 28
– textual 221
development, grammatical 64, 66, 187
developmental psycholinguistics 159, 170
developmental sequences 186, 188, 190
Dewell, R. B. 31
Diachronic Construction Grammar 109, 114, 125–8
diachronic semantics 33–4
dialectal/dialectic relationships 137, 146–7
dialectology 137, 142–4, 148
dialects 8, 10–12, 14, 16, 41, 133, 136, 150–1
direct objects 38, 67–8
directed speech 166
directive speech 53
direct-object relatives 65–6
Dirven, R. 34–6, 38, 82–3, 85–7, 96, 139, 141, 145
discourse 37, 63, 81–103, 185, 209–11, 214, 221
– analysis 209, 217
– beyond the sentence 97
– ideology in 84, 87
– markers 119
– metaphor in 84, 143
– political 81, 85, 89, 97, 102
– space 87, 97, 100–101

– model 98
– world 97, 99–100
discursive contexts 85, 87, 103
discursive strategies 87, 89, 103
– and construal operations 88
dispersion 125, 127
distance 41, 71, 96–7
– objective linguistic 145
ditransitive 63, 70–1, 118, 184, 196
diversity 136–7, 141, 145
– contextualised 210
– experiential 137
Divjak, D. 34, 40, 73, 110, 147, 183, 197
Dixon, R. M. W. 67–8, 215
doen, causative 126–7
domain-general cognitive processes 51, 75, 103
domain-general socio-cognitive processes 109, 114, 117
domains 35, 39, 86, 108–9, 114, 117, 122, 139
– source 83–5
Donegan, P. J. 1, 6, 8, 15, 17, 20
double perspectives 133, 149
drama 208, 210–11
dramatisation 223

Early Modern English 116, 124
ecology of factors 123–4
embodied experience 89
embodied perception 2, 14
embodiment 41, 139, 142, 197, 199, 211, 223
– situated 142
emergence 73–4, 109, 114, 119, 122, 125, 134–5, 190
emergent categories 51, 69, 76
emergentism 199
empirical analysis 198–9
empirical evidence 38, 109
empirical poetics 215–17
empiricism 215, 217–18, 220
enactment 213, 223
energy 91–4
English
– American 3, 7–10, 71, 123
– British 71
– Canadian 147

– Early Modern 116, 124
– verbs 172
entrenchment 38, 40, 50, 72, 110
– cognitive 193, 197
epistemic capacity 99–100
epistemic proximisation 100–102
equivalence, semantic 144
ergative morphology 68
errors 14, 65–6, 172, 184
– over-regularisation 172
– speech 4, 9, 63
Eskildsen, S. W. 189–90
euphemisms 115–17
evaluation 89, 97, 101–2
Evans, N. 7
Evans, V. 31, 33, 89, 225
events 37, 86, 89–91, 95–6, 115, 121, 160, 198
– causative 55–6
– intransitive 67
– transitive 67
– usage 111, 137, 159, 190
evidence 7, 13–14, 56–7, 102, 167–9, 187–8, 190, 217–20
– empirical 38, 109
evidential value 218, 224
evidentiality 101
exemplar clouds 111, 127
exemplar theory 11, 20, 199
exemplar tokens 111, 126
exemplar-based categories 6, 112
exemplar-based memory 117
exemplars 11, 117, 147, 193–6
expansion 25, 119–20, 122
– grammaticalization as 120
– host-class 119–20
– pragmatic 119–20
– syntactic 119–20
expectations 174–6, 198, 226
experience 72–3, 83–4, 86, 136–7, 197–9, 212, 220, 223–5
– embodied 89
– input 185, 191
– language users 69, 72, 75
– literary 215–16
– reading 215–16, 220
experiments 57, 163, 167–70, 184, 216, 219, 224, 226

expressions 35–7, 60, 101–2, 116–17, 120, 141–2, 149–50, 190
– idiomatic 56, 191
– lexical 52, 54, 59–60, 62–4, 69, 72, 74, 113
– non-idiomatic grammatical 56
– referring 174–5
– regular 56
extensions 10, 99–100
– meaning 115, 143
– metaphorical 115
– metonymic 20, 116, 120
external world 160
extrapolation 25–6, 39
eyes 17, 160–1, 196, 213

family resemblances 27, 30–1, 112
Ferreira-Junior, F. 185, 191, 194, 196–7
Fillmore, C. J. 37–8, 53, 56, 114, 188
finger tapping 19
finite verbs 67, 188
first language acquisition 59, 110, 115, 159–76
– communication before words 160–1
– cue competition model 173
– developing a lexicon 162–4
– and formulaic language 185–6
– grammar 164–73
– inflectional morphology 169–73
– pragmatic skills 159, 174–5
– and second language acquisition compared 197–8
– word order 168–9
flexibility and change 32–4
fluency 183–4, 188, 192
focus 20, 81, 124–5, 135–6, 142–4, 167, 182–3, 211
force schemas 90–1, 93
force-dynamic construals 90–1
force-dynamic schemas 90, 92–3
form-function contingency 196–7, 199
form-function mapping 196
forms
– grammatical 109, 117, 120, 122
– grammaticalizing 118–19
– linguistic 110, 112, 118, 122, 163, 176, 226
– regular 170, 172

– variant 12, 113
– word 161, 171–2
formulaic frames 61, 191
formulaic language
– and first language acquisition 185–6
– methodological considerations 190–1
– and second language acquisition 187–92
formulaic sequences 184, 188, 191–2
formulaic-creative continuum 190, 192
formulas 165, 184, 186, 188–92
Foucault, M. 82–3
frame semantics 37–8
frame theory 37–8
frames 34, 37–8, 56, 83, 86, 94, 139, 191
– commercial transaction 37
– formulaic 61, 191
framing 87, 218, 222
– strategies 88–9
frequency 73–4, 121–2, 125, 127, 171–2, 183–6, 192–4, 199
– effects 110, 172
– fundamental 14, 16
– low 186, 192
– role in phonology 13–15
– text 125–6
– token 172, 185, 193–4, 196
– type 172, 185, 189, 193
functional linguistics 83, 135
functions 37, 52–3, 64, 135–8, 167–8, 173–5, 190–1, 195–7
– bodily 115–16
– grammatical 118, 120
– ideological 87, 89, 95
– pragmatic 175, 187
– syntactic 66, 68

gender 14, 118, 124–5, 146
generalisability 216–17
generalisations 30, 59, 69, 113, 125, 147, 165–7, 209
generative grammar 5, 54–5, 57, 73, 75, 135–6, 182, 189
generative linguistics 58, 69, 75, 135
generative phonology 1, 5–6, 8, 147
genitive choice 123–4
genres 89, 102, 123, 185, 190, 221, 224
Gestalt 87–9
gestalt psychologists 50, 213

Gibbs, R. W. 35, 41, 83, 86, 115, 223–4
girls 2, 57, 65, 174
glottal stops 3, 10, 12, 18
Goldberg, A. E. 51, 53–4, 58, 64, 113, 117, 194, 196–7
grammar 50–2, 58–9, 73, 75, 117–18, 144–5, 164–72, 188–9
– artificial 60
– construction 52–4, 56–7, 66, 109, 113, 125, 127, 182
– development 161, 170
– first language acquisition 164–73
– generative 5, 54–5, 57, 73, 75, 135–6, 182, 189
– mental 110, 149
– systemic-functional 222
– usage-based construction 50–76
grammatical analysis 51, 58, 69
grammatical categories 50, 118
grammatical change 117, 121–3
grammatical constructions 63, 85, 89, 94, 142, 195
grammatical cues 167
grammatical development 64, 66, 187
grammatical forms 109, 117, 120, 122
grammatical functions 118, 120
grammatical knowledge 50, 69, 167
grammatical markers 114, 173
grammatical patterns 37, 54–6, 62–3, 167
grammatical relations 57, 65–9
grammatical rules 165, 188
grammatical signs 51, 53–4, 58
grammatical structures 62, 109
grammatical theories 51, 66, 68
grammatical units 52–4
grammaticalization 20, 51, 109, 112–14, 116–22, 125, 128
– as expansion 120
grammaticalizing constructions 114
grammaticalizing forms 118–19
grammaticalizing units 118–19
gravity, center of 111–12
Gries, S. T. 63, 70–1, 113–15, 124, 150–1, 184–5, 197, 199
groupings 75, 184
groups 25, 123, 184–5, 216
– social 97, 145–6
– of speakers 137, 145

hammering 19
hearers 14, 87, 97, 110, 193
hearing 14–15, 17, 169, 175
here-and-now 108
Herman, D. 219, 221
hierarchical organization 59, 73, 75
high token frequency 185, 193–4
high type frequency 185, 193
historical linguistics 108–28
historical sociolinguistics 122–5, 128
historiography 214
history 1, 126, 134–5, 139–40, 199, 208, 214, 222
– of lexical semantics 25, 42
– of phonology 4, 7
holistic properties 55–6
holistic structures 88–9
homogeneity 136, 138, 142, 145
horizontal links 59, 63, 72
host-class expansion 119–20

idealized speakers 109, 113
identification 37, 87, 93–5
– strategies 88, 93
identity 4, 11, 18, 137, 146
– semantic 33
– social 137, 146
identity-of-sense anaphora 33
ideological discourse research 81, 85–6
ideological functions 87, 89, 95
ideological properties 81, 83, 103
ideological properties of text 81, 89, 103
ideology 81–7
– conceptual parameters 89–102
– in discourse 84, 87
idiomatic expressions 56, 191
idiomaticity 56, 183, 191–2
idioms 53, 56, 192
idiosyncratic properties 55–6
image schema transformations 8, 10, 17
image schemas 8, 10–11, 17, 86, 89–90
image schemata 89–90, 93
images 11, 20, 84, 162
imperative construction 53
imperative sentences 53–5
implicit knowledge 183
indeterminacy 25, 28
indirect objects 64

indirect-object relatives 65–6
infants 60, 149, 159–64
inferences 37, 83, 87, 90
- pragmatic 163–4
inflectional morphology 119, 159, 167
- first language acquisition 169–73
inflections 118, 165, 167, 169–70, 172–3, 195
informants 216–17, 219
information, mutual 184
input 149–50, 165–6, 168, 170–1, 185–6, 191, 193–5, 199
- experience 185, 191
instantiations 8, 11, 18, 87, 96, 103, 189, 223–4
instigators 91–2
instructions 53–4
intelligence reports 98, 101–2
intentions 17, 99, 160–3, 208, 211, 218
interaction 91–2, 94, 96, 109–10, 136–7, 150–1, 160, 162
interactional sociolinguistics 146
interconnected signs 51, 58
interlinguistic variation 136–9
intermediate learners 188–9
internal structures 27, 83, 90
intersubjective explicit 102
intersubjective opaque 102
intralinguistic variation 136–9, 141, 147
intransitive events 67
intraspeaker variation 109
introspection 138, 208, 219–20
invariance 2
- problem 7–8
- and variation 2–3
Israel 113, 125–7
items, lexical 32, 35–6, 40, 108–9, 115–16, 118, 122, 125
Itkonen, E. 142

Johnson, M. 34, 36, 38, 82–3, 86, 89–90, 210, 212
joint attention 109, 122, 160, 162–3

Kay, P. 26, 53, 114, 139
Kirby, S. 143
knowledge 102, 113, 172, 175, 183, 185, 197–8, 211–12
- grammatical 50, 69, 167
- implicit 183

- linguistic 86, 111, 113, 117, 125, 190, 192
- productive 168, 170
- underlying 186, 189
Koller, V. 82, 84, 86, 89
Kövecses, Z. 35, 140
Krashen, S. 187–8

L1 language acquisition see *first language acquisition*
L2 language acquisition see *second language acquisition*
L2A, naturalistic 194–5
labels 11, 87, 116, 122
Lakoff, G. 8, 10, 34–6, 82–3, 85–6, 140, 210, 212
Langacker, R. W. 12, 50–1, 53–5, 85–7, 94–6, 100–101, 222–3, 225
language, native 15, 161, 169, 183, 187
language change 51, 68, 108–11, 113–14, 124–5, 127–8, 145, 171
- and usage-based model 109–14
language learning, constructionist model 183, 192
language processing 110, 183–4, 191, 195
language use 33, 50–1, 72–3, 75–6, 81–2, 108–9, 113–14, 136–7
language users 28, 36, 50, 66, 69, 72, 137–8, 144–6
- experience 69, 72, 75
language varieties 40–1, 108, 133, 145, 150
language-external factors 123, 125
Larkin, P. 225
Larsen-Freeman, D. 185, 199
learners 19, 173, 183–5, 187–96, 198
- adult L2 185, 187, 190–1
- intermediate 188–9
learning 159, 161–2, 165–6, 172–5, 182, 191–3, 195, 198
- second language see *second language acquisition*
- word 162–3
lectal competence 145
lectal factors 138, 148, 150
lectal variation 41, 133, 138–9, 141, 143, 145, 147
lects 41, 133, 142, 145
Lehmann, C. 109, 119, 121

lexemes 52–4, 63, 69–70, 72
– and constructions 54, 69–72
lexical constituency 199
lexical expressions 52, 54, 59–60, 62–4, 69, 72, 74, 113
– concrete 59, 69
lexical items 32, 35–6, 40, 108–9, 115–16, 118, 122, 125
lexical links 59, 69, 72
lexical meanings 33, 37, 108
lexical network 58
lexical priming 63
lexical relations 34, 38, 83
lexical semantic change 108, 112, 114–17, 120–3, 125, 128
lexical semantics 1, 20, 25–43, 90
– current developments 41–2
– history 25, 42
lexical signs 51, 54
lexical structure 38
lexical variation 41, 143
lexical verbs 112, 120
lexicography 38
lexicology 34, 209
lexicon 5, 32, 34–5, 58, 117, 122–3, 164–5, 170–1
– adult-like 159
– developing 162–4
– mental 56, 58, 63–4, 171
lexis 117–18, 144–5, 182
Lieven, E. V. M. 60–2, 160, 166–7, 173, 186, 191
linguistic behavior 20, 72, 137, 151
linguistic community 135, 138
linguistic competence 165, 183–4
linguistic elements 53, 58–9, 72–5, 144, 183
linguistic forms 110, 112, 118, 122, 163, 176, 226
linguistic knowledge 86, 111, 113, 117, 125, 190, 192
linguistic phenomena 86, 143, 145, 150
linguistic relativity 141
linguistic representations 20, 97, 197
linguistic signs 51–2, 58, 76
linguistic structure 50–1, 55, 58–9, 69, 75–6, 83–4, 185, 191
linguistic systems 40, 136, 138, 142, 159
linguistic units 6, 20, 112, 119, 161

linguistic variables 123, 146, 150–1
linguistics see *Introductory Note and Detailed Entries*
links 34, 51, 58–9, 62–3, 66, 72, 76, 143–4
– associative 63, 69, 72, 74
– horizontal 59, 63, 72
– lexical 59, 69, 72
– syntactic 59, 66, 72
– taxonomic 59, 69, 72
literariness 215, 221, 224
literary criticism 209, 217, 224
literary critics 209–10, 213, 217, 221, 225
literary experience 215–16
literary language 210, 218
literary texts 208–9, 214–15, 218, 220–2, 224–6
literary works 209–10, 214–18, 221–4
literature 32, 35, 69, 101, 142, 212–15, 221–4, 226
– and cognition 214–20
– and linguistics 208–10
location 36, 86, 90, 93, 99
longitudinal data 185, 189
long-term memories 8, 11, 147, 182
Louwerse, M. M. 215, 220, 222

MacWhinney, B. 173, 196
mapping
– form-function 196
– metaphorical 121
Marín Arrese, J. 87–9, 96, 102
markers 68, 118, 120–1, 169, 173, 189
– discourse 119
– grammatical 114, 173
marking 67, 167–9, 173
mass nouns 50
meaning extensions 115, 143
meanings
– causal 120–1
– lexical 33, 37, 108
– social 146
– temporal 121
media representations 91
Mellow, J. D. 189
memory 13, 62, 111, 170–2, 192, 209, 211, 220
– exemplar-based 117
– long-term 8, 11, 147, 182

– schemata 194
– short-term 182
mental grammar 110, 149
mental lexicon 56, 58, 63–4, 171
mental representations 82, 147, 195, 221
mentally-stored sound images 4
metaphor studies 35–6, 41, 81, 87, 140
metaphor theory 35, 86, 182
metaphorical mappings 121
metaphorical models 140, 145
metaphorical patterns 139
metaphors 30–1, 34–7, 81–6, 88–9, 115, 123, 140, 143
– conceptual 34–6, 83–4, 86, 108, 121, 139–40, 220–1
– and metonymy 31, 36–8, 41, 117, 145
methodology 134, 138, 144, 148, 151, 190, 215, 219
metonymic extensions 20, 116, 120
metonymical patterns 36–7, 143
metonymy 11, 20, 31, 36–8, 41, 108, 115–17, 123
– conceptual 34, 36–7
– and metaphors 31, 36–8, 41, 117, 145
– referential 37
modal axis 97, 99–100
modal positioning 88, 101
models 5, 26–7, 37, 145, 149, 171–3, 195, 217–18
– cognitive 83, 86, 97, 209, 211
– conceptual 37, 225
– cue competition 173
– cultural 35, 139–40, 145
– discourse space 98
– general 26, 147
– metaphorical 140, 145
– network 12, 31, 58, 171–2
– prototype 26, 32, 38
– prototype-based 25, 32, 145
– recontextualizing 137, 147
– Rescorla-Wagner 195–6
– usage-based see *usage-based models*
morphemes 70, 74, 127, 187, 193, 195
morphological change 150
morphological constructions 54, 117
morphological schemas 118, 171
morphologization 119–20, 122

morphology 1, 57, 68, 167, 170, 172–3, 182, 209
– agreement 67
– ergative 68
– inflectional 119, 159, 167, 169–73
morpho-syntactic properties 56, 110
morpho-syntax 182
motion 71, 86, 89–90, 93
– path of 90, 93
– schemas 90–2
– verbs 121
multi-word sequences 167, 187
multi-word utterances 60, 167
mutual information (MI) 184

names 18, 39–40, 118, 162, 170
– novel 162, 170
narratology
– cognitive 219, 221
– post-classical 221
natiolects 150–1
national varieties 41, 133
native language 15, 161, 169, 183, 187
native speakers 3, 7–9, 14, 147, 160, 183–5, 187–8
natural phonology 1, 5
naturalistic L2A 194–5
neighboring sounds 5, 14
Nerlich, B. 34, 38, 112, 115
network architecture 58–9
network models 12, 31, 58, 171–2
networks
– dynamic 51, 76
– lexical 58
– radial 31
nominalisation 85, 95–6
non-equality 27
non-formulaic phrases 184
non-idiomatic grammatical expressions 56
non-linguistic systems 35
noun phrases 51, 53, 70, 168–9
nouns 62, 66, 75, 118, 120, 127, 169, 191
– count 50
– mass 50
novel names 162, 170
novel objects 162–3
novel verbs 168–9, 173

novel words 163, 170
Nycz, J. 147

objects 3–4, 14–15, 62, 66, 115, 160, 163–4, 212
– direct 38, 67–8
– indirect 64
– novel 162–3
– prepositional 110
O'Donnell, M. B. 194, 198
onomasiological grouping 36–7
onomasiological salience 38–42
onomasiological structure 34–5, 41
onomasiological variation 40–1, 144
– conceptual 40–1
onomasiology 34–41
open slots 60, 70
oppositions 4, 83, 85, 91, 118, 135–8
Optimality Theory (OT) 1, 8
order, word 55–7, 60, 64–5, 68, 167–9, 173
ordering, relative 185, 191
OT see *Optimality Theory*
over-regularisation errors 172

Panther, K.-U. 36–7
parole 51, 135
participant roles 91, 96, 222
participants 67–8, 85, 91–5, 99, 184
passive constructions 55–7, 63, 67–8, 70, 94–5, 119
past tense 118, 169, 171–2, 193
path of motion 90, 93
pathways 20, 118–20, 125
patients 62, 91–4, 168, 173
patterns 17–18, 61, 111–12, 114, 147, 151, 198, 224
– common 188, 220
– general 170, 224
– grammatical 37, 54–6, 62–3, 167
– metaphorical 139
– metonymical 36–7, 143
– regular 111, 170
– sound 52
– structural 51–2, 56–8, 60, 70
pejoration 116–17
perception 1, 5, 7, 13, 15–17, 195, 197, 219
– embodied 2, 14
– nature 15–17

– phonemic 3, 10
– phonetic 9
– speech 15, 146
– visual 50
perceptual dialectology 144, 148
permission 53–4
perspectives 37–8, 87, 89, 96, 111, 138–9, 143, 150–1
– constructionist 198–9
– cultural 139–40
– double 133, 149
– sociolinguistic 149, 216
– usage-based 73, 118, 141
perspectivisation 86
phenomena 32, 94, 98, 124–5, 140, 145, 151, 215–16
– cognitive 35, 50, 74, 123
– linguistic 86, 143, 145, 150
– social 123, 142
phoneme inventories 6
phonemes 4–11, 13–14, 74, 112, 114, 183
– single 3, 13
phonemic perception 3, 10
phonetic features 63, 223
phonetic perception 9
phoneticians 3, 7
phonetics 2, 7–8, 64, 147, 209
phonological change 20
phonological representations 6, 147
phonological storage 20
phonological variation 13–14
phonology 1–21, 147, 182, 194, 209
– generative 1, 5–6, 8, 147
– history 4, 7
– natural 1, 5
– role of frequency 13–15
– usage-based 147
phrases 54, 66, 73, 110–11, 183, 185, 193, 225–6
– coordinated 110
– formulaic 188, 192
– non-formulaic 184
– noun 51, 53, 70, 168–9
– prepositional 38, 53, 119
– structure 72–5
– verb 75
Pierrehumbert, J. 1, 6, 11, 147
pivot schemas 60–1

pivot words 60–1
poetics 208–27
– classical 211
– cognition and literature 214–20
– cognitive see *cognitive poetics*
– developments in cognitive poetics 220–6
– empirical 215–17
– introspection 219–20
– linguistics and literature 208–10
– precursors to cognitive poetics 210–13
– textual analysis 214, 218–19, 222
poetry 208, 211, 218, 223–6
poignancy 223, 225
police 13, 84, 91–3
Polish 169, 173
political discourse 81, 85, 89, 97, 102
political protests 89, 91
polysemic context 26, 30
polysemous clusters 31–2
polysemy 25, 31–3, 41, 108
– and contextual dynamics 32–4
– criteria 32
– development 112, 115
– synchronic 109, 116
Port, R. F. 4, 11, 86, 147
positioning 42, 87, 96–7
– modal 88, 101
post-classical narratology 221
pragmatic expansion 119–20
pragmatic functions 175, 187
pragmatic inferences 163–4
pragmatic skills 159, 174–5
pragmatics 141, 163, 182, 209
precursors 161, 210–13
predictions 26, 147, 166–7, 173
prefabricated routines 187–8
preferences 19, 40, 135, 137, 140, 150, 184, 189
– generativist 138
– subcategorization 185
prepositional object 110
prepositional phrases 38, 53, 119
present tense 195
primed recognition 184
priming 63, 124, 194
– constructional 63
– lexical 63
– syntactic 63, 150, 185

primitive categories 51, 57, 66
primitives
– atomic 54–5, 68
– conceptual 50
processes
– automatic 74
– learning 171–2, 175, 189, 192
– reading 215–16
processing 3, 5, 15, 57, 182, 184, 194, 197
– language 110, 183–4, 191, 195
– units 73–5
– visual 85, 197
production 1–2, 13, 15–16, 63, 110, 184, 186, 190–1
– early 188
– speech 5, 17, 60, 63, 110, 183
productive knowledge 168, 170
productivity 125, 172, 193
pronouns 118, 174–5, 189, 191
properties 55–6, 84, 159–60, 188, 218
– holistic 55–6
– ideological 81, 83, 103
– idiosyncratic 55–6
– morpho-syntactic 56, 110
prose 208, 211
– fiction 214, 224
prosody 12, 17, 19, 161
– semantic 226
protestors 85, 91–3, 95
protests, political 89, 91
prototype effects 26, 28, 31, 42
prototype models 26, 32, 38
prototype structure 12, 29, 33, 142
prototype theory 11, 25, 87, 108, 195
prototype-based models 25, 32, 145
prototypes 12, 25, 31, 38, 195–6
prototypicality 32–3, 40, 113, 122, 139, 145, 193
– effects 26, 145
– in monsemic context 26–30
– in polysemic context 30–1
– semantic 218
proximisation 98, 100
– conceptual 100
– epistemic 100–102
– spatial 99–100
– temporal 99–100

psycholinguistic factors 149, 193
psycholinguistic research 57, 59, 63, 74, 148
psycholinguistics 57, 128, 133, 149–50, 183
– developmental 159, 170
psychological mechanisms 1, 50, 74
psychological reality 94, 183
psychology 26, 42, 209, 215
– cognitive 74, 172, 194, 212–13, 217, 219–22
– empirical 213

radial networks 31
radial prototype categories 6, 8, 10
radial sets 26–7, 30–1
Ramscar, M. 11, 59, 86, 147
range 26, 28, 30, 56, 58, 86, 89, 222–3
reader-control 215–16
reader-response 216–17
readers 84, 86, 208–9, 213, 215–18, 220–1, 223, 225–6
reading 27, 30, 161–2, 184, 208–9, 215–18, 220, 223
– community 208, 216
– experience 215–16, 220
– process 215–16
reality 82–4, 88, 97, 100–101, 213
– external 15
– psychological 94, 183
recency 194
recognition 41, 191
– primed 184
recontextualizing models 137, 147
redundancy 159, 193, 195
referential boundaries 27
referential metonymy 37
referents 32, 39–40, 113, 116, 160, 174
referring expressions 174–5
regiolects 41, 133
regional domination 98–9
regular expressions 56
regular forms 170, 172
regular patterns 111, 170
relations 81–2, 85, 88, 90, 95, 97, 99, 109
– grammatical 57, 65–9
– lexical 34, 38, 83
– oppositional 92
– spatial 120

relationships 27, 30, 35, 59, 63, 66, 69–72, 81–2
relative clauses 54, 57, 64–6, 68, 175
relative ordering 185, 191
relative pronouns 64–5
relatives, indirect-object 65–6
relativity, linguistic 141
repetitions 74, 110, 122, 166, 185, 225
representations 6, 83–4, 144, 147, 165, 172, 219, 223
– cognitive 108, 114, 145, 149
– linguistic 20, 97, 197
– media 91
– mental 82, 147, 195, 221
– phonological 6, 147
– schematic 59, 62, 193
– spatial 97
– syntactic 62, 68
representative examples 139, 146
requests 53–4, 113
Rescorla-Wagner model 195–6
rhetoric 210–11
rhyme 9
rhythms 17–20
Richards, I. A. 213
Robinson, J. A. 34, 41, 123, 143, 182, 185, 197–8
roles 67–8, 90–2, 140–1, 145, 147, 150, 191, 193
– participant 91, 96, 222
Rosch, E. 10, 26–7, 42, 112, 139, 195
routines 162, 187, 197
– prefabricated 187–8
rules 2, 5, 9, 55–6, 117, 170–2, 183, 187
– abstract 164–5, 170
– combinatorial 54
– general 55, 57
– grammatical 165, 188

salience 34, 38–40, 86, 88, 93–5, 101, 145–6, 193–5
– effects 32, 41
– onomasiological 38–40, 42
– semantic 26
– semasiological 40
Sapir, E. 1, 4–5
Saussure, F. de 1, 4, 52, 88, 134, 142
scale 97, 99–100, 199

scanning 88, 95–6
– modes 95–6
– sequential 95–6
– summary 96
Scarcella, R. C. 187–8
scenes 38, 63, 85–6, 88–9, 94, 96, 108, 168–9
– commercial transaction 37–8
Schank, R. C. 211–12
schemas 11–13, 20, 90, 93–4, 171–2, 209, 211, 220–1
– force 90–1, 93
– force-dynamic 90, 92–3
– image 8, 10–11, 17, 86, 89–90
– morphological 118, 171
– motion 90–2
– pivot 60–1
– sound 5–6
– syntactic 118
schemata
– image 89–90, 93
– memory 194
schematic representations 59, 62, 193
schematicity 53, 118, 120
schematisation 59, 86, 88, 90–1, 109, 121, 147, 165
schwas 13
scope 5, 15, 35–6, 114, 119–20, 133
– of attention 94
– categorical 116
– decrease 119
second language acquisition 182–99
– and constructionist model of language learning 183, 192–7
– constructions 183–92
– first v second language learning 197–8
– and formulaic language 187–92
– future priorities 198–9
second person 37
segments 3–4, 7, 9, 12–13, 17, 161, 175
semantic background 94
semantic change 33, 36, 115–16, 121
– lexical 108, 112, 114, 116–17, 120–3, 125, 128
semantic coherence 71, 73
semantic descriptions 25, 28
semantic equivalence 144
semantic fit 71–2

semantic identity 33
semantic prosody 226
semantic prototypicality 218
semantic salience 26–31
semantic shifts 116
semantic structure 25, 27, 32, 36
semantics 35, 56, 63–4, 85–6, 118–21, 123, 139, 149–50
– cognitive 31–5, 83
– constructional 143
– diachronic 33–4
– frame 37–8
– lexical 1, 20, 25–43, 90
– spatial 143
semasiological salience 40
semasiological structure 31, 38, 40
semasiology 25–34
Semino, E. 37, 85, 143, 213, 218, 221
senses, word 115–16, 123
sentence types 56, 63, 66, 70
sentences 33, 61, 63–4, 66, 164–5, 167–9, 184, 186
– active 57, 63
– cleft 57, 118
– complex 50, 67–8
– imperative 53–5
– passive 55–7, 63, 67–8
– transitive 56–7, 68, 167, 169
sequences 66, 74–5, 110, 119, 167, 186, 188, 190–1
– developmental 186, 188, 190
– formulaic 184, 188, 191–2
– multi-word 167, 187
sequential scanning 95–6
sets 6, 8, 26–7, 86, 141–2, 146–7, 159–60, 223–6
– radial 26–7, 30–1
sex 32, 144
s-genitive 113, 121, 123–4
Sharifian, F. 139
shifts 109, 125–6, 138–9
– semantic 116
– vowel 5, 8
Shirai, Y. 189
short-term memory 182
signs 52, 54, 58, 76
– grammatical 51, 53–4, 58
– interconnected 51, 58

- lexical 51, 54
- linguistic 51–2, 58, 76
- notion 52, 54
Simpson-Vlach, R. 184
simulations 172, 199, 223–4
singularity 221, 224
Sinha, C. 142–3
situated embodiment 142
situatedness 224
skills, pragmatic 159, 174
Slobin, D. I. 57, 172–3, 198
slots 53, 56, 70, 191
- open 60, 70
Soares da Silva, A. 34, 41, 143
social factors 122–4, 137, 141–2, 150
social groups 97, 145–6
social identities 137, 146
social meanings 146
social phenomenon 123, 142
social practices 81–3
social structure 82, 150–1
social turn 112–13, 148
social variation 135, 146
sociolects 41, 146, 150–1
sociolexicology 38
sociolinguistic change 109, 123, 125
sociolinguistic perspectives 149, 216
sociolinguistic variables 144, 146, 149–50
socio-linguistic variables 144
sociolinguistic variation 148–9
sociolinguistics 112, 134, 137, 141–4, 146, 148–50, 209, 217
- historical 122–5, 128
- interactional 146
- mainstream 143, 146
- third wave 146
- variationist 113, 144
sociophonetic variation 149
socio-spatial axis 97–8
Soukup, B. 146
sound patterns 52
sound schemas 5–6
sounds 1, 3–10, 12, 15–17, 160–2, 171, 175, 223
- neighboring 5, 14
- speech 1, 12, 15, 160–1
source domains 83–5
spatial proximisation 99–100

spatial relations 120
spatial representations 97
spatial semantics 143
speakers 2–4, 9–15, 101–2, 110–11, 113–17, 123, 141, 197–8
- idealized 109, 113
- native 3, 7–9, 14, 147, 160, 183–5, 187–8
- non-native 184
- present-day 111, 113, 116, 128
speech 3–4, 7, 15–16, 123–5, 161, 164–5, 208, 211
- community 20, 146, 159
- directed 166
- directive 53
- errors 4, 9, 63
- naturalistic 194
- perception 15, 146
- production 5, 17, 60, 63, 110, 183
- sounds 1, 12, 15, 160–1
- stream 3, 159, 161, 175
Speelman, D. 41, 140, 143–4
Stampe, D. 4, 6, 9, 13, 15, 17, 19–20
Steels, L. 53, 143
Steen, G. J. 35, 213, 221
Stefanowitsch, A. 53, 70–1, 150, 218
stimuli 14, 194–6, 216
stops 7, 17, 87, 121
- aspirated 3, 8, 14
- glottal 3, 10, 12, 18
- syllable final voiced 10
- Thai 7
storage 1–6, 8, 13, 15, 17, 148
- phonological 20
- and units 3–7
storyworlds 219, 221
strategies
- discursive 87–9, 103
- identification 88, 93
- positioning 88–9, 96, 98–9, 101
- structural configuration 88, 90, 93
stress 5, 17–19
strings 3, 17, 59–60, 74–5, 110, 184
- formulaic 192
- frequent 62, 73
structural configuration 87–93
- strategies 88, 90, 93
structural patterns 51–2, 56–8, 60, 70
structural schematicity 118

structuralism 1, 6, 35, 69, 83, 134–6
structured inventory of constructions 165–6
structures 34, 55–8, 62, 64, 73, 82–6, 137, 185–6
– complex 187, 189, 192
– conceptual 50, 82, 85–6, 94, 97
– constituent 73–5
– grammatical 62, 109
– higher levels 17–19
– holistic 88–9
– internal 27, 83, 90
– lectal 142, 145, 151
– in lexicon 34–8
– linguistic 50–1, 55, 58–9, 69, 75–6, 83–4, 185, 191
– onomasiological 34–5, 41
– phrase 72–5
– prototype 12, 29, 33, 142
– semantic 25, 27, 32, 36
– semasiological 31, 38, 40
– social 82, 150–1
– syllable 13, 18
– syntactic 54, 134–5
students 4, 9, 84, 190, 215–16
stylistic analysis 214, 218, 222
stylistic variation 144, 214, 221
stylisticians 209, 218, 223
stylistics 142, 209, 214, 218–19, 222, 224
– cognitive 208, 218
– corpus see corpus stylistics
subcategorization preferences 185
subjective explicit 102
subjective implicit 102
subjectivity 101–2, 220
subtlety 218, 224–6
suffixes 124, 127, 193
Sugaya, N. 189
summary scanning 96
surface form 2
syllable structure 13, 18
syllables 4, 7, 12–13, 18–20, 161
– closed 3
– open 3
symbolic units 58, 117, 125
synchronic polysemy 109, 116
synergy 81, 83, 87
synonymy 34, 41

syntactic categories 59, 72, 75
– and constructions 66–9
syntactic constructions 112, 114, 119
syntactic expansion 119–20
syntactic functions 66, 68
syntactic links 59, 66, 72
syntactic priming 63, 150, 185
syntactic representations 62, 68
syntactic schemas 118
syntactic structures 54, 134–5
syntactic units 73
syntax 135, 159, 170, 182, 194, 209
systemic-functional grammar 222
Szelid, V. 41
Szmrecsanyi, B. 63, 113, 123–4, 143, 149

Talmy, L. 50, 82, 86, 90, 94, 101, 197
taxonomic links 59, 69, 72
taxonomical levels 38–40
taxonomy 38–9, 62, 87, 96, 98
Taylor, J. 25, 32–3, 112, 197
temporal meaning 121
temporal proximisation 99–100
tenses 118, 195
– past 118, 169, 171–2, 193
– present 195
text frequency 125–6
texts
– ideological properties 81, 89, 103
– literary 208–9, 214–15, 218, 220–2, 224–6
textual analysis 214, 218–19, 222
textuality 209–10, 213–14, 216, 218–19
thematicity 123–4
theoretical framework 42, 103, 113, 138, 159
theory formation 134–5, 139
third person 124, 195
Thornburg, L. 36–7
to-dative constructions 63, 70–1
tokens 111, 128, 147, 189–90
– exemplar 111, 126
– frequency 172, 185, 193–4, 196
– repeated 121
Tomasello, M. 52–3, 60–2, 64–6, 109, 160, 162–3, 168, 186
transactive clauses 94–5
transfer 71, 191, 193
– act of 63, 70–1
– theories 198

transformations 5, 55, 90
- complex 17
- gradual 140
- image schema 8, 10, 17
- mental 11
transition 16, 32, 159, 161
transitional probabilities 74, 161, 185
transitive clauses 54, 57
transitive constructions 57, 70, 168-9
transitive events 67
transitive sentences 56-7, 68, 167, 169
transitive verbs 55-6, 127
transitivity 86, 222
Traugott, E. C. 51, 109, 113-14, 117-20
Trousdale, G. 51, 53, 113, 145, 183
Tsur, R. 212, 219
Turner, M. 35, 212
turns
- cognitive 81, 209, 214-15
- social 112-13, 148
Tyler, A. 31, 182
type frequency 172, 185, 189, 193

underlying form 2, 8, 10
units 2, 4-7, 9, 19-20, 40, 73-4, 161, 191
- grammatical 52-4
- grammaticalizing 118-19
- linguistic 6, 20, 112, 119, 161
- and storage 3-7
- symbolic 58, 117, 125
- syntactic 73
Universal Grammar 2, 182
universality 137, 139
unrelated languages 15, 109, 120
usage 50, 53, 111-14, 118-22, 125-7, 135, 183, 185
- data 42, 138
- events 111, 137, 159, 190
usage-based approach 50-3, 59, 62, 66, 73, 75, 108-9, 147-8
usage-based construction grammar 50-76
usage-based models 5, 12, 20, 51, 58, 122, 128, 137
- and language change 109-14
usage-based perspectives 73, 118, 141
usage-based phonology 147
use, language 33, 50-1, 72-3, 75-6, 81-2, 108-9, 113-14, 136-7

users, language 28, 36, 50, 66, 69, 72, 137-8, 144-6
utterances 110, 112, 159, 166-7, 169, 174, 193, 195
- concrete 59, 69, 75
- multi-word 60, 167

vagueness 25, 32-3, 41
Van Dijk, T. A. 81-2, 84, 95, 102
van Peer, W. 213, 215, 220, 222
Vandeloise, C. 31
variables
- linguistic 123, 146, 150-1
- sociolinguistic 144, 146, 149-50
- socio-linguistic 144
variant forms 12, 113
variants 8, 124, 144, 146, 215
variation 2-3, 6-8, 32, 112-13, 136, 138-9, 142-5, 150
- analysis 138, 144
- interlinguistic 136-9
- intralinguistic 136-9, 141, 147
- intraspeaker 109
- and invariance 2-3
- lectal 41, 133, 138-9, 141, 143, 145, 147
- lexical 41, 143
- of meaning 143, 146-7
- meaning of 143-4, 147
- onomasiological 40-1, 144
- phonological 13-14
- semasiological 41
- social 135, 146
- sociolinguistic 148-9
- sociophonetic 149
- stylistic 144, 214, 221
variationist Cognitive Linguistics 133-4, 137, 148
- motivations for 134-8
variationist linguistics 41, 133-51
- challenges 147-51
- domains of investigation 138-47
- motivations for 134-8
variationist sociolinguistics 113, 144
varieties
- language 40-1, 108, 133, 145, 150
- national 41, 133
- standard 122

verb argument constructions 61, 66, 185, 191, 194, 196–7, 199
verb phrases 75
verb-object-locative 196
verbs 61–2, 66–7, 70–2, 126, 185–6, 188–91, 193–4, 196–7
– finite 67, 188
– lexical 112, 120
– novel 168–9, 173
– transitive 55–6, 127
Verhagen, A. 87, 113, 126–7, 142
visual perception 50
visual processing 85, 197
vocal tracts 15–17, 20
vowel shifts 5, 8
vowels 4–7, 10, 12, 16–17, 160

way-construction 70, 125–6
WH-constructions 62

Wodak, R. 81–2, 87, 94
word classes 50, 66, 69, 191
word forms 161, 171–2
word learning 162–3
word order 55–7, 60, 64–5, 68, 167–9, 173
– first language acquisition 168–9
word senses 115–16, 123
words 7–16, 30, 39–40, 60–1, 63, 114–18, 159–62, 164–75
– communication before 160–1
– content 70, 186
– novel 163, 170
– pivot 60–1
wug test 170

Zenner, E. 41, 143, 146, 150
Zipf's Law 194

www.ingramcontent.com/pod-product-compliance
Lightning Source LLC
Chambersburg PA
CBHW021122300426
44113CB00006B/253